GAZETTEER OF MANIPUR

GAZETTEER
OF
MANIPUR

BY

E. W. DUN

GYAN

Published by

Gyan Publishing House
5, Ansari Road
Daryaganj, New Delhi-110002
Phone: 011-47034999, 9811692060
E-mail: books@gyanbooks.com

Distribution Network
gyanbooks.com
India, USA, Canada, UK, Australia

ISBN: 978-93-6280-173-9 (PB)
First Published, 1886

2nd Impression 2024

Printed at: Gyan Press, Delhi.

GAZETTEER OF MANIPUR
Author: E. W. DUN

GAZETTEER OF MANIPUR

GAZETTEER OF MANIPUR

By

Captain E.W. DUN, B.S.C.

CONTENTS

GAZETTEER OF MANIPUR.

CHAPTER I.

PHYSICAL GEOGRAPHY.

THE country inhabited by the Manipuris is, by the Burmans, called Kathay, which term they also apply to the people; by the inhabitants of Cachar, it is named Moglie; by those of Assam, Mikli; and by the Shans and those who inhabit the country east of the Ningthee or Khyndwen, it is known as Kassay, of which term the Burmese word Kathay is a corruption.

It lies between* 24° and 26° north latitude and 93° and 95° east longitude, and in the centre of the large tract of mountain country between Assam, Cachar, Burma and Chittagong.

* To be accurate, the latitudes should be 23·47 and 25·41; longitudes 93·6 and 94·48.

The territory which now constitutes the Native State of Manipur consists of a large tract of hill country and the valley proper of Manipur.

BOUNDARIES.

It is bounded on the west by the British district of Cachar and the Naga Hills District; to the north by the Naga tribes, yet unsubdued, and the Naga Hills District; to the east by the Kubbo valley, a portion of Upper Burma; and to the south by the collection of Kuki tribes called by various names, and in various states of barbarism. Some of these latter tribes are pushing forward towards the north-east, and in a few years will probably, together with the Tankhool Nagas and Burma, form the eastern boundary. This was demarcated in 1882 as follows :—

EASTERN FRONTIER.

The demarcation of this part of the Manipur frontier had become necessary for several reasons, the principal being that, while no definite line existed, the Burmans were able to support some villages of Kukis, whom they had sent with the intention of annoying Manipur, to settle on lands claimed by Manipur, from which they raided on and enslaved the Manipur Naga tributaries, and from whence they could not be dislodged without the probability of bringing on a war, which, as it would have involved us also, it was the policy of Government to prevent. Since the time when Manipur, much more powerful than now, made raids on Burma, and carried their arms to the

Irrawaddy, and Burma in retaliation raided on Manipur, and slaughtered men, women, and children indiscriminately, the two peoples have been bitter enemies, and it became necessary to clearly define the boundary between them. The boundary, as laid down in 1834, prescribes that the whole of the Kubbo valley should be given to Burma, and that the boundary line north of it should be drawn so as to separate the Ungoching hills in the east (which are in Burma) from the continuation of the western range of the Yumadoung or Malain hills, which are in Manipur. Looking at the map of the country as now surveyed, it is clear that the line drawn from near the Kongal thánà eastward to the Tuileng river, then up that stream, and northward along the Nissanga and Kassom range, most nearly agrees with the terms of the agreement. This boundary was laid down in 1882.

AREA.

The arm of the Himalayas, which sweeps round the southern side of the Assam valley dividing this province from Upper Burma, throws off in latitude 26° longitude 94° a southern branch. This southern branch divides Cachar from Upper Burma and further south Chittagong and Arrakan from Lower Burma.

In the latitude of Cachar, a section, 120 miles in breadth, has been brought under Manipur rule.

The range is here some 100 miles in breadth from east to west, and is deeply gashed with valley running north and south. A central stream has been blocked by some convulsion of nature just below the points at which two streams join, alluvium has been deposited instead of being carried off, and the flat and elevated valley of Manipur proper has been formed.

This valley is 25 miles long and nearly 25 miles broad.

GENERAL APPEARANCE OF VALLEY.

Immediately on crossing the last ridge from Cachar the tree-jungle disappears, and the eastern slope of the hill range is bare and covered with grass; scarcely a tree is to be seen, save in the ravines which occur at intervals along the range.

It is early morning. The mist, which throughout the night has been brooding over the marshy portion of the valley in the south, is just rising, and through rents and windows in the veil, caused by the fresh morning breeze, we see the glassy surface of the Logtak mirroring clearly the hills upon its margin.

The mist has cleared. Before us lies an oval flat valley, enclosed by long even ridges rising towards their northern and southern ends.

All within the valley is of a uniform warm reddish tint, contrasting strongly with the dark-green shadowy forests through which we have been passing. At our feet lies the Logtak; from its southern end the ground slopes upwards very gradually towards the foot of the hills. There are no villages in this tract; it is one wide savannah of tall grass.

On the far eastern side a few dark specks mark the presence of bamboo-shaded homesteads, and away to the north and north-east wide dark-green patches show where the major part of the population has established itself.

The white and glistening point in the principal dark patch is the Raja's palace and the capital.

Lines of low hills in the valley running north and south are evidently the highest points of a range of which the greater portion has been submerged in the alluviums which have formed the level plain.

Towards both north and south, range upon range, peak upon peak, is painted in faintest blue upon the horizon.

We descend the eastern face of the Laimatol range by an easy winding road. From the base of the hills it lies through wide stretches of rice cultivation, which shares the surface of the plains with grass jungle or miles of tall reeds.

There are no forests, woods or hedgerows; neither rock nor stone show above the ground. In the steady glare of the sun, which we find trying after the cool dark forest, the peaceful little bamboo-shaded homesteads, lying in belts along the course of the streams we cross, afford the only relief to the eye.

At midday we cross a sluggish stream by a high wooden bridge. On the far side of the stream the road is bordered for several hundred yards by a bazaar; each shop a basket shaded by a large bamboo umbrella. A village lies along the edge of the stream.

Again we traverse wide, open rice-fields.

As we approach the northern end of the valley, the setting sun lights up the already warm tints of the eastern hills with an intenser glow. The fine peak of Kopru, rising sheer 7,000 feet above us, is purple from base to summit, and throws a deep violet shadow across the level plain, contrasting strongly with the pale primrose tint of the ripened grain.

All the air is resonant with song and laughter. The whole family, both girls and boys, are at work, getting in the harvest. The busy housewife, returning from the market with her little purchases of fish, fruit, and snowy cotton, is dressed in colours at once as bright and harmonious as those in the landscape around her.

The ponderous buffalo, marching with solemn measured stride, drags homeward across the open fields the quaint cart, peculiar to the country, heaped with the garnered grain. On his shoulders is perched a little naked urchin, quavering out the pathetic national operetta of Khamba and Thoibi. He already knows his part, and will form one of the village chorus when the harvest is all gathered in.

And now the trumpet note of the geese is heard as in great V-shaped squadrons, and with gathering darkness, they wing their way from lake to field, there to feast upon the fallen rice grain. A flight of duck comes whizzing past our heads, and, as the yellow harvest moon rises gloriously over the eastern hills, we enter the capital.

FRONTIERS.

The frontier on every side present lines of natural defence.

On the west the Jiri river is backed by the Nunjaibong range. The latter is clothed from foot to summit with dense forest, and but one road and a few paths penetrate through it.

On the north-east the river Barak is backed by mighty cliffs. On the north the passage of the spur from Khunho forms a natural barrier as also the line of the Lanier and the hills behind.

Along the eastern side, from Somrah to Moray thanna, it presents the front of a rugged forest-clad mountain slope, over which there are no roads but only narrow paths capable of being blocked at many points.

On the south advances, along the longitudinal valleys, are not met by any natural obstacles; but the frontier here cannot be drawn with any approximate correctness.

Hills and Mountains.

The hill ranges found within the area under Manipur rule run north and south, with occasional connecting spurs and ridges of lower elevation between. Their greatest altitude is attained to the north-east, about fifteen days' journey from the Manipur valley, and here hills are found upwards of 13,000 feet above the level of the sea. From this point south, until the sea is reached towards Chittagong and Arrakan, there is a steady decrease in the height of the hill ranges. To the north, again, until the Assam valley is reached, there is the same gradual decrease in height. The general aspect of the hill ranges is that of irregular serrated ridges, occasionally rising into conical peaks and flattened cliffs of bare rock. Sometimes, as in the western range of hills overlooking the Manipur valley, the summit of the hills presents a more open and rolling character.

The ranges on the west are—

(1) Nunjaibong.
(2) Kala Naga.
(3) Chakka-Nungba.
(4) Kaupum (really only a spur from the Laimatol).
(5) Kopru-Laimatol.

On the north—

(1) The Khunho spurs.
(2) Thumion—Mayang-khang.
(3) Laisom.
(4) Sirohifarar.

On the east—

(1) Sarameti or Ching-angauba.
(2) Somrah.
(3) Kassom.
(4) Nupitel or Maphitel.
(5) Yomadung.

On the south—

(1) Hawbi.

Peaks.

	Elevation. Feet.		Elevation. Feet.
Angoching range		Langól	3,727
Arui or Sómrah . . .	8,639	Longtival	3,040
Chakka	9,337	Manchuibung	
Chingamukka	2,680	Maphitel or Nupitel . . .	6,716
Ching-angauba or Sarameti .	12,557	Maram	6,167
Chore		Nameh	5,585
Hawbi		Nenphong	5,815
Itahmi	5,150	Nongmaiching . . .	5,133
Kabalong		Nangshigum	
Kachauphung	8,070	Phunán	3,717
Kala Naga		Rasibúng	5,656
Kambang		Sanaching	5,860
Kamongla		Saraméti or Ching-angoba . . .	12,557
Karao	6,457	Sirohifarar	8,421
Kassóm	6,543	Somrah (North Peak) . .	10,079
Kaupum	6,200	Tangching	
Khayangphung	9,295	Thanga	
Khomjom	5,985	Thumión	5,801
Khunho	8,809	Tusóm	8,252
Kopamedza	8,375	Yongbalang-kong . . .	5,527
Kopru	8,409		
Laimatol			
Laisen	5,173		
Laisom	7,091		

See Gazetteer.

Gaz

RIVERS.

The rivers in the Manipur valley proper all take their rise in the hills to the north and north-west, and are insignificant in size and breadth, although carrying a large body of water with a rapid current during the rains. The chief are named the Imphal, Iril, Thobal, Nambul, and Nambol. The first three, rising in the hills to the north, flow eastward to the Logtak, and do not fall into it; the other two, which rise to the north and north-west, fall into the Logtak, from which one stream, the Kortak, emerges. This eventually joins with the others to form one river, usually called the Imphal or Achauba, and flows south past Shugnon. Here it enters the hills and joins the Ningthi below the town of Kendat in Upper Burma.

These rivers have cut deep into the alluvial deposit which has filled up and united the two valleys of which at one time Manipur must have consisted.

In the hills they are bright and sparkling; but as soon as they enter the plains they take up and carry along a quantity of sand, which makes them, if not absolutely deleterious to health, all the better for filtration.

They are only navigable for dug-out canoes, and for them only within the limits of the valley.

The Imphal is stated to be navigable for two days down-stream; but it is probably navigable as far as the Chingdan Hut—*vide* page 94,—which is said to be seven or eight days down-stream.

HILL RIVERS.

The hill rivers on the western portion of Manipur territory have one common type—long rocky pools, containing, even in the cold weather, 30 and 40 feet of water, alternate with stretches of shingle, over which there is frequently but 4 or 5 inches of water. The valleys they flow in are deep-cut rocky gorges, whose sides are clothed with forest wherever it is possible for a tree to grow.

The Barak alone is fordable with difficulty in the cold weather. During this season, bamboo matting, laid on pontoons constructed of large bundles of bamboos, form bridges, easily passable by laden animals.

During the rains the only means of crossing are cane suspension bridges, strengthened with wire and stretching across from trees on either side at a height of 100 feet above the water.

They are only passable by laden coolies in single file, but are quite safe for them. The currents during the rains are very swift.

On the north the rivers are not so swift, nor so large. The valleys are open, flat-bottomed, and not so thick with forest.

They do not contain the same masses of large boulders, but flow easily in almost uniformly shingly beds.

On the east there are small hill streams flowng in deep steep-sided but not rocky valleys.

The Máglang is the only one which is at all difficult to ford in the cold weather.

All are liable to sudden floods, and are difficult to cross after heavy rain.

LAKES.

The Logtak is the only piece of water which properly deserves the name of lake.

It is one of the chief and perhaps most striking features of Manipur.

It is 8 miles long from north-west to south-east and 5 miles broad at its greatest breadth from east to west. Its edges are swampy or are floating beds of reeds and aquatic plants.

Towards the southern end there are some small islands which rise steeply from the water. The largest is named Thanga. Excellent oranges of two kinds are grown here.

The surface is everywhere dotted with floating islands composed of the matted roots of aquatic plants. They are made use of by the inhabitants for fishing purposes.

The lake is stated to be very shallow.

The Lamphél jheel is important from its position on the edge of the capital.

The Ikók jheel, south and a little east from Thobál, is a piece of water of some size, and receives several of the streams from the Yomadoung hills. There are many other smaller pieces of water in different parts of the valley.

FORESTS.

The whole of the hill ranges lying between the valleys of Cachar and Manipur, and far to the north and south, are densely clothed to their summits with tree-jungle. Almost the only exception to this has been already stated in the description of the Manipur valley, and refers to the hill slopes facing it. These slopes have been steadily cleared of their timber, and present a denuded appearance. The tree-forest presents a great variety; and in the ranges lying west of the Manipur valley there are large forest tracts of trees comprising nágesar, jarul, India-rubber, tún, oak, ash, &c. Fir trees do not exist in the hills immediately adjoining the Cachar road.

Bamboo of the commoner kinds is plentiful between Cachar and Manipur. On the higher ranges to the north ringals and thorny bamboo are found. Round all the villages in the north-east portion of the hill territory the giant variety is grown, but is not common in other parts of the State.

In the Yomadung range, lying between Burma and Manipur, the jungle is much more open, very large trees are rarer than either towards the west or north, and the bamboo is confined to the low-lying ground and ravines. Fir trees are occasionally seen, but are not plentiful. The tea plant is found in this range, and apparently spreads over a large area. Teak is common to the slope overlooking the Kubbo valley. The cinchona would most likely grow well on the slopes of the hills, especially those lying nearest to the Manipur valley and in the Hirok range. The tea plant is common in the hills to the north. The only part of the immense forest tracts which are utilised are those of the Jiri forest and the hill slopes lying nearest to the valley. From the hills to the south of the valley, most of the wood used in building is obtained; some of the varieties are said to be proof against the ravages of the white-ant. From a tree found to the north-east in the hills in considerable numbers a black resinous fluid is obtained, which is used for japanning by the Manipuris. The fir tree is found to be highly resinous, and the trees are of large size. Near the salt wells to the north-east of the valley, on the first low range of hills rising from it, are numerous clumps of firs. To the south, the fir is plentiful. Palm trees are

This probably refers to the varnish tree, called in Manipur Kheo; it is found bordering on the Kubbo valley.

found on the eastern slope of the Yumadoung range, near Tumu in Burma where a few supari trees grow; on the Kaupum peak and the Nunjaibong, range, where the fan-palm is plentiful; and all over the hills on the north and east, where a kind of palmetto is common.

The wood most in request among the Manipuris is one they call U-ning-thau. Wild apricot,* plum, apple, and pear are common both in the valley and on the hills, and the willow is found in many places in the north.

* I believe the apricot to be confined to the valley; it must have been imported from China in past ages. The peach is common in the hills.

The Somrah basin and the valley to the north of it contain magnificient forests of the *Pinus longifolia*.

The red rhododendron all over the hills to the north and a white-flowered kind is found in a few places.

Except that it grows on high ground.

Perhaps the commonest tree about Mau and the southern spurs from Khunho is a tree which both in leaf, fruit, and habitat closely resembles the alder.

SOIL.

The soil of the valley is a cold, blue clay which does well for rice, but requires an immense deal of manure for any high cultivation.

Round the base of the hills the soil is, as a rule, better, being lighter and richer, and wheat, oats, and barley would thrive.

Higher up the hills, where not enriched by the débris from forests, is decidedly poor.

MINERAL RESOURCES.

The region under description is very poor in mineral of economic importance; but iron, copper, salt, lime, and edible earth are found in small quantities.

IRON.

Iron is found in more than one locality in the valley of Manipur, but, so far as I know, is confined to the swampy alluvial bays, where it is found in the shape of small pisolitic nodules of hydrated oxide of iron (bog iron ore), intermixed with clayey matter. The bed in which the ore is found is never at the surface, but covered with alluvium to the depth of 2 to 5 feet, and is itself from 3 to 12 inches thick. To procure it pits are dug, the barren soil above is thrown aside, and the land containing the ore carefully collected and washed to separate the ore from the useless clay.

COPPER.

Copper is worked in the south-eastern corner of Manipur territory, the ore being obtained from the hills bordering the Kubbo valley. I was not able to visit this locality, but was shown a specimen of malachite and copper pyrites mixed.

LIME.

The supply of lime is very deficient. Manipur is supplied by the produce of the beds mentioned in paragraphs 7 *et seq.* (close to Kassóm, between

Khangoï and Lumpui, near Hundung, below Rapvo on the east), which has to be carried three days' journey. Here, as elsewhere in India, the solid limestone is not burnt, tufa being preferred.

Edible Earth.

In the valley of Manipur, in a small tila to the left of the main road leading northwards from the city, there is exposed an unctuous clayey rock, which is dug out and sold in the bazaar, being esteemed a delicacy, to which medicinal virtues are also attributed.

Salt.

Salt is in Manipur territory tolerably abundant; it is derived from brine wells.

Coal.

The Kassóm ridge is composed of regularly-bedded sandstones * * * The sandstones have a moderate dip to the east, averaging about 20°, and in them plant remains and patches of coaly matter, which have given rise to the rumours of coal in the Angoching hills noticed by more than one of the Political Agents stationed at Manipur, are not infrequent. There is, however, but little hope of finding workable coal, the beds corresponding to the Kahan band of the sub-Himalayas, in which similar fragments of lignite have but too often raised false hopes of mineral wealth.

Serpentine.

The trappean intrusions are confined to the eastern portion of the Tanku country, and, if we except variations in texture, due to unequal rates of cooling, substantially all of but one kind. It is a characteristic dark-coloured serpentine. It frequently becomes a gabbro and contains bronzite, and is intersected by veins of gold-coloured chrysolite or sometimes carbonate of magnesia. The former was not found by me in Manipur.

The hills formed of serpentine may be distinguished at a distance by their barrenness. They appear to support little except grass and a few bushes.

(*Oldham*, 1882.)

COMMUNICATIONS.

Hill Roads.

Lying as Manipur does between ranges running north and south, the lines of communication from Cachar on the west and Upper Burma on the east necessarily cross these ranges at right angles; on the other hand, those from north and south run along the course of ridges and valleys. Every village is connected with those nearest to it by some kind of path.

Those coming across the run of the hills, *viz.*, from east and west, are all formed upon one plan.

A convenient spur is selected and followed up, probably to one of the highest peaks on the range, and then down any convenient spur on the other side. The hillman prefers ascending a spur where the jungle is, as a rule, light and no scarping is required, even though he may have to ascend very high, to scarping a path along the face of a hill and over a low kotal.

Scarped village paths are only found occasionally in the north-east.

The routes between Manipur and Burma are all of the above kind, and are therefore more difficult than they need be.

There are several points at the heads of the streams which are not raised more than 1,000 feet above the level of the Manipur plain. The sides of the valleys on either side are earthy, and roads could be easily scarped and at gentle gradients; whereas there are excessively steep places on all the present routes, and though they are passable by, would prove very trying to, laden animals.

There are only two roads, properly so called, between British territory and the Manipur valley—one from the Cachar district on the west, the other from Assam on the north, passing through Kohima. The first lies through a country of exceptional difficulty. It starts from the Cachar valley at an elevation of 100 feet above the sea, and within a longitudinal distance of 50 miles ascends five steep-sided forest-covered ranges, crossing them at elevations averaging 4,000 feet above the sea. It descends between the ranges to four rivers, the bed of one of which has an altitude of 1,000 feet above the sea; but all the others are less than 350 feet above the sea.

It will be easily seen that, however well the line of road may have been selected, difficulties in the way of moving wheeled vehicles and finding camping grounds must occur.

The Kohima road, on the other hand, runs along the gently-sloping sides of hills or in broad flat-bottomed valleys. A good cart-road or tramway could easily be constructed along it, and there is unlimited camping-ground and water at every point.

A cart-road trace exists, but it is to be regretted that the Manipur Durbar have made many deviations from it, and it is liable to be lost sight of.

Rivers.

As lines of communication, the hill rivers may be left out of consideration. The Lanier alone of them all affords a good highway for foot passengers during the cold weather.

The rivers in the valley will admit the passage of dug-out canoes carrying 15 to 20 maunds each, throughout the year, between Imphal and Shugunu except when streams are very low; but they will always carry 5 or 6 maunds.

Roads in the Valley.

The roads in the flat portion of the valley are exactly like those o Assam, Burma, and other rice-growing countries. That is to say, they ar simple earthen banks, raised a few feet above the rice-fields through which they pass. The earth of which they are constructed is dug out of ditches on each side.

Width.—They are in all cases wide enough for one cart, but frequently not sufficiently broad to allow of two carts passing one another.

Surface.—A little rain makes them very slippery, and cart traffic would soon make them impassable.

Edges.—They are never enclosed by walls or hedges, and there are no trees along them.

Bridges.—The bridges are frail, bamboo structures, fit for laden mules, but not for carts. In many places the road is led over swampy places on bundle of grass or straw.

CLIMATE.

Seasons.—The rainy season commences in April* and lasts till the end of September. July, August, and September are the wettest months.

* There are generally long breaks of fine weather up to the middle of June.

The cold season commences in October and lasts till the end of February.

The hot season commences in March and continues until the end of September.

Prevailing winds.—The prevailing winds are from the south and west.

Range of thermometer.—The thermometer† ranges from 32° to 90° during the year.

† The lowest I have seen in the valley is 30°; the highest in the shade 92°.

The variation during the day in the hot weather is slight. In the cold weather, however, it is considerable, for the following reasons. All the low ground (below 3,000 feet) in Manipur, whether in the main valley or among the hills, is covered in the cold season with a dense fog. This fog lasts till 11 o'clock in the morning, and under its influence the thermometer remains low; but when it does dissipate, which it does rapidly, the thermometer rises very quickly.

The tops of hills too will be found to be 5° to 10° warmer than the valleys below them.

Rainfall.—The rainfall of the main valley and of the hills appears to be very considerable. In the valley it does not exceed 60‡ inches,§ while at Khang-jhoop-khool on the Laimatol range it reaches 120 inches. It is, however, very probable that Khang-jhoop-khool, situated at the head of a valley running down towards the west and in a gap in the hills, receives more rain than most places; but the rainfall in the hills may certainly be estimated at 100 inches.

‡ In the hills of the north-east of Manipur firs grow 600 feet higher up in the eastern than in the western side of the range.

§ This is much above the average, which cannot, I think, be put above 50 inches.

A little rain usually falls about the end of December; the remainder in the five months of the rainy season.

Effects of Climate on the Country.—The climate, at once rainy and temperate, covers the hills in the western portion with thick forest and induces the inhabitants to grow rice; causes numerous rivers, streams, and marshes; and encourages aquatic and water-loving plants.

The forest on the hills east of the valley is not nearly so thick as that on the hills to the west, and differs in character.

Oaks replace bamboos, firs are substituted for negassar,|| and, judging from the collateral evidence of the lower rainfall in the valley as compared with that of the hills further east, we may suppose that a drier climate has produced a lighter and different kind of jungle on this side.

|| The negassar is not a hill tree, properly speaking, and seldom grows at a higher level than 1,000 to 1,200 feet.

Health.—At any elevation greater than 3,500 feet above the sea, the climate of Manipur is suitable and favourable to Europeans and natives of India throughout the year. Below this elevation, it is good only from the 1st January to the 30th March. During the rest of the year, persons other than natives of the country are

The climate of the valley is decidedly bad for European children.

Diseases.

very liable (below 3,500 feet) to malarial fever, and in months of October, November, and December to pneumonia. These three months too are the worst for fever. The country has been frequently visited by cholera and small-pox, usually between August and November.

Fever.
Pneumonia.
Cholera.
Small-pox.

Precautions.—It is very necessary that the rule of wearing warm clothing at night and light clothing by day should be rigidly observed. It should, moreover, have this extension, *viz.*, warm clothing should not be laid aside at sunrise, but be retained until the fog has cleared off, as the chief change in temperature occurs, not at sunrise, but when the fog rises.

Troops should not be required to march before the fog has cleared, especially in the hills. Even if the camp has been placed for the night upon a hill, to descend rapidly in the early morning into the cold damp mist, is to make sure of cases of cold, fever, and pneumonia. Starting late* enables the men to prepare and eat a meal before exposing themselves to a climate which is always to a certain extent *malarial*.

* *Very true*: the Manipuris think it a great hardship to be made to start a march early in the cold season.

The two rules above noticed—*viz.*, wearing warm clothing at night and continuing it until the fog has cleared, and not doing any labour until the sun begins to shine upon the ground—are observed by the inhabitants with good effect.

Sanitaria.—There are no existing sanitaria; but along the whole of the interior faces of the ranges, bounding the main valley on the east and west, there are innumerable positions above 3,500 feet which would answer the purposes of sanitary camps. It is difficult to conceive the circumstances in which they could be used; but it may be as well to mention that in the northern portion of the country, the vicinity of the villages of Ukrul, of Jessami, and Wakhong offer good sites for sanitaria, and that the Somrah basin is admirably suited for such a purpose. The peaks surrounding this valley average rather more than 8,000 feet. The spurs are very broad and slope gently. They are well wooded (chiefly with fir) and well supplied with water, even on the tops of the spurs at 6,000 feet.

There is excellent grazing for the greater portion of the year, and the rainfall, judging from the appearance of the hills, is not nearly so great as in Cachar or Burma.

It is proposed to construct a direct road to it from the Manipur main valley, which will bring it within a nine days' march.

It is situated two days' journey from the Ningthi (Khyendwen) river. East of the Lanier there is a fine range, with peaks of 11,000 and 12,000 feet, which in the winter have 1,000 feet of snow. The nearest peak is called Sarameti. In some maps this range is placed within Manipur territory.

Seasons for Military Operations.

Troops should not, if possible, be moved along the Cachar road before the 1st December. The deep narrow valleys retain their malarial character till late in the season, and the change of temperature between the hill-tops, on which the sun shines, to the river-beds, where the forest is thick and the sun only touches for a few hours, is trying until the forest has had time to dry. The Naga hill route (within Manipur) is quite sufficiently healthy from the 1st November.

In the main valley and hills nothing should be done before the 1st December,* if possible. The roads and forests retain their dampness almost till that date.

* The Manipuris never, if possible, go on a military expedition till about the 10th December, as it would interfere with the rice harvest.

From the month of March the weather is unsettled, and the rains may be expected, which would of course render military operations difficult.

They should be limited to the period from the 1st November to the 1st April at latest.—(*Lieut. Dun, 1885.*)

CHAPTER II.

THE PEOPLE.

ETHNICAL DIVISIONS.

As the State of Manipur consists of both tangled forest-covered hills and of open cultivated plain, so do its people include both civilized Hindus and barbarous tribes.

The name Manipur is only applicable, properly speaking, to the Hindu dwellers of the plains. The wild tribes are divided generically into the two classes of Naga and Kuki.

There is not apparently any racial* difference between the Hindus and the savages—the dwellers in the plains and the dwellers in the hills,—but only a difference of religion.

The Manipuris are supposed to be the descendants of four old tribes, called Kamal, Luang, Moirang, and Maithai, which are known to have inhabited the valley of Manipur at no very distant period. They still call themselves Maithai, which tribe appears to have absorbed the rest, and are divided into seven families, the members of which do not intermarry, and whose names perpetuate the memory of the original tribal divisions.

* I do not agree with Captain Dun. All the hill tribes differ, more or less, from each other, and it cannot be said that the Manipuris resemble one more than another, unless it be the Tankul Nagas; probably the Manipuri partaking slightly of all with an admixture of Hindu Dravidian and other foreign blood. They are daily becoming more mixed, and dark blood comes from the west.

They are called—

Kumal.	Ningthaūja.
Luang.	Angom.
Moirang.	Mangáng.
Kabágnalba.	

These families are further subdivided into castes, as follows:—

Brahman.	Dhloi.
Ganak.	Kayastha.
Kshatriya, called Khettree.	Mehter, or Hari.

Besides the Maithai, there live in the valley a race of helots called Phungnai, divided into Hitakphalba and Potsungba, Tengkul, Ayokpa and Kei. The Phungnai perform various duties about the Raja's person. Tengkul and Ayokpa are gardeners, and Kei pounders of rice to the Raja's household.

All appear to have been at one time slaves, and are probably mixed tribes of Maithai and Nagas. Another class is called Loi; another Maiyang, or men from the west

The ranks of the Loi have been largely recruited by persons deprived of caste; but many (the Sengmaie people, for instance, who speak a separate language or dialect) appear to belong to a tribe distinct from the Maithai. The Lois are also being constantly elevated into the ranks of the Khettrees.

Caste.

A strange custom prevails in Manipur by which a man of low caste marrying a woman of high caste is adopted into her tribe, and the children are considered as full-blooded members of their mother's caste. Cases of this kind are often seen where a man in favour with the Raja makes his way rapidly to the top of the tree. The present prime minister and virtual ruler of the State, Tangal Major, is an instance of this. He is by birth low caste and the descendant of Bengali goldsmiths. He is now adopted into the Khettree caste, and professes to be of the "Ningthauja" or royal tribe. A low caste man may even marry a Brahmin woman, and his children become Brahmins. It is needless to say that all this is utterly opposed to all orthodox Hinduism.

The Maiyangs are descendants of Hindus who originally emigrated from the west. They formerly occupied the site of Maiyang Imphal, which remained deserted for 30 years, but has since been occupied by another class of immigrants from the west, the Mussulmans.

The Chief of the Maiyangs, called Kalaraj, or Maiyang Ningthau (western chief), lives at the village of Ningthaukong, to the south of Bishenpur; but the Maiyangs are scattered over the valley.

The name Maiyang, which simply implies a western man, is frequently applied to the Muhammadan immigrants; but it appears evident that there were two classes of these immigrants, and that the name Maiyang was, in the first instance, applied to, and was appropriated by, the Hindu settlers.

The Mussulmans are the descendants of Bengali immigrants; retain a knowledge of Hindustani and Bengali,* and are hardly distinguishable in appearance from the Bengalis, who have never left Cachar.

* Not one percent of those born in the country speak either.

Population.

The population of Manipur, distributed according to religion, stood in 1881 as follows:—

Hindus	130,892
Muhammadans	4,881
Christians	7
Buddhists	2
Hill tribes	85,288
Total	221,070

Distributed according to language, as follows:-

Bengali	16
Sengmaie	7,151
English	7
Kuki	25,384
Manipuri	128,526
Naga	59,901
Hindustani	83
Total	221,070

We may state the table thus :—

Plains population	Foreigners	Bengali	15	
		English	7	
		Hindustani	83	
				105
	Manipuris	Maithai		117,103
		Kei, Loi, Maiyang, Muhammadans		18,574
				135,782
Hill tribes	Kuki		25,384	
	Naga		59,904	
				85,288(a)
		Total		221,070

The Maithai, or Manipuris proper, constitute therefore rather more than half the entire population of the State.

(a) NOTE.—From an examination of the detailed papers in the office of the Manipur Agency, it appeared that 17,204 Kukis had been accidentally included with Nagas of the Khoirau or Kolya clan. This error has been corrected here.

PHYSICAL CHARACTERISTICS OF THE MANIPURIS.

Although the general facial characteristics of the Manipuris are of the Mongolian type, there is a great diversity of feature among them, some of them showing a regularity approaching the Aryan type. Among both men and women the stature is very various, differing about as much as is found among Europeans. Some of them are very good-looking and fair. It is not uncommon to meet with girls with brownish black hair, brown eyes, fair complexions, straight noses, and rosy cheeks. The Manipuris are decidedly a muscular race, some of the men particularly so; they are generally spare in habit of body, and fat people are rare. They have good chests and well-formed limbs.—(*Brown.*)

PERSONAL HABITS.

In their habits generally the Manipuris are cleanly, and they bathe their bodies frequently. The women have a disagreeable habit of cleaning their hair with putrid rice water, which, if not carefully removed (which it usually is) by washing, leaves a very offensive smell. Their houses are kept clean.—(*Brown.*)

RELIGION.

The religion of the country is ostensibly Hinduism, and this is apparently of comparatively recent introduction,* or, according to pundits and authorities,

* We have no direct proof of Hinduism having existed in Manipur previous to the 18th century; but there can, I think, be no reasonable doubt that a great Aryan wave of very pure blood passed through Manipur into Burma in prehistoric times. I often think I see traces of this in the finely cut features seen now and then among the Manipuris, and even among the hill tribes, notably among the Tankhuis. The Hinduism of those remote times was probably free from caste prejudices, and very different to what it is now; but I think it extremely probable that a tradition of it remained when the new missionaries from Bengal arrived. These latter for their own purposes distorted the history of Manipur; the Burmese invasion put the finishing touch and killed off the old traditions.

a revival. The proof of the revival is so meagre, and the statements in support of the idea that the Hindu religion existed in the country at a very ancient period are so contradictory and unsatisfactory, that there is no hesitation in stating that in every probability, although a spurious and imperfect form of Hinduism may have existed in individual cases previous to the reign of Gharib Newaz, about A.D. 1750, it was during his reign that the Hindu religion became general, and was adopted by him and by the majority of the people. The Manipuris quote the Mahabharat in support of their statement that they were originally Hindus; but, beyond the mention of Arjun's coming into Manipur and marrying a daughter of the Raja of the country, there is nothing further bearing on the subject. They theorise that Arjun being a Hindu, the country must consequently, from the birth of his son Babrubaba, who became Raja, have become Hindu, of which there is no proof whatever. When questioned as to what occasioned their backsliding,—for all are agreed that previous to its revival the Hindu religion had fallen into abeyance,—they some time ago ascribed it to the ravages made on the country by the Burmans, which, by dispersing the inhabitants, caused them to forget their religion, they not taking into account, apparently, that Burmese ravages are almost things of yesterday, and that the Burmese occupation of the country only lasted for a very short period on each occasion of invasion. But the latest and most astounding reason assigned is to the effect that, after the death of Babrubaba, their religion assumed a monotheistic form; in fact, they became Brāhmoists, or worshippers of one God. This form, they say, continued until the reign of Charairomba, about A.D. 1715 to 1720, when Hinduism began again to be professed by a few. This continued until the advent of Raja Gharib Newaz about A.D. 1750, when all, or nearly all, reverted to their original faith, in which they have since continued. The real history of the conversion of the Manipuris to Hinduism appears to be as follows. During the reign of Gharib Newaz, a wandering fakir, according to the Manipuris, had a mysterious call to proceed to Manipur and re-admit the backsliding Hindus into their former faith. He arrived there, and professed to have discovered traces of the former existence of the Hindu religion, and converted the Raja and the people, and admitted them into the Kshatriya caste. Since then they have remained Hindus; but even at this date they are very ignorant of the faith they profess. The various Hindu festivals have of late years had greater attention paid to them. All the Manipuris are "Baishnabs," or the followers of Vishnu.*

* At least 10 per cent. of the so-called Hindus have become so since Colonel M'Culloch's time, *i.e.*, since 1867.

The Muhammadans of this country are very ignorant of their religion, and there is but one sect amongst them, *viz.*, Sunni. The Brahmins are well-to-do; they are provided with lands by the Maharaja, and live generally by cultivation and trade. The Kshatriyas are generally employed in military duties and other works in the palace.† They, and all the other castes in the country, live by cultivation and have to work, according to the lallup system, ten days in a month for the Raja.

† Not more so than others.

VILLAGES.

The villages are placed in long lines on either banks of a river or on the edges of jheels, and are ^{"its"} always placed so that every man has some water immediately adjoining his compound. Every house stands in about an acre of land, which the owner surrounds with a mud wall, and further plants an interior fence of cactus, bamboo, plantain, babool, and other indigenous trees.

Houses.

The houses do not differ essentially from those of the Bengalis in Cachar; the shape is somewhat different, but the material used is the same. The houses of the better sort are constructed of wood, bamboo, &c., while those of the poorer class are entirely, as regards the framework, of bamboo. The walls are usually of reed, plastered over with mud and cowdung. The dwelling-houses are all of the same form, but those of the rich are larger and constructed of better materials than those of the poor. The roofs of all are thatched with grass. All the dwelling-houses face to the eastward, in which direction they have a large open verandah. In this verandah the family sits during the day, and in it all the work of the household is carried on, except cooking, which is performed inside. In the south side of the verandah is the seat of honour: here a mat or cloth is laid for the head of the family, upon which no one intrudes. Inside, the house is without partitions. The bed of the head of the family is placed in what is called the "Luplengka," close to the wall on the south side about the middle. It is usually screened with mats. The daughters usually sleep on the north side. There are no windows in the houses, the only light admitted being by two doors, one opening into the open verandah, the other to the north near the north-west corner of the house. The fireplace is on the floor towards the north-west corner. There is no chimney at all. The fuel used is generally dry reed jungle; this answers every purpose in the warm weather, but is a sad substitute for wood in the colder months. Connected with the making of their houses are many superstitious practices: first, the house must be commenced on a lucky day; and that day having been fixed by the astrologer, on it (it makes no difference whether the other materials are ready or not) the first post called the "jaltra" is erected. The post is bound towards the top with a band of cloth, over which is tied a wreath of leaves and flowers; milk, juice of the sugarcane, and ghee are poured in the lower extremity, and into the hole in the ground in which it is to be fixed are put a little gold and silver. The number of bamboos forming the body of the frame for the thatch must not be equal on the south and north sides. If they were so, misfortune, they consider, would overtake the family.

Social Position of Women.

The women of Manipur, married or unmarried, are not confined in zenanas, as they are in Bengal or Hindustan; all classes are alike in this respect; neither do they cover their faces before strangers. They are very industrious; in this respect the opposite of the men, who are lazy and indolent. The most of the work of the country, except the heaviest, is performed by them, and they are consequently the mainstay of the family circle. All the marketing is done by women, all the work of buying and selling in public, and the carrying to and fro of the articles to be sold; whilst at home they are busily employed in weaving and spinning. It would be difficult to find a more industrious woman in India than the Manipuri. With all their industry and usefulness, women hold but a very inferior social position, and are considered more in the light of goods and chattels than as persons to be treated with honour and consideration. This is partly owing, no doubt, to the laxity of their marriage customs, which are loose in the extreme, but still more to the baneful system of domestic slavery which is the prevailing custom of the country.

Marriage Customs.

Although to become man and wife it is not necessary that the marriage ceremony should be performed, still it is usually performed; but as often after as before cohabitation. A man can put away his wife without any fault on her part, and, if a person of influence, he may do so without its being noticed. The rule, however, is that if a man puts his wife away without any fault of hers, she takes possession of all his property, except a drinking vessel and the cloth round his loins. A man and wife may separate by mutual consent, and a wife may quit her husband on giving him the value of a slave. Women are really the slaves of their husbands; they are sold in satisfaction of their debts, and it is said that men often pawn their wives to purchase some office or even a pony.*

* Till within the last few years, wives were often sold to buy a pigeon. Pigeon-fighting and the gambling consequent thereon is now strictly forbidden.

Polygamy.

This is common among the well-to-do part of the population; but the lower orders do not often indulge in it.

Adultery

Is punished by the offending male who receives the wife of another man being condemned to pay a fixed sum of Rs. 50 for all classes of the population, besides fines to the court that tries such cases. Should the offender not be able to pay, his family are seized and sold as slaves for the satisfaction of the claim. Both the male and female offenders are arrested and confined until the claim is satisfied, after which they are free. For carrying off a woman living under a man's protection, but not married, the expenses incurred by the man on account of the woman must be paid by the party who takes the woman.

Early Marriages.

Early child-marriages are unknown; widows, except those of the Brahmins, may re-marry. In contracting marriage, as a general rule, the young couple are allowed to see and approve of each other. When the parents approve of a marriage, the heads of the families arrange matters; presents are sent by the young man's parents to the house of the girl; no return presents are made at this stage; money presents are not given. Food, fish, fruit, &c., constitute the gifts sent, which must be presented three times before the arrangement is considered concluded. After marriage there is no rule about living separate from the parents or otherwise.

Hair how worn by Men.

The men wear their hair, which is coarse and black, long and combed back from the forehead, which is occasionally shaved; the hair is gathered into a coil behind. Moustaches are uncommon, although now and then a man with a thick straight moustache will be seen; beards are very uncommon. Boys' heads are generally shaved, leaving only a straggling quantity of hair on the back.

Women's Hair how worn.

The hair of the females is worn in three different ways, according to age. When quite young, up to the age of about 10, the front part of the head is shaved, the back part from about the level of the ears round the head being allowed to grow loose behind. The next fashion is that for unmarried girls, and is very peculiar; the hair behind from about the middle of each ear round is allowed to grow long, is combed back and tied in a knot or left loose. In front of this the hair is combed forwards, and cut equally so as to reach over the forehead an inch or so above the eyebrow. In front of, and over, each ear is a lock of hair two inches broad and reaching down to the angle of the jaw. In married women the hair is allowed to grow long, and is combed back from the forehead in Bengali fashion, and tied in a knot behind, leaving a few inches dependent upon the knot. All who can afford the luxury wear a false hair, which, as with the Bengalis, is incorporated with the knot of back hair.

Dress of the Men.

The dress of the men does not differ materially from that of the Bengali, and consists of the dhoti, a kurta, or shirt, only occasionally worn, and a chudder, or sheet. In winter, those who can afford it wear a quilted and padded coat,* like that worn in the Punjab, generally having long uncomfortable sleeves and enormously high collars. Shoes are seldom worn. The puggree is shorter than that worn by Hindustanis, but is put on in the same manner. The Manipuri generally wears small rings of gold in his ears when he can afford it, and the well-to-do among them have necklaces of coral and gold and hollow chased armlets of gold called "k'huji" on their wrists.† They are very fond of carrying flowers in their earrings or in holes in the ears and in their head-dress.

* Every man who can get one wears an English coat. The importation of second-hand coats must be great.

† These can only be worn when given by the Raja.

Dress of the Women.

The dress of the women, when of good quality, is picturesque and pleasing. During the hot weather it consists of a piece of cloth open except at the bottom, where it is stitched together by the edges for a few inches; this is folded round the body under the armpits and over the breast, and tucked in by the hand at the side of the body; in length it reaches to the ground; but as this would be inconvenient in walking, it is hitched up about half way to the knee, and tucked in again at the waist. This piece of cloth is called a "fanek," is only wide enough to go one and a half times round the body; this gives enough room, however, for the legs in walking. The fanek is made of cotton and silk, and the only patterns are stripes of various colours, the width running across the material, the ground-work being of different colours. The commoner patterns are red, with green stripes, green and black, blue with black and white stripes, yellow and brown, dark-blue with green and white stripes, &c. At the top and bottom of the garment is a broad margin, on which geometrical figures or patterns of various kinds are sewn by hand with floss silk in various colours. Over the fanek is worn a white sheet, which is folded in the usual native fashion, the face, however, being left uncovered. In the cold season, a short jacket with long sleeves is worn; this reaches below the bust over the fanek, and is worn tight-fitting; the material is usually velvet or satin—black, blue, and green being favourite colours. The great drawback to their dress in a European's eyes is its tendency to spoil the figure; the whole weight of the fanek resting on the breast soon ruins the shape. Female children, until puberty or near it, wear faneks round the waist, the upper part of the body being bare.

(*Brown, 1873.*)

Ornaments.

The ornaments are earrings, necklets, and bracelets; ankle ornaments are never worn, or rings in the toes; nose ornaments are limited to a small piece of gold wire in the side of each nostril. The only ornaments which may be worn without restriction are earrings; these may be worn by anyone. With regard to other ornaments of gold, permission for all but the upper classes to wear them must be obtained from the Raja. Gold-embroidered clothes are also forbidden. Ornaments of other metal than gold may be worn freely.

Manners and Customs.

In their intercourse amongst themselves, the Manipuris are ceremonious. They address one another by the name of the office they may hold, or as younger or elder brothers. To call a man "Angang" (literally child) is most respectful, and, when called by a superior, to answer "Agya" is the most respectful response. The Raja and members of the royal family call all male Manipuris "Eepoo," grandfather, and females "Eebel," grandmother. The male members of the royal family are all called "Sunnaor," golden, the females "Soja." Their actions are described in a different style of language from that of the rest of the people: thus, they do not walk, but move; they do not sleep, but recline. A common Manipuri, if riding, would be spoken of as "Sagontonglai," a prince as "Sagon-telli"; the eating of the commoner would be designated "Chuk-chaba," of the prince "Look-haba"; and so on.

Diet.

The usual diet of the Manipuris differs in no important particular from that of the Bengali in the adjacent district of Cachar. Children up to about the age of nine years, when they receive the sacred thread of the Hindus, may eat what they choose without loss of caste; after that period they require to be more strict, and eat only what is allowed by the Hindu religion, to which the Manipuris professedly belong; the staple food of the Manipuris being rice, dhall, and fish. They do not eat any flesh whatever; ghee and milk are seldom used.

Cost of Living.

The cost of living in Manipur is cheap, and said to be about one-half of that in the British province of Cachar.

Use of Tobacco, Betelnut, &c.

The Manipuris, both male and female, are inveterate chewers of pán and supari. The whole of this is brought from the neighbouring district of Cachar, and forms a considerable trade. The betelnut tree will not grow in Manipur territory. Tobacco is also used by all classes and ages, and the tobacco is manufactured and smoked as in Bengal. Opium is not used by the Hindu part of the population; neither is there any consumption whatever of ganja (Indian hemp) or any other intoxicating drugs; drinking is most strictly prohibited, but said to be indulged in in private to a great extent.

Games and Amusements.

The out-door games of the Manipuris are few; indeed, the only one, it may be said, which has any popularity, is hockey on horse back—a game formerly peculiar to Manipur, but which of late years has spread over and become popular throughout a large portion of British India. This is the game named polo, which is so fashionable now. The traditions of Manipur have it that the game of hockey was first introduced by a Raja named Pakungba, who flourished 500 years ago. According to some, the introduction is given as late as the reign of Gharib Newaz, about 120 years ago. The game, it is said, has not altered since that time, and, as it is now so generally understood, a brief description of it will suffice. In the more important games as played in Manipur, seven men on either side is considered the correct number; but in ordinary games any number can play. As might be expected in the place of its birth, the play is much superior to what can be seen elsewhere; it is much faster, and the hits are delivered with greater precision. The games are always started from the centre of the ground by the ball being thrown into the middle of the players; it is frequently struck before reaching the ground. The pace is kept fast from the commencement of the game, and such a thing as a player being allowed to spoon a ball along before delivering his stroke is unknown; an attempt at this kind of play would result in the ball being at once taken away by a stroke from one of the opposite party. When an evening's play has commenced, the games succeed each other quickly. So soon as the ball is driven to goal, the players hurry back to the centre of the ground, and a fresh game is begun. When a ball is sent off the ground to either side, it is flung as at starting among the players opposite the point of exit. The Manipur riding costume for the game is a scanty dhoti, well tucked up, and a pair of thick woollen gaiters reaching from the ankle to the knee; a whip is carried in the left hand suspended from the wrist, to allow free motion of the hand. The saddle is furnished with curved flaps of enamelled leather, suspended from the sides opposite the stirrups and stirrup leathers. The ball used is made of bamboo root, and is large and light. The clubs have handles of well-seasoned cane; the angular striking part is of heavy wood. As might be expected, a good hockey pony is a valuable animal and is parted with reluctantly. All classes, from the Raja, who is a good player, down, play the game, and an unusually good player is sure of royal favour. Hockey on foot is played by the juveniles.

The polo of Manipur differs in certain respects from the polo of British India. There is no off-side. Each player has his position in the field relatively to the others defined, and each player is attended by an opponent who never leaves him. Thus the backs on each side find themselves at every turn opposed by the advanced guard (as it were) of the opposing party.

There are no goal posts. A man may catch the ball and run with it as in Rugby football, and there is absolutely no limit as to crossing and hitting of hooking sticks.

In-door Games.

Of in-door games there are many, mostly resembling those popular in Bengal, as chess, cards, &c. The game called "Kang-sanaba" is very popular, both amongst men and women. A modification of this game is common also in the hills, but is simpler than that practised among the Manipuris. There is another game called "Kekri-ke-sanaba," only played by the women.

In it a number of them join hands, dancing round in a circle, and chanting the praises of Raja Chingtung Komda in his fights with the Nagas to the south. The in-door amusement in its season most enjoyed is Kang-sanaba—a game as peculiar to Manipur as hockey on horseback was. It is played only in the spring, the players being generally young women and girls, with a sprinkling of men on each side. The game seems to cause great excitement, and there is great emulation between the sides. The kang is the seed of a creeper; it is nearly circular, about 1½ inches in diameter, and about ⅜ of an inch in thickness. This is placed upon the ground upright, at one time with its broad side towards the party by whom it is to be struck, at another edgewise. When the kang is placed with its broad side to the party, it is to be pitched at with an ivory disk; when it is placed edgewise, it is to be struck by the disk propelled on its flat side, along the surface of the ground, by the force of the middle finger of the right hand acting off the forefinger of the left. A good player can propel the disk in this way with great force and precision. The side having most hits wins. The whole is closed by a feast at the expense of the losers.

"Conundrums" are a fertile source of amusement. They appear usually far-fetched, and sometimes not over-delicate. The tale of Khamba and Thoibi, sung by their Eesai Sokpa, or bards, never fails, with a popular singer, to rivet attention. The scene of this tale, and the place where it was originally sung, is Moirang. The hero and heroine are persons said to have flourished hundreds of years ago. Thoibi is the daughter of the Moirang Chief's brother; she loves Khamba, a lad poor in worldly riches, but rich in personal beauty, of good descent, of great modesty, courage, strength, and agility. Thoibi herself is a lady of surpassing beauty, and Khamba, having seen her by chance while boating on the Logtak, loved her at first sight. But the course of true love never yet runs smooth, and it was no exception with these lovers. A person named Kong-yamba saw Thoibi's love for Khamba, and, wishing to gain her for himself, he used all the means that a powerful connection gave him to crush Khamba.

"The various perils through which Khamba has to pass, and the constancy of Thoibi, form the subject of the song. After having won his foot-race, speared his tiger, caught a wild bull, and been tied to the foot of an elephant, Khamba gains Thoibi, who has also passed through various troubles. The end is tragical. Khamba doubts his wife, and wishing to try her fidelity, she, not knowing who he was, spears him. Having discovered what she had done, she spears herself. Some of the characters introduced in the story are very good. The constant repetition of this story only seems to increase the desire to hear it. Thoibi is regarded as a goddess; and that Khamba was a man of giant proportions, is held to be incontestible. This idea of the great size of Khamba is not, however, derived merely from his celebrity in song; that their ancestors were giants is believed by all. Some of the language used in their songs is quite different to that usually spoken. The same is the case in their writings; but the meaning of songs is known to most, whereas the writings are intelligible only to the initiated. Amongst the hill tribes there is the same difference between the common language and that in their songs. The singers of the adventures of Khamba and Thoibi accompany their songs with the notes of the 'pena,' the solitary musical instrument of Manipur, a sort of fiddle, with one string of horse-hair, the body of which is formed of the shell of a cocoanut. On the bow of the fiddle is a row of little bells, which jingle in harmony with the air. The singing of the Manipuris is not agreeable, *i.e.*, is harsh, shrill, and quavery; a few of the songs have, however, more pleasant airs. Some of them are of interminable length, and the longest of these have a spoken part, alternating with the song proper. Besides the 'pena,' above described, the Manipuris use cymbals, drums, &c., differing in no respect from those used in Bengal."*—(*M'Culloch.*)

Festivals, Games.

There are three public festivals or games held annually in Manipur, and which are peculiar to the country, are of great antiquity, and are unconnected with religious matters. The first of these is held in July, and consists chiefly of foot-races. This is called the "Lumchel" (Lum or Lumbi, a road; Chelba, to run). The next in September, called "Heeyang," lasts five days. The chief sport is boat-racing on the moat in front of the Raja's palace. The third is an assembly of the hillmen under the Manipur Government, called the "Haochangba."

Lumchel.

This is a competition between the different "pannahs" or classes among the Manipuri population. Brahmins, as also the lowest class of Manipuris, the Lois, are not allowed to compete, but Mussalmans may. The distance is under half a mile. The first part of the races consists of trials of speed by two pannahs at a time; the winners in these races run again when all have had their trial, and the first man in of the whole wins the race of the year. The first man receives as his reward sundry presents, and is excused from lallup, or forced labour, for the rest of his life; he becomes a hanger-on about the Raja usually after his victory. Old winners are allowed to run again for the honour of the thing; when they win more than once, they get presents. The first in at the preliminary races between the pannahs are allowed three months' exemption from lallup. These races cause great competition, and for months before they come off various lanky-looking men, with scanty proportion of clothing, may be seen morning and evening trotting along the roads, getting themselves into training for the important event. The Raja is always present at these and the other games, seated in a sort of gateway which bounds the straight road along which the races are run.

Wrestling.

After the races there is an exhibition of wrestling. This presents nothing very peculiar; the only thing that need be mentioned regarding it is a curious custom which prevails. The victor over the wrestler who competes with him before salaaming to the Raja leaps up in the air, alighting on his left foot; as he descends, he gives his right buttock a resounding slap with his right hand; having thus asserted his superior skill, he salaams in the usual manner.

Heeyang or Boat-races.

The boat-races occupy five days in September, and take place on the moat which surrounds on three sides the Raja's enclosure. This ditch is about 25 or 30 yards broad, and at the season when the boat-races come off contains

* This story is copied *verbatim* from Colonel M'Culloch's account of Manipur.

plenty of water. This festival is the most important held in Manipur, and great preparations are made for it; stands are erected on both sides of the moat, the one for the Raja being of considerable size and height. The women occupy stands on the opposite side of the moat. The boats used in the races are two in number, of great length, and hollowed out of a single tree; the rowers number about 70 men, each with a short paddle. Besides the rowers are several men attending to the steering and urging on the crew. One of these stands in the front of the boat, and, leaning on his paddle, encourages the efforts of the men by stamping violently with his right foot at intervals. The race itself differs from most boat-races, in the fact that here the great object is for the one boat to foul the other and bore it into the bank so that one side of the boat is disabled, the men not being able to use their paddles; the boats are thus always close together until the finish, when the race is usually won by a foot or two only. The distance paddled is about a quarter of a mile. Each race is rowed twice, whichever wins, and the results are carried on from year to year. As in the Lumchel, the competitors are men belonging to the different pannahs. There are no rewards for the races, they being rowed merely for the honour of the thing. The Raja in his boat, which is like the others, but ornamented with a carved deer's head and horns gilt at the prow, accompanies the race, the Raja on the chief race day steering his own boat in an ancient Manipuri costume. The boat-race, in the opinion of many, is not a fair race, but a struggle between the rowers on either side, in which those who can deal the hardest blows are usually the victors. That fights occasionally happen is correct, but they arise from accidental causes, and are really not a premeditated part of the performance. While the boats are paddling down to the starting place, a good deal of chaffing, flinging weeds, water, &c., between the rival boats takes place; but all seems to be conducted in a good-humoured way. One very peculiar custom in vogue at this boat-race is the following.

If one boat succeeds in swamping another, the headman of the swamped boat becomes the property of the headman of the boat that caused the trouble. All his personal ornaments and clothing go with him, and before he can be freed he has to pay Rs. 60, the value of an adult slave.

Hockey Matches after Boat-races.

On each of the five days devoted to the boat-race, important hockey matches take place. Immediately after the races, an adjournment takes place to the hockey ground close by, and the game at once commenced, the play being much better than can be witnessed at any other time. The ground at that season not being in good condition, many falls take place, which are not allowed, however, to interrupt the sport. The scoring is carried on from year to year also in this case, and many sporting gentlemen may be seen in various parts of the field carefully marking the results with pieces of pebble. The excitement and interest manifested in the result are very great. In the first day's hockey match a male member of the royal family heads either side of the players.

Hawchongba.

This festival in October lasts for only one day; it is a gathering of the hill tribes under the Manipuri Government, and is a curious sight on account of the great number of different tribes assembled, with their curious dress and weapons, differing from each other in feature and language, but all unanimous in one particular, to get drunk as speedily, and remain so as long, as possible. The hillmen indulge in feats of strength before the Raja, such as carrying heavy weights, &c. They also indulge in war dances and sham fights. The sports of the day conclude with a feast, at which they are regaled with the flesh of cows, buffaloes, dogs, cats, &c., which may have died in the valley. The flesh is dried and preserved on purpose for this feast.

SLAVERY.

Another of the institutions of the country which will now be briefly described is slavery. The name of slavery, however, as it appears to European ideas, is, perhaps, too harsh a name for the mild form which in most, if not in all, instances obtains in Manipur.

Its forms.

The slavery which exists in that country may be properly divided into two classes: *1st,* that in which any one becomes a slave either temporarily or permanently of his own free will; and, *2nd,* when he or she is made a slave of forcibly and against the will. Debt is perhaps the most general cause of voluntary slavery. In this case a man in debt will confess his inability to pay and agree to serve his creditor until such time as the debt can be paid; his services thus are credited as interest on the original debt, although it does not follow that the original debt is in all cases taken; a greater or less sum may be taken as may be agreed on. Men not in debt also become slaves for a money consideration of which they may have need, often, as they are fed and clothed at their owner's expense, as M'Culloch observes, from "sheer laziness." Nothing can be said in favour of the system under which people may become slaves not of their own free will. A not uncommon form of this kind of slavery is that of parents disposing of their children either temporarily or permanently—a fruitful source of immorality. It is said that this is only resorted to in extreme cases, such as want of food, &c., and is looked upon as a disgrace; but this is somewhat doubtful. For certain crimes people are made slaves. In cases of theft, when the culprit is caught, but the goods not recovered in full, he and his family may be seized and sold until the claim for the stolen goods is recovered. In cases of debt, when the claim for damages cannot be realised, the same may happen. The Ràja's slaves number about 1,200 or 1,500. The classes who are the Raja's slaves are the Ayokpa, Lengpul, and Kei. On a change taking place in the rulers of the country, it was formerly the custom to seize the slaves of those who had held office, and to divide them amongst the adherents of the new ruler. This practice, when the changes of rulers became so frequent as it latterly did, was found to entail upon individuals more hardship than the worth of the slave. Slaves, therefore, when seized, were not distributed amongst adherents, but made to work for the Raja under the name of "Ayokpa." The present Raja has, it is said, ordered that slaves shall remain, in case of a change of officers, the property of their owners under all circumstances. Ill-usage of slaves does not seem common; they are generally treated as part of the family with whom they reside, and do not hesitate to run away when they are ill-treated, which creates a scandal, and is carefully avoided. Cases of cruelty do, however, occur; but such cases are exceptional.—(*Brown, 1873.*)

EDUCATION.*

The question of education may be dismissed in a very few words. In 1872 a vernacular school was established in Manipur at the suggestion of the late Political Agent, Major-General W. F. Nuthall, and the Government of Bengal presented books and maps, &c., to the value of Rs. 400 or 500, but, for want of encouragement on the part of the authorities, it has been nearly closed. Some few boys attend occasionally. The Manipuri prefers remaining ignorant. So illiterate are they, that some of the highest officials can neither read nor write, and are not a whit ashamed for their want of knowledge.

WRITTEN CHARACTER OF THE MANIPURIS.

The Manipuris possess a written character of their own, which seems a modification of the Nagri. This character is said to be very ancient; only a few can write it. Of late years the Bengali character has been chiefly used, except in cases relating to Manipur proper itself. (*Brown, 1873.*)

LALÚP OR LABOUR SYSTEM.

The inhabitants, instead of taxes, give labour on the same principle as used to obtain in Assam.

With the object of carrying out this duty systematically, the Maithai population is divided into four parts, called Pannahs, which are designated, in the order of their seniority, Kaphum, Laipham, Ahallúp, Niharúp.

The Pannahs perform *lalúp,* or service, for ten days in rotation, thus bringing every male above sixteen years of age on duty ten days in forty.

This service is a due to the State. None are remunerated for it. The head of each family or tribe furnishes the proper persons for the different services required of that tribe in his own Pannah. The immediate family of the *Pipa,* or head of the tribe, is not called upon to perform any heavy duty. Its post is near the Raja, acting as *Ningthau zelba,* or personal attendants.

The family next in seniority has a heavy duty to perform in the Lai Kai; the third has the Látoní, and the fourth the Súngsa toi. The lalúp of the second and fourth families work generally in unison. Their chief duty is to make houses and bridges, for which they cut and bring the materials. The Lálmi was in former days the soldier of Manipur. But, since the raising of the troops in the time of Gambhir Sing, the Lálmi's duties have become civil.

Of the families after the fourth, the places are not fixed; some are *Khootnaiba,* or artificers, as goldsmiths, blacksmiths, carpenters, workers in brass and bell-metal, &c., who all have their lalúp, in which they perform any work in their respective lines they may be called upon to do. Some again attend to the Raja's ponies; some to his elephants, &c. The Brahmins even have their lalúp, during which they cook for the Raja and their idol Govindji. In fact, except the lowest kinds of service, there is scarcely any which is not performed by some part of the Maithai population. The heads of the Pannahs,

* An English school was established in Manipur nearly 50 years ago by the then Political Agent, Captain Gordon, and maintained at his own expense; it was very successful, but was not carried on after his death. After ceasing for years, an English school is again being started; the Raja is giving the building which is now being erected in the Residency ground, and the Assam Government gives a grant-in-aid. The Rajas and others will subscribe. There is every prospect of it being successful.

and all officers required in connection with them, are appointed by the Raja from among his favourites, and generally without reference to their origin. The appointment to office exempts the holder's immediate family from the performance of any heavy duty.

The particular duty of the Phungnai Tenskul, Ayokpa, and Kei has already been mentioned (page 13).

The Loi population alone pay tribute. They also manufacture silk, smelt iron,* distil spirits, make earthen vessels, cut posts, beams, and canoes, manufacture salt, catch fish, and cut grass for the Raja's ponies.

* Most of the iron-workers have now become Brahmans.—J. Johnstone, [illegible]

The Maiyang are employed as grass-cutter.

The Mussalmans are employed as gardeners, carpenters, and potters, but [illegible] as sepoys and buglers.

They serve lalúp with the Pannahs.

Occupations.

The following extracts from the census of 1881 throw light upon the taste and habits of the Manipuris :—

	Males.	Females.	Both sexes.
Professional class	12,169	2,858	15,027
Domestic class	7,324	7,672	14,996
Commercial class	572	14,861	15,433
Agricultural class	51,057	52,880	103,937
Industrial class	2,125	917	3,042
Indefinite and non-productive	36,310	32,315	68,635
Total .	109,557	111,513	221,070

The professional class includes the "Officers of the National Government," amounts to 187 persons, including the Maharaja, his heir-apparent, 59 officers of State, 103 headmen of villages, and others.

Secondly, the army which numbers 6,624, commanded by 250 officers.

Thirdly, priests and temple officers, of whom there are 1,754 males and 143 females. Of these, 1,465 get their living as expounders of the Vedas.

There were 5,000 musicians, 6 school teachers, and 53 astrologers.

In the industrial class there were 39 persons employed in the mint (22 males and 17 females); 110 carpenters and 101 masons, all males; 326 dealers in silk; 236 cotton dealers; 37 thread dealers (all females); 41 cloth dealers (all males); 173 persons (41 males and 133 females) engaged in weaving; 7 workers in leather; 2 paper-manufacturers; 470 potters; 2 glass-manufacturers; 1,163 salt-makers; 136 goldsmiths; 148 workers in brass; 326 iron-mongers; 356 blacksmiths; 130 pán-sellers.

The agricultural class has more females than males. Of the non-productive and indefinite class, 2.484 are described as general labourers (1,108 males and 1,379 females). There are 4 courtiers; 1 female pensioner; 125 female garland-makers; 62 beggars; and 117 prisoners.

HILL TRIBES.

Ethnical Divisions.

The hill tribes of Manipur, though divided into innumerable clans and sections, may be considered generally under the two great divisions of Kuki and Naga.

The Nagas are scattered over the hill districts of Manipur, but chiefly to the west, north, and north-east.

The derivation of the name "Naga" is doubtful, and may be derived from *nanga* "naked,"* but the name is used in the Mahábharat, and they are described as beautiful dragon-like beings against whom the hero Arjun fought.

* The Assamese word for naked is "*naga*," and they called the Nagas so, because in old days most, if not all, of them were naked. The word as a tribal name certainly came from Assam. The Manipuris call all hill tribes by the general term "How," unless they know the particular tribe, in which case they give the tribal name.—(*J. Johnstone, 1885.*)

Amongst themselves they have no generic name, but use the tribal names only. They scout the name of Naga.

The Nagas residing under Manipur rule are (by the census of 18[illegible])—

	Souls.
Lahúpa	28,552
Tankul	4,400
Kolya (Khoiran)	17,992
Kaupai	8,476
Marring	484
Total	59,904

Allowing 4 individuals per house and 1 fighting-man per house, we get a fighting strength of 14,976 men.

Lahúpa and Tankul.

There is no perceptible difference between these two tribes.

The Manipuris as a rule, apply the name Tankul to both indifferently.

The men in a few villages round the Nupitel peak resemble Marrings in appearance, but declare themselves to be Tankuls.

The inhabitants of Khairan and of a few villages in the vicinity resemble Kukis in appearance, but also claim to be Tankuls.

These two tribes (Tankul and Lahúpa) are now perfectly peaceful and contented.

They have no stockaded villages, and, with the exception of the Somrah villages, which are thrown together by their geographical position, each village is a separate community.

Even the Somrah villages have very little cohesion.

There is no one leader of the tribe in any sense whatever.

Characteristics.—They are not particularly athletic or muscular, and not in the least warlike. They are thoroughly subject to the Manipuris. They submit to the inroads of the Chussad Kukis, and never attempt reprisals.

Villages.—They always build their villages just above the spot where the spur of the hill commences its last and steepest descent, where the sides of the spur are as precipitous as possible, so that it is usually only possible to enter the village, without climbing, by the upper or lower end. Generally they make a ditch across the spur at the upper entrance and a fence of sticks at both ends in place of a stockade. Unlike most of the hill tribes, the sites of their villages are permanent. They are small in the south and increase in size further north.

Houses.—Their houses are of the usual Naga pattern, with roofs nearly down to the ground, and boarded walls. East of the Toyungba, most of the verandahs are enclosed with stockade work.

Weapons.—They have no guns and use only the spear and dhao.

Cultivation.—The southern Tankuls jhum the hills round their villages; in the north terrace cultivation is universal.

Crops.—They grow rice, múm, arums, pumpkins, and yams; occasionally tomatoes and a little cotton. They estimate the annual produce at from 10 to 20 maunds for each family or house. They have only one crop.

Live stock.—Pigs, poultry, and dogs; they keep no cows or metna.

Transport.—As carriers they are inferior somewhat to the Konjai Kukis. They are noisy and rather given to drink.

Location.—They inhabit the Yomadoung range, and also the country north-east of Sirohifarar. The latter portion are akin to the southern Tankuls and similar to them in appearance, but speak a different dialect.

(*Lieut. Dun, 1881-82.*)

Kolya.

The Kolya Nagas, or, as the Manipuris frequently call them, the Khoirau, present a less united body than the Tankuls. They are broken up into nine sections, some of which do not understand the language of others.

The subdivisions are—

Tangál.	Threngba.
Mau.	Maithaipham.
Marám.	Maiyáng kháng.
Upurul.	Tokpa.

Kacháng or Katcha (includes Liyáng).

But, besides these, there are many isolated villages, such as Gaziphimi, Jessami, and Mellomi, which are all independent communities, and have no common bond but that of subjection to the Manipuris. Each of these villages along the northern frontier fears and dislikes its neighbour. The largest communities are—

(1.) Mau, which numbers 750 houses, in six villages.
(2.) Maram, which numbers 368 houses, in seven villages.
(3.) Mellomi, which consists of 700 houses.

The Mau section has one large village, called Razameh, on the left bank of the Thetzirr, which is said to contain 700 houses, and is classed as Kolya of the Mau section. It is, however, situated on debateable ground, and, as it is at present (1885) uncertain whether it is on British or Manipuri territory, the Manipuris have nothing to do with it.

The same may be said of the village of Mellomi on left bank of the Lanier.

The chief Maram village which lies to the west of Maithaipham thanna on the Kohima road is a shadow of its former self.

The Kolya tribes may be grouped ethnically midway between the Angamis of British territory and the Kaupuis of Manipur territory, as they are situated geographically between them on the northern frontier of Manipur. They partake of the outward characteristics and appearance of each.

Appearance.—They are slight men, small of limb and stature, but possessed of great activity.

Their features vary from decided Mongolian to equally decided Aryan.

They cut the hair square in front over the forehead and draw that on the back of the head up into knot, round which they twist white wool.

They wear the kilt, like the Angamis; a blue cloth, with a red stripe, is thrown over the shoulders, and they ornament their ears and necks with fantastic decorations of brass, gay birds' feathers and grass, dyed red and yellow.

Villages and Houses.—The villages are usually placed on a commanding point on a ridge. The houses are of the usual gable-ended kind, common to all the tribes on the north-east frontier, but the roof-tree slopes backwards rather less than in Kaupui houses.

The eaves come down almost to the ground. The front wall is made of boards and the front gable decorated with an enormous conventional representation of buffalo horns.

Cultivation.—They have terraced fields of great extent round their villages, in which they cultivate rice. Very soon after the crop is off the ground, they turn on water from an irrigation channel; the rotting straw makes good manure, and the labour of breaking up the soil is much lightened.

This system, however beneficial it may be to the cultivation, prevents the fields being used as camping-grounds, unless special precautions are taken beforehand.

Weapons.—The spear, dhao, and panji are their only weapons, and they do not seem to use the concealed pitfall to anything like the extent the Tankuls do.

Village defences.—None of their villages are defended either with stone walls or stockades.

KAUPUI.

The Kaupuis, a tribe of Nagas, are located in the hills between the Cachar and Manipur valleys.

Their subdivisions are—

(1) Sungbu. | (2) Pooron.

In 1881 they numbered 8,476 souls.

Villages.—Their villages are permanent and are not stockaded, but are usually placed on the top of steep peaks.

Houses.—Their houses are large and comfortable; are placed on the ground, and consist almost entirely of roof, the eaves coming down to within a few feet of the ground.

Cultivation.—They adopt the "jhum" style of cultivation, and never terrace their fields.

Weapons.—They frequently carry a small spear, or dhao, but only as a protection against wild beasts. Their warlike tendencies have long since died* out.

* Apparently so; but it is said that they still nourish old feuds, and, but for Manipuri supremacy would again murder each other.—(*J. Johnstone.*)

Appearance.—They are small men of no great muscular development, and their features vary from decided Mongolian to equally decided Aryan.

Characteristics.—They are very peaceful and contented.

Dancing and drinking occupy every moment of their leisure. Their good temper and geniality are remarkable, and they are thoroughly subject to the Manipuris.

Powers of combination.—They have no large villages or any recognized chief; and there seems no probability of their combining for any object.

MARRINGS.*

A tribe of Nagas who occupy the western watershed of the Yumadoung hills, together with different Kuki tribes. Indeed, there appears a certain amount of doubt whether they should not be classed as Kukis themselves; but they are generally classed as Nagas.

Characteristics.—As a tribe, the men are short and of a muscular development, nearly equal to that of Kongjai. They are distinguished from both Kukis and others by wearing their hair long and confined in a bunch, like a horn rising from the front of the head. There are a few villagers on the north-east corner of the Manipur valley who wear their hair in this fashion and call themselves Tankuls,—possibly Marring emigrants or captives.

Villages.—They build permanent villages, but do not stockade them.

Arms.—Spears and dhaos.

Occupations.—They are very seldom employed as carriers, being excellent cultivators, and appear to be the most thriving by far of any of the hill tribes. They place their fields on the hillsides without terraces, but drain them very ingeniously, so as to retain both the soil and the moisture for a longer time. The average yearly produce per house is—

100 baskets of dhall,
50 ditto of paddy,
5 to 10 ditto of múm,

a basket containing a little less than a maund. They also grow a large quantity of coarse plantains on the hillsides; also arum, yam, and pumpkins.

Live-stock.—Comparatively large herds of metna and cows; also pigs and poultry. They do not usually milk their cows and metna.

Manufactures.—The great industry is the manufacture of baskets, which are used universally by Manipuris in Manipur, Cachar, and Sylhet.

History.—The tribe appears at one time to have been settled in or near the Kubbo valley.—(*Lieut. Dun, 1881-82.*)

The Marrings are subdivided as below; but, as the tribe numbers less than 500 souls in all, the fact of their being so divided is not of very great importance:—

(*a*) Saibu, the eldest branch. | (*b*) Marring, or the western branch.

The subdivisions have the same name in each:—

(1.) Khulbu.
(2.) Churungna.
(3.) Kemsowa.
(4.) Makunga.
(5.) Tangsowa.
(6.) Tungtangna.
(7.) Klaya.

* The Marrings assert that they came from Burma.—(*J. Johnstone.*)

THE MELLOMI, LAPVOMI, AND PHOZAMEH GROUP.

The people of these three villages, though classed by the Manipuris, for the sake of convenience in administration, with the Kolya section, differ greatly in dress, appearance, and language from the rest of the tribes included within it.

They are usually designated "Naked Nagas," from their habit of going about in a state of nature. This is, however, an uncertain distinction, as in winter they wear two cloths, knotted on each shoulder and making a perfectly decent dress.

Each village fears and dreads its neighbour, and the nearest villages of other tribes fear all three, because they are armed with cross-bows.

They are small men, of inferior physique, and are perfectly barbarous savages.

Their villages (*vide* Gazetteer) are weakly defended with stockades.

KUKIS.

The origin of the term Kuki is not certainly known; but it is said to be derived from a word applied to the system of cultivation by the Bengalis.

The whole of the wild tribes who dwell in the mountain district contained between Bengal and Burma, Cachar and Manipur and Arrakan, have received this designation. In other cases where a large number of tribes have been classed together (Abors, Singphos, Nagas), the differences between tribes separated socially and geographically from one another have, since the imposition of the name, been discovered to be so great as to suggest doubts as to the advisability of attempting any such wide generic classification; but in the case of the Kukis, all the tribes (with indeed the exception of the Pois) have so many common grounds of affinity, that the classification seems to have been, however accidental, correct.

The Kuki race is at present moving northwards. The progress can be easily traced within the memory of man, and they have even moved across the valleys of Cachar and Manipur, and occupied the lower slopes on either side of the Barrail range. The people on the spot have thus been led to classify them as old arrivals and new arrivals—or Old Kukis and New.

This system has been carried out independently, but simultaneously both in Cachar and Manipur. Lieutenant Stewart, half a century ago, spoke of old and new Kukis; and the Manipuris, while they designate each section or clan of the old arrivals in their country by a distinctive name, give the general name of Kongjai to all new arrivals.

The word "clan" is undoubtedly the best to apply to the Kuki subdivisions. It is evident from the genealogies of their chiefs, which have been preserved from the earlier times, that each clan has simply called itself after the name of its chief, and the process may be observed going on at the present day. Fifty years ago the Chussáds were only known as Haukibs; now they are only known by the former name, though they cannot deny being a branch of the older clan.

Census of 1881.—The census of 1881 gave 17,204 souls (*vide* note (*a*) on page 15) as the total strength of the Kongjai or New Kukis.

Clans.—The best known clans are—

Thádo.	Khlangam.
Vúngsón.	Chungloe.
Changsen.	Changput.
Shingsól.	Haukib.
Mangvung.	Simmté.

Kamhau.

The Kamhau are also called Sukti and Wité.

The Chussáds, of whom much has lately been heard, are an off-shoot of the Hawkib.

The old Kuki clans are—

(1) Kom.	(5) Koireng.
(2) Anál.	(6) Chohté.
(3) Namfau.	(7) Purum.
(4) Chiru.	(8) Mantak.

(9) Hiroï or Lamgáng.

They numbered in 1881 8,180 souls. It has been stated that the Kuki race is on the decrease rather than the increase, and there is considerable *primâ facie* evidence to be found in Manipur in support of this statement.

The old Kuki clans are mere remnants, and the first eight new Kuki clans above enumerated are very small.

The chief strength of the Kongjai lies in the Hawkib and Simmté, who are the latest arrivals in Manipur.

There is little to be said about the older clans of new Kukis. They are much quieter and more settled than the last three; indeed, two villages—one of the Vungson, and another of the Mangvung clan—have settled on the plain at the south of the valley, in permanent villages, and have adopted the use of the plough,—a great innovation on Kuki customs.

Ancient lineage is much prized by all Kukis, and Kutingmáng, head of the Thádos, and Lankapau, head of the Chángputs, occupy high places in their estimation. Tanghu, chief of the Hawkibs, and Sumkám and Pumlal, both Simmté chiefs, are more powerful, but in affairs of importance Kutingmáng would undoubtedly be consulted.

The clans are now too much disintegrated for any probable combination; but the fact must not be lost sight of, as they regard the persons of their chiefs as sacred, and an injured chief of ancient lineage could enlist the sympathies of a very large number of villages.

Simmté.

The Simmté, being strange to the country, hold pretty well together. They can muster about 850 fighting-men, of which about one-half are said to possess guns, and their villages are all clustered together in the south-west corner of Manipur. The chief, by name Sumkam, is a young man, of not very friendly bearing.

He has a rival in a chief, named Pumlal, an older man and to all appearance more friendly.

Suktis, or Kamhaus.

The Suktis, who appear to be identical with the Chins of the Burmese, inhabit the hills overlooking the southern portion of the Kubbo valley. They are quite independent of Manipur, and are the terror of the Burmans along their western frontier, on account of their raids on their villages.

At one time the Suktis used to furnish armed men for the assistance of the Khambat Wun, but this arrangement has long since been discontinued. Of late years they seem to have shown less disposition to annoy the subjects of Manipur, and they would not be likely to interfere with the passage of any force across the Yumadoung range of hills.

Their capital or head-quarters is Kamhau, moving from whence, in bands of 200 to 300 men, armed with muskets, they pounce upon some village, generally at night, but sometimes in open day, and, firing recklessly into the house, take advantage of the general panic to carry off men, women, children, and whatever else they can lay hands on. In this manner they carry off the Burmans, and keep them in slavery in the hills till they are redeemed, leaving very wisely the husband or head of the family to amass the required amount by his labour.

Some time ago a Phungyi was carried off, and is now living in a Chin (Sukti) village, from whence he sends warning letters to the villages to be attacked, or arranges terms concerning captives.

Some of the captives are sold into slavery in Chittagong, and possibly parts of Arrakan : the latter astounding statement appearing more than probable.

All attempts to subdue them, whether made by Manipur or Burma, have hitherto been unsuccessful.

In 1856 the Maharaja of Manipur sent an expedition, and in 1879 the Burmese Government sent the Nat-Chins-oung Myay Wundouk with 1,500 men.

Unless Manipur and Burma will combine to subdue them, which, in the present state of their relations, seems highly improbable, there appears very little chance of their altering their ways, but rather they will continue, as now, every year to grow more fearless and more aggressive.

(*Phayre, 1881-82*; *Lieut. Dun, 1881-82.*)

The Suktis or Kamhau or Wité clan is now (1885) being pressed hard by the Pois.

They have frequently asked the Manipuris for help against their powerful enemies.

It is probable that many of them will soon migrate to Manipur.

The name of their present chief is Yatol.

They are said to be able to muster 8,000 fighting-men, a large proportion of whom are armed with guns.

CHUSSÁDS.

The Chussáds, or more properly speaking the Choksads, who are an offshoot of the Hawkib Kukis, left their old home to the south of the valley of Manipur between 10 and 20 years ago, and settled themselves in the hills bordering on the Manipur valley near the Kongal route to Burma. Previous to their settling there, a foul act of treachery had made them, at heart, deadly enemies of Manipur. On a certain occasion, when the chief of the tribe, the father of the present chief Tonghu, was coming in to Colonel Mc'Culloch, the then Political Agent, by his invitation and under safe conduct, he was murdered by a high Manipur official, the brother-in-law of the present Raja. In the end of 1877 they began to move, and determined to leave Manipur altogether. Chunyang apparently went first, and, crossing the Ungoching range, began to settle down in Burmese territory. Others began to follow, but, together with Chunyang, were told by the Samjok Tsaubwa to settle down in their present place, the latter promising his protection in case of any objection from Manipur. And so they have established themselves on the low hills which form the northern boundary of the Kubbo valley. The proximity of the defenceless Tankuls proved too great an attraction to their young warriors, and, aided by the Samjok people, they attacked Chattik thanna, which had been established to overawe them.

Political position.—Appreciating the fact that the British Government is on the side of Manipur, they appear to rather fear us. The ground has been assigned to Manipur; but Chunyang stated his intention of remaining where he was, whether the land might be allotted to Burma or Manipur.

From being nearer to Samjok than Manipur, the Tsaubwa of the former place must necessarily exercise more or less influence over them; also, as we have seen, they have a rooted dislike to the Manipuris, who are rather afraid of them.

Fighting-men.—They cannot muster more than 250 fighting-men.

Appearance.—Exactly like, but fairer than, Eastern Lushais.

Principal men.—Their chief Tonghu is a boy; he has no brothers. The heir-presumptive is his cousin, Yangapow, aged 25. The chief mantri or minister is Kabyang, a fine intelligent man. Chunyang is a lesser chief, ruling three villages.

Language.—The language appears to be identical with that spoken by the Thadoe Kukis.

Weapons.—They are said to possess guns (which are flint-locks) to the extent of 20 per cent. They manufacture their own powder. The only other arm in use is the dhao.

Houses.—Their houses, unlike those of other Kukis, are built on the ground, but like them are small and built of bamboo, and have not the permanent character of Naga houses.

Crops.—Their crops are those of the Kongjais, except that they grow more cotton.—(*Lieut. Dun, 1882.*)

The Chussads, who in 1881 presented a united front, have now (1885) split up into two factions.

The largest faction, under Tonghu, has definitely thrown in its lot with Manipur.

Chunyang still holds somewhat aloof.

Tonghu has now established a village on a south-east spur of the Makku peak without any stockade or defence.

Chunyang remains on his old ground.—(*Lieut. Dun, 1885.*)

SINPHOS.

The Sinpho tribe is unknown in Manipur, even to the most north-eastern villages. The clans most likely to be found near Manipur are the Mirip and Tisan.

POIS.

Although no individuals of this tribe have yet been seen in Manipur, the time appears to be approaching when they will force themselves upon our attention.

Lewin divides them into—

(1) Shindus. | (2) Banjogies. | (3) Kumies.

They all (unlike the other Kukis) tie their hair in a knot on the forehead, and fasten it with two brass brooches in the shape of Jew's-harps. The Lushais use a similar securing pin, but like their cousins, Thados, Kamhaus, &c., tie their hair in a knot on the nape of the neck.

Of the Shindus, Lewin says: They seem to be more a nation than a tribe. Both sexes are in stature above the ordinary height of hill people, and of a fairer complexion.

The faces of those I have seen do not bear any signs of the prevailing Mongolian type of physiognomy. I am told that they do not cultivate with the dhao in jhum fashion, but are acquainted with the methed of form-cultivation common among the Himalayan hill tribes. Field labour is, as a rule, performed by men; only the wives of very poor men labour in the fields.

The Shindu houses are raised from the ground and built entirely of logs and planks of wood.

They have iron in the country, and possess brine springs. Like other tribes around, they make their own gunpowder. Their guns do not appear to be of European manufacture.

Colonel (then Captain) Lewis narrowly escaped with his life when attempting to visit this tribe.

A decided superiority over the Lushais was noticed in the few individual Pois seen by Lieutenant Dun during a visit to Lushai country in 1881.

The Labour System as applied to the Hill Tribes.

The more distant hill tribes, instead of giving labour, pay a small tribute in whatever is easiest for them to supply.

The more distant Tankuls,* the Mao and Maram tribes, the Marrings, and a few Kuki villages pay tribute.

* The Tankuls within five or six days of Manipur come in to work at the capital or on road in the valley. They are the ditch and tank diggers of the place, and work by contract for private individuals.

Of these, however, the Mao and Maram men have to work on the Kohima road, build the rest-houses, and carry loads for officers or officials passing along it. The Marrings are very clever at making baskets, and do a certain amount of labour in that manner. They also collect leaves, which are useful as a blue dye, and several other wild products.

Wherever there is a road, the villages near, if accustomed to digging, are forced to keep it in order, and look after the condition of rest-houses.

The chief labour, however, which is imposed upon hillmen is that of carrying up articles for trade or for the Raja's private use. Tankuls, being good hands at spade work, are usually employed in making tanks, &c., about the Raja's own grounds or on canals; but every other hillman is bound to make two journeys per annum to Cachar to bring up loads on the Raja's account.

A vast amount of tact and ingenuity is displayed by the Manipuris in getting work out of the hill tribes, and many tasks are performed by them in addition to their regular quantum.

CHAPTER III.

HISTORY.

ORIGIN OF THE MANIPURIS.

THE origin of the Manipuris is obscure, and the written records, having been mostly composed since they became Hindus, are not worthy of much credit. Their claim to a Hindu origin has been rejected by Pemberton, who considers them to be the descendants of a Tartar colony which probably emigrated from the north-west border of China during the sanguinary conflicts for supremacy which took place between the several members of the Chinese and Tartar dynasties in the thirteenth and fourteenth centuries, at which time there was an extensive kingdom called Pong, occupying the country between the frontier of Yunnan and the hills separating the Kubbo valley from Manipur, extending north apparently to the mountains which bound Assam on the south-east and south, as far down as the parallel of 23° 35′. In the records of Manipur, however, their history is traced from the 30th year of the Christian era down to the year 1714, in which period they number a succession of 47 kings, the average length of whose reigns is thus made to amount to upwards of 35 years. In this long period we have but one event of any importance recorded, said to have taken place in the year 1475, during the reign of the Raja Kyamba, when the refractory tributary of Khumbat, at that time dependent upon the kings of Pong, was attacked and expelled from his territory by the united forces of Pong and Manipur, and the Kubbo valley was formally annexed to the latter country, in virtue of an alliance which had then taken place between a daughter of Kyamba of Manipur and the king of Mogoung, the capital of the Pong dominions. From 1475 to 1714, the date of the accession of the Raja Gharib Newaz or Pam Haibaba, nothing of any importance is recorded in the meagre annals of Manipur. From this period we find the people assuming a position of peculiar interest: emerging from their mountain strongholds, they wage war successfully in the fertile valley of the Irrawaddy, attack and reduce the most important Burmese towns and villages on the banks of the Moo, Chindwin, and Irrawaddy rivers, and at last plant their standard in the capital itself. The truth of this portion of their historical annals receives most unexpected and satisfactory corroboration from the records of Ava, in which all the principal circumstances are narrated nearly as we find them in the chronicles of Manipur, with a trifling variation of three or four years in the dates assigned to them, for the knowledge of which we are indebted to the researches of Lieutenant-Colonel Burney, the Resident at Ava. Very shortly after Gharib Newaz ascended the throne, he commenced that career of conquest which we find recorded in the Burmese annals.

Raja Gharib Newaz or Pam Haibaba ascended the throne of Manipur, A.D. 1714.

Gharib Newaz attacks and defeats a Burmese force, 1725.

In 1725 he attacked and defeated a Burmese force at the mouth of the Maglang river; the following year repulsed an army of 30,000 men, which had penetrated into the valley, and captured three divisions. In 1735 he crossed the Ningthee river, attacked and destroyed the town of Myedu, on the banks of the Mu river, and carried off numerous captives. Two years subsequently he successively defeated two Burmese armies, amounting to

7,000 foot, 700 horse, and 20 elephants, and devastated the whole country from the banks of the Khodoung Choung to Dabayen. In 1738 he again crossed the Ningthee river, attacked and dispersed a Burmese army of 15,000 foot, 3,000 horse, and 30 elephants; and at the termination of the rains of the same year, at the head of a force of 20,000 men, marched between the Burmese army, three divisions of which occupied the towns of Matsen, Dabayen, and Myedu, and, to use the language of the Burmese historians, "without stopping" attacked and carried the stockaded positions around the ancient capital of Sagaing, of which he obtained possession. Religious fanaticism appears to have stimulated the Manipuris to this last act of successful daring; for the Burmese chronicles record the name of a Brahmin who is said to have assured them that they would be preserved from all evil by drinking and bathing in the waters of the Irrawaddy river. In 1739, Gharib Newaz, aided, it is said, by the Cacharis, again invaded Ava with a force of 20,000 men; but failing in an attack on a Burmese force, stockaded at Myedu, he was deserted by his allies, and, after suffering much loss, was compelled to retire to the strongholds of his own country. He appears to have remained inactive on the frontier until the year 1749, when he again crossed the Ningthee river, and, marching along its left bank with an army of 20,000 foot and 3,000 horse, encamped near the confluence of the Chindwin and Irrawaddy rivers, waiting for a favourable opportunity to cross the latter river and attack the capital. The most formidable preparations were made to oppose him, and he appears to have been shaken from his purpose by one of those trifling incidents which, to the superstitious mind of the savage, are proofs of the will of Heaven. During the night his standard was blown down, and, under the influence of this sinister omen, he was glad to negociate rather than to fight, and, presenting a daughter about 12 years of age to the king of Ava, immediately returned and commenced a retreat by the road of Myedu to his country. Near the Mu river he was attacked by the Koees, a fierce tribe belonging to that part of the country, whom he quickly subdued, and resuming his journey reached the Maglang river, called by the Burmans the Yoo-Choung. Here he was met by his son Oogut Shah, or Kakeelaltbaba, who upbraided him with the unsuccessful termination of his expedition, and with having tendered homage to the king of Ava by the presentation of his daughter. The result of these remonstrances was that Gharib Newaz was deserted by all but 500 men, with whom he again retired, for the avowed purpose of soliciting aid from the king of Ava against his rebellious son. He resided for a short time at Tsingain, and gave a daughter in marriage to the Toungoo Raja, under whose protection he remained until Ava was destroyed by the Peguers; when in an attempt to re-enter Manipur, he was met by the emissaries of Oogut Shah at the mouth of the Maglang river, and cruelly murdered, together with his eldest son, Shamshaee, and all the principal men of the court who had shared his compulsory exile. Oogut Shah was, however, soon expelled from the throne by his brother, Burut Shah, who was raised to the regal dignity by the unanimous voice of his subjects. He reigned but two years, and on his death was succeeded by Gouroosham, the eldest son of Shamshaee, an act of justice by which the direct succession of the line was again restored.

Gharib Newaz invades Ava with 20,000 men, but is repulsed, A.D. 1739.

Gharib Newaz is attacked by the Koees, but subdues them, A.D. 1749.

Gharib Newaz is murdered by the emissaries of his son, Oogut Shah, who succeeds him.

Oogut Shah driven from the throne and succeeded by his brother, Burut Shah.

Gouroosham succeeds to the throne.

The victorious career of Gharib Newaz clearly proves that during his reign the Manipuris had acquired very considerable power; and as the events just narrated are drawn almost exclusively from Burmese historical works, and are the acknowledgments of a defeated enemy, all suspicion of their truth must cease to exist. With Gharib Newaz the power of Manipur seems to have entirely deserted her; very shortly after his death, the first great invasion of the country by a Burmese army, commanded by a relative of Alompra, took place in 1755; and this is known in Manipur at the present day as the "Koolthakahalba," or primary devastation, and is rendered the more remarkable as being the first occasion on which the Burmese appear to have owed their success entirely to the use of firearms, their weapons, like those of the Manipuris, having up to this period consisted almost entirely of the dhao, spear, and bow and arrow. In 1758, Alompra in person undertook the conquest of this devoted country, and, proceeding up the Chindwin with a fleet of boats, laid waste its western bank, which was inhabited by the Kathay Shans, or Shans tributary to Manipur, where he disembarked, and, crossing the Ungoching hills by the Khumbat route, marched through Kubbo, and entered the Manipur valley by the Imole pass, at Palel. He was here met by the Manipuris under Burut Shah, and, after a sanguinary conflict, proved victorious. He remained thirteen days in possession of the capital, and intelligence being then received of the revolt of the Peguers, he returned with the utmost expedition to Ava.

First great invasion of Manipur by a Burmese army in 1755.

Alompra in person attacks Manipur, A.D. 1758.

The invasion of Manipur by Alompra must have been most disastrous to the inhabitants of that country, as they then, for the first time, sought external aid, and appeared a few years afterwards as supplicants for British protection. Oogut Shah, having been expelled from the throne two years before the invasion of Alompra, appears, from the communications of Mr. Verelst, who was then Chief at Chittagong, in the course of the year 1762, to have endeavoured to interest the British Government in his behalf, and by representing himself as unjustly driven from the throne had created a feeling of sympathy for his misfortunes. Jaee Sing, brother of Gouroosham, who was then in Manipur, becoming acquainted with these negociations, deputed a confidential messenger, named Hurree Doss Gossein, with a letter to Mr. Verelst, in which the real character of his uncle and the crimes of which he had been guilty were depicted. Of the truth of these statements, the Tripurah Raja appeared perfectly satisfied, and the British authorities not only withdrew from any further communication with Oogut Shah, but prepared to support Jaee Sing against his machinations and the aggressions of the Burmese.

A treaty of alliance, offensive and defensive, was negociated on the 14th September 1762 with Hurree Doss Gossein, on behalf of his master Jaee Sing, by Mr. Verelst, in which the aid of a contingent of British troops was promised, whenever the Raja might find it expedient to attempt the recovery of such portions of his territory as had been wrested from him by the Burmese; and he promised, in return, to make such grants of land to the English as might suffice for the establishment of a factory and fort, and a distance of country round such factory and fort, of 8,000 cubits, free of rent for ever. He was further to afford every facility for the prosecution of the trade with China, and when put in possession of the Burmese country by the six companies of sepoys whose aid had

Offensive and defensive alliance between the British and Manipuris negociated, 14th September 1762.

been promised, he was to indemnify the English for the injuries they had sustained at Negrais and in Pegu from Burmese violence and treachery.

No communication appears to have been received from Jaee Sing, when the troops destined for the enterprise started from Chittagong early in January 1763. Marching by routes along the eastern frontier of Bengal, they reached Casspoor, the then capital of the Cachar country, in the month of April, when they suffered severely from heavy rain, which had continued to fall from the 21st of March: their progress to Manipur was, in consequence, arrested, and finding Casspoor unhealthy, they were compelled to return to Jeynugur, a pergunnah on the left bank of the Barak river at the eastern foot of the Telyn hill. Circumstances of a political nature rendering the recall of the force necessary, a letter was despatched to Mr. Verelst, who returned with it to Chittagong. The treaty had been conveyed to Manipur by Hurree Doss, for the information of Jaee Singh; but some change in the administration of that country must have taken place, for in October of the following year, three accredited agents arrived at Chittagong, deputed by Gouroosham, who is represented as again in possession of the regal power; he confirms the treaty entered into with Jaee Sing, but states his inability to pay, in specie of gold or silver, the expense incurred by the troops to be employed in his service, the Burmese having destroyed a great part of the dominions of Meklee: he agrees, however, to refund whatever sums may have been already expended by the British Government on his account, and to repay, in the produce of his country, the charges for military assistance. As an earnest of the sincerity of his intentions, he makes an immediate offer of 500 Meklee gold rupees, to be valued at 12 silver rupees each. Allusion is also made in this document to the gold mines on the banks of the Burhampooter, in the dominions of Meklee, as well as any other mines of gold, silver, lead, iron, tin, copper, and precious stones which were known to exist, or might hereafter be recovered. The concluding article of the treaty enumerates the following products, which are to be paid annually by Gouroosham, in addition to the contingent privileges already mentioned:—

Gouroosham confirms treaty with British, October 1764.

	Maunds.				Rs.
Silk	10	at Rs.	5	per seer	2,000
Iron	1,000	"	4	per maund	4,000
Kupass	1,000	"	$1\frac{1}{2}$	"	1,500
Dammer	1,000	"	$1\frac{1}{2}$	"	1,500
Wood-oil	1,000	"	$1\frac{1}{2}$	"	1,500
Wax	500	"	20	"	10,000
Elephants' teeth	100	"	20	"	2,000
Agar (sandalwood)	100	"	4	per seer.	16,000
Camphor	10	"	80	per maund.	800
Black thread	100	"	20	"	2,000
Red do.	100	"	20	"	2,000
Blue do.	100	"	20	"	2,000
White do.	200	"	20	"	4,000
Black coss	100	"	2	per seer.	8,000
Meklee cloths	5,000 ps.	"	$1\frac{1}{2}$	per pc.	7,500
Meklee gold rupees	500	"	12	each	6,000
					70,800

With this treaty all communication between the British and Manipuri authorities appears to have ceased. The death of Gouroosham, with whom it had been concluded, soon followed,

Death of Gouroosham.

and Jaee Sing had resumed the reins of government but a short time, when another invasion of the Burmans under Schembegwen, in 1765, overwhelmed his unhappy country. The Manipuris were defeated, Jaee Sing fled into Cachar, and the horrors of captivity were superadded to the sufferings inflicted upon them by their relentless enemies. As soon as the Burmans had retired, which they did after raising a man remotely connected with the royal family, called Keringha, to the throne, Jaee Sing returned, and dispossessed the usurper, whose life was spared. From 1765, the date of the last great invasion mentioned by Symes, Jaee Sing had been actively engaged in attempts to restore the country to some degree of prosperity, and his efforts would appear to have been but too successful, as the knowledge of its improved condition promised a fresh harvest of slaves and cattle, and stimulated the Burmans to renew their aggressions. Their forces advanced in two divisions, one of which proceeding by water devastated the villages on the western bank of the Ningthee river, while the other, penetrating through the valley of Kubbo, their united forces entered the Manipur valley and were met by the troops of Jaee Sing near Lungthabol. A bloody conflict, which lasted for three days, terminated in the total discomfiture of the Manipuris, and Jaee Sing fled across the hills into Assam. The Burmans raised the Moirang Raja to the vacant throne, and returned to their own country. Jaee Sing having obtained assistance in Assam, and relying on the attachment of the people, again returned to Manipur, devastated Moirang, and resumed the government of his country. Between 1775 and 1782, Jaee Sing had made no less than four successful attempts to regain his throne, but was as often expelled by a fresh Burmese force, and on each occasion was compelled to fly into Cachar, where he obtained a temporary refuge. In 1782, he, however, appears to have made some compromise with his enemies, and from that period until 1798, he seems to have been allowed to remain in quiet possession of his devastated country. In January of that year, he left his eldest surviving son, Robinchundruh, in charge of Manipur, and set out on a pilgrimage to Nuddea. Distrusting the Cachar Raja, who refused him a passage through his territories, he travelled towards Tipperah, and, giving a daughter in marriage to the Raja of that country, resumed his journey and died near Bhagovangola on the banks of the Ganges in October 1799. From this period the history of Manipur presents an unvarying scene of disgusting treachery between the numerous sons of Jaee Sing, who, in their contests for supremacy, arrayed the unhappy people of the country in hostile warfare against each other, and inflicted miseries upon them, little if at all inferior to those they had suffered at the hands of their common enemy and the Burmans. Of these sons, Nobinchundruh, the eldest, who had been left in charge of the country by his father, was murdered in 1801. Modoochundruh, the next in succession, shared the same fate in 1806. When Choorjet Sing ascended the throne, his brother Marjeet almost immediately afterwards conspired against him, but, being unsuccessful in an attack, fled to Wuqueel and supplicated assistance from the king of Ava, who despatched a Tummoo to Manipur on his behalf, and he was pardoned by Choorjet. Received into favour, he again rebelled, and, being repulsed in two attacks upon the capital, fled into Cachar, from whence, with a few followers, he made his way to Ava through the province of Arakan. In this country he remained six or seven years, and at

Another invasion of Manipur by the Burmans under Schembegwen, A.D. 1765.

Manipur again conquered by the Burmans.

Death of Jaee Sing, October 1799.

the end of that time, in 1812, succeeded in inducing the king of Ava to espouse his cause, and to place him on the throne of Manipur, for which he agreed to renounce all claim on the Kubbo valley, and to acknowledge his dependence on the king of Burma. To the friendship of the monarch of Ava was he indebted for the interest shown on his behalf; and it will be subsequently seen how he requited the good offices of his young protector. In the cold weather of 1812, a considerable army marched from the Burmese territory to establish Marjeet on the throne of Manipur. At Tummoo, in the Kubbo valley, two divisions were formed, one of which, accompanied by Marjeet Sing, entered Manipur by the Imole pass, and debouched in the valley near Kokshingkhoolel; the second, under the Samjok Raja, entered by the Muchee route, and encamped near Hueerok. This division was totally routed, and its leader killed by Petumber Sing, a nephew of the Raja Choorjet Sing, who, with the main army, had advanced to Kokshing. A conflict, which lasted for five days, terminated in his discomfiture; he fled into Cachar with a few of his followers, and the country submitted to the yoke of the usurper. Marjeet, at the expiration of ten days, dismissed his Burmese friends, and continued for five years in undisturbed possession of the country. During this period, Manipur is represented as having regained almost all its former prosperity. The friendship existing with the Court of Ava tended to encourage trade. The prosperity of the inhabitants was proved in the numerous herds of buffaloes and bullocks which grazed in the plains, and a considerable accession of people had taken place from the return of those who had accompanied Marjeet in his flight. Marjeet and his principal officers had, from their long residence in Ava, adopted many of the luxurious habits of that Court, and they affected a degree of splendour in dress and the equipments of their horses which contrasted very strikingly with their former simplicity. Nothing, however, but terror of the Burmans could have induced the principal families in Manipur to tolerate the presence of Marjeet, whose sanguinary disposition was early shown in the execution of almost all Choorjet's followers and the attempted murder of many of his nephews. In 1818 he invaded Cachar with a large force, which penetrated the hills in three divisions, and would have effected the conquest of that country with ease, had its Raja, Gobindchunder, not interested Choorjet Sing in his favour. This prince had been residing for some time at Jynteea, and, on learning the situation of affairs in Cachar, immediately came to Govinchunder's assistance; and Marjeet, hearing of his arrival, was so much afraid of his influence amongst the Manipuris, that he made a precipitate retreat across the hills into his own country. Choorjet, with the assistance of Gumbheer Sing, succeeded in obtaining possession of the greater portion of the Cachar territory, in which he finally established himself with all his followers.

In 1819, when the king of Ava ascended the throne, it was determined to commemorate the event with an unusual degree of splendour, and all the tributary princes, as is customary on such occasions, were summoned personally to do homage to the new sovereign. Amongst others, Marjeet Sing of Manipur was ordered to attend, and as it was to the friendly exertions of this very king that he was entirely indebted for his present position, it was natural to suppose that such a summons would have been gladly obeyed. Some circumstances, however, such as the forcible cutting of timber in the Kubbo valley, and the erection of a richly-gilded palace, had been the subject of remonstrance from the Court of Ava a short time before; and distrusting their intention, Marjeet declined obeying the order for his appearance at the installation of the king; but anxious to avert the consequences of a more explicit refusal, he pleaded the hostile intentions of his brothers in excuse for his disobedience. A Burmese army was immediately despatched to seize the rebel; they were encountered by the Manipuris at Kokshing, the scene of many former struggles between the same troops, and the contest was at length terminated by the retreat of Marjeet, who, deserting his troops, fled precipitately towards Cachar, followed by so large a proportion of the population of the country that the Burmans gained little more by their conquest than the glory of having vanquished a force greatly inferior in numbers. Marjeet, on reaching Cachar, was kindly received by his brother Choorjet, to whom he made a formal resignation of the regal authority, by giving into his charge the sacred images of Govinduh and Burnamchundruh, which he had brought away with him from Manipur. Heerachundruh, the son of Robinchundruh and nephew of Marjeet, continued at the head of a small body of horse to annoy the Burmese garrison left in Manipur, who in vain attempted to capture him. He was secretly supported by his countrymen, who admired his gallantry, and by keeping him acquainted with the movements of the enemy, enabled him to cut off many of their small detachments.

In 1822, Petumbhur Sing, another nephew, was despatched from Cachar by Choorjet to his assistance, and they succeeded in drawing a large Burmese detachment into an ambuscade, every man of which was cut to pieces. The country had been so much devastated by the long continuance of hostilities, that the leaders of these parties found themselves unable to sustain the force they kept up, and consequently withdrew into Cachar. In the following year Petumbhur Sing was again detached by Choorjet to depose a man called Shoobol, who had been placed on the gadi by the Burmans, and having effected that object Petumbhur assumed the dignity himself. To dispossess him, Gumbheer Sing left Cachar with a small force, and Petumbhur having been worsted in an action near Jeynugur, fled to the Court of Ava, where he remained. Gumbheer Sing, from the extreme difficulty of obtaining supplies, was compelled to return almost immediately to Cachar, when, in consequence of disagreements with his brother Choorjet, the latter retired to Sylhet, leaving Marjeet and Gumbheer in possession of nearly the whole of that territory of which Govinchundruh had been unjustly deprived. In this state of affairs the Burmese war commenced; the forces of Ava again occupied Manipur, and when our frontier was threatened through Cachar, negociations were opened with the three Manipuri brothers, who supplicated to be taken under our protection. The proposition was acceded to, and the Burmese authorities, though made acquainted with the fact, persisted in their original design of invading it, and eventually overran the province with a very considerable body of troops. Gumbheer Sing, the most enterprising of the three brothers, with whom we had negociated, raised from among his own followers a body of 500 men, who actively co-operated with our troops in expelling the Burmese force from Cachar; and in June 1825 he compelled them to evacuate the Manipur valley. In the following year, having obtained some reinforcements, he entered Kubbo, attacked the Burmese forces in their stockaded position at Tummoo, and pursuing them across the Ungoching hills, cleared the western bank of the Ningthee river of every opposing detachment. At the conclusion of the peace by the treaty of Yandaboo in February 1826, Gumbheer Sing was recognised as the Raja of Manipur, where he continued to reign until January 1834, when he suddenly expired, leaving an infant son, the Raja

Burmese war.

Treaty of Yandaboo, A.D. 1826.

Kirti Singh, who was formally acknowledged by the British Government, and a regency, of which the Sunaputtee, Nar Sing, his late father's most confidential and faithful friend, governed the country. During the regency of Nar Sing, numerous attempts were made to upset the government. The first occurred in 1838. In that year Tarring Komba, eldest son of a former Raja Robinchundruh, made a raid with 300 followers from Cachar. They were met by 500 men of Nar Sing's on entering the valley of Manipur. In the fight which ensued, Tarring Komba and his brother, with many followers, were killed, 100 were taken prisoners, the remainder fled. The prisoners were released after being detained one year. Within the next few years the following attempts at securing the raj took place: Marjeet's eldest son named Jogendra Sing, tried to invade the country; but he and his brother were both killed in the hills on their way to the valley. Two sons of Choorjet Sing, Tribhubunjet and Ram Sing, also made an attempt; they managed to get inside the Raja's enclosure at night, but in the fight which ensued in the morning both were killed. After Nar Sing had declared himself Raja, another attempt was made, not long before his death, by one Melai Ramba and his brother, descendants of Raja Churai Romba. They invaded the valley from Cachar. In an engagement which took place in the valley, Melai Ramba's brother was killed and himself taken prisoner; he was executed by being put into a basket and flung into the river. This was the last political execution. It will be readily understood that these continued disturbances and fights rendered the position of the Political Agent anything but pleasant; however, he was never interfered with, although sometimes rather awkwardly situated, as when, in the progress of one of the skirmishes, a cannon ball coming from the Raja's enclosure struck his house. On the Rani reaching Cachar, as before mentioned, she placed herself under British protection, and had a small guard of sepoys told off for her security. An allowance of Rs. 100 a month was allowed her from the Kubbo compensation money for her and the young Raja's support. During a stay of five years in Cachar, she made many applications to Government to regain the gadi for the Raja; but these were not listened to, Nar Sing having become Raja. She then proceeded to Assam with a view of consulting with Captain Jenkins, the Commissioner, who she supposed would be able to aid her in her efforts to regain the gadi for her son. Some correspondence went on, it is believed, on the subject, but the Rani was finally referred to the Manipur Political Agent. After remaining one year in Assam, she returned with the Raja to Cachar, where she remained until the death of Nar Sing in 1850. After the death of Nar Sing, which took place from cholera, an epidemic of that disease then raging in the valley, his brother Debendra Sing, a man of less firmness and talent than Nar Sing, assumed the raj, it is said in the Political Agent's correspondence of the time, at the request of Nar Sing. He is said also to have exhorted his three sons to proceed to Cachar and render every assistance in their power to further this end. Be this as it may, there is no doubt that the three sons of Nar Sing, almost immediately after his death, fled to Cachar, and put themselves in communication, together with other influential men who had left Manipur, with Chandra Kirti Sing. Fearing disturbances after the flight of Nar Sing's sons to Cachar, a guard was placed over the Raja Chandra Kirti Sing. About this time the Raja petitioned for the restoration of his raj; but before he had time to receive an answer, he had contrived to elude his guards, and was in full march for Manipur,

Death of Nar Sing, 1850.

accompanied by Nar Sing's three sons and about 100 followers. Halting at the Jiri river, where he was joined by more recruits, he sent a letter to the Political Agent, intimating his intentions of coming on to Manipur. He met with but little opposition on the way, and reached the valley safely. After another trifling skirmish, he established himself in a former residence of the Raja's situated three miles from the captial to the south, and commanding the most fertile part of the valley. During five days matters remained quiet; many of the followers of Debendra Sing's deserted him and went over to the young Raja, whose advent was apparently approved of by the majority of the people. After this period, Debendra Sing's prospects became hopeless, and he was forced to fly, after having been attacked by the troops who had up to this time adhered to his cause. Debendra Sing made his way with his family to Cachar, where he remained, making no doubt preparations for the attempts he afterwards made to recover the raj. It would appear, both from the opinions of the then Political Agent and the present statements of the Manipuris, that Debendra Sing was not popular, and that, when a son of Gumbheer Sing appeared on the scene, the prestige of his being the only male descendant of the Raja, who had freed the country from the hated Burman, told immensely in his favour. The fact of Chandra Kirti Sing having been accompanied in his expedition by Nar Sing's sons had also a favourable effect, as tending to unite the two great factions of the country—the supporters of Gumbheer Sing's family and that of Nar Sing. Debendra Sing having fled after only occupying the gadi for three months, Chandra Kirti Sing assumed the raj, naming as joboraj, or successor, the eldest son of Nar Sing, another son, to be senaputi. The attitude of the Political Agent at this period was of simple expectancy, and, with the exception that the Kubbo compensation money was withheld, nothing was done. He stated, as his opinion, that the above arrangement with Nar Sing's son was not likely to continue, and feared that, from his ignorance of the country, the young Raja would fall entirely into the hands of his advisers, and great oppression and misery result. Not more than a fortnight had elapsed after the flight of Debendra Sing, when disturbances, as the Political Agent feared, broke out. A younger brother of Debendra's who had remained behind on his flight, united with Nar Sing's sons, and with 600 followers attacked the Raja; but they were defeated, and fled towards Cachar. When Debendra Sing assumed the raj, apparently by desire of Nar Sing, the Political Agent recommended that he should be recognised by Government. This recognition was accorded; but as it arrived eleven days after Debendra's flight, it could not be acted on, and was not made known. Before the above orders were received, however, and to add to the complications of the situation, Debendra Sing had made known his intentions of making an attempt to recover the raj. The first attempt was made about two months after his flight from Manipur, and was unsuccessful, his adherents being dispersed by the Raja's troops in the hills about half-way to Manipur. Another attempt was made after this, but was defeated by Government sepoys, who followed up and dispersed the raiders. After the last raid, Debendra Sing was seized by the Cachar officials, and conveyed first to Sylhet, and afterwards to Dacca, where he died in November 1871. He was supported by an allowance from the Kubbo compensation money of Rs. 70 a month. In the meantime, matters in Manipur were going on from bad to worse, and great oppression was caused by the reckless behaviour of the authorities, unchecked apparently by the Raja. These unscrupulous men, fearing the success of Debendra Sing's plans for regaining the raj, only thought of enriching themselves at the expense of the unfortunate inhabitants, who by this time had become so dissatisfied with the rule of Chandra Kirti Sing that the majority of them would have gladly welcomed back Debendra Sing, who would doubtless have succeeded in reaching the valley in his second attempt, had he not been attacked and routed by the British forces. Not content with oppressing the people, the attitude of the Raja and his advisers was at this period one of decided hostility to the Political Agent, who was accused unjustly, it need scarcely be said, of keeping back the Kubbo compensation allowance, which the Raja and his harpies constantly clamoured for, and which was withheld until it could be clearly shown that the Raja was able to hold his own. So insolent had they become, although they had been assured that the Political Agent, in withholding the Kubbo allowance, was only acting up to the orders of Government, that they openly gave out that, if they did not receive the allowance when the next instalment became due, they would re-occupy the Kubbo valley. The whole of the conduct of the Manipur Government at this time is characterized by the Political Agent as being "unbecoming from the Court of the son of the man who owed his throne to the British Government." The Political Agent, writing to Government at this time, states: "I have met with some petty acts of annoyance indicating a bad spirit in the authorities, who (at least many of them) seem to think that the presence of the representative of the British Government ought to be no check on them; that by their prowess they gained the throne for the young Raja in spite of the British Government, and now they have got it, they may do exactly as they choose. I trust, however, as they cool down, they may understand their position. The young Raja, I believe, does." Again, in October 1850, the Political Agent fears that the unsettled state of the country may induce the Burmans to interfere and assist a prince named Nibirjit, who was then in high favour with the Court of Ava. In December 1850, matters at length reached a climax demanding interference. At this time, it was clearly shown that the Manipur Government had supplied arms and men to a tribe of Nagas to the north at that time hostile to the British Government. All the remonstrances of the Political Agent failed in eliciting any satisfactory explanation of this transaction, and the matter was reported to Government. In reply, Government administered a rebuke to the Manipur Raja, and reminded him that his State only existed by the sufferance and countenance of the British Government. At this the state of affairs improved considerably, the Raja evidently being recalled to a proper sense of his position, and ruling with a greater regard to the rights and feelings of his subjects.

In February 1851, the orders of Government recognising the succession of Chandra Kirti Sing to the raj of Manipur were conveyed to him, and shortly afterwards another assurance of stability was given by Government undertaking still further to guarantee the raj to him and his descendants, and to prevent, by force of arms if necessary, any attempts by rival chiefs to dislodge him. Very shortly after the above recognition, other raids on Manipur took place, which are related briefly as follows.

In 1851, Debendra Sing's and Nar Sing's sons made an attempt. In the subsequent fight which ensued, Debendra Sing's eldest son was killed and two of Nar Sing's sons taken prisoners; these were afterwards made officials and forgiven. One year after the above, two sons of Madu Chandra and one of Marjeet Sing's, named Kanai Sing, made an attempt. Madu Chandra's two sons were captured, and afterwards died in Manipur; Kanai Sing escaped, and subsequently made other attempts. Up to the time of the outbreak of the

Indian mutiny of 1857, no other raids took place. At the latter end of 1857, or beginning of 1858, the sepoys stationed at Chittagong mutinied and made for Cachar; they were met and defeated at Latu on the borders of the Sylhet and Cachar districts by a detachment of the Sylhet Light Infantry, now the 44th Native Infantry; they afterwards continued on their way east in the direction of the Manipur frontier. The Political Agent, on hearing of the Chittagong mutiny, asked the Raja to send a body of his troops to the frontier to prevent the mutineers entering his country; this was at once done, and 400 men under two majors despatched. These troops did good service, and captured a number of the mutineers, who were given up to the British officials. It is supposed that nearly, if not all the mutineers were killed, captured, or perished miserably in the jungles of the Manipur and Kuki hills. During the whole of the period of the mutiny, the Political Agent, in his reports to Government, states that the conduct and feelings of the Raja and the majority of the officials and inhabitants were at that time good, and the Raja's offers of assistance to the British Government, in case of need, sincere. Advantage was taken of the arrival of the mutineers by some of the Manipuri chiefs in Cachar, and several joined them, with a view of getting their aid in overthrowing the Manipur Government. Among them was Nurendrojit or Chai Aham ("Chai Aham," three years, so called as he was supposed to have been three years in his mother's womb), a younger son of Choorjet Sing's; he was made prisoner and handed over to the British officers; he was eventually transported.

During the mutiny, an attempt was made by Government to enlist men as sepoys for general service; but it quite failed, as the Manipuris did not like the idea of serving in the North-Western Provinces, more especially as disturbances were still going on. In 1859, at the recommendation of the Political Agent, the Raja was presented with a dress of honour, sword, and belt; at the same time, eight of his chief officers received khilluts. These gifts were expressive of approval of the conduct of the Raja and his officers during the mutiny. One Major Roma Sing also received the mutiny medal, he having been actually engaged with the mutinous sepoys from Chittagong. In 1859 Mypak, a descendant of Gharib Newaz, made an attempt; he reached the valley, but was defeated under the western hills and fled. In 1862 he again invaded the valley; his party was followed up by sepoys from Cachar, who had skirmishes with the raiders in the hills, but did not succeed in stopping them. Mypak succeeded in eluding the parties sent against him, including a guard of 50 men of the 44th Sikh Light Infantry under a European officer and attached to the Political Agency at that time, and got inside the Raja's enclosure at night. In the morning he and his party were easily overcome by the Manipuris, and Mypak wounded and taken prisoner.

The sepoys were not called upon to act. Mypak died in Manipur some two or three years afterwards. Several of his descendants and followers are still alive in the valley. Towards the end of 1864 or beginning of 1865, Kanai Sing made his second attempt, accompanied by about 200 followers. He only got as far as the Jiri river, where he was overtaken by a party of the 33rd Native Infantry and police, who completely defeated and dispersed the raiders, Kanai Sing making his escape.

In December 1866, the last of these raids took place, led by Gokul Sing, a younger son of Debendra Sing, who had not accompanied his father to Dacca. With about 100 followers he managed to reach the valley unmolested, though closely followed up by a party of sepoys and police from Cachar. The

Manipuris sent out a party to meet him as soon as the news came in; this party came up with the raiders under the hills to the west, about 10 miles from the capital. It being nearly dark when they came in contact, little was done, and the Raja's men proceeded to entrench themselves, proposing to attack the raiders in the morning. In the meantime, unknown to the Manipuris, the sepoys from Cachar were approaching; their advance being observed by Gokul Sing, he and his adherents fled. The British force coming suddenly in the dark upon the force of entrenched Manipuris, and supposing them to be the enemy, at once attacked them. The Manipuris, on their side, were under the impression, the night being dark, that they in their turn were being attacked by Gokul Sing and his men, defended themselves. An irregular firing on both sides was kept up all night, and in the morning the mistake was at once discovered. In the meantime Gokul Sing and his adherents had got clear off. In this unfortunate affair several men were wounded on either side; one man, a sepoy of the British force, afterwards died. Gokul Sing eluded pursuit until 1868, when he was apprehended by the police in Kuch Behar; he was afterwards tried in Cachar and sentenced to seven years' imprisonment. The number of Manipuri princes now resident in the British provinces who are influential enough to make raids on Manipur are few. Debendra Sing died last year,* and his nephew, a son of Nar Sing's, named Shaikar Sing, is detained at Dacca under British surveillance, as a political detenue, on an allowance of Rs. 20 a month. Kanai Sing, who has been at large since his last raid in 1865, was captured in 1871, and he, as well as Gokul Sing, are at Hazaribagh as exiles, and receive from the Manipur Durbar an allowance of Rs. 30 each per mensem. Kala, *alias* Dayabant Sing, a grandson of Choorjet Sing, is also at Hazaribagh under British surveillance. Nirjit Sing, another son of Debendra Sing, is living at Dacca with Shaikar Sing. Kanai Sing has an elder brother who resides in Angartolah in Tipperah, named Durjai Sing; but there is nothing against him. Quirakpa, a grandson of Marjeet, formerly resided in the valley; but as he wanted to raise disturbances, he was made to leave the country by the present Raja; he now resides in Sylhet. Fourteen Manipuris, exiled from time to time for adhering to the cause of the raiders, have been released by Government at the request of the Maharaja. There seems to be no apprehension of any attempts to seize the raj from the Burmese side. Before the introduction of firearms at the time of the Burmese war, the numerous hill tribes now under control were then almost entirely independent, they being constantly at feud amongst themselves and with Manipur. The inhabitant of the valley had to meet the hillman with his own weapons, the spear, bow and arrow, &c. Amongst the whole of the hill tribes at this period, the Tankuls and Luhupas were the most troublesome, occasionally making raids into the valley itself, but, like all hillmen, afraid to quit the shelter of their hills for any distance, and easily beaten back by the pony cavalry of the State. Communication with the west at this time had scarcely any existence, and only large armed bodies of men could go with safety from the Manipur valley towards Cachar. The Kaupois and Marrings were then, as now, the most under control; during the invasion of the Burmans, the hillmen on the line of the road invariably fled, and none of the Burmese operations involved the subjection of the hill tribes away from their lines of route. The whole of the hill tribes were unfriendly to the Burmans; and although no organised attempt at resistance to their march was ever made by them, they lost no opportunity of annoying them and cutting off stragglers.

* 1878.

After the defeat of the Burmans in Cachar, on their retreat they lost a number of men in the hills. As soon as the country became somewhat settled after the Burmese war, Raja Gambheer Sing turned his attention to the subjugation of the hill tribes. He, by the aid of the firearms now in his possession, speedily reduced the major portion of them to subjection. Before his death he reduced the Kaupuis completely, and brought the Tankuls, Luhupas, and Angami Nagas into fair order. During this period it was undoubtedly found necessary to resort occasionally to severe measures, and it may be supposed that the Manipuris, smarting under all that they had suffered from the hands of the tribes, made fatal use of their weapons; but this excessive punishment has long ago ceased. During the time of Raja Gambheer Sing two British officers, the late Captains Jenkins and Pemberton, accompanied by some 1,000 Manipuri sepoys, crossed the hills between the Manipur and Assam valleys; they met with much opposition from the warlike tribe of Angamis. Raids by any of the hill tribes have long ceased. Although it would not be profitable to detail every little raid or disturbance that has taken place of late years, some particulars with regard to raids by the Lushai tribe of Kukis may be found of interest. Until some 32 years ago, the tribes to the south in contact with the Manipuris were the Khongjai and Kom Kukis. On these being driven out by the Lushais, a series of raids and annoyances by the latter commenced, and continued until 1870-71. Disturbances have always been confined to the hills occupied by the Kaupui tribe of Nagas, although they once on their first appearance invaded the valley. This raid, the first by the Lushais, occurred about 32 years ago, when Raja Nar Sing occupied the gadi. The leader was Chief Vonolail, now dead. A village of Khongjais near the south of the valley was first destroyed, after which the Lushais entered the valley. The Manipuris in the villages adjacent turned out to the number of 500 with one mounted man armed with a spear to oppose them, and the Lushais were driven back with a loss of 10 men killed, the Manipuri loss being only 2. It is said that the one mounted man behaved with great bravery and inflicted great damage upon them; after this raid, the only thing done was to establish a post at the point where they had entered the valley. About three years after the above occurrence, a village, named Nomidong or Nungdang (the same village as was destroyed by the Lushais in October 1868, and in which they awaited the attack of the Manipuris sent against them), was cut up; but it was never clearly ascertained whether the outrage was committed by Khongjais or Lushais. After an interval of about two years, during the incumbency of the Raja Chandra Kirti Sing, the thana of Kala Naga, containing only 10 men at the time, was suddenly attacked, the sepoys making good their escape. The Lushais numbered about 500, and the thana and surrounding villages were destroyed. The Lushais after this retreated, but returned in three months and committed great ravages in and around the Kala Naga range of hills, the few sepoys in the thana which had not been strengthened again retreating. Three hundred men were at once despatched from Manipur on this occasion, but they arrived only to find that the Lushais had gone. The Kala Naga post was now strengthened, 300 men being posted in it. Shortly after this the Lushais returned for the third time and burnt a village close to the thana, evidently unaware of the reinforcement that had been thrown into the post. The Manipuris having concealed themselves, a party of them entered, and the Manipuris, rushing from their concealment, captured ten of them before they could offer any resistance, the rest escaping. The prisoners were brought into Manipur, where they were detained for three or four years, after which nine of them succeeded in escaping from custody; but they were all killed by Khongjai Kukis while trying to make their way back to their own country. After this, negociations were opened with the Chief; Vonolail, the surviving prisoner, who was a relative of his, was released on the Chief's giving a promise not to molest Manipur for the future. This promise the Lushais faithfully kept until 1868, when they again broke out and made raids on Mukti, Nungdang, &c., and attacked and burnt Kala Naga stockade. In 1872 the British Government sent an expeditionary force into the Lushai country, and punished the tribes that committed raids in the Cachar district. The Manipur Government, at the instance of the Government of India, also sent a force of 2,000 sepoys under two majors, with a view to co-operate with the Cachar column. They were detached at Chibu, in order to restrain Kamhow's tribe and guard the southern frontier. Though they were not employed in any active service, yet they succeeded in assisting and escorting some captives and refugees into their camp. On the return of the force in March 1872, some eight Lushai Chiefs, consisting of Dambum and others, came into Manipur and entered into a treaty with the Maharaja. The Government of India has also acknowledged the services rendered by the Manipur Dubar during the expedition, and presented the Raja with 500 Victoria muskets and 12 sporting rifles for himself and his princes. Three of his officers, Bolaram, Tangal, and Gokul, have also received khilluts from Government in recognition of their services.

Although the origin of British influence in the affairs of Manipur has been already referred to, it may be well here to give a connected account of its rise and the benefits it has conferred on the country. Up to the time of the first Burmese war, or rather shortly before it, little had been heard of the Manipuris. During the reign of Jaee Sing, Chingtung Khomba, negociations were entered into with the British Government about 1762, with a view to obtain its assistance against the Burmans; but nothing was effected. There is no knowledge among the Manipuris of the present day of any actual treaty, as mentioned in Aitchison's Treaties, page 121, having been concluded. In 1833 the following treaty was concluded with Gambheer Sing. Of this treaty the Raja has no copy, and never seems to have possessed one.

TREATY WITH GAMBHEER SING.

"The Governor General and Supreme Council of Hindustan declare as follows:—

"With regard to the two ranges of hills, the one called the Kala Naga range, and the other called Nungjai range, which are situated between the eastern and western bends of the Barak, we will give up all claim on the part of the Honourable Company thereunto, and we will make these hills over to the possession of the Raja, and give him the line of the Jiri and the western bend of the Barak as a boundary, provided that the Raja agrees to the whole of what is written in this paper, which is as follows:—

"*1st*—The Raja will, agreeably to instructions received, without delay remove his thana from Chadrapur and establish it on the eastern bank of the Jiri.

"*2nd*—The Raja will in no way obstruct the trade carried on between the two countries by Bengali or Manipuri merchants. He will not exact heavy duties, and he will make a monopoly of no articles of merchandise whatever.

"*3rd*—The Raja will in no way prevent the Nagas inhabiting the Kala Naga and Nungjai ranges of hills from selling or bartering ginger, cotton, pepper, and every other article, the produce of their country, in the plains of Cachar, at the Banskandi and Oodherban bazaars, as has been their custom.

"*4th*—With regard to the road commencing from the eastern bank of the Jiri, and continued *viâ* Kala Naga and Kowpum, as far as the valley of Manipur, after this road has been finished, the Raja will keep it in repairs so as to enable laden bullocks to pass during the cold and dry seasons. Further, at the making of the road, if British officers be sent to examine or superintend the same, the Raja will agree to everything these officers may suggest.

"*5th*—With reference to the intercourse already existing between the territories of the British Government and those of the Raja, if the intercourse be further extended, it will be well in every respect, and it will be highly advantageous to both the Raja and his country. In order, therefore, that this may speedily take place, the Raja, at the requisition of the British Government, will furnish a quota of Nagas to assist in the construction of the road.

"*6th*—In the event of war with the Burmans, if the troops be sent to Manipur either to protect the country or to advance beyond the Ningthee, the Raja, at the requisition of the British Government, will provide hill porters to assist in transporting ammunition and baggage of such troops.

"*7th*—In the event of anything happening on the eastern frontier of the British territories, the Raja will, when required, assist the British Government with a portion of his troops.

"*8th*—The Raja will be answerable for all the ammunition he receives from the British Government, and will, for the information of the British Government, give in every month a statement of expenditure to the British officer attached to the Levy."

All the provisions of the above treaty, with the exception of the last, remain in force. The only other arrangement carried out between the British and Manipur Governments in the form of a treaty relates to the handing over of the Kubbo valley to the Burmans, and the payment of the monthly allowance in lieu. This arrangement bears date January 25th, 1834, and stipulates that, should the Kubbo valley, from any circumstances, again revert to Manipur, the allowance shall cease. In 1835, the British support in pay was withdrawn from the force constituting the Manipur Levy, and the British Government established the Political Agency. The objects of the establishment of the Political Agency were, to preserve a friendly intercourse with the Manipur Government, and, as occasion may require, with the Burmese authorities on the frontier, and more especially to prevent border feuds and disturbances which might lead to hostilities between the Manipuris and Burmese. Such were the original duties of the Political Agent. It took many years to bring about the general peace that now prevails on the Burmese frontier; but any relaxation in the endeavours to keep the tribes on that border quiet would be followed by infractions of the peace, such as were formerly so frequent, and which might lead to hostilities between Manipuris and Burmese.

From this sketch of the history of Manipur and the vicissitudes through which it has passed, the determined character of the people and their rooted aversion to the yoke of the Burmans are clearly shown. Religious prejudices have served still more strongly to keep alive the feeling of hatred produced by so many years of persevering aggression, and we may rely implicitly on the attachment of the Manipuris to the power which has effectually rescued them from their state of degradation and suffering. Their country is to be regarded principally as an advanced military position for the defence of the eastern frontier, and its utility must entirely depend upon its natural resources and the efficiency of its military force. The materials for forming a correct opinion on the first of these points have been furnished in the preceding paragraphs.

The Local Force in 1837.

The whole local force in that year consisted of infantry 3,000 men, cavalry 100 men, and 100 golandauz attached to four 3-pounders, and, if required emergently, another battalion of 1,000 men could have been raised. In lieu of pay, grants of land were made to the officers and men, while the arms and accoutrements were supplied by the British Government.

(*Capt. Pemberton, 1835.*)

Manipur Militia.

The present Manipur army had its origin in the old Manipur Levy, a body of 500 men raised by Raja Gambheer Sing in 1824, during the Burmese war. This body was armed and paid by the British Government and served under its directions. The original force of 500 was shortly increased to 1,000 and afterwards to 2,000, and two British officers were attached to it to superintend drill and discipline. These troops did good service in 1825. They cleared Manipur of the Burmese, and in the following year took the valley of Kubbo. In 1835 the one British officer which remained with the force was withdrawn, and since that date the efficiency of the Manipur troops has considerably deteriorated. The soldiers of Manipur receive no pay, but have land assigned to them according to rank, the value of a private sepoy's holding being about Rs. 7 per annum. Nominally, every man serves 10 days out of each 40; but were this rule strictly adhered to, the garrisoning of the more distant posts would be practically impossible. At such places, therefore, it is usual for the men to serve several months consecutively. Service may be said to be hereditary, the land with its obligations descending from father to son, so* that the army increases with the population, and now numbers about 7,000, including 700 irregulars. The troops are supposed to be organised in regiments (battalions ?). These are all infantry, except about 500 artillerymen, who have charge of eight old 3-pounder brass field guns, which are quite useless. The once celebrated Manipur cavalry, which performed brilliantly in the Burmese war, has practically disappeared, though a body of 400 still nominally exists. The reason for this extinction of the cavalry arm is that the breed of native ponies has very greatly deteriorated, while the import of ponies from Burma has been stopped since 1871 by the Burmese Government, without any apparent reason, so that to

* There is much vacant land and cultivation, and new holdings are being constantly increased. – (*J. Johnstone, 1885.*)

mount a force efficiently is now impossible. This is the more unfortunate as Manipur was originally formidable principally on account of the number of mounted troops it could put into the field, and in a war with Burma the old pony cavalry would still be of immense service. According, however, to the Assam Trade Report of 1879-80, the Raja has stopped the export of ponies from his dominions, with the view of resuscitating the old breed. There is, therefore, some hope of the Manipur cavalry being in time re-established. The men of the infantry are of good physique, capable of bearing great fatigue, patient, willing, and obedient. They are always ready to march, carrying their own provisions, building their own huts, and, if necessary, entrenching themselves. Their independence, says Lieutenant-Colonel Johnstone, the Political Agent, is in striking contrast to the requirements of our own troops, who cannot move without a great number of coolies. The British officers who served with the Manipuris in the Burmese war thought well of their fighting qualities. If organised and again placed under British leaders, the Manipur troops would soon become a serviceable body. Their own officers are very incompetent, and the present drill and training of the men is at the lowest ebb. About half the infantry are armed with smooth-bore muskets. In addition to the regular State troops, some 700 Kuki irregulars are kept up. These act as scouts, &c., during expeditions. They are naturally more courageous and better soldiers than the Manipuris. Their arms are old muskets of various descriptions.

Colonel Johnstone writes :—

"Service in the army is said not to be popular; but I doubt if any of the men would change with those performing ordinary 'lalúp,' and I feel sure that a low rate of pay would make a soldier's calling the most popular of all. It is well known that service in the old levy was much sought after. The Maharaja formerly took much pride in his army, and used to personally superintend the drill of the men; latterly, however, he has neglected it.

"At present the Manipur troops may be considered useful as a body of men always in readiness and always at the disposal of the British Government for service on this frontier when required, and their services could be utilised at a minimum of cost, as it would only be necessary to pay them during the time they were embodied."

CHAPTER IV.

NATURAL HISTORY.

Wild Animals.

Those that inhabit the valley are few in number—tiger, a species of wild cat, pig, and two species of deer. The jackal is unknown to Manipur.

Wild fowl, comprising geese, duck, teal, snipe, &c., abound all over the valley.

Tiger.—This animal is common in the Manipur valley, and frequently attains a large size; they generally confine their depredations to carrying off cattle and ponies, but man-eaters are not uncommon. The tiger and wild hog are at times destructive to human life. In one instance a tiger got into a house, killed seven individuals, and was not destroyed until he had eaten one of them.

Mode of capturing tigers.—As in Bengal, when the lair of a tiger has been noted and marked, it is surrounded by a strong rope net, and information is at once given to the authorities. The officer of the "lalúp" in which the tigers are found makes arrangements for their destruction, first, however, informing the Raja in case he might like to kill one himself. Villagers are rewarded for the destruction of tigers, according to circumstances, the rewards varying in value from a present of land and a robe of honour to small rewards of money, cloth, and salt.

In order to keep down the number of tigers, an arrangement is in existence all over the country for trapping them. This is done by "karrups" or tiger parties, who surround the tiger with a net. There are also scouts called "whiroi," whose duty it is to mark the lair of the tiger which is then surrounded by the "karrup." Now that firearms are common in the country, they are always used in despatching the tiger. Spearmen are also always present, but their services are seldom required. Formerly, when spears alone were used, many fatalities occurred. When the Raja is present at the killing of a tiger, great crowds assemble of both sexes, and all the headmen with sepoys, &c., are present.

Deer.—The best time for deer-shooting is about March, at which time the grass jungle is burnt, and the young grass shoots up; at other times the deer retire into the hills.

Sambhar and Cervus Eldii or the Pegu swamp deer, ravine, barking deer, and hog deer.

Wild Fowl.—The valley towards the Logták lake during the cold season positively swarms with wild fowl, especially geese. Both the geese and ducks met with in the valley are fine birds and make good eating. The wild fowl, especially the geese, nearly all migrate to the hills during the hot weather.

Of other birds there are mostly the varieties common to Eastern Bengal. The only crow seen is the large black variety. Kites are few in number. Singing birds, varieties unknown by name, are common; their song is chiefly heard in the early morning.

The wild animals found in Manipur hill territory may now be briefly enumerated.

Elephant.—This animal exists in large numbers both to the north and south of the Manipur valley; also to the south of the Cachar road and in the Jiri forest. The hillmen hunt and kill them for the flesh and tusks.

Leopards.—These are few in number.

Wild Cats.—Of these there are several varieties.

Bears.—Of these there are two varieties, one small and one large and fierce. They are both black, and are mostly found to the north.

Wild Goat.—The Goorat, found on the hills to the north.

Wild Pig.—Plentiful and very large; tusks very long and curved upwards.

Porcupine.—Plentiful.

Wild Buffalo.—This animal is found to the south of the valley only.

Wild Methna or Hill Cow.—This animal in a wild state is now rare, and is found to the south only.

Rhinoceros—Is found only in the hills to the south and east.

Flying Lemurs—Are said to be not uncommon.

Mole or Mole Rat.—This animal is said to be found of a reddish colour. Should a Manipuri meet this animal on the road, he will not pass the place until he has caught and killed it; he afterwards splits the animal lengthways, and flings the halves on either side. If the animal cannot be caught, it is considered a very bad omen, and the journey is resumed reluctantly.

Rat.—This animal is very plentiful in the hills, and is of large size. Rats often occasion great destruction of the hillman's crops; they appear in immense swarms at times, and their coming is said to be simultaneous with the flowering of the bamboos. These swarms are common in the west and south; they appear suddenly, it is said, at night, and eat up the ripened but standing grain and the stores in the villages, and disappear as rapidly and mysteriously as they come. Their last appearance was in 1868, when they invaded the Naga villages lying close to the Manipur road, and committed so much damage that supplies of rice had to be sent to the sufferers from the Manipur valley. Besides this rat, there are also found the common brown and musk rat. Mice are also common.

Otter.—Of this there are two varieties, one large and the other small.

Monkeys.—Hoolook—these are plentiful; lungoor, a large monkey resembling the ourang-outang, is said to be found to the north; the common brown monkey; and a small reddish monkey, which is said to hide its face when observed by men.

Bats and flying-foxes, birds, jungle fowl, partridge, quail, snipe, hawks, kites, black crow, doves, eagles of a black colour, are said to be found in the highest peaks; owls, parrots, small birds in great variety, mostly without song.

Snakes.—The boa-constrictor is found in the dense jungle to the south, and is said frequently to attain a large size; other small varieties of the snake tribe are found in the jungles; they are all or nearly all innocuous.

Domestic Animals.

Those kept by the Manipuris are the horse or rather pony, the cow, buffalo, goat, fowls, ducks, geese, pigeons, cat. Dogs are only occasionally kept by them. They look upon them as unclean, and therefore have to bathe if touched by them.

Breed of Ponies.—The breed of ponies in Manipur is similar to that in Burma; they are generally small, under 12 hands high, but strong and hardy. Good ponies are decidedly scarce, and the Manipuris show a remarkable carelessness in breeding them. They are allowed to graze about the country in herds; consequent upon this good ponies are becoming more and more rare every year, and threaten to become altogether extinct at no distant date. Some 43 years ago, an attempt was made to breed horses in the valley, but the experiment failed. In 1859, Government, at the request of Nar Sing, then Regent, sent an Arab stallion and 8 mares, apparently stud-bred, to Manipur. In a few years, however, they and their progeny had all died. No other experiment of the sort has since been tried. It is likely, however, that Cabul horses would thrive, as that breed is the one that stands all climates in India probably the best. Arabs, as a rule, do not thrive in the climates of Assam or Eastern Bengal, which Manipur resembles.

Breed of Cattle.—The ordinary breed of cattle is the same as that of Bengal. They are, however, a better looking class of animals, probably from the climate being more favourable, and grazing ground being of better quality. They have lately decreased to a great extent owing to the murrain of 1870-71. There is also a variety resembling the Brahmini breed. Buffaloes were plentiful and formed the chief trade of the country; but they also were killed by the murrain; as many as 95 per cent. of all the buffaloes perished. Sheep are not bred in the valley, although imported ones thrive well, the ewes giving as many as two, three, and four lambs at a time. The other domestic animals resemble in all points those common in Bengal.

Domestic Animals kept by Hillmen.—The domestic animals kept in common by the hillmen are buffaloes, cows, methnas, goats, pigs, dogs, cats, fowls, ducks, and pigeons. The methna or hill cow is an animal peculiar to the hills bordering on the north-east frontier. It is a large animal, and in shape of body closely resembles the buffalo; its horns are shorter, however, like the cow, and thick at the base; it is also seen, unlike the buffalo, with the hide marked in coloured patches, although black is the ordinary colour; neither is it half amphibious like the buffalo. This animal is highly valued by the hillmen, and is consequently expensive; the cost of a methna being from Rs. 40 to Rs. 70, thus very few can afford to keep them. No use is made of the animal while alive, it not being worked like the buffalo. It is killed for feasts and sacrifices. The goat common in the hills is the long-haired variety. The dog, except to the north, is similar to the Bengali pariah. The same with the other animals mentioned above.

Cultivation.

Rice.—No fewer than 19 varieties of rice are grown in the country. These may be divided into early and late crops. The early crop ripens in three months and is ready for cutting in September. Of late years a large quantity of the early sort has been sown. Of the early there are four varieties, *viz.*, Sujikhong, Dumai, Kubbo Phow, and Phowrel Anulbah. The late crop ripens in six months and is reaped about November. The great bulk of rice grown in the country is of the late varieties, which comprise 15 kinds, chiefly distinguished by size of grain and colour. Their names are as follows :—

Phorail.	Towthubi Phow.
Yenthik.	Chahow Puritole.
Moirang Phow.	Chahow Munkhang.
Phowkuk Chahow.	Kuckcheng Phow.
Chahow Mussapalbi.	Haidup Phow.
Laining.	Sugole Yangba.
Phongang.	Chahow Erikole.

Chahow Sempak.

Rice is mostly transplanted, and the land suitable for it is moist and marshy.

Dhall.—The following is a list of the dhalls procurable in the country :—

Mung.	Nunghasye.
Sugole Hasyeor Kulye.	Murrambasye.
Hasye Moirungbi.	Mungul or Mutter.
Khesari.	Cha Hasye.

Haoye Tuchumbi.

The vegetable productions of the country are as follows: Potatoes of inferior quality, sweet-potatoes or sukurkunds, kalindri, kolee hasye, haoye, assungba, brinjals, cucumber, pumpkins, onions, pepper, and tobacco of good quality. English vegetables, peas, indigenous, and English cabbage, cauliflowers, beans, &c. Wheat is grown in the cold season in small quantity, but thrives splendidly.

FRUITS.

Fruits are scarce, and few in number. Plantains of fair quality, pineapples, mangoes* (some of large size and fine quality) are almost the only fruits procurable which would be relished by a European. The stone of the mango at Manipur seems wonderfully prolific, for each seed often produces as many as three or four seedlings, which, if separated when young, would all grow into healthy trees. A plum resembling an English variety is common, but, as met with in the bazaars, is excessively bitter. Peaches grow, but of poor quality. Apples grow on the slopes of the hills, of fair appearance externally, but quite uneatable. Throughout the valley and the neighbouring hills, the bramble and wild raspberry are common. Jack, guava, and raspberry are procurable. Palm† and cocoanut trees are quite unknown. Cotton does not grow in the valley. The cultivation of sugarcane is very limited, but it thrives well.

* All the mangoes are full of insects. In the Kubbo valley they are free from them.

† There are several wild palms. I have introduced English mulberries which thrive exceedingly; English apples which are doing well and bear tolerable fruit; plums which now and then bear; Himalayan apricots, pears and cherries not as yet successful; also Spanish chestnuts.—(*J. Johnstone.*)

The crops raised by the inhabitants of the Manipur hill territory comprise rice, cotton, oil-seeds, pepper, tobacco, vegetables of various kinds, potatoes of small and inferior quality, ginger, sweet-potatoes of very superior quality, Indian-corn, pân leaves, &c. There are numbers of jungle roots and plants used also as food by the hillmen. The yam is plentiful. Jute, flax, hemp, are not cultivated. Opium is cultivated by the Muhammadan population only to a small extent.

CHAPTER V.

AGRICULTURE, &c.

AREA OF LAND FIT FOR CULTIVATION.

A DESCRIPTION of the cultivation of the ground, also of the crops produced by the inhabitants of the Manipur territory, has been given in the preceding chapter. It is impossible to ascertain with any precision the amount of land cultivable in Manipur; but it is believed about one-half of the whole area of the valley is fit for raising crops of various kinds; of this only about one-half is under cultivation.

SYSTEM OF LAND-HOLDING.

The whole land system of the valley starts with the assumption that all the land belongs to the Raja, and is his to give away or retain as he pleases. Under the Raja is an official named the Phunan Salungba, whose duty it is to superintend all matters connected with land cultivation. He looks after the measurement, receives the rent in kind, and transacts all business matters connected with land on behalf of the Raja. The land is subdivided into villages and their surroundings; the headman of each division or village looks after the cultivation, and is responsible for the realisation of the tax payable in kind by each cultivator; he holds no interest in the land, and is merely an agent of the Raja.

GRANTS OF LAND GIVEN TO FAVOURITES, &c.

Besides the land thus directly, as it were, cultivated for the Raja, grants of land are given to officials and favourites, sometimes for their own lives only, or for a specified time, sometimes for themselves and descendants. These hold their lands on payment of the usual tax in kind.

PROPORTION OF LAND CULTIVATED BY DIRECT SYSTEM.

The proportion of land cultivated under what may be called the direct system on account of the Raja is about one-third of the whole; rather more than a third is in possession of the ruling family, Brahmins, and sepoys; the remainder is in the hands of the headmen, officials, &c., who hold it by favour from the Raja. Each individual liable for lalúp or forced labour for the State is entitled to cultivate for his support one parri of land, equivalent to about 3 English acres, subject to the regular payment of the tax in kind.

TAX IN KIND UPON LAND CULTIVATED.

The tax in kind realised from each cultivator and which goes to the Raja is liable to many modifications, although in theory the tax is a fixed one. The tax varies from 2 baskets to 13 from each parri. It is said that the 2 baskets which nominally should only be taken from every one alike is realised from favourites, and that the average from others may be set down at 12 baskets yearly; this is seldom exceeded, except in rare emergencies, as war, &c. This again will only apply to land cultivated for the Raja or held by those subject to lalúp. In cases where lands are held by officials, &c., as the middle class of men, the burdens are more severe, running as high as 24 baskets per parri, which is said to be the outside limit. Considering, however, that the worst parri of land yields 160 baskets, and the best from 160 to 200, the 13 baskets is not a high rent; but so long as the rent taken by the State is given out as 2, every basket over this is an exaction, and may be made a matter of grievance as it is now. The average yield per pari, or 3 acres, is about 150 baskets annually; each basket contains about 60 lb.

Cultivation extending or otherwise.

The Raja, as already said, is the absolute proprietor of the soil, and can dispose of it as he likes. No one is prohibited from cultivating, but rather the contrary; for every male who comes on duty is entitled to cultivate one parri of land, paying in rent for the same in kind. The tax taken over 2 baskets is considered a matter of grievance; but this grievance can only be one as long as the parri of the cultivator is of the standard measure, which is seldom the case. Indeed, it has sometimes been found nearer two, and until a survey has been made, neither the Raja nor the people can be satisfied. Seeing the necessity for a survey, the Raja commenced one in 1868, but it was much disliked. Several persons connected with it have been punished for taking bribes; but bribes will still be taken, and so the measurement will not be honestly done, even if the people employed were qualified to survey it, which is doubted. The land under cultivation yields sufficient for the wants of the people; but the action of the Keiroithau is against the extension of cultivation, and, unless steadily looked to, would lead to its diminution. For some time past attention has been directed to the improvement in the Keiroithau; and as the Raja is anxious to bring more land into cultivation, for which purpose he has caused watercourses to be dug, he will see clearly the necessity of so managing the Keiroithau as to make the people willing to take up the land which will be thus rendered fit for cultivation. It has been ascertained from all sides that, within the last few years more especially, cultivation has been considerably increased, watercourses have been extensively constructed, the survey is still being carried on, and with more satisfaction to the people, and the Keiroithau has been so modified as to be no longer a cause of dissatisfaction to the cultivators.

Mode of Land Cultivation.

The mode of cultivation of the soil does not, from what is the practice in Bengal, materially differ so far as tillage is concerned. The operation of scratching up the soil and preparing the field for the reception of the rice seed commences in February, and in May they sow what is called "pung-hul," or dry seed cast in dry ground. In June, the rains having set in, the field is brought by successive ploughings and harrowings into a state of liquid mud, and in this the "pung-hul" is cast. The seed for the "pung-hul is first quickened by being moistened with water and kept in a covered basket until it shoots. As this seed floats on the surface of the mud, it has to be carefully watched until it takes root and three or four leaves spring up in order to protect it from wild ducks and other birds. After this comes the "Ling-ba" or transplanting. The seed for the plants which are destined to be transplanted are usually sown very close in plots carefully prepared for the purpose. When the transplanting season arrives, the plants are pulled in handfuls out of the ground; the roots are by washing divested of all the earth attached to them, and having been taken to the field, they are, one by one, separately inserted in the mud. For a time after transplanting they look as if they were all withered up; but they soon spring up and afford an excellent crop. If the ground has been carefully deprived of weeds before sowing the crops, weeding afterwards is not required. The only cultivation of any importance is that of rice; not a particle of manure is ever placed on the ground, and yet, year after year, good crops are raised on the same spot. The yield has, of course, lessened from what it was, but its being still so considerable as it is evinces a very rich soil. The mainstay, however, of Manipur is the crop raised at Thobal and its vicinity. There the river, once at least in the year, inundates the rice-fields, giving them amazing fertility. About Thobal they weed with a harrow, which, drawn by a buffalo over the rice-fields, uproots indiscriminately weeds and rice. The former die, and the rice-plants take root again and are not injured. When the rice begins to ripen, it has to be watched against the depredations of immense flights of birds. Deer and other wild animals also do a great deal of mischief, and against them precautions have to be taken. The rice having ripened is cut with a knife, slightly curved at the top, and having a rough edge like a saw. As it is cut, it is laid in handfuls on the ground, and when dry tied in sheaves. These sheaves are carried to the part of the field most convenient for the purpose, and the rice beat from them on a large reed mat. After having been winnowed by means of fans, the rice is ready for the granary and removed to it. This sun-dried rice keeps very well in husk, but when cleared of the husks, it can be kept for a short time only. The straw is left lying in a pile round the place where the paddy was beat out. Except as fuel, no use is made of it.

It will be seen from the above description that the mode of cultivation, the planting, and transplanting the rice, &c., is the same as that followed in Eastern Bengal.

The fertility of the soil, which continues without manure to yield good crops, is doubtless owing to the fact that the rivers flowing through the valley are in the rainy season enormously loaded with mud which becomes annually deposited in the rice-fields. The Manipuris themselves seem, however, to be unaware of the value of the rivers in this respect, and attribute the fertility of the soil to its own inherent richness. The soil of the valley is nearly all throughout of excellent quality and of great depth. The general run of it is a blackish loam towards the hills, and on the hills themselves this becomes reddish and of inferior quality. The low hills in the valley, as a rule, have a poor soil, clayey and pebbly; on some of them, however, the soil is good and of fair depth.

TRADE.

Most of the trade of the country is carried on with Cachar. Below is given an account of the tax levied on various articles imported and exported, which will show fairly well the amount of trade carried on with that country. It is for one year, 1868-69 :—

Imports from Cachar.

	Tax levied.		
	Rs.	A.	P.
Betelnut and pân	721	8	0
Cloth	562	13	0
Yarns	203	6	3
Brass and other metals	228	7	0
Hukas	206	15	9
Miscellaneous	52	5	9
Total	1,975	7	9

Exports from Manipur to Cachar.

	Tax levied.		
	Rs.	A.	P.
Cloths	505	14	3
Yarns	127	3	6
Manipur buffaloes	1,500	0	0
Burma ditto	500	0	0
Manipur ponies	900	0	0
Total	3,533	1	9

	Rs.	A.	P.
Silk is also exported from Manipur to Burma, and the tax levied upon this article in the above year amounted to	100	0	0
A further sum of money was obtained by granting licenses for cutting wood, bamboo, and cane in the Jiri forest amounting to	406	2	3
Also by the sale of elephants caught in the Jiri forest	7,000	0	0
Total	7,506	2	3

(*Brown, 1873.*)

Although during the year 1878-79 the monopoly* of four articles has been abolished, *i.e.*, of bees'-wax, tea seed, ivory and India-rubber, yet the trade does not increase; piece-goods and betelnuts still seem to be the chief articles imported. Trade with Burma had been entirely stopped throughout the above year, owing to the passes being closed, pending the settlement of the Kongal affair. The trade with the Naga Hills was about the same as in past years; but the chief drawback is the want of good carriage, men's backs being the only means of conveyance for goods.—(*Political Agent's Report, Manipur, 1879.*)

* It has been again established, 1885.—(*J. Johnstone.*)

MANUFACTURES.

As might be anticipated from the isolated position of Manipur, its manufactures are few and unimportant; they comprise—

Cloth.—These are manufactured of cotton of various kinds, chiefly a coarse quality called "kess." These coarse cloths are purchased by the hill tribes chiefly; some, however, find their way into Cachar. Of late years finer qualities of cloth have been made from English yarns. The Political Agent, writing in 1879, states: "The more I see of them, the more I am impressed with the excellence of the Manipur cotton manufactures, which are all of first-rate quality and very cheap, when their weight is considered."

Leather.—In leather manufactures, it is said, there has been of late years a great improvement. Formerly tanning was a matter of great difficulty, and the results inferior. Now they use the bark of a tree which is found in plenty in the jungles; by this they make leather superior to any formerly known in the country; they also enamel the leather very nicely in black. The skins used are those of deer and calf; and the articles made, saddles, shoes, belts, pouches, &c., for the use of the troops.

Cooking-pots.—Cooking-pots,* &c., are made in brass, copper, bell-metal, &c.; they do not differ from those in use in Eastern Bengal.

* They are almost all peculiar to the country. —(*J. Johnstone, 1885.*)

Pottery.—In clay only ordinary pots and water ghurras are made. Stone bowls are also found nicely made and polished; the stone used is ordinary sandstone artificially blackened.

Jewellery.—Jewellery manufactured is of fair workmanship, but not distinguished by any special merit; rings, bracelets, necklets are the articles chiefly made; a large number of brass and bell-metal armlets are made, which are disposed of to the hillmen.

Iron and Steel.—In iron and steel are made dhaos of various kinds, spear and arrow-heads, &c. Firearms are not made in any form.

Carpentry.—The Manipuris have a great reputation as carpenters in the adjoining provinces of Cachar and Sylhet, specially for the better kinds of work; here good workmen few, and are entirely monopolised by the Raja. The good carpenters there are, however, are capable of turning out first-rate work, and can imitate English work successfully.

Turning, &c.—Turning in wood and ivory is common. They can make also silver glass and electroplate, good serviceable locks, and can at a pinch repair and clean a clock.

Dyeing.—Dyeing in a few colours is practised; a yellow dye is commonly procured in the hills.

Fine Arts.—The Manipuris have some taste in the arrangement of colours, but of drawing or painting they have little or no idea.

Silk Culture.—The cultivation of silk, which, if properly developed, would form a most important article of export, is unfortunately much restricted. The silk culture is entirely in the hands of the Loi part of the population, and only five villages to the west and north-west of the valley close to the hills rear the worm. The fact of the Loi being the cultivator of the silk is fatal to its extension, as by the custom of the country, which so much associates position or caste with the nature of the various employments pursued, anyone wishing to engage in the silk culture must lose position and will become a Loi; thus it is that the production of silk is on a very limited scale. The food of the silk-worm is the mulberry leaf, and the species is common in Bengal, although the silk yielded is of a decidedly superior equal quality. About 300 persons are employed in the silk culture, and they pay for the privilege some Rs. 300 annually; they are for this payment excused from the operation of lalúp or forced labour.

The raw silk is disposed of by the above to a weaver class called "Kubbo," they having originally, it is said, emigrated from the Kubbo valley in Upper Barma. These weave it into various clothes,—dhotis, pagris, kamarbands, presses for the women, &c. A small quantity of silk cloths find their way into Cachar. The Burmese traders who frequent Manipur buy up greedily all the raw silk they can get. This speaks well for the quality of the silk, as the silk-worm is plentiful in and near the Kubbo valley.—(*Brown, 1873*.)

Glass.—Since 1878 a successful attempt has been made to manufacture glass, the Maharaja having imported a man from Calcutta to teach some of his people, and several articles of glassware having been made, although they cost ten times more than they would in Calcutta.—(*Political Agent, Manipur, 1879*.)

Bazaars and Market Places.

All the marketing of the country is conducted by women in the open air. Many of these collections of women are to be found throughout the Imphal or capital; but the principal meeting-place for women trading there is on a vacant spot of ground to one side of a brick bridge; here, during the early part of the day, the women congregate with their wares for sale. In the afternoon this market place is deserted, and the women all migrate to the side of the road leading to the Raja's enclosure, quite close to the gate, and a very short distance from the bridge.

There is no attempt, in any of the market places at the erection of shelter of any kind and the women remain exposed to rain or sun, as the case may be. The same custom prevails in the British provinces of Cachar and Sylhet among the Manipuri population settled there. There is very little to interest a European in the contents of the various market-places, which consist of food, such as dry fish, rice, vegetables, pân, supari, clothes, ornaments for the hillmen, and sweetmeats. Here, however, especially during the cold season, the curious observer will be rewarded by seeing large numbers of hillmen, from the northern hills especially, in their curious costumes. About 3,000 women assemble in the afternoon bazaar. Men, with the exception of foreigners, are not allowed to enter the market-places; all the buying and selling is conducted by women.

Curious customs in the large Bazaars.—There is a curious custom in connection with this afternoon bazaar deserving of mention, as illustrating the sort of petty oppressiveness which is so characteristic of Manipur rule. A certain number of the Raja's house servants called "Haomacha," ten in number, daily visit this bazaar, and take from the women enough food to last for one day; this is bitterly complained of by the women, who suffer much from the indiscriminate plundering which is carried on, and which comes hard on some of them. The amount of food thus carried off by the servants amounts to about Re. 1-8 per diem in value; but so wedded are the Manipuris to their customs, that successive Political Agents have failed in inducing them to carry out any reform in this, although the women express their willingness to submit to any small regular tax that may be imposed to avoid the irregular plundering that is thus openly carried on. This custom was supposed to have been abolished in 1871 on representations being made by the Officiating Political Agent, a small tax being substituted on all the women frequenting the bazaar with articles for sale. After a time, however, the custom was revived, the Raja's mother getting the credit of making daily requisitions on the bazaar, instead of the Raja's retainers. Thus matters are actually worse than before, as the poor women find themselves saddled with a tax, and get robbed, to some extent at least, as before into the bargain.—(*Brown, 1873.*)

CHAPTER VI.

REVENUE.

As might be expected from the isolated position of the country and the poverty of its inhabitants, the money revenue of the State is but small. Were it not the policy of the Government to render no assistance, nay, to cramp any efforts to make anything of the natural resources of the country, this need not be. The money revenue of the State, including the compensation of R6,370 per annum paid by the British Government for the surrender to the Burmans of the Kubbo valley, is estimated from R25,000 to R30,000 annually, from all sources.

TAXES ON IMPORTS AND EXPORTS.

The Manipuri authorities have furnished an account of taxes levied on goods imported and exported for one year, 1868-69, the particulars of which have been given before, in describing the trade of the country. The total tax levied on imports amounted to R1,975-7-9; on exports, to R3,633-1-9. The amount of revenue received on account of licenses for cutting wood, &c., in the Jiri forest, and by the sale of elephants caught in the Jiri forest, was R7,406-2-3. It is impossible to get anything like a correct idea of the revenue realised from the Manipuri inhabitants of the valley; the estimate of the authorities themselves is between R12,000 to R15,000 per annum.

CURRENCY AND COIN OF THE COUNTRY.

The only coin proper to the country is of bell-metal, and small in size, being only about 16 grains. This is coined by the Raja as required, goods or money being taken in exchange. The metal is obtained chiefly from Burma and consists of old gongs, &c.; some of it is also procured from the British provinces. The process of coining is very primitive; the metal is first cast in little pellets; these are then softened by fire and placed on an anvil; one blow of the hammer flattens the pellet into an irregular round figure; a punch, with the word "Sri" cut on it, is then driven on it by another blow, which completes the process. The market value of the "Sel," as it is called, varies. When rupees are plentiful, then "Sel" is cheap; when scarce, the opposite. The value of the coin in 1873 was 428 to one British or Burmese rupee, and its usual variation is said to be from 420 to 450. There is no evidence whatever of there having been, at any time, a gold coinage in existence; but it is stated that Choorjet Sing, about 1815, coined silver of a square form and of the same value and weight as the British rupee. The British and Burmese rupee, both representing the same value, circulate freely; also the smaller silver coins, as four-anna and two-anna pieces. About seven years ago an attempt was made by the then Political Agent to introduce copper coinage, and a large quantity was supplied by Government. The experiment totally failed, as the women in the bazaars positively refused to have anything to do with it, and the coin had to be returned. The bell-metal coin, in conjunction with rupees and smaller silver coins, are amply sufficient for the wants of the country. Besides coin, bartering articles in the bazaar is quite common.—(*Brown, 1873.*)

CHAPTER VII.

ADMINISTRATION OF JUSTICE.

THE chief courts are two in number,—the Chirap and the Guard or Military Court. There is also a court for the trial of cases in which women are concerned, and other minor courts for cattle disputes, &c. Cases decided by any of the courts may be appealed to the Raja, who decides the case as he thinks proper. The Chirap, which is the chief court, consists of 13 senior members, all of whom are appointed by the Raja. The two senior members of the court, as at present constituted, are the Joobraj or eldest son of the Raja, and a chief of a district, named the Dola Raja. The Guard or Military Court is composed of the eight senior army officers, named Majors, and other officers of the army. In it all cases in which sepoys are concerned are heard; it also occasionally takes up other cases. The Paja or Woman's Court consists of six members appointed by the Raja from no particular class. In this court all cases of family disputes in which women are concerned—wife-beating cases, adultery, &c.—are in the first instance heard. Serious cases may afterwards come before the Chirap. The other courts are unimportant. In former times the membership of the various courts was hereditary; now all the appointments are made by the Raja.

VILLAGE PUNCHAYETS.

In the villages situated in the Manipur valley are clubs named "Singlup" or wood clubs, resembling the punchayets of Bengal. These clubs, under the sirdar, or head of the village, have the general control of it, and adjudicate in trifling cases arising in the village. In the event of a villager sinking into a state of extreme poverty, these clubs supply him with necessary food. In sickness they look after him, and when dead, provide the wood, &c., for his last rites. In this way, although many of the inhabitants are very poor, actual starvation or fatal neglect is rendered impossible.

PUNISHMENT FOR OFFENCES.

The punishments inflicted for the various offences are numerous. Treason or conspiracy against the Raja is the highest offence that can be committed. Before the advent of the present Raja, who has relaxed the severity of the punishments awarded in such cases, death was the penalty not only to the chief offender, but to all his followers. If the chief culprit belonged to the royal family, he was put in a basket and thrown into a river, and there kept until drowned. (This kind of punishment is believed to be common in Bhootan.) The predecessor of the present Raja Nar Sing carried out the punishment in its integrity. Murder is the next offence in point of magnitude. For this crime the punishment is death, except in the case of Brahmins (whose punishment is simple banishment from the country for murder) and women. Execution in its form varies with the nature of the murder. Should the deed have been done by beating, then the punishment is being beaten to death with clubs. If by cutting or stabbing, the head is cut off. Hanging is also mentioned as one of the means of executing. No executions took place for four or five years up to 1873. Cases of assault and petty theft are punished by flogging with a cane on the shoulders, the culprit on his face on the ground, and by exposure in the bazaar; also imprisonment. The hair is occasionally cut off as a punishment, but rarely. Fining is the commonest of all punishments, and leads to gross abuses. Women are not confined in the jail; their usual punishment is shaving the head and exposure in the bazaars, the offender being walked round them on successive days; they in the event of not answering freely before the court may be tortured with thumb-screws. They are also, as a punishment chiefly for loose behaviour, made prostitutes of occasionally. In the cases where imprisonment is carried out as a punishment, in a good many instances, as in the cases of arms stealing, which is reckoned a very serious offence, and debt, no time for the imprisonment to expire is mentioned. In the case of the debtor, release follows payment of the debt. Political offences come under the same category, the term of imprisonment not being defined; specified terms of imprisonment vary from one week to twelve years.

Jail.

The jail is situated within the Raja's enclosure; it is surrounded by a high sun-dried brick wall, and is calculated to accommodate 150 prisoners. The sanitary conditions seem as bad as they could be, and yet, since its construction, some nine or ten years ago, among an average of 100 prisoners, only five deaths have occurred. The prisoners are freely employed on the roads, &c., outside, which may help to account for the small mortality. The interior discipline of the jail is looked after by the guards, &c. Breaches of discipline are punished by flogging, increased weight of irons, lengthened term of imprisonment, &c. Most of the prisoners are ironed, but not heavily.

Cattle-wounding.

Before quitting the subject of offences, some allusion may be made to cattle-wounding or killing, which are serious crimes according to the Manipuri code of law. In every case where a cow dies, the authorities have to be informed of the circumstance, and an enquiry takes place, followed in a good many instances, if not in all, by the fining of the individual to whom the cow belonged, or, in doubtful cases, the village in which it is found. This gives rise to a great deal of rascality, as anyone having a spite against another has only to smuggle a dead cow into his premises, or wound some of his cattle, to get him into trouble. The members of the court for trying such cases, like the others, receive a share (about 30 per cent.) of the fines inflicted; so it may be imagined few escape. In cattle cases, according to the authorities, fines vary from 14 annas to Rs. 100.—(*Brown, 1873.*)

CHAPTER VIII.

GAZETTEER.

A

ACHAMBIKI—

A Manipuri village on the Tiki river, 6 miles north of Imphal.

AIMOL—

An Aimol village, built after the usual Aimol pattern; about 4,815 feet above the sea-level. It is situated 5½ miles east-south-east of Pallel on the Pallel-Moray road, which it commands. There are 30 houses.

Camping-ground.—At each end of the village there is sufficient space in all for two regiments to encamp.

Approaches.—The village is approached from the west up a steep hill, which therefore commands the road; but from the south-east, the road approaches along a level ridge, which commands the village at 1,000 yards.

Nature of Outskirts.—Between the village and the peak of the same name the jungle is very much thicker than in other parts of the Pallel-Moray route.

Inhabitants.—The inhabitants* are a subdivision of the Kom-Kuki tribe. Population 130, of whom 30 are fighting-men.

* The people of Aimol are immigrants from Tipperah. They say they came about 100 years ago. Their language is akin to that of the Kukis, but the appearance of many of them very different.—(*J. Johnstone.*)

Climate.—The climate is unhealthy from beginning of August to end of October.

Water.—Supply very scanty to south of village.

Supplies.—Rice-straw procurable. Good grazing. The principal grains are rice and múm. Firewood plentiful. Plantains, yams, and pumpkins. Harvest in November and early part of December.

Live-stock.—Pigs, poultry, and buffaloes.

Transport.—For coolie purposes, 10 men and women.

Timber.—Chiefly small oaks; no firs.—(*Lieut. Dun, 1881-82.*)

AIMOL PEAK—

A peak near the Pallel-Moray road, situated 2¼ miles south-east of the village of the same name. Would be suitable as a heliograph station to communicate with the hills in the Logták lake.—(*Lieut. Dun, 1881-82.*)

AKHAM—

A small Manipuri village at the foot of a western spur of Langol hill.

AKHNI—

A small Kaupai Naga village on the Northern Cachar valley route, and between the rivers Barak and Irang.

AKPAL—

A small Tangal Naga village at the northern end of the Manipur valley and close above the Tiki stream on the east.

ALOUN-MYO—

A town on the left bank of the Ningthee.

AMYEN-MYO—

One of the principal towns on the left bank of the Ningthee. The chief trade consists in cloth, cotton goods, cutlery, &c., and from the northern provinces rice is brought in large quantities; teak timber, jack, sapan, and kio; and varnish or lacquer which is extracted from the kio tree.

ANAH—

ANAL OR ANAL NAMFOW KUKIS—

A division of the Kuki tribe; they occupy a large tract of country to the south-east of Manipur. Lieutenant Dun writes:—

> "South of the Moray route lie the Anal Namfow Kukis. These men are short in stature and rather slight in build; they are more civilised and intelligent than the Kongjai Kukis. They appear to be most peacefully inclined, and quite subject to the Manipuris. Their villages are not stockaded and have permanent sites. Their houses are of the Kuki pattern. They are good cultivators and keep metna and cows. They cultivate the same grains as the Kongjai Kukis." By the latter they are called Hol.

ANDRO—

A Manipuri village of the Loi caste and employed in making earthenware. It is situated close under Nongmaiching Hill on the east, and is about 2,700 feet above the sea.

Houses.—It has forty houses built in the usual Manipuri pattern, and numbers 200 souls.

Carriage.—Sixty coolies and forty carts.

Water and Camping-ground.—There is plenty of water of fair quality, and unlimited camping-ground on the lower slopes of Nongmaiching.

Approaches.—It is approached by rough tracks over open rice-fields, from east and south, and by a path over the northern spur of Nongmaiching from the north.

Climate.—Like all villages in the Manipur valley, it is unhealthy from the 1st May to the 1st December.

Grazing and Forage.—There is good grazing, and the usual forage of unhusked rice (dhan) and rice-straw. The oil-cake produced is used for fuel.

Grains, Vegetables, &c.—There is little or no variation in the products of Manipuri villages. This village produces rice, oil-seed, dhall, plantains, pumpkins, potatoes, kamrac, peas, onions, mustard, and beans.

Timber.—Bamboo.

Firewood and Fuel.—Firewood is scanty near the village, and the villagers have to ascend Nongmaiching some distance to get it. A little oil-cake is obtainable.

Harvest.—Rice, the principal crop, is gathered in by the 1st to 15th December.

Live-stock.—Sixty buffaloes and eighty cows.

ANGAMI OR GNAMEI—

A Naga tribe situated on the northern frontier of Manipur. It is subject to the British Government.

ANGO-CHING RANGE—

A rocky, forest-clad range bordering the Kubbo valley on the east. Its name signifies white hill in Manipuri, but there is no apparent reason for its having received this name, unless it has been given in mistake for the Sarameti range, which is known to the Manipuris as Ching-ango-ba, which has the same signification.

APHOMA—

A Kolya Naga village of the Mau section, situated due east of Maithaipham thanna, and between the Lanier and the Barak.

It is 4,500 feet above the sea, and in January the thermometer registered 33° at sunrise. It is healthy at all seasons of the year.

There are 100 houses of the ordinary Naga pattern. Four hundred persons and 100 fighting-men.

There is very little camping-ground, and the water-supply is scanty.

It is approached up a gently sloping spur from the Lanier, and up a steep hill-side from the west by narrow hill paths.

For forage there is unhusked rice, rice-straw, and oil-cake.

Firewood is plentiful.

The grains grown are rice and múm.

Fruits and Vegetables.—Yams and pumpkins.

Live-stock.—Ten cows, pigs, and poultry.

Carriage.—One hundred and fifty coolies.

Timber.—Chiefly fir and oak.

ARAVATI—

A Manipuri village close to the Pallel-Moray road on the south bank of the Leelong river.—(*Lieut. Dun, 1882.*)

ARUI OR SOMRAH—

A peak, elevation 8,639 feet, above the sea on the range which encloses the Somrah basin on the southern side. The southern exit from the Somrah basin leads straight over this peak by a very gradual easy ascent on the north side, and a rapid drop on the south side (*vide* Route No.). It is covered with thick forest, the trees in which are of considerable size.

ARUNG—

A muddy slow stream flowing from the Yumadoung range into the Ikok jheel and crossed by the eastern valley road at the village of Thobal Atokpam.

It is 40 yards broad with 4 feet perpendicular banks, and has one foot of water in the cold weather, with a soft muddy bottom.

(*Lieut. Dun, 1882.*)

ATONGLO—

A stream crossed by the Manipur-Kohima route, about 5 miles from Kaitemabi. At this point the Atonglo flows through a broad bed of shingle; in the cold weather it has only a few inches of water in each channel, but apparently becomes of considerable width after heavy rain.—(*Lieut. Dun, 1882.*)

AWANGKUN—

A small Kaupui Naga village on the Northern Cachar valley route between the Laimatak and Irang rivers.

AWANG KUNAO—

A Manipuri village, 3 miles west of Imphal.

B

BADOUN—

A town on the Chen-dwen, 30 leagues from Sagaing.

BALET—

A village, containing 20 houses, a few miles from the left bank of the Ningthee, on the route from Ava to Kendat.

Supplies.—There are some paddy-fields.

Live-stock.—A few buffaloes.—(*Lieut. Dun, 1881-82.*)

BARAK—

The Barak, the largest and most important of the rivers in the Manipur hill territory, rises east of the Mukru under the Barrail range of mountains; flowing south-east, it receives in its course, besides several small unnamed streams, first the Mukru, next the large river which rises further east than the Barak, the Irang; still pursuing a southerly course, it receives at the southern spur of the mountain range, continuous with the Kalá Naga range of hills, the Tipai river which flows north from the Lushai country. The Barak now makes a sudden bend, and flows nearly due north until it receives the waters of the Jiri, after which the one river thus constituted, still named the Barak, enters the British territory and flows west through the Cachar valley. The Barak is named by the Manipuris the Quaee, and is said to be navigable for canoes for about one day above its junction with the Tipai river. This river is fordable in the dry weather, the water thigh-deep; the bed of the river is filled with boulders, and the stream at the ford is about 60 yards wide, with a moderately strong current. Immediately above the ford the river expands into a wide pool, and above this again contracts between high banks. The forest jungle at this part is heavy and dense; below the ford of the Barak, on its right bank, the hill is almost perpendicular and densely clothed with trees; so high and steep is this hill, that it is sunset on the river some hours before the sunshine fades away from the summit of the hill. Like the Mukru, the Barak is well stocked with fish, and the fishing-ground below the ford is remarkably good for a considerable distance.

There is a cane suspension bridge, exactly similar to that over the Mukru, by which traffic is kept up during the rains.

BENTHE—

A halting-place in the jungle on the road from Ava to Kendat; no village and little water; road good.

BENUNG—

A village on the road between Pallel and Moray.—(*Lieut. Dun, 1882.*)

BISHENPUR*—

A Manipuri thannah, situated where the Cachar road leaves the Manipur valley, and on the edge of the village of Lamlangtong.

* This is the Hindee name of the village of Lamlangtong. The thannah is called so by foreigners, but the Manipuris call it Sebokthannah.

BOLON—

A Hawkib village, built after the usual Kuki pattern; about 4,500 feet above the sea-level. It is situated east of Kambang, about a mile to the north of the Hytuk-pokpi-Yanga-pokpi road. There are 10 houses.

Camping-ground.—From the general character of the country, there is not likely to be much ground situable for camping.
Approaches.—There is a steep ascent from the west of the village, which commands that side.
Inhabitants.—The inhabitants belong to the Hawkib subdivision of the Kangjoi Kuki tribe. Population 50, of whom 10 are fighting-men. The chief and most influential man is Howle.
Climate.—The climate is unhealthy from beginning of August to end of October.
Water.—Supply scanty.
Supplies.—Rice-straw procurable. Fair grazing. The principal grains are Indian-corn, rice, múm, and chayan. Firewood plentiful. Pumpkins, beans, and arum. The rice harvest is in November; that of the múm in December.
Live-stock.—Pigs, poultry, and metna.
Transport.—For coolie purposes, 15 men and women.
Timber.—Oaks, &c.; no firs.—(*Lieut. Dun, 1881.*)

BORRHI—

A small confluent of the Barak, which falls in a short distance above Maithaipham.

BUNGBUL—

A Hawkib village, built after the usual Kuki pattern, about 4,000 feet above the sea-level. There are 40 houses.
Inhabitants.—The inhabitants belong to the Hawkib subdivision of the Kangjoi Kuki tribe. Population 200, of whom 60 are fighting men. The most influential man is Hawam, an interpreter.
Climate.—The climate is unhealthy from beginning of August to end of October.
Water.—Supply scanty.
Supplies.—Rice-straw procurable. Fair grazing. The principal grains are Indian-corn, rice, múm, and chayan. Firewood plentiful. Pumpkins, beans, and arum. The rice harvest is in November; that of the múm in December.
Live-stock.—Pigs, poultry, and metna.
Transport.—For coolie purposes, 60 men and women.
Timber.—Chiefly oak; no firs.—(*Lieut. Dun, 1881.*)

BUNGLI—

A Mangvung village, built after the usual Kuki pattern; about 4,000 feet above the sea-level. There are 30 houses.
Inhabitants.—The inhabitants belong to the Mangvung subdivision of the Kangjoi Kuki tribe. Population 150, of whom 45 are fighting-men. The chief and most influential man is Chambúm.
Climate.—The climate is unhealthy from beginning of August to end of October.
Water.—Supply scanty.
Supplies.—Rice-straw procurable. Fair grazing. The principal grains are Indian-corn, rice, múm, and chayan. Firewood plentiful. Pumpkins, beans, and arum. The rice harvest is in November; that of the múm in December.
Live-stock.—Pigs, poultry, and metna.
Transport.—For coolie purposes, 45 men and women.
Timber.—Chiefly oak; no firs.—(*Lieut. Dun, 1881.*)

C

CHADONG—

A Tankul village, built after the usual Tankul pattern; about 3,000 feet above the sea-level. There are 25 houses.

Inhabitants.—The inhabitants belong to the south-western section of the Tankul Naga tribe. Population 125, of whom 25 are fighting-men.

Climate.—The climate is unhealthy from beginning of August to end of October.

Supplies.—A plentiful supply of rice-straw. Scanty grazing. The principal grains are rice and múm. Firewood plentiful. Arum, yams, and pumpkins. Harvest in November and early part of December.

Live-stock.—Pigs and poultry.

Transport.—For coolie purposes, 25 men and women.

Timber.—Oaks and firs plentiful; bamboos scarce.—(*Lieut. Dun, 1881.*)

CHAIBA—

A Kaupui Naga village on the eastern slope of the Laimatak range, south of the Cachar road.

It is about 4,500 feet above the sea, and the thermometer registered in January 37° at sunrise.

Houses.—Twenty.

Population.—Eighty.

Fighting-men.—Twenty.

Carriage.—Twenty-five coolies.

Timber.—Oak and toon.

Supplies.—As in all Naga villages. No cows.

Water.—Probably a fair supply. No level camping-ground.

CHAIIKONG—

A small mountain stream which joins the Phaiikong below Chattik on the east. It is 6 inches deep at its mouth in the cold weather.

CHAIREL—

A Manipuri (Loi) village on the Imphal river, a few miles north of Shugunu

Houses—Thirty-five of the usual Mainpuri pattern.

Inhabitants.—One hundred and seventy-five.

Products, Harvest, &c.—*Vide* Andro.

Water and Camping-ground.—Unlimited.

Approaches—Over open grassy plain from all sides. From Kunbi on the west it is necessary to cross the Imphal, which is here 40 yards wide and 50 feet deep. There is no ford, and the current is very slow indeed. There are few dug-out canoes available in the village for crossing.

Live-stock.—70 cows, 50 buffaloes.

Transport.—30 men, 5 boats, 35 carts.

Timber.—Oaks, firs, bamboos.

CHAKKA—

The cliffs washed by the Barak, in the bend to the south which it takes in the upper part of its course, have received this name from the village situated on their summit. Along the same range and to the south there is a peak with an elevation of 9,337 feet, which bears the same name.

CHAKPI—

A mountain stream draining the country in the south-east corner of Manipur. One of its sources commences close by Aimol to the south of that village, and it empties itself into the Imphal, 3 or 4 miles below Shugunu. It is everywhere fordable during the cold weather.

CHAKPI (THANNA)—

A small Manipur frontier post, situated in the Yumadoung hills, 9 miles from the mouth of the pass into the Kubbo valley, by the Nasinga route. Very little is known of this route.

CHALAO OR TARAO—

A Kom village, built after the usual Kom pattern; about 3,000 feet above the sea-level. There are 5 houses.

Approaches.—The village is approached from the west by a steep path which is commanded by it.

Inhabitants.—The inhabitants belong to the Kom Kuki tribe. Population 25, of whom 7 are fighting-men.

Climate.—The climate is unhealthy from beginning of August to end of October.

Supplies.—Rice-straw procurable. Fair grazing. The principal grains are rice, múm, chayan, and oil-seed. Firewood plentiful. Plantains, yams, and pumpkins. Harvest in November and early part of December.

Live-stock.—Pigs and poultry.

Transport.—For coolie purposes, 5 men and women.

Timber.—No heavy timber; small oaks; no firs.—(*Lieut. Dun, 1882.*)

CHALLO—

A Tankul village, built after the usual Tankul pattern; about 4,000 feet above the sea-level. It is situated on the eastern edge of the Yumadoung range, and forms one of the third or outer line of frontier posts. There are 10 houses.

Inhabitants.—The inhabitants belong to the north-eastern section of the Tankul Naga tribe. Population 25, of whom 5 are fighting-men. The chief's name is Koito.

Climate.—The climate is unhealthy from beginning of August to end of October.

Supplies.—A plentiful supply of rice-straw. Scanty grazing. The principal grain is múm. Firewood plentiful. Arum, yams, and pumpkins. Harvest in November and early part of December.

Live-stock.—Pigs and poultry; a few buffaloes or metna.

Transport.—For coolie purposes, 10 men and women.

Timber.—Oaks and firs plentiful; bamboos scarce.—(*Lieut. Dun, 1881.*)

CHAMMU KULEL—

A Tankul Naga village on the eastern slope of the Kassom range.

Houses.—Twenty-five, of the usual Naga pattern; inhabitants 100.

Fighting-men.—Twenty-five.

Water.—Plentiful.

Camping-ground.—Sufficient clear ground for 200 men only.

Elevation.—5,500 feet.

Temperature.—36° at sunrise in February.

Supplies.—Rice, múm, yams, and pumpkins. Firewood plentiful. Grazing scanty.

Live-stock.—Pigs and poultry only.

CHAMMU KUNAO—

A Tankul Naga village near the head of the Nelekong valley on the western face of the Kassom range.

Elevation.—5,000 feet.

Temperature.—34° at sunrise in February.
Houses.—Twenty-five, of the usual Naga pattern.
Inhabitants.—One hundred.
Fighting-men.—Twenty-five.
Water.—Scanty.
Camping-ground.—Very little open ground.
Approaches—Up a steep slope from the west by a narrow path through thick jungle.
Grains.—Rice, múm, oil-seed.
Forage.—Rice-straw, unhusked rice, oil-cake.
Firewood.—Plentiful.
Fruits and Vegetables.—Yams, arums, pumpkins
Harvests.—Completed 1st December.
Live-stock.—Pigs and poultry only.
Carriage.—Forty coolies.
Timber.—Plenty of heavy timber of unknown kinds.

CHAMOL—

A Mangoung village, built after the usual Kuki pattern, about 3,500 feet above the sea-level. There are 7 houses.

Inhabitants.—The inhabitants belong to the Mangoung subdivision of the Kongjai Kuki tribe. Population 35, of whom 10 are fighting-men. The chief and most influential man is Limyam.

Climate.—The climate is unhealthy from beginning of August to end of October.

Supplies.—Rice-straw procurable. Fair grazing. The principal grains are Indian-corn, múm, and chayan. Firewood plentiful. Pumpkins, beans, and arum. The rice harvest is in November; that of the múm in December.—(*Lient. Dun, 1881.*)

CHANAO—

A small Kaupui village in North-West Manipur.

CHANAO—

A deserted Tankul Naga village in the Nelekong valley in North-East Manipur.

CHANDRAKONG—

A Manipur (Loi) village at the western foot of the Yumadoung hills, a little south of the exit of the Thobal river from the hills.

Houses.—Twenty-five, of the usual Manipuri pattern.
Inhabitants.—One hundred and twenty-five, engaged in making salt.
Carriage.—Forty coolies, 25 carts.
Live-stock.—Thirty-seven buffaloes, 50 cows.
Water.—Plentiful and good.
Camping-ground.—Unlimited in cold weather; no level ground in the rains.
Forage.—Rice-straw, unhusked rice (dhán).
Grazing.—Scanty.
Grains.—
Fruits.—
Timber.—
Harvests.— } As on page 70, Andro.

Approaches—Over open rice-fields by narrow path from the west; by fair road from north and south along the base of the hills; by steep but open path from the hills on the east.

CHANGANGAI—

A Manipuri village, 3 miles from Imphal on the Cachar road.

Elevation.—2,600 feet above the sea.

Temperature.—34° at sunrise in December.

Climate.—Unhealthy from 1st May to 1st December.

Houses.—Seventy, of the usual Manipuri pattern.

Inhabitants.—Three hundred and fifty (sepoy class).

Fighting-men.—Seventy.

Water.—Scanty and indifferent.

Camping-ground.—Between the 15th December and the 1st April there is unlimited encamping ground in the rice-fields. None at any other season.

Grazing.—Scanty.

Forage.—Rice-straw, unhusked rice (dhán), oil-cake.

Grains.—Rice, dhall, mustard.

Fruits and Vegetables.—Plantains, peas, pumpkins, potatoes, beans, onions, kamrac.

Live-stock.—One hundred and forty cows, 105 buffaloes.

Carriage.—Seventy carts.

Approaches.—By Cachar or western valley road from north and south.

CHANGLÉ—

A Chussad village, built after the usual Chussad pattern. It is by the side of Chunyang (which see below). There are 20 houses.

Inhabitants.—The inhabitants belong to the Chupad subdivision of the Kangoï Kuki tribe. Population 100, of whom 30 are fighting-men. The headman and most influential man is Vumyam.

Climate.—The climate is unhealthy from beginning of June to end of October.

Water.—Supply plentiful.

Supplies.—Rice-straw procurable. Scanty grazing. The principal grains are Indian-corn, rice, múm, and chayan. Firewood plentiful. Pumpkins, beans, and arum. The rice harvest is in November; that of the múm in December.

Live-stock.—Pigs and poultry.

Transport.—For coolie purposes, 40 men and women.

Timber.—No oaks or firs; other trees plentiful.—(*Lieut. Dun, 1881.*)

CHANGLÉ—

A Hawkib village, built after the usual Kuki pattern, about 400 feet above the sea-level. There are 10 houses.

Inhabitants.—The inhabitants belong to the Hawkib subdivision of the Kangoï Kuki tribe. Population 50, of whom 15 are fighting-men. The chief and most influential man is Yamthow.

Climate.—The climate is unhealthy from beginning of June to end of October.

Supplies.—Rice-straw procurable. Fair grazing. The principal grains are Indian-corn, rice, múm, chayan. Firewood plentiful. Pumpkins, beans, and arum. The rice harvest is in November; that of the múm in December.

Live-stock.—Pigs and poultry.

Transport.—For coolie purposes, 15 men and women.

Timber.—Chiefly small oaks.—(*Lieut. Dun, 1881.*)

CHANGPUT KUKIS—

A subdivision of the Kangoï Kuki tribe.

CHANJANG—

A Kuki village of the Simmté section on the Manipur source of the Tipai river.

Elevation.—2,800 feet.

Temperature.—42° at sunrise in December.

Climate.—Unhealthy from 1st May to 1st December.
Houses.—Five, of the usual Kuki pattern.
Inhabitants.—Twenty.
Fighting-men.—Eight.
Water.—Scanty.
Camping-ground.—Very little cleared ground.
Grazing.—Good.
Forage.—Rice-straw, unhusked rice (dhán).
Grains.—Rice, múm, oil-seed (*sesamúm*).
Fruits and Vegetables.—Yams and pumpkins.
Timber.—Oak and Toon.
Harvests.—Completed 1st December.
Live-stock.—Pigs and poultry only.
Carriage.—Ten coolies.

CHANNO—

A Chussad village containing 20 houses.—(*Lieut. Dun, 1881.*

CHAPA—

A small Manipuri (Sengmail) village at the north-west corner of the valley.

CHAPAPAN—

A small Manipuri (Sengmail) village, 7 miles to the north-west of Imphal.

CHARO—

A Kaupni Naga village on the eastern face of the Laimatak range, and south of the Cachar road.

Elevation.—About 4,600 feet above the sea.
Temperature.—36° at sunrise in January.
Climate.—Healthy at all seasons.
Houses.—Fifteen, of the usual Naga pattern.
Inhabitants.—Sixteen.
Fighting-men.—Fifteen.
Water.—Probably scanty.
Camping-ground.—Probably plenty.
Grazing.—Good.
Forage.—Rice-straw, unhusked rice (dhán).
Grains, &c.—Rice, múm, oil-seed, pumpkins.
Timber.—Oak and toon.
Harvests.—Completed 1st December.
Live-stock.—Pigs and poultry only.
Carriage.—Twenty coolies.
Approach.—Up easy open spur from the Manipur valley.

CHARUIKULEL—

A small (chiru) village in North-West Manipur, west of the Thobal stream.

CHATTIK—

A range of hills in the north-east of Manipur, running nearly due north and south, and forming part of the Yumadoung range.

CHATTIK (JATRIK)—

A Tankul village, built after the usual Tankul pattern; 3,800 feet above the sea-level. It is situated on the ridge of the same name, on the eastern edge of the Yumadoung range, and is on the Pong-Kongal route. Half a mile from it is the Chattik thanna (which see below). There are 50 houses.

A Manipur force was sent to the village in 1878 to check the Chussads, who were assembling there in great numbers.—(*Manipur Précis, 135, p. 64.*)

Camping-ground.—There is camping ground on the ridge for two regiments.

Approaches.—There are open approaches along the ridge from both sides, both being perfectly easy. The roads up from the Meié on the east, and the Konookong on the west, are excessively steep and rather difficult occasionally. They meet the southern approach 300 yards from the village.

Signal Station.—The ridge would be a suitable station from which to signal to Makku peak.

Inhabitants.—The inhabitants belong to the south-eastern section of the Tankul Naga tribe. Population 250, of whom 50 are fighting-men. The chiefs are Chapoug and Chadde; and Soté and Lendo have considerable influence, and are friendly.

Climate.—The climate is unhealthy from beginning of August to end of October.

Water.—Supply plentiful.

Supplies.—A plentiful supply of rice-straw. Fair grazing. Principal grains are rice and múm. Firewood plentiful. Arum, yams, and pumpkins. Harvest in November and early part of December.

Live-stock.—Pigs, poultry, and two buffaloes.

Transport.—For coolie purposes, 50 men and women.

Timber.—Oaks and firs plentiful; bamboos scarce.—(*Lieut. Dun, 1881-82.*)

CHATTIK (THANNA)—

A Manipur frontier post, forming one of the third or outer line along the eastern edge of the Yumadoung range. It is situated on the Cháttik ridge, half a mile south of the village of the same name. The part of the ridge on which the stockade stands is very narrow and steep on both sides, descending to deep ravines.

The stockade is about 40 yards long and 25 broad. It is made of poles 20 feet high and 3 or 4 inches in diameter. There are no panjies or obstacles round the stockade. The doors are situated at the north and south ends.

Camping ground.—Camping-ground for two regiments between the thanna and village (*vide* Chattik).

Surrounding Country.—There is rising ground close to the stockade on the north, from which at about 100 yards it is partially commanded. The height of the stockade obviates this, however, to a great extent. On the south also there are knolls at about 250 and 600 yards distance respectively. They do not command the inside of the stockade, though they are slightly higher than the ground on which it stands.

The jungle on the ridge is light and has been cleared back from the stockade to an average distance of 500 yards.

The most advantageous point of attack would be from the rising ground on the north.

Garrison.—The ordinary strength of the garrison is:—1 subadar, 1 jemadar, 1 havildar, 1 bugler, and 60 sepoys.

Water.—Water-supply is obtained down the hill to the east (*vide* also Chattik).

(*Lieut. Dun, 1881-82.*)

CHERUI-PANDUMBA—

A small Chiru village in North-West Manipur, on the right bank of the Thobal stream.

CHESABA—

A Manipuri village, at the junction of the Imphal and Thobal rivers.

Elevation.—
Temperature.— } *Vide* page 77, Changangai.
Climate.—
Houses.—Twenty-five, of the usual Manipuri pattern.
Inhabitants.—One hundred and twenty-five, of the sepoy class.
Water.—Plentiful.
Camping-ground.—*Vide* page 77, Changangai.
Grazing.—Scanty.
Forage.—
Grains.—
Fruits, &c.— *Vide* page 70, Andro.
Timber.—
Harvests.—
Live-stock.—Fifty cows, 37 buffaloes.
Carriage.—Twenty-five carts, 12 boats.
Approaches—By a fair mule path along the Imphal and Thobal rivers, from both north and south.

CHIBEK—

A village in Manipur south of Huerok.

CHIN-DWEN—(*Vide* Ningthee.)

CHINGAI—

A Tankul village, built after the usual Tankul pattern; about 5,000 feet above the sea-level. There are 50 houses.
Inhabitants.—The inhabitants belong to the south-eastern section of the Tankul Naga tribe. Population 250, of whom 50 are fighting-men. The chief's name is Mikram.
Climate.—The climate is healthy at all seasons.
Supplies.—Rice-straw procurable. Scanty grazing. Principal grains—rice and múm. Firewood plentiful. Arum, yams, and pumpkins. Harvest in November and early part of December.
Live-stock.—Pigs, poultry, and a few metna.
Transport.—For coolie purposes, 50 men and women.

CHINGA MUKKA—

A small hill in the southern portion of Imphal; its summit is 60 feet above the level of the valley.

A good view of the city can be obtained from it, and it would form a good signalling station.

It is, with the exception of four or five very large mango trees, quite bare of vegetation.

It commands three southern exits from the city, and extends almost from the Nambol on one side to the Imphal river on the other; so that it blocks the section between them.

CHING-ANGO-BA—(*Vide* Sarameti.)

HINGSAU—

A Tankul village, built after the usual Tankul pattern; about 5,000 feet above the sea-level. It is on the Manipur-Ningthee route *viá* Poshing. There are 65 houses.
Camping-ground.—There is plenty of camping-ground in terraced rice-fields, if dry; also a little in the valley to the south.

Inhabitants.—The inhabitants belong to the north-eastern section of the Tankul Naga tribe. Population 325, of whom 65 are fighting-men. The chief's name is Yunang.

Climate.—The climate is healthy at all seasons.

Water.—Plenty on the east of the village.

Supplies.—Rice-straw plentiful. Scanty grazing. Principal grains are rice and múm. Firewood plentiful. Arum, yams, and pumpkins. Harvest in November and early part of December.

Live-stock.—Pigs, poultry, and a few buffaloes or metna.

Transport.—For coolie purposes, 65 men.

Timber.—Oaks and firs plentiful; bamboos scarce.—(*Lieut. Dun, 1881-82.*)

CHINS—(*Vide* Kyens.)

CHIRU—

An old Kuki tribe.

CHITENG—

A Tankul village, built after the usual Tankul pattern; about 4,000 feet above the sea-level. There are 10 houses.

Inhabitants.—The inhabitants belong to the north-eastern section of the Tankul Naga tribe. Population 50, of whom 10 are fighting-men.

Climate.—The climate is unhealthy from beginning of August to end of October.

Supplies.—Rice-straw plentiful. Scanty grazing. Principal grains are rice and múm. Firewood plentiful. Arum, yams, and pumpkins. Harvest in November and early part of December.

Live-stock.—Pigs, poultry, and a few buffaloes or metna.

Transport.—For coolie purposes, 10 men and women.

Timber.—Oaks and firs plentiful; bamboos scarce.—(*Lieut. Dun, 1881.*)

CHITTAH—

A Hawkib village, built after the usual Kuki pattern; 4,800 feet above the sea-level. There are 40 houses.

Approaches—By clear level road from the south, which is commanded by the village.

Inhabitants.—The inhabitants belong to the Hawkib subdivision of the Kongjai Kuki tribe. Population 200, of whom 60 are fighting-men. The chief and most influential man is Vomyil.

Climate.—The climate is healthy at all seasons.

Water.—Supply scanty.

Supplies.—Rice-straw procurable. Fair grazing. Principal grains are Indian-corn, rice, múm, and chayan. Firewood plentiful. Pumpkins, beans, and arum. The rice harvest is in November; that of the múm in December.

Live-stock.—Pigs, poultry, 10 goats, and 40 metna.

Transport.—For coolie purposes, 60 men and women.

Timber.—No oaks or firs; other forest trees in plenty.—(*Lieut. Dun, 1882.*)

CHONGVEL—

A new Kuki village of the Simmté clan, at present situated in the Turbung valley in south Manipur.

Elevation.—2,700 feet above the sea.

Temperature.—44° at sunrise in December.

Climate.—Unhealthy from 1st May to 1st December.

Houses.—Five of the usual Kuki pattern.
Inhabitants.—Twenty.
Fighting-men —Seven.
Water.—Plentiful.
Camping-ground.—Unlimited.
Grazing.—Plentiful.
Forage.—
Grains.—
Fruits and Vegetables.— *Vide* page 77, Chanjang.
Timber.—
Harvests.—
Live-stock.—Pigs and poultry only.
Carriage.—Ten coolies.
Approaches.—Up easy slopes through open oak forest from the north and east.

CHORO—

A peak overlooking the Kubbo valley on the west. It has an elevation of 3,440 feet, and is the southernmost point of the range, whose culminating peak is Sirohifarat. It is covered with forest.

CHOWHUM—

Is a Tankul Naga village, built after the usual pattern, 4,000 feet above the sea-level. It is situated 7 miles from Chattik on the Kongal road, which it partly commands. Together with the village of Mankot, it covers any advance on the Chussad chief's village, Tonghu, from the north. There are 20 houses.

Camping-ground.—There is plenty of open ground, a mile from the village, on the north.
Approaches.—The village is approached along a ridge from the north and up a ravine from the south, both being covered with thick jungle.
Inhabitants.—The inhabitants belong to the Tankul tribe. Population 100, of whom 20 are fighting-men.
Climate.—The climate is unhealthy from beginning of August to end of October.
Water.—Plentiful supply close to the village.
Supplies.—Rice-straw and bamboo leaves plentiful. Scanty grazing. Principal grains, rice and múm. Firewood plentiful Arum, yams, and pumpkins. Harvest in November and early part of December.
Live-stock.—Pigs and poultry.
Transport.—For coolie purposes, 20 men and women.
Timber,—Oaks, firs, and bamboos plentiful.—(*Lieut. Dun, 1881-82.*)

CHUITAR-KULEL—

A Tankul village, built after the usual Tankul pattern, about 6,000 feet above the sea-level. There are 60 houses.

Inhabitants.—The inhabitants belong to the south-western section of the Tankul Naga tribe. Population 300, of whom 60 are fighting men. The chief's name is Sowkum. Mimyang, who is friendly, has much influence.
Climate.—The climate is healthy at all seasons.
Water.—There is a small supply close by on the east.
Supplies.—Rice-straw plentiful. Scanty grazing. Principal grains, rice and múm. Firewood plentiful. Arum, yams, and pumpkins. Harvest in November and early part of December.

Live-stock.—Pigs, poultry, and a few metna or buffaloes.
Transport.—For coolie purposes, 60 men and women.
Timber.—Oaks and firs plentiful.—(*Lieut. Dun, 1881.*)

CHUITAR-KUNAO—

A Tankul Naga village in North-East Manipur, an offshoot of above.

CHUMMU-KULEL—

A Tankul village, built after the usual Tankul pattern, about 3,000 feet above the sea-level. It is on the road from Manipur to the Ningthee river *viâ* Poshing. There are 60 houses.

Camping-ground.—There is plenty of camping-ground in the rice-fields in the vicinity.

Approaches.—There is a steep ascent and descent by the road.

Inhabitants.—The inhabitants belong to the north-eastern section of the Tankul Naga tribe. Population 300, of whom 60 are fighting-men. The chief's name is Jempung. Sicha, who is friendly, has much influence.

Climate.—The climate is unhealthy from beginning of August to end of October.

Water.—Supply plentiful.

Supplies.—Rice-straw and bamboo leaves plentiful. Scanty grazing. Principal grains, rice and múm. Firewood plentiful. Arum, yams, and pumpkins. Harvest in November and early part of December.

Live stock.—Pigs and poultry.
Transport.—For coolie purposes, 60 men and women.
Timber.—Oaks, firs, and bamboos plentiful.—(*Lieut. Dun, 1881-82.*)

CHUMMU-KUNAO—

A Tankul village, built after the usual Tankul pattern, about 3,000 feet above the sea-level. It is on the road from Manipur to the Ningthee *viâ* Poshing, a little above the Nelekong stream. There are 15 houses.

Camping-ground.—Plenty of camping-ground in the vicinity.

Inhabitants.—The inhabitants belong to the south-eastern section of the Tankul Naga tribe. Population 75, of whom 15 are fighting-men. The chief's name is Motra. Masessar, who is friendly, has much influence.

Climate.—The climate is unhealthy from beginning of August to end of October.

Water.—Supply plentiful.

Supplies.—Rice-straw plentiful. Fair grazing. Principal grains, rice and múm. Firewood plentiful. Arum, yams, and pumpkins. Harvest in November and early part of December.

Live-stock.—Pigs and poultry.
Transport.—For coolie purposes, 15 men and women.
Timber.—Oaks and firs plentiful.—(*Lieut. Dun, 1881-82.*)

CHUNBANG—

A Chohté village in South-East Manipur.

Elevation.—3,500 feet above the sea.
Temperature.—40° at sunrise in February.
Climate.—Unhealthy from May to 1st December.
Houses.—10, Naga pattern.
Inhabitants.—40.
Fighting-men.—10.
Water and Camping-ground.—Probably plentiful.

Grazing.—Good.
Forage.—
Grains.—
Fruits and Vegetables *Vide* page 156, Machi.
Timber.—
Harvests.-
Live-stock.—A few metna, pigs, and poultry.
Carriage.—15 coolies.

CHUNGAI—

A Tankul village, built after the usual Tankul pattern, about 3,000 feet above the sea-level. There are 6 houses.

Inhabitants.—The inhabitants belong to the south-western section of the Tankul Naga tribe. Population 30, of whom 6 are fighting-men.

Climate.—The climate is unhealthy from beginning of August to end of October.

Supplies.—Rice-straw procurable. Scanty grazing. Principal grains, rice and múm. Firewood plentiful Arum, yams, and pumpkins. Harvest in November and early part of December.

Live-stock.—Pigs and poultry.

Transport.—For coolie purposes, 6 men and women.

Timber.—Oaks and firs plentiful.—(*Lieut. Dun, 1881-82.*)

CHUNGSE—

A Kuki village in Burmese territory.

CHUNYANG—

A Chussad village, built after the usual Chussad pattern, 2,000 feet above the sea-level. It is by the side of another village, Changlé, which, together with it, covers any advance on the Chussad chief's village, Tonghu, from the south, being situated on the road from Kongal Thana. There are 15 houses.

Camping-ground.—There is fair camping-ground, with water about 2 miles north of the village; also 200 men could encamp in the village.

Approaches.—The village is approached from the north and from the south. Both approaches are level and good, winding along a ridge on alternate sides. That to the south is defended by a palisade at a ravine 1½ miles from the village.

Inhabitants.—The inhabitants belong to the Chussad subdivision of the Kongjai Kuki tribe. Population 75, of whom 22 are fighting-men. Their chief is Chunyang, who rules also the villages of Changlé and Molhuri. It is believed that most of the late damage done to the Tankuls was by his people.

Climate.—The climate is unhealthy from beginning of June to end of October.

Water.—Near the village there is but a scanty supply.

Supplies.—Rice-straw procurable. No grazing. Principal grains are rice, múm, and chayan. Firewood plentiful. Arum, beans, pumpkins, and plantains. Harvest in November and early part of December.

Live-stock.—Pigs and poultry.

Transport.—For coolie purposes, 20 men and women.

Timber.—No oaks or firs; other kinds plentiful.—(*Lieut. Dun, 1882.*)

CHURUNGNA—

A subdivision of the Marring Naga tribe. (*Vide* Naga.)

CHUSSAD—

The chief village of the Chussad Kuki tribe. (*Vide* Tonghu.)

CHUSSAD KUKIS—

A subdivision of the Kongjai Kuki tribe, who inhabit the country lying between Chattik and Kongal Thana on the north and south, and between the Ungochings and main portion of the Malaya range on the east and west. They inhabit 12 villages, some of which are mere off-shoots of others.

COMPANI—

A Manipuri hamlet just outside Imphal on the west.

G

GANDABI—

A Manipuri hamlet in the north-east portion of the valley.

GAZI[illegible]HIMI—

(*Vide* Laiee.)

GE[illegible]AT—

(*Vide* Kendat.)

GNA[illegible]U—

A Tankul village, built after the usual Tankul pattern, about 4,000 feet [illegible] the sea-level. There are [illegible] houses.

Inhabitants.—The inhabitants belong to the north-eastern subdivision of the [illegible] Naga tribe. Population [illegible], of whom 60 are fighting-men. The [illegible] name is Maiyor.

[illegible].—The climate is unhealthy from beginning of August to end of October.

Supplies.—Rice-straw plentiful. Scanty grazing. Principal grains are rice and múm. Firewood plentiful. Arum, yams, and pumpkins. Harvest in November and early part of December.

Live-stock.—Pigs and poultry.

Transport.—For coolie purposes, 60 men and women.

Timber.—Bamboos scarce; oaks and firs plentiful.—(*Lieut. Dun, 1881.*)

GNARAIKONG—

A mountain stream which drains a very sequestered valley between the Arni Peak and Kachaophung. Its bed is full of large boulders; it is (between these two peaks) not more than 20 yards broad, and easily fordable by man and beast during the cold weather. It is sometimes called the Guamei. (*Vide* Angami.)

H

HAIDRUNG—

A Manipuri village on the Thobal River above Yarapok.

Elevation.—
Temperature.— } *Vide* page 77, Changangai.
Climate.—
Houses.—50, Manipuri pattern.
Inhabitants.—250, sepoy class.
Fighting-men.—50.
Water.—Plentiful.
Camping-ground.—
Grazing.—
Forage.—
Grains.— } *Vide* page 77, Changangai.
Fruits and Vegetables.—
Timber.—
Harvests.—
Live-stock.—100 cows, 75 buffaloes.
Carriage.—50 carts.
Approaches—By fair mule path along the bank of the Thobal from both north and south.

HAIENGKHANG—

A small Manipuri village at the south-western corner of Longtival Hill on the central valley road.

Elevation.—
Temperature.— } *Vide* page 77, Changangai.
Climate.—
Houses.—20, Manipuri pattern.
Inhabitants.—100. Have charge of a shrine in their village.
Fighting-men.—20.
Water.—Plentiful (Achawba River).
Camping-ground.—Sufficient for 200 men on a small mound, at all seasons of the year.
Grazing.—Good.
Supplies.—*Vide* page 77, Changangai.
Live stock.—40 cows, 30 buffaloes.
Carriage.—20 carts.
Approaches—By the central valley road from north and south.

HAIGROJAM—

A small Chiru village 7 miles south-west of Imphal.

HAIROK—

A Manipuri village on the Ingorok stream, between its exit from the Yumadoung Hills and the eastern valley road.

Elevation.—
Temperature.— } *Vide* page 77, Changangai.
Climate.—
Houses.—25, Manipuri pattern.
Inhabitants.—100, sepoy class.
Fighting-men.—20.

Water.—Good and plentiful.

Camping-ground.— } *Vide* page 77, Changangai.
Grazing.— }
Supplies.— }

Live-stock.—37 buffaloes, 50 cows.

Carriage.—25 carts.

Approaches—By a fair mule path along the Ingorok stream from east and west.

HAITUK-POKPI (THANNAH)—

On the Manipur-Yanga-popi road, 29 miles from Manipur and 18 miles from Kambang. It forms one of the inner lines of frontier posts which lie along the western foot of the Yumadoung range, as in the Manipur valley at the mouth of one of the passes leading into the Kubbo valley. The thannah is little more than a police post, an officer and 10 men being stationed there.

Camping-ground.—There is fair camping-ground for two regiments.

Approaches.—The hills on each side are grassy, rounded, and easily ascended.

Water.—Supply of water plentiful.—(*Lieut. Dun, 1881-82.*)

HANGO—

A Tankul village, built after the usual Tankul pattern, 4,800 feet above the sea-level. There are 10 houses.

Camping-ground.—There is a small amount of camping ground available above the village.

Approaches—From below; on the west by path 6 feet broad winding along the face of the hill and passing through jungle. No natural difficulties; gradient easy.

Inhabitants.—The inhabitants belong to the south-western subdivision of the Tankul Naga tribe. Population 50, of whom 10 are fighting-men. The chief's name is Nánu.

Climate.—The climate is unhealthy from beginning of August to end of October.

Water.—Scanty supply at the village.

Supplies.—Rice-straw plentiful and bamboo leaves. Scanty grazing. Principal grains are rice and múm. Firewood plentiful. Arum, yams, and pumpkins. Harvest in November and early part of December.

Live-stock.—Pigs and poultry.

Transport.—For coolie purposes, 10 men and women.

Timber.—Oaks, firs, and bamboos plentiful.—(*Lieut. Dun, 1881.*)

HAOHOYAM—

A new Kuki village of the Changsen clan, situated a day's journey south of the Kaupúm Valley.

Elevation.—About 3,000 feet above the sea.

Temperature.—About 40° at sunrise in January.

Climate.—Unhealthy from 1st May to 1st December.

Houses.—15, Kuki pattern.

Inhabitants.—60.

Fighting-men.—15.

Water.—Probably distant and scanty.

Camping-ground.—Probably very little open ground available.

Grazing.—Most probably very poor.

Supplies.—*Vide* page 77, Chanjang.

Live-stock.—A few metna, pigs, and poultry.

Carriage.—20 coolies.
Timber.—Heavy forest of unknown species and bamboo.
Approaches.—The village is surrounded with heavy forest, and the hill-sides are steep.

HAUBI—

A well-marked forest-clad peak in Southern Manipur.

HAUKA—

The eastern portion of the large Manipuri village of Thobal.

Elevation.— }
Temperature.— } *Vide* page 77, Changangai.
Climate.— }
Houses.—75, Manipuri pattern.
Inhabitants.—375, sepoy class.
Fighting-men.—75.
Water.—Plentiful.
Camping-ground.—None at the village. But 2 miles to the east along the high road there is sufficient ground for four battalions, and appears sufficiently well raised to be available throughout the year.
Grazing.—Fair.
Supplies.—*Vide* page 77, Changangai.
Live-stock.—150 cows, 110 buffaloes.
Carriage.—75 carts, 50 boats.
Approaches—By main road (Route No. 10 from east and west).

HAUKCHONG—

A small Kaupui village in North-West Manipur.

HAUKIL KUKIS—

A subdivision of the Kongjai Kuki tribe.

HAUREBI—

A Manipuri village on the Achanba River near the centre of the valley.

Elevation.— }
Temperature.— } *Vide* page 77, Changangai.
Climate.— }
Houses.—75, Manipuri pattern.
Inhabitants.—375, Mussulman sepoys.
Fighting-men.—75.
Water.—Plentiful.
Camping-ground.— }
Grazing.— } *Vide* page 77, Changangai.
Supplies.— }
Live-stock.—105 cows, 105 buffaloes.
Carriage.—75 carts, 35 boats.
Approaches—By fair mule-path along the banks of the Achauba (or Imphal)

HEBUBVOMAH—

A Kolya Naga village of the Mau section, situated on the northern frontier of Manipur between the head-waters of the Sijjo and the Zullo streams.
Elevation.—5,000 feet above the sea.
Temperature.—40° at sunrise in December.
Climate.—Healthy at all seasons.
Houses.—150, Naga pattern.

Inhabitants.—600.
Fighting-men—150.
Water.—Plentiful.
Camping-ground.—Plenty of the terraced rice-fields to be kept unflooded. If flooded, as is usual during the cold weather, there would be no level, and very little cleared ground available.
Grazing.—Good.
Supplies.—*Vide* page 78, Charo.
Live-stock.—180 cows, pigs, and poultry.
Carriage.—200 coolies.
Approaches.—Not actually visited.

HELEN—

A large village of about 150 houses and 750 inhabitants on the Ava-Kendat road. Country in vicinity well cultivated. Road good, light, and sandy. Salt made about here.

HEMKAIE—

A Hawkib village, built after the usual Kuki pattern, about 3,500 feet above the sea-level. There are 3 houses.
Inhabitants.—The inhabitants belong to the Hawkib subdivision of the Kongjai Kuki tribe. Population 15, of whom 4 may be fighting-men. The headman is Langdum.
Climate.—The climate is unhealthy from beginning of August to end of October.
Water.—Scanty supply.
Supplies.—Rice-straw procurable. Scanty grazing. Principal grains are Indian-corn, job's-tears, and rice. Firewood plentiful. Arum and pumpkins. Harvest in November and early part of December.
Live-stock.—Pigs and poultry.
Transport.—For coolie purposes, 4 men and women.
Timber.—Oaks and firs plentiful.—(*Lieut. Dun, 1882.*)

HINGLAM—

A new Kuki village of the Simmté clan. The name of the chief is Haukúmáug. It is situated on the Manipur source of the Tipai river in Southern Manipur.
Elevation.—3,000 feet above the sea.
Temperature.—42° at sunrise in December.
Climate.—Unhealthy from 1st May to 1st December.
Houses.—30, Kuki pattern.
Inhabitants.—120.
Fighting-men.—30.
Water.—Probably scanty.
Camping-ground.—Probably scanty.
Grazing.—
Products.—
Timber.—
Harvests.— } *Vide* page 77, Chanjang.
Live-stock.—10 metna, pigs, and poultry.
Carriage.—60 coolies.
Approaches.—Not personally visited.
Forest-covered country, and steep hill-sides.

HUINING—
A Tankul village in North-Eastern Manipur.

HÚISSU—
A Tankul village, built after the usual Tankul pattern, about 5,000 feet above the sea-level. There are 20 houses.
Inhabitants.—The inhabitants belong to the north-eastern subdivision of the Tankul Naga tribe. Population 100, of whom 20 may be fighting-men. The chief's name is Asáwah.
Climate.—The climate is healthy at all seasons.
Supplies.—Rice-straw plentiful. Scanty grazing. Principal grains are rice and múm. Firewood plentiful. Arum, yams, and pumpkins. Harvest in November and early part of December.
Live-stock.—Pigs and poultry.
Transport.—For coolie purposes, 20 men and women.
Timber.—Bamboos scarce; oak and fir plentiful.—(*Lieut. Dun, 1881.*)

HUMI—
A Tankul Naga village at the source of the Thobal river in Northern Manipur.
Elevation.—4,800 feet above the sea.
Temperature.—34° at sunrise in January.
Climate.—Healthy at all seasons.
Houses.—Seventy-five, Naga pattern.
Inhabitants.—Three hundred.
Fighting-men.—Seventy-five.
Water.—Scanty.
Camping-ground.—Very little, except on rice-fields, which are always flooded by the inhabitants during the cold weather.
Grazing.—Fair.
Products.—
Timber.— } *Vide* page 78, Charo.
Harvests.—
Live-stock.—Ten cows, pigs, and poultry.
Carriage.—One hundred coolies.
Approaches.—Not personally visited, but apparently easy and open from the east.

HUNDUNG-KULEL—
A Tankul village, built after the usual Tankul pattern, 4,000 feet above the sea-level, situated on the Chattik-Kongal route, between Thobal and the village of Pong. The village contains 10 houses, and is built on the edge of the Hundung-Kulel ridge.
Camping-ground.—There is a little on the west of the village.
Approaches.—The village is approached from the west by a path along a narrow ridge; from the east up a steep spur. Both could easily be defended.
Inhabitants.—The inhabitants belong to the south-western subdivision of the Tankul Naga tribe. Population 50, of whom 10 are fighting-men. The Chief's name is Kotakul. Phowoonlyen has much influence.
Climate.—The climate is unhealthy from beginning of August to end of October.
Water.—Scanty supply of water.

Supplies.—Rice-straw plentiful. Scanty grazing. Principal grains, rice and múm. Firewood plentiful. Arum, yams, and pumpkins. Rice harvest in November; múm in December.

Live-stock.—Pigs and poultry.

Transport.—For coolie purposes, 12 men and women.

Timber.—Oaks and firs plentiful.—(*Lieut. Dun, 1881-82.*)

HUNDUNG-KULEL—

A ridge, crossed by the Chattik-Kongal route, on the end of which the village of the same name is situated.

HUNDUNG-PANDA—

A Tankul village, built after the usual Tankul pattern, 4,500 feet above the sea-level, situated between Leireng and Konjai on the Manipur-Ningthee northern route *viâ* Poshing. There are 200 houses.

Camping-ground.—There is camping ground for a large force below the village to the south-west.

Inhabitants.—The inhabitants belong to the south-western subdivision of the Tankul Naga tribe. Population 1,000, of whom 200 may be fighting-men. The Chief's name is Thowai-Chowba. Pheiomalot has much influence.

Climate.—The climate is healthy at all seasons.

Water.—Plenty of water on north and west of village, and also at camping-ground on south-west.

Supplies.—Rice-straw plentiful. Scanty grazing; none at camping-ground. Principal grains, rice and múm. Firewood plentiful. Arum, yams, and pumpkins. Rice harvest in November; múm in December.

Live-stock.—Pigs, poultry, and a few metna.

Transport.—For coolie purposes, 200 men and women.

Timber.—Oaks and firs plentiful.—(*Lieut. Dun, 1881-82.*)

HUNDUNG-TANKUL—

A Tankul village, built after the usual Tankul pattern, about 4,500 feet above the sea-level. There are 45 houses.

Camping-ground.—There appears from a distance to be a little at either end of the village.

Approaches.—The ground from a distance looks easy.

Inhabitants.—The inhabitants belong to the south-western subdivision of the Tankul Naga tribe. Population 225, of whom 45 may be fighting-men.

Water.—Scanty supply of water.

Supplies.—Rice-straw plentiful. Scanty grazing. Principal grains, rice and múm. Firewood plentiful. Arum, yams, and pumpkins. Rice harvest in November; múm in December.

Live-stock.—Pigs and poultry.

Transport.—For coolie purposes, 20 men and women.

Timber.—Oaks, firs, and many other kinds plentiful.—(*Lieut. Dun, 1881.*)

HUNGOO—

A Mangoung village, built after the usual Kuki pattern, about 4,000 feet above the sea-level. There are 27 houses.

Inhabitants.—The inhabitants belong to the Mangoung subdivision of the Kongjai Kuki tribe. Population 135, of whom 40 may be fighting-men. The chief's name is Mangjung.

Climate.—The climate is unhealthy from beginning of August to end of October.

Supplies.—Rice-straw procurable. Scanty grazing. Principal grains are rice, job's-tears, and Indian-corn. Firewood plentiful. Pumpkins, yams beans, and sugarcane. Harvest in November and early part of December.

Live-stock.—Pigs, poultry, 5 goats, and 30 metna.

Transport.—For coolie purposes, 54 men and women.

Timber.—Not many oaks; no firs; other kinds plentiful.—(*Lieut. Dun, 1881.*)

HYTUK-POKPI—

A small stream crossed by the Manipur-Yanga-pokpi road.

I

IARONG—

A small Kaupui Naga village in North-West Manipur.

ICHAIC—

A small tributary.

ILANG—

A Manipuri village on the south-east corner of the valley, about 20 miles north of Shugurm.

Elevation.—
Temperature.— } *Vide* page 77, Changangai.
Climate.—

Houses.—20, Manipuri pattern.

Inhabitants.—100, Loi caste.

Fighting-men.—20.

Water.—Plentiful.

Camping-ground.—Plenty between 15th December and 1st April; none at other seasons.

Grazing.—Good.

Products.—
Timber.— } *Vide* page 77, Changangai.
Harvests.—

Live-stock.—40 cows, 30 buffaloes.

Carriage.—20 coolies, 20 carts.

Approaches—By narrow path through high grass jungle from the eastern

IMNAM—

A Manipuri village, on the south-east corner of the valley, about 25 miles north of Shugurm.

Elevation.—
Temperature.— } *Vide* page 77, Changangai.
Climate.—

Houses.—25, Manipuri pattern.

Inhabitants.—125, Loi caste.

Fighting-men.—25.

Water.—Plentiful.

Camping-ground.—Fair amount. Wants clearing of grass jungle.

Grazing.—
Products.—
Timber.— } *Vide* page 77, Changangai.
Harvests.—

Live-stock.—50 cows, 35 buffaloes.

Carriage.—25 men, 25 carts.

Approaches—By narrow paths over rice-fields and through grass jungle.

IMPHAL—

Name.—The chief town of Manipur is called Imphal, which in the Manipuri language signifies "capital town."

No part of the valley seems to be so hot or so unhealthy as the capital. A large part of it must have once formed part of the Lamphel, and sites for houses have been raised by digging tanks and trenches. The mosquitoes are worse than I have ever known elsewhere.

Position.—It is situated near the northern end of the valley and almost equidistant from the watersheds of the main ranges on east and west.

Geographically speaking, it is in 94° east longitude and in 24° 22′ north latitude. It is 2,619 feet above the sea.

Other insects abound, and in the evenings the eyes suffer sadly.—(*J. Johnstone.*)

Population.—It contains between fifty and sixty thousand inhabitants, or one-third of the plains population and one-fourth of the total population of the territory.

Size.—It is 6 miles long from north to south and 4½ miles broad from east to west.

* I put the distance at 132, which is, I think, the least it can be estimated at.—(*J. Johnstone.*)

Distances.—It is 104* miles from Silchar, 89 from Kohima, 114 from Samjok, and 141 from Kendat.

Appearance.—In order to give a clear idea of its appearance, it will be necessary first to describe a Manipuri village, as it is nothing more than an unmodified collection of villages.

The favourite position for a village is on the banks of a river in a single row on each bank, and this for two reasons,—firstly, because the banks of the rivers are higher than the country behind them; and secondly, on account of the fondness Manipuris have for the proximity of water.

The villages are thus all length and no breadth, and they are made longer by the custom of placing every house in at least half an acre of compound.

The householder surrounds his half acre with a mud wall, 4 feet high and 1 foot thick; plants cactus and aloes on the wall, and bamboos, kagra reed (which attains a height of 20 feet), and indigenous trees, of which the most common are the mango, the babul, and the kaddam behind it.

In front of the house, which is an oblong hut on a framework of wooden post and beams, with walls of reeds and bamboos and a thatched roof, there is a small well-beaten patch of open ground; but the whole of the rest of the little estate is carefully cultivated with vegetables, sugarcane, tobacco, &c. The Manipuri thus ensures to himself a great amount of privacy, as well as a supply of building materials and vegetables, and the village from a distance presents the appearance of a long bamboo grove.

At the spot where the capital is now placed, three of the main streams which drain the valley converge, and three villages have thus been placed in juxtaposition.

Land being still in excess of the demand, the size of compounds has not been reduced or bamboo clumps and hedge-row trees cleared away.

Viewed from the top of Langol hill, which is situated on the north-west corner, and stretches protecting arms round the city on west and north, it presents the appearance of a dense forest having a large square clearing in the centre.

Entering it, we find no streets and no shops, no paved or metalled roads. There are no masonry walls or buildings visible. The city has no enclosing walls or gates. There is no system of lighting, drainage, or artificial water-supply.

Surroundings.—Every cultivable inch within five miles is laid out in rice-fields. It is not, however, equally approachable from every direction.

The Langol hill and the Lamphel jheel forbid access to it at the north-western corner, and the Langol hill sends spurs down across the northern and western entrances.

From the east the road crosses a swamp and the Iril and Kongba rivers; the north-eastern road crosses the two last.

The southern approaches are covered (at a distance of 5 miles from the centre of the town) by the hill of Longtival. The south-western approach alone is open.

At the north-western corner, and both on the western and the eastern sides there are swampy lakes of considerable size.

Arrangement.—In the centre is the Raja's enclosure or, as it is called in Manipuri, the Pāt. Every road converges upon it, and it is in every sense the heart of the city and of the country.

In front of the Pāt is a large open square, down the centre of which passes a broad road; the remainder is occupied by bazaars, polo-ground, and a piece of waste land.

On the southern edge of this square (which is on the western face of the Pāt) is situated the Residency and the lines of the escort.

Divisions.—The city is divided into four quarters under officers called the heads of the Punnahs. The divisions are—

(*1*) *Khwai*—From the Kohima road westerly to the Cachar road.

(*2*) *Yaiskul.*—From the Cachar road to the southern section of the Atchowba river.

(*3*) *Wankei.*—From the Atchowba to the eastern road.

(*4*) *Khurai.*—From the eastern road to the Kohima road.

Communications.

Roads.—Ten main roads issue from the town:—

(1) The Naga Hills and Assam road on the north.

(2) The Tankul country road on the north-east.

(3) The eastern road.

(4), (5), and (6) Three Thobal and Burma roads on the south-east.

(7) and (8) Two Longtival or central valley roads on the south.

(9) The western road.

(10) The Konjupkul, Acqui or Upper Cachar road.

They issue at first from the Pāt in four roads only—to north, south, east, and west,—and throw off branches.

In addition to the above, there are a great number of cross-lanes connecting the main arteries. No roads are metalled, but the ten principal (above enumerated) are 20 yards broad (in some cases more), are well raised when not situated on the bank of a river, have broad ditches on either side, and within the city have fairly level surfaces.

The soil being clayey, they become slippery and difficult to traverse in the rains.

Rivers.—There are three rivers—the Nambol, the Atchowba (called higher up the Tiki), and the Kongba.

They run parallel to one another from north to south.

The two former have cut deep into the soil, and in the rains hold 20 feet of water, though in the winter they are not (within the town) more than 2 or 3 feet deep.

Their banks are steep and raised about 3 feet above the ground behind them.

They average 40 yards broad at the top.

Their currents run at about 3 miles an hour in the winter.

The two former are much used as lines of communication with the southern portion of the valley.

The Kongba is a shallow sluggish stream. In the rains it cannot contain more than 4 feet of water.

It is 20 yards broad.

Canals.—The canals are all shallow, the banks being not more than 3 feet high. They can only be supplied with water by rain or the overflow of the rivers.

That constructed along the eastern road was intended for the conveyance of firewood from Nongmaiching hill, but it becomes, like the rest of the canals, almost dry by the month of January.

Bridges.—There is only one brick bridge in the town, though there are many brick culverts. It is situated at the western end of the square, and is thrown across the Nambol.

Three roads branch off from it—the western road, the Southern Cachar road, and the western of the central valley roads.

It is very massive. It has a 20 feet roadway with 3 feet high bounding walls. It has five arches, of which the three centre alone remain open.

The bricks of which it is made are, like all the bricks of Manipur, very soft and bad, and, in spite of its massive appearance, it could be easily destroyed.

There are about a dozen wooden bridges of a semi-permanent character and practicable for laden animals. They are constructed as follows. Pairs of wooden posts, usually 1 foot in diameter and 6 feet apart, are driven vertically into the bed and banks of the river, the interval between pairs being about 5 yards. Each pair of posts is connected at the top by cross-beams. On these cross-beams poles or bamboos are laid longitudinally, and over these again a roadway of bamboo matting. They rise slightly in the centre, and the central pair of poles is sometimes 25 to 30 feet high.

* The cows are a curse to the country, as they are turned loose to commit any devastation they like. When they can they crowd on the bridges and often break them down by their numbers.—(*J. Johnstone.*)

To prevent cows * straying on to these bridges, the roadway usually stops a few feet short of the bank, and its place supplied by couple of bamboos.

This defect could be remedied in a few minutes from the bamboo clumps of the neighbouring compounds.

Fords.—During the cold weather, *i.e.*, from the 1st November to the 1st April, the rivers within the city are fordable anywhere.

Lakes and Marshes.—The Lamphel lake does not apparently dry up at all in the cold weather. It is very deep and is always full.

It is almost entirely covered with vegetation, too thin however to support the weight of a man.

No stream flows into it, and only 1 foot by 4 inches of water issue from it. The exit is close to the brick bridge on the edge of the Konjupkul road. It has a fall of some 15 feet, and is used to turn a grindstone.

The swamp to the south of the Lamphel between the two western roads never completely dries up. In January it holds about 4 acres, and is 4 feet deep in the middle. The swamp on the east of the town between the Kongba and the Iril dries up completely in the winter; that on the left bank of the Iril never dries up. The road across it has sunk down and become impassable in two places. Throughout the year it is a quivering morass.

Entrances.—There are nine entrances to the town. They have no artificial defences.

The northern entrance is defended naturally by an eastern spur of the Langol hill, called on the east of the road Ching Mairong.

The Langol hill, which is very steep, covered with small bushes only, and has a swampy nala along its eastern base, flanks the approach to a considerable distance. The ground in front of this entrance is absolutely without cover.

The Ching Mairong hill is terraced and flat at the top. Guns could be easily taken up to and placed on it.

To force this entrance with a minimum of loss it would be advisable to ascend the Langol hill at its northern end near Sengmaie or at Koirengi.

The western entrances have similar natural defences. In this case a southern spur from Langol. They are suitable for artillery, but they only give direct fire. The ground in front is perfectly open.

The south-western (Southern Cachar) road entrance has no natural defences. All the southern roads are covered by the Longtival and Hyenkhang hills. The central valley roads encounter at Hyenkhang a barrier exactly similar to that at the northern entrance to the town. The Hyenkhang hill is, moreover, supported by a marsh in rear, which would render its turning difficult.

The Burma road entrance has in its front the Lilong river: on its left flank the Iril, the Atchowba, and a broad canal 4 feet deep (used originally for boat racing); on its right the Longtival hill, with a marsh along its eastern base. From the east, a dangerous morass, the Iril, and the Kongba have to be crossed, and on the edge of the town proper an earth bank at right angles to the road, 4 feet high and 10 feet thick.

From the north-east, the Iril and Kongba have to be crossed. There are no other natural defences at this entrance. The Kongba is crossed on a causeway, 20 yards broad, over which the river flows in the rains, but which is quite dry in winter.

Defences.—The only attempt at defences are :—

(1) A triple line from Chingmairong to the Atchowba stream consisting of a mud wall 4 feet high and 1 foot thick, a ditch 6 feet broad and 2 feet deep, and an earthen bank 5 high and 10 feet thick; the latter being in rear of the two first.

(2) This bank is continued along the eastern face inside the Kongba.

(3) The enclosing walls of compounds, which are usually 4 feet high, 1 foot thick, and planted with cactus and aloes.

(4) The Chingba hill, which stretches from the Nambol river almost to the Atchowba, and across one of the central valley routes, is a strong natural defence. It is about 150 feet higher than the plain, commands 800 yards of the eastern and western central valley roads. Guns could be placed on it easily by the help of coolies or elephants.

(5) The Pāt is the only portion of the town which possesses any serious attempt at artificial defence. It is surrounded by a moat 20 yards broad and 6 feet deep at the deepest part, near the western gate. During the cold weather this moat only contains water round the south-eastern and south-western corners. It is divided into sections by the bunds over which the roads pass as they enter the four gates. The water round the south-western angle can be drawn off by a culvert (now closed up) and partially filled up, cutting across the main road which runs along the edge of the moat outside it. There are partially-filled up cuttings, but no other culverts near each of the other corners.

The Pāt or Raja's enclosure.

Inside the moat there is a 10 feet berm crossed by thick traverses at 50 yards interval. The bank inside the berm is constructed of earth. It is about 20 feet thick at the base, has a ramp and loop-holes for musketry fire, but has no arrangement for securing flanking fire. The portion above the level of the ramp is about 4 feet thick. For 150 yards at the north-eastern corner the earth-work has disappeared. In rear of the open space left by the river on the south face there is a mud wall. The houses on every side are not more than 100 yards from the crest of the earthwork.

There is, I believe, an inner enclosure, similiar but smaller in profile to the outer one.

The western entrance has a strong brick gateway and a door in two leaves. They are closed like the flats of a theatre scene and by means of horizontal beams attached to them at the back and working in female screws.

There is a small brick gateway at the southern entrance, but (at present) no door.

At the eastern and northern entrances there are wooden gateways and doors.

None of them have any arrangement for their defence in the way of loop-holes, &c.

Buildings.—The national temple and the Raja's and princes' house, built of brick and situated inside the Pāt.

Two brick temples of no great size belonging to the two ministers, both to the south of the Pāt.

The Residency, the Quarter-Guard, and Hospital.—The Residency stands in acres of ground, and is surrounded by a mud wall 5 feet high and 1 foot thick.

It measures 112 feet by 46 feet.* The dwelling portion is raised 7 feet above the level of the ground upon† strong brick walls, inside which are several rooms for stores, &c. The walls of the upper portion are made in the Elizabethan style on a framework of wood filled in with brick. The roof is thatched. Both in front and rear are deep varandahs, up to which lead flights of steps.

* There is also a projection in front 45 feet by 42 feet.

† The lower rooms were designed as a refuge for non-combatants in case of civil tumults when shell have occasionally, though undesignedly, struck the Residency. These rooms, with a few sand-bags, could be made perfectly shot-proof.—(*J. Johnstone, 1885.*)

The Quarter-Guard, which is also the main entrance gate, is 65 feet by 25½ feet. It is built in the same style as the Residency. It has two stories and four rooms.

The Hospital is 64 feet by 27 feet, is raised upon a solid masonry foundation, and has three rooms and a verandah all round.

The escort lines contain barracks, each by , and are built of bamboos and reeds with thatched roofs.

The only other building of any size in the town is a large "nautch" house on the northern edge of the great square in front of the western entrance of the Pāt. It is built of wooden posts, bamboos and reeds, and thatched.

Places of Rendezvous and Camping-grounds.—The square in front of the western gate of the Pāt is the best place of rendezvous. A division could parade upon it.

There is camping-ground for a regiment of infantry at the north-western corner of Chingba hill on the left bank of the Naobol.

The Mahawali, a sacred grove on the left bank of the Atchowba, 1,000 yards south of the Pāt, would afford ground for two regiments of infantry.

A strip of ground, 100 yards deep, is available all along the left bank of the Atchowba, southward from the Pāt.

A battalion of infantry could be disposed, though not compactly, in the brick-fields on the eastern edge of the Pāt.

At the north-west corner of the Pāt, where the Kohima road issues from it, and in a sacred grove, called the on the eastern edge of the Langthel lake, there is in each place ground for a couple of companies.

Outside the town, there is unlimited camping-ground everywhere in the cold weather, but on the north along the Kongba, and on the south on the plain between the Longtival and the city, there is excellent and unlimited ground at all seasons of the year, with plenty of water and as good grazing as the northern part of the valley affords.

Signalling Stations.—Any point in or on the edge of the Pāt can be placed in communication with almost any point on Langol.

Langol can communicate with Longtival, Chingba, and the outer end of its southern spur. There are no other prominent points.

Bazaars.—It has been already stated that there are no shops. Their place is supplied by open bazaars, to which every vendor brings a basketful of wares. The stock-in-trade of each consists of this one basketful, which is an easy load for a woman. There are about two dozen of these bazaars, large and small.

The largest are two on the square—one held in the morning, the other in the evening; two on the central valley road; one on the south face of the Pāt; one at the north-east corner, and one on the north-east road; one at the northern entrance to the city.

There are no large traders, and the process of collecting trifling quantities of food-stuffs from individuals would not work practically.

There is no butcher's meat; a few fowls* and ducks. No milk; a very little ghee; oil, a few vegetables, and a little fish. Any large quantity of supplies must be obtained through the Durbar, who would collect what was wanted outside the town.

* Also pigeons.—(*J. Johnstone.*)

Under this heading (*viz.*, supplies) it may be as well to mention that at the exit of the Lamphel, close to the brick bridge, there is a water-wheel used for turning a corn-grinding mill. Two more mills could be constructed at this point if required.

Shelter.—Every house has a front verandah and a shed or two in the compound. Accommodation could therefore be supplied for at least 4 men per house. It would not, however, be advisable to billet men, as the Manipuris have a custom (nominally a caste rule) which prevents their admitting foreigners into their houses. This does not, however, apply to Mussulmans, of whom there are about 5,000 (or 1,000 houses) in the capital. The only other places are the Residency Quarter-Guard, an old hospital, and the nautch house.

Firewood.—There is a small firewood* depôt at the brick bridge; but in ordinary times not more than 5 maunds would be found there.

* Chiefly reeds. Wood is very scarce and expensive throughout the valley.—(*J. Johnstone.*)

The chief firewood depôt is two miles south of Longtival, between the two central valley roads which diverge at Hyenkhang.

No stacks of firewood are seen in private houses.

There are two canals, one leading from the north-east corner of the town, the other from the eastern gate of the Pāt to the foot of the hills on the east, which were specially constructed for bringing in firewood; but they dry up in the cold weather and seem to be quite out of use.

Nongmaiching hill is the nearest place in which dry wood could be obtained.

Timber.—The Mahawali is the only place where any considerable quantity of timber is procurable in one place.

There are fine pipal trees along the rivers, and mangoes and small trees and quantities of bamboos in the partition fences of the houses.

The Raja has a timber depôt on the eastern road, where it crosses the Iril, but there is not a large quantity usually obtainable there.

Transport.—There are 200 coolies available in the town at a moment's notice, all hillmen. Two hundred ponies might be produced; but none of them are accustomed to carrying loads.

There are 400 dug-out canoes, each of which will carry 3 maunds of grain and travel at 6 miles an hour down-stream, and 3 miles an hour up.

There are about 1,000 carts, of the kind peculiar to Manipur (*vide* sketch). They carry 4 maunds of grain and travel at 2 miles an hour.

Grazing-ground and Fodder.—In and around the capital the grazing is very poor, as is shown by the attenuated condition of the cows. There is a grassy swamp just beyond the Iril on the Tankul country road; those on the east, west, and north-west, already mentioned, and one west of Longtival. Those on the north-east and east are the best, but are more suitable for buffaloes than for any other animal.

Bhoosa is never made anywhere in the valley, and the rice-straw is frequently burnt.

Oil-cake is procurable in small quantities, but is generally used for fuel. The Manipuris seem to have an objection to feeding cattle with it, and have been known to decline selling it for that purpose.*

* The objection to selling it is that they never have done so before, and, if asked to sell, they demand an enormous price.—(*J. Johnstone.*)

The most suitable points.—There are two conditions which stand out prominently as difficulties in attacking Imphal:—

(1) The extremely open and flat ground to be traversed in approaching the town.

(2) The walls and ditches and lines of trees and bamboos which surround every house, and which would prevent the observer outside from discovering where the defenders were in force and where weak, and which would equalise any disparity which might exist in armament.

There are other conditions, such as the manner in which the town is cut up into sections by the rivers, preventing lateral communication—the hills covering some of the entrances; the straightness of the roads which enables them to be raked for a considerable distance; the contour of the edge of the town which provides excellent flanking fire; the possibility of flooding the fields on the west from the Lamphel lake; the good and direct interior communications which would enable parties to be transferred rapidly from an unthreatened to a threatened point.

Moreover, the Manipuris, themselves expert at digging, are excelled by the Tankul Nagas in this art, and very strong works could be constructed at a week's notice, and from the large quantities of bamboos available excellent obstacles could be constructed.

That line then will be best in which there is least open ground to be traversed and least city to be fought through.

Such a line is found in the Langol hill and the northern portion of the town. The Langol hill in the possession of the defenders, is their chief source of strength; lost to them, their chief source of weakness. With a proper system of trenches, this hill could be made exceedingly difficult to take; but in any case the assailants would probably suffer less loss in its capture than in advancing over flat open and flooded fields. It can be ascended almost anywhere, but best at the northern end and at Koirengi, which is situated half-way between Sengmail and the town.

From the Langol hill the Pāt could be breached, if not rendered untenable, by artillery, and the northern part of the town by infantry fire. The assailant could then approach to within 150 yards of the Pāt under cover.

Failing the northern side of the town, the eastern side would be the easiest to attack. The fields are not liable to be flooded, and there is less depth of enclosed country.

The southern side presents most obstacles—Longtival hill flanked by a canal, a river and a marsh, an open stretch of ground, Chingha hill, and a great depth of town would have to be encountered.

Such are the natural difficulties to be overcome in carrying out an attack on the chief town of Manipur. Whether the Manipuris have the skill and intelligence necessary for the construction of strong works, or the resolution to defend them when made, is another question. It is considered very improbable that they would display either or any of these qualities.

IMPHAL—

A river of Manipur, on which the capital is situated. At this point it is about 50 yards broad at the top, with steep banks, about 15 feet high, and in the cold weather has about 2 feet of water. The road to Chattik *viá* Poshing, used by the Manipuris, crosses it by a small bamboo bridge.

INGOROK (THANNAH)—

A Manipur village on the Manipur-Kongal road, 26 miles from the capital; it is situated at the foot of the Yumádoung range, and forms one of the inner line of frontier posts. The thannah is little more than a police post, being garrisoned by an officer and 10 men.

Camping-ground.—There is good camping-ground for two regiments.

Approaches.—The village lies in a little valley close under the hills.

Water.—Plentiful supply of good water.

IRAM—

A Manipuri village on the Thobal river, below the Thobal villages and Waito.

Elevation.—
Temperature.—
Climate.— } *Vide* page 77, Changangai.

Houses.—25, Manipuri pattern.

Inhabitants.—125, sepoy class.

Fighting-men.—25

Water.—Plentiful

Camping-ground.—
Grazing.-
Products.—
Timber.—
Harvests.— } *Vide* page 77, Changangai.

Live-stock.—50 cows, 35 buffaloes.

Carriage.—25 carts, 12 boats.

Approaches—By fair mule-path along the banks of the Thobal, from north and south.

IRANG RIVER—

The Irang river flows in the next valley east of the Barak. Like the Barak and Mukru, it consists of long deep pools flowing between rocks, alternating with broad shallows, where in the cold weather not more than a few inches of water cover the shingle.

The valley through which it flows almost deserves the name of gorge, so steep and high are the sides.

They are clothed thickly with forest, and the scenery, specially at the crossing, where the river begins to wash the base of the great Kaupúm cliffs, is very beautiful.

There is an easy ford in the cold weather, and a bamboo matting roadway, laid on pontoons of bundles of bamboos, over the pool. A cane bridge, similar to those over the Mukru and Barak, is the means of crossing in the rains.

IRIL—

One of the principal rivers of the Manipur valley. Among the hills it flows through flat-bottomed valleys, and in the plains has cut a deep nala for itself. As far down as the point where the road from Imphal to Yarapok crosses it, it is easily fordable during the cold weather.

At the point where the Manipur-Chattik road crosses it, it is 30 yards broad at the top, with perpendicular banks, about 30 feet high, and about 2 or 3 feet depth of water in the cold weather. The stream is not very fast.

IRING—

A mountain stream in North-West Manipur, a tributary of the Irang.

IRING—

A small Kaupui Naga village in North-West Manipur.

IRINGPAL—

A Manipuri village on the Sengmail stream in South-East Manipur.

Elevation.—
Temperature.— } *Vide* page 77, Changangai.
Climate.—

Houses.—40, Manipuri pattern.
Inhabitants.—200 (grass-cutters).
Fighting-men.—40.
Water.—Good and Plentiful.

Camping-ground.—
Grazing.—
Products.— } *Vide* page 77, Changangai.
Timber.—
Harvests.—

Live-stock.—80 cows, 60 buffaloes.
Carriage.—40 men, 40 carts.
Approaches.—Over rice-fields by narrow paths from the eastern valley road.

IROÏ—

A Kolya Naga village of the Marám section, situated in Northern Manipur, just above the Tiki stream on the east.

Elevation.—3,400 feet.
Temperature.—36° at sunrise in December.
Climate.—Unhealthy from 1st May to 1st December.
Houses.—8, Naga pattern.
Inhabitants.—32.
Fighting-men.—8.
Water.—Plentiful.
Camping-ground.—Probably very little.

Grazing.—
Products.— } *Vide* page 78, Charo.
Timber.—
Harvests.—

Live-stock.—2 buffaloes, pigs, and poultry.
Carriage.—15 coolies.
Approaches.—Not visited, but most probably up a steep fairly open spur from the west.

IRONG—

A Tankul village, built after the usual Tankul pattern, about 3,000 feet above the sea-level. There are 4 houses.

Inhabitants.—The inhabitants belong to the south-western subdivision of the Tankul Naga tribe. Population 20, of whom 4 may be fighting-men.

Climate.—The climate is unhealthy from beginning of August to end of October.

Supplies.—Rice-straw procurable. Scanty grazing. Principal grains are rice and múm. Firewood plentiful. Arum, pumpkins, and yams. Rice harvest in November; múm in December.

Live-stock.—Pigs and poultry.

Transport.—For coolie purposes, 4 men and women.

Timber.—Oaks and firs plentiful.—(*Lieut. Dun, 1881.*)

ITAHMI—

The southern peak of the south spur from Japvo. The summit is 5,150 feet. It is covered with light oak forest. The present Kohima road between Karong and Maithaipham traverses its western face. The old path passed over the summit.

ITHOÏ—

A small tributary of the Iril.

ITHU—

A small Kaupui Naga village in North-West Manipur.

ITUK—

A small Shan village in the Kubbo valley, one day's journey from Tamoo.

IYE—

A tributary of the Irang in North-West Manipur. Where crossed by the Aqui route, it is fordable in the cold weather.

J

JAKHAMA—

An Angami village on the road from the Manipur frontier (Mao) to Kohima. It is built after the usual Angami pattern, about 4,500 feet above the sea-level, and contains 180 houses.

Camping-ground.—There is plenty of ground for camping in terraced rice-fields.

Approaches.—There are steep inferior paths up to the village on each side of the ridge; the village commands the Kohima road to a small extent, but there are no defensive works.

Inhabitants.—The inhabitants belong to the Angami Naga tribe, and are divided into three subdivisions or sections, *viz.*, Nakema, Viama, and Zerma. There is no chief or headman, but the most influential man is Mazalhu.

Climate.—The climate is healthy at all seasons.

Water.—Small supply at the village, but plenty near.

Supplies.—Rice-straw plentiful. Fair grazing. Principal grains are rice, múm, and chayan. Moderate supply of firewood. Arum and pumpkins. Harvest in November and December.

Live-stock.—Cows in large numbers, pigs, and poultry.

Transport.—For coolie purposes, 180 men and women.

Timber.—Very little fir or oak; near village small pollarded alders; bamboos scarce.—(*Lieut. Dun, 1882.*)

JALAIN—

A new Kuki village of the Simmté clan, situated in the Turbúng valley, at the south of the valley.

Elevation.—2,700 feet.

Temperature.—44° at sunrise in December.

Climate.—Unhealthy from 1st May to 1st December.

Houses.—9, Kuki pattern.

Inhabitants.—35.

Fighting-men.—9.

Water.—Good supply.

Camping-ground.—Unlimited.

Grazing.—
Products.—
Timber.—
Harvests.— } *Vide* page 77, Chanjang.

Live-stock.—Pigs and poultry.

Carriage.—20 coolies.

Approaches.—Up easy open slopes from the Turbung.

JATRIK—

The Manipur name for Chattik (*vide* Chattik).

JESSAMI OR PUNGTAR KULEL—

A Kolya Naga village in Northern Manipur, a few miles west of the junction of the Thetzirr and the Lanier.

Elevation.—4,000 feet.

Temperature.—35° at sunrise in January.

Climate.—Healthy at all seasons.

Houses.—200, Naga pattern.
Inhabitants.—800.
Fighting-men.—200.
Water.—Plentiful and good; one stream on the west of the village and two on the east.
Camping-ground.—Sufficient for 3,000 men and transport, north of the village.
Grazing.—Good.
Products.— } *Vide* page 71, Aphoma.
Timber.— }
Harvests.— }
Live-stock.—Pigs, poultry, and a few buffaloes.
Carriage.—200 coolies.
Approaches—Up steep sides of hills from the Lanier, both on east and west. Light jungle on both roads.

JIRI—

Coming from the west, the first river met with after leaving Lakipur is the Jiri, which forms the boundary between British and Manipur territory from its source to its termination in the Barak. The Jiri rises in the hills to the north-east of the Cachar district, and flows nearly due south until Godam ghaut is reached; here it makes a bend and flows west to Jiri Ghát, where the Government road crosses; making another bend here, it flows south again, and, after a course of about 12 miles, falls into the Barak river. From its junction with the Barak, it is said to be navigable for small boats for five days. In the dry weather the Jiri is fordable; it is also crossed by a propped foot-bridge of bamboo; during the rains a ferry-boat conveys passengers across. The river is about 40 yards wide, and its bed is full of snags and trunks of trees. On the Manipur side of the Jiri commences a large and valuable area of dense forest, which extends on either side, but especially in a southerly direction, for many miles; this forest contains much valuable timber, india-rubber, &c.

JIRI—

A Manipuri Thannah on the Cachar frontier, where the Cachar road crosses the river of that name.

There is a rest-house for officers.

K

KABALONG—

A peak on the range bounding the Mayangkhang and Tiki valleys on the west.

KABYANG—

Chussad village, which, together with the village of Punjoong, covers advance on Tonghu from the west.

The chief, whose name is Kabyang, is montri or minister of the tribal chief Tonghu.—(*Lieut. Dun, 1881-82.*) (*Vide* Chussad Kuki tribe.)

KACHAI—

A Tankul Naga village in Northern Manipur, at the source of the Thobal.

Elevation.—4,600 feet.
Temperature.—33° at sunrise in January.
Climate.—Healthy at all seasons.
Houses.—60, Naga pattern.
Inhabitants.—2,100.
Fighting-men.—60.
Water.—Scanty.
Camping-ground.—
Grazing.—
Products.—
Timber.—
Harvests.—
} *Vide* page 78, Charo.
Live-stock.—10 cows, pigs, and poultry.
Carriage.—90 coolies.
Approaches.—Up easy open spurs from the east and south.

KACHAO—

A Tankul Naga village, situated at the head of the Nelekong Valley in North-east Manipur.

Elevation.—4,400 feet.
Temperature.—36° at sunrise in February.
Climate.—Unhealthy from 1st May to 1st December.
Houses.—25, Naga pattern.
Inhabitants.—100.
Fighting-men.—25.
Water.—Plentiful on south and east.
Camping-ground.—Unlimited.
Grazing.—
Products.—
Timber.—
Harvests.—
} *Vide* page 78, Charo.
Live-stock.—Pigs and poultry.
Carriage.—35 coolies.
Approaches.—Along level piece of ground through open forest from the main plateau on the east.

KACHAUPHUNG—

A peak at the head of the Cháttik valley, having an elevation of 8,070 feet above the sea.

The road from Somrah to Cháttik ascends it from the north by a very gently sloping spur, but the southern descent is precipitous.

There is sufficient water and camping-ground on the south side of, and a few hundred feet below, the peak for 500 men and transport.

A very extended view on all sides is obtainable from the peak which was cleared by the Survey in 1851.

KAIENO—

A Manipuri village, 13 miles from Imphal, on the Cachar road.

Elevation.—
Temperature.— } *Vide* page 77, Changangai.
Climate.—

Houses.—30, Manipuri pattern.
Inhabitants.—160, sepoy class.
Fighting-men.—50.
Water.—Scanty and indifferent.
Camping-ground.—
Grazing.—
Products.— *Vide* page 77, Changangai.
Timber.—
Harvests.—
Live-stock.—60 cows, 15 buffaloes, 5 ponies.
Carriage.—30 carts, 5 ponies.
Approaches.—Along the Cachar road.

KAIHEPOVMAH—

A Kolya Naga village, on the northern frontier, a mile east of the Manipur-Kohima road.

Elevation.—5,000 feet.
Temperature.—40° at sunrise in December.
Climate.—Healthy at all seasons.
Houses.—130, Naga pattern.
Inhabitants.—520.
Fighting-men.—130.
Water.—Plentiful.
Camping-ground.—
Grazing.—
Products.— *Vide* page 89, Hebubvomah.
Timber.—
Harvests.—
Live-stock.—150 cows, pigs, and poultry.
Carriage.—130 coolies.
Approaches.—Along gently rising ridge from Phunamah on the west. Up a steep open hill-side from the south.

KAILET—

A new Kuki village of the Simmté clan on the Manipur source of the Tipai river, Southern Manipur.

Elevation.—3,000 feet.
Temperature.—42° at sunrise in December.
Climate.—Unhealthy from 1st May to 1st December.
Houses.—7, Kuki pattern.
Inhabitants.—28.

Fighting-men.—7.
Water.—Scanty.
Camping-ground.—Very little clear ground.
Grazing.—
Products.—
Timber.—
Harvests.—
} *Vide* page 77, Chanjang.
Live-stock.— Pigs and poultry.
Carriage.—15 coolies.
Approaches.—Not visited, but the village is situated in heavy forest and the hills are steep.

KAIPHUNG—

A Kolya Naga village, of the Máram clan, on the range west of Karong Thana, Manipur-Kohima road.

Elevation.—4,500 feet.
Temperature.—36° at sunrise.
Climate.—Healthy at all seasons.
Houses.—26, Naga pattern.
Inhabitants.—84.
Fighting-men.—26.
Water.—Plentiful.
Camping-ground.—Good and plentiful. (Jungle very open.)
Grazing.—
Products.—
Timber.—
Harvests.—
} *Vide* page 78, Charo.
Live-stock.—30 cows, pigs, and poultry.
Carriage.—30 coolies.
Approaches—Up easy slopes from the east through very open jungle.

KAITÉMABI (THANA)—

A village on the Manipur-Kohima road, about 24 miles from the capital, situated on the top of a plateau.

The thana is in a good position, is not commanded, but commands the road, and has a good view up the valley to the north.

Defences.—It is not stockaded or defended in any way.
Camping-ground.—There is unlimited and excellent camping-ground.
Water.—Water-supply plentiful.
Supplies.—If the grass is burnt at a favourable time, there is in March sufficient grazing for 2,000 mules for one day.—(*Lieut. Dun, 1881-82.*)

KAKSA—

A Shan village on the Ningthee river. A steam-launch drawing 4 feet of water got up to this point, but was stopped by rapids. Above Kaksa small boats only are used; they are able to ascend to a point distant two months' journey by water, one month by land.

KALA NAGA—

A forest-clad range of hills between the Mukru and Barak Rivers, Western Manipur.

KALA NAGA—

A Manipuri stockade on the Manipur-Cachar road, just below the village of the same name. The stockade is placed on a spur, where the road bends round and becomes very narrow. It quite commands the road and the approach from the west for 800 yards. It is about 40 yards square, is not itself commanded except from the village, and is usually kept in repair. The garrison consists of 1 officer, 1 non-commissioned officer, and 10 sepoys.

KALA NAGA—

A Kaupui Naga village on the Cachar road, between the Mukru and Barak Rivers.

Elevation.—3,400 feet above the sea.

Houses.—About 75, Naga pattern.

Inhabitants.—300.

Fighting-men.—75.

Water.—Scanty below the village on the east.

Camping-ground.—Scattered bits of level ground east of the village.

Grazing.—
Products.—
Timber.—
Harvests.—
} *Vide* page 78, Charo.

Live-stock.—Pigs and poultry and a few metna.

Carriage.—100 coolies.

Approaches.—Up easy slope from the south through the Manipuri stockade Up steep open path from the east.

KALASOM—

A Tankul village, built after the usual Tankul pattern, about 5,000 feet above the sea-level. There are 40 houses.

Camping-ground.—There should be ground available in the terraced rice-fields.

Inhabitants.—The inhabitants belong to the north-eastern subdivision of the Tankul Naga tribe. Population 200, of whom 40 may be fighting-men. The most influential man is Yamang; he is friendly.

Climate.—The climate is healthy at all seasons.

Supplies.—Rice-straw procurable. Scanty grazing. Principal grains, rice and múm. Firewood plentiful. Arum, yams, and pumpkins. Rice harvest in November; múm in December.

Live-stock.—Pigs, poultry, and a few metna.

Transport.—For coolie purposes, 40 men and women.

Timber.—Oaks and firs plentiful.—(*Lieut. Dun, 1881.*)

KALAY—

The most southerly of the four districts to the east of the Ningthee. It is governed by the Aloung Woon, who resides at Aloung.

KALHANG KULEL—

A Tankul village, built after the usual Tankul pattern, about 5,000 feet above the sea-level. There are 150 houses.

Camping-ground.—There should be ground available for camping in terraced rice-fields.

Inhabitants.—The inhabitants belong to the north-eastern subdivision of the Tankul Naga tribe. Population 750, of whom 150 may be fighting-men. The most influential man is Kougyana, who is friendly.

Climate.—The climate is healthy at all seasons.

Supplies.—Rice-straw procurable. Scanty grazing. Principal grains are rice and múm. Firewood plentiful. Arum, pumpkins, yams. Rice harvest in November; múm in December.

Live-stock.—Pigs and poultry.

Transport.—For coolie purposes, 150 men and women.

Timber.—Oaks and firs plentiful.—(*Lieut. Dun, 1881.*)

KALHANG-KUNAO—

A Tankul village, built after the usual Tankul pattern, about 5,000 feet above the sea-level. There are 60 houses.

Camping-ground.—There should be camping-ground available in terraced rice-fields.

Inhabitants.—The inhabitants belong to the north-eastern subdivision of the Tankul Naga tribe. Population 300, of whom 60 may be fighting-men.

Climate.—The climate is healthy at all seasons.

Supplies.—Rice-straw procurable. Scanty grazing. Principal grains are rice and múm. Firewood plentiful. Arum, yams, and pumpkins. Rice harvest in November; múm in December.

Live-stock.—Pigs, poultry, and a few metna.

Transport.—For coolie purposes, 60 men and women.

Timber.—Oaks and firs.—(*Lieut. Dun, 1881.*)

KAMBANG (THANA)—

A small Manipuri frontier post, forming one of the second line of defences, situated 20 miles from Yanga-pokpi in the Yomadoung range, 4,600 feet above the sea-level, on the spur coming down from the Kambang peak, in a slight hollow. There is no stockade or defences of any kind.

Camping-ground.—A regiment could find camping-ground on the south-east, but would have to clear away much brushwood.

Approaches.—The road from the west would thoroughly command the post if the forest were cleared. Only a few yards of the eastern approach can be seen, owing to some mounds, which would materially assist and advance from that quarter.

Defence and Attack.—Thick forest jungle comes close up to the huts on every side but the east-south-east, where there is a large piece of open grass. Since the Kongal outrage, the direct road to Tamoo has been closed and is now quite overgrown with brushwood. On the peak of the same name, a signal-station might be formed, from which to communicate with Mungsa, Tamoo, and any point between Sawamba and Kongang.

Water.—Small supply close to the thana on the north; a better supply to the south, but far down the hill-side.

Garrison.—The garrison consists of one jamadar, one havildar, and six sepoys.

A much better site for a stockade could easily be selected, the position being naturally a commanding one and of considerable importance.—(*Lieut. Dun, 1881-82; Phayre, 1882.*)

KAMBÁNG—

A peak on the watershed between the Manipur and Kubbo valleys. Elevation 5,282 feet above the sea. Route No. VII passes close under it.

KAMBASOL—

A Tankul village, built after the usual Tankul pattern, about 5,000 feet above the sea-level. There are 120 houses.

Camping-ground.—There should be camping-ground available in the terraced rice-fields.

Inhabitants.—The inhabitants belong to the north-eastern subdivision of the Tankul Naga tribe. Population 600, of whom 120 may be fighting-men. The most influential man is Konkeibah, who is friendly.

Climate.—The climate is healthy at all seasons.

Water.—A small supply of water to south of village.

Supplies.—Rice-straw procurable. Scanty grazing. Principal grains are rice and múm. Firewood plentiful. Arum, yams, and pumpkins. Rice harvest in November; múm in December.

Live-stock.—Pigs, poultry, and a few metna.

Transport.—For coolie purposes, 120 men and women.

Timber.—Oaks and firs.—(*Lieut. Dun, 1881.*)

KAMBIRONG—

A Manipur thannah and stockade on the Manipur-Cachar road.

It is situated at the top of the rise from the Barak river, where the road passes between two elevated portions of the spur.

It blocks the road without commanding it, and is itself commanded on north and south-east.

The stockade is kept in good repair and the garrison consists of 1 native officer, 1 non-commissioned officer, and 15 sepoys.

There is a bungalow for officers on the high part of the spur north of the stockade, whence an extensive view can be obtained towards the west.

KAMHAU—

A hill district south of Manipur, where the Sukti Kukis are settled.

KAMHAU—

A Kuki tribe, called also Sukti and Wíté by the Manipuris, and Khyen (pronounced Chin) by the Burmese. (*Vide* Kuki.)

KAMPA—

A small Naga (Tankul) village, two miles north of the Charo Peak, on the western edge of the Kubbo valley.

Elevation.—2,700 feet.

Temperature.—44° at sunrise in February.

Climate.—Unhealthy from 1st May to 1st December.

Houses.—5, Naga pattern.

Inhabitants.—20.

Fighting-men.—5.

Water.—Scanty.

Camping-ground.—None.

Grazing.—
Products.—
Timber.—
Harvests.—
} *Vide* page 78, Charo.

Carriage.—8 coolies.

Approaches.—Not personally visited, but apparently a steep rise along a spur from the west.

KANGBOM (THANNAH)—

A Manipur frontier post, forming one of the second line, situated in the Yomadoung hills, on the Ingorok-Kongal route, at a distance of one-third of a day's journey from the Maglang river.

Camping-ground.—A force of 400 men might encamp at that part of the spur on which the thannah is situated, which rises in front near the village of Konggum. The village is out of sight at about 800 yards distance.

Approaches.—The thannah commands the Kongal road and also a road to the Kubbo valley, which comes out opposite Táp, and by which Kangbom is only one day's journey from the Kubbo valley. It would be most easily approached by an attacking force from the west by the Manipur road.

Defences.—It is stockaded with small logs, not in very good repair, outside which there is a fence covered with pointed bamboos.

Surrounding Country.—The ridge in front of the stockade is very narrow, and it could be made a strong position. It is commanded by the hill behind it on the east.

Good station from which to signal to Makku peak.

The jungle has been cleared away to a considerable distance on all sides.

Garrison.—The garrison consists of 1 subadar, 1 jemadar, one havildar, and 20 sepoys.

Water.—Water is procured from a little way down the hill on the south side of the spur.—(*Lieut. Dun, 1881-82.*)

KANG-GUM—

A very small Tankul village, built after the usual Tankul pattern, 3,000 feet above the sea-level; about 800 yards from Kangbom thannah on the Ingorok-Kongal route. There are but two houses.

Camping-ground.—Camping-ground for 400 men between the village and Kangbom thannah.

Approaches.—The village is out of sight of the thannah, and does not command either the road passing north to Kongal or that passing south to the Kubbo valley.

Inhabitants.—The inhabitants belong to the south-western subdivision of the Tankul Naga tribe. Population 10, of whom 2 may be fighting men. Ako is friendly.

Climate.—The climate is unhealthy from beginning of August to end of October.

Water.—Plentiful supply of water close to village.

Supplies.—Rice-straw procurable. Scanty grazing. Principal grains, rice and múm. Firewood plentiful. Arum, yams, and pumpkins. Rice harvest in November; múm in December.

Live-stock.—Pigs and poultry.

Transport.—For cooly purposes, 2 men and women.

Timber.—Oaks and other kinds; no firs.—(*Lieut. Dun, 1881-82.*)

KANG-OÏ—

A Tankul village, built after the usual Tankul pattern, about 6,000 feet above the sea-level; situated on the road to Chattik *viâ* Poshing, near the Nunshangkong river. There are 120 houses.

Camping-ground.—There is sufficient camping ground for a regiment in the valley below the village. *

* The valley is most charming, 5,000 feet above the sea, with a meandering stream fringed with willows and wild pears; the hills are covered with firs and rhododendron.—(*J. Johnstone.*)

Inhabitants.—The inhabitants belong to the north-eastern subdivision of the Tankul Naga tribe. Population 600, of whom 120 may be fighting-men. Kongshangba and Allah have much influence and are both friendly.
Climate.—The climate is healthy at all seasons.
Water.—Plentiful supply of water.
Supplies.—Rice-straw procurable. No grazing. Principal grains, rice and múm. Firewood plentiful. Arum, yams, and pumpkins. Rice harvest in November; múm in December.
Live-stock.—Pigs, poultry, a few buffaloes, and metna.
Transport.—For coolie purposes, 120 men and women.
Timber.—Chiefly oaks and firs.—(*Lieut. Dun, 1881.*)

KANG-OÏ—

A very small Marring village, built after the usual Marring pattern, about 4,000 feet above the sea-level. There are but two houses.
Inhabitants.—The inhabitants belong to the Marring Naga tribe. Population 10, of whom 3 may be fighting-men.
Climate.—The climate is unhealthy from beginning of August to end of October.
Water.—Fairly good supply of water.
Supplies.—Rice-straw procurable. Fair grazing. Indian-corn, rice, múm, and chayan. Fire-wood plentiful. Arum, beans, pumpkins, and plantains. Harvest in November and early part of December.
Live-stock.—Pigs, poultry, and metna.
Transport.—For coolie purposes, 3 men and women.
Timber.—Chiefly oaks; no firs.—(*Lieut. Dun, 1881-82.*)

KANJUP—

A small Chiru village on the range of hills forming the western boundary of the valley.

The summer residence of the Political Agent is situated close to this village.

* 5,170 feet by survey.

Elevation.—5,000* feet above the sea.
Temperature.—34° at sunrise in December.
Climate.—Healthy at all seasons.
Houses.—20, Naga pattern.
Inhabitants.—80.
Fighting-men.—20.
Water.—Scanty at the village.
Camping-ground.—None at the village.

NOTE.—There is plenty of excellent water, camping-ground, and a firewood reserve at the foot of the range where the ascent to this village commences.

Grazing.—
Products.—
Timber.—
Harvests.— } *Vide* page 78, Charo.
Live-stock.—Pigs, poultry, and a few metna.
Carriage.—30 coolies.
Approaches—Up a very steep open slope from the east. By a narrow path along steep hill-sides from the west and north.

KANTI (KAMPTI)—

The most northerly of the four districts along the Ningthee. Kanti (or

Kampti, as the Assamese call it) is two months' journey by river or one month by land from Thoung-thwoot (Samjok). It is governed by a Shah Tsawbwa, who is more independent than those of the other districts, owing to the distance of his capital from Mandalay. He pays a visit to Mandalay once in two or three years.—(*Phayre, 1882.*)

KAPRANG—

A Tankul Naga village situated on the eastern slopes of the Nongmaiching hill.

Elevation.—3,500 feet.

Temperature.—36° at sunrise in February.

Climate.—Unhealthy from 1st May to 1st December.

Houses.—10, Naga pattern.

Inhabitants.—40.

Fighting-men.—10.

Water.—Scanty.

Camping-ground.—Enough for 200 men.

Grazing.—
Products.—
Timber.—
Harvests.— } *Vide* page 78, Charo.

Live-stock.—Pigs and poultry.

Carriage.—15 coolies.

KARÂM—

A Manipuri village, on the old course of the Imphal river, just below its junction with the Iril.

Elevation.—
Temperature.—
Climate.— } *Vide* page 77, Changangai.

Houses.—50, Manipuri pattern.

Inhabitants.—250, sepoy class.

Fighting-men.—50.

Water.—
Camping-ground.—
Grazing.—
Products.—
Timber—
Harvest.— } *Vide* page 77, Changangai.

Live-stock.—100 bullocks and cows, 75 buffaloes.

Carriage.—50 carts, 25 boats.

Approaches.—By a good mule path along the banks of the river from north and south.

KARAO—

A forest-clad range, the highest peak of which is 6,457 feet above the sea, between the Thobal and the Iril rivers.

KARMAKARAKUL—

KARONG (THANA)—

A Manipur thana between Mayang Khang and Meitheipham on the road to Kohima.

Camping-ground.—There is unlimited good camping-ground.

Defences.—The thana is not stockaded. It is commanded on the east and west at about 600 yards, otherwise its position is naturally very strong, being situated on the flat end of a spur which comes down from the hills to the east of it.

Water.—Good supply of water.—(*Lieut. Dun, 1881-82.*)

Grazing.—Good.

Karong in the Manipuri language means "fork of a river." There is a camping-ground of the same name on the Lanier river.

KASSÓM—

A precipitous rocky range of hills bounding what is known as the Cháttik valley on the east. It is in reality a southern spur sent down from Kachaophung peak and has been cut off from its natural prolongation, the Angoching range, by the Námpágna river.

Its highest peak has an elevation of 6,543 feet.

North of the Napanga river, this range now forms the boundary between Manipur and Burma.—(*Col. Johnstone, 1881; Lieut. Dun, 1881-82.*)

KASSÓM-KULEL—

A Tankul village, built after the usual Tankul pattern, on the western face of the Kassóm ridge, about 5,000 feet above the sea-level. There are 60 houses.

Inhabitants.—The inhabitants belong to the north-eastern subdivision of the Tankul Naga tribe. Population 300, of whom 60 may be fighting-men. Kongyambah has much influence and is friendly.

Climate.—The climate is healthy at all seasons.

Supplies.—Rice-straw procurable. Scanty grazing. Principal grains are rice and múm. Forage plentiful. Arum, yams, and pumpkins. Rice harvest in November; múm in December.

Live-stock.—Pigs and poultry.

Transport.—For coolie purposes, 60 men and women.

Timber.—Chiefly oaks; no firs.—(*Lieut. Dun, 1881.*)

KASSÓM-KUNAO—

A Tankul village, built after the usual Tankul pattern on the eastern face of the Kassóm ridge, about 4,500 feet above the sea-level. There are 25 houses.

Inhabitants.—The inhabitants belong to the south-western subdivision of the Tankul Naga tribe. Population 125, of whom 25 may be fighting-men. Mungshiba and Maro have much influence and are friendly.

Climate.—The climate is unhealthy from beginning of August to end of October.

Supplies.—Rice-straw procurable. Scanty grazing. Principal grains are rice and múm. Firewood plentiful. Arum, yams, and pumpkins. Rice harvest in November; múm in December.

Live-stock.—Pigs and poultry.

Transport.—For coolie purposes, 25 men and women.

Timber.—Chiefly oaks; no firs.—(*Lieut. Dun, 1881.*)

KASSONG—

A small Tankul village, built after the usual Tankul pattern, situated in the Huerok hills, above 3,000 feet above the sea-level, on the Thobal-Taap route, containing 5 houses.

Camping-ground.—Camping-ground in rice-fields.

Inhabitants.—The inhabitants belong to the south-western subdivision of the Tankul Naga tribe. Population 25, of whom 5 may be fighting-men.
Climate.—The climate is unhealthy from beginning of August to end of October.
Water.—Scanty supply of water.
Supplies.—Rice-straw procurable. Scanty grazing. Principal grains are rice and múm. Firewood plentiful. Arum, yams, and pumpkins. Rice harvest in November; múm in December.
Live-stock.—Pigs and poultry.
Transport.—For coolie purposes, 5 men and women.
Timber.—Oaks and firs plentiful.—(*Lieut. Dun, 1881.*)

KASSOW—

A small Tankul village, built after the usual Tankul pattern; about 3,000 feet above the sea-level. There are 10 houses.
Inhabitants.—The inhabitants belong to the south-western subdivision of the Tankul Naga tribe. Population 50, of whom 10 may be fighting men. The chief's name is Thodai-chouba. Pheiomatol has much influence.
Climate.—The climate is unhealthy from beginning of August to end of October.
Supplies.—Rice-straw procurable. Scanty grazing. Principal grains are rice and múm. Firewood plentiful. Arum, yams, and pumpkins. Rice harvest in November; múm in December.
Live-stock.—Pigs and poultry.
Transport.—For coolie purposes, 10 men and women.
Timber.—Bamboos, a few oaks, and firs; other kinds plentiful.
(*Lieut. Dun, 1881.*)

KASSUNG—

A small Tankul village, built after the usual Tankul pattern, about 3,000 feet above the sea-level. There are 5 houses.
Camping-ground.—A little camping-ground at either end of the village.
Approaches.—Along almost level spur from both east and west, with no natural difficulties.
Inhabitants.—The inhabitants belong to the south-western subdivision of the Tankul Naga tribe. Population 25, of whom 5 are fighting-men. Máraba has much influence, and is friendly.
Climate.—The climate is unhealthy from beginning of August to end of October.
Water.—Scanty supply of water.
Supplies.—Rice-straw procurable. Scanty grazing. Principal grains are rice and múm. Firewood plentiful. Arum, yams, and pumpkins. Rice harvest in November; múm in December.
Live-stock.—Pigs and poultry.
Transport.—For coolie purposes, 5 men and women.
Timber.—Oaks and firs plentiful.—(*Lieut. Dun, 1881.*)

KAUPUM—

A peak a mile south of the Cachar road. It forms the western wall of the Kaupum plateau, and lies on the left bank of the Irang river.
Elevation.—6,200 feet.

It would form an excellent signalling station, and would connect Kala Naga and any point on the Laimatol range. The plains of Cachar are visible from it.

KAUPUM—

A Kaupui Naga village, situated just below the peak of the same name, and 3,000 feet above the Kaupum plateau on the west.

Elevation.—5,600 feet.

Temperature.—38° at sunrise in January.

Climate.—Healthy at all seasons.

Houses.—Forty-eight, Naga pattern.

Inhabitants.—One hundred and ninety-two.

Fighting-men.—Fifty.

Water.—Very scanty, below the village on the east.

Camping-ground.—Sufficient clear and level ground close to the village for 200 men.

Grazing.—
Products.—
Timber.—
Harvests.— } *Vide* page 78, Charo.

Live-stock.—Thirty buffaloes, pigs, and poultry.

Carriage.—Seventy coolies.

Approaches—Up very steep open slopes from the east, in parts precipitous; from the west, up precipitous hill-side through jungle; from the north, along a narrow ridge, very steep in some places; from the south, along a narrow ridge, very steep in some places.

KAUPUM—

An elevated plateau on the Cachar-Manipur road between the Irang and Laimaták rivers.

It is perfectly flat, surrounded by steep, jungle-covered, and in some places precipitous, hills; measures 4 miles in length from north to south, and 2 miles in average breadth from east to west.

Two-thirds of its surface is under rice cultivation, the remainder being covered with grass and reed jungle.

At intervals along the surrounding hills there are small Kaupui villages, each perched upon a peak somewhat difficult to ascend, and the inhabitants of which till the fields on the plateau.

The surface of the plateau is 2,400 feet above the sea, 2,000 feet higher than the bed of the Irang, and 1,400 feet higher than the bed of the Laimaták river.

The ring of hills which encloses it varies from 2,600 feet above the sea at the point where the Cachar road enters on the north-west to the Kaupum peak, 6,200 feet above the sea. The general run of the ridge is about 4,000 feet above the sea.

The sluggish stream which drains it cuts an exit for itself through a ridge of rock at the south side of the surrounding ring of hills, and thence drops down in a succession of falls through a narrow gorge with precipitous sides to the Irang river.

It resembles very closely the Manipur valley on a small scale, and may be compared to a flat-bottomed basin.

Viewed from the village of Nungba, it presents the appearance of a huge natural fortress, barring the approach to Manipur.

The western entrance is placed at the head of a re-entering angle at the north-western corner.

From this point southwards the outer face presents a series of precipices, alternating with steep earth slopes covered with the densest jungle.

Northwards, though not precipitous, the hill-sides are exceedingly steep and clothed with thick forest and undergrowth.

The Laimaták and Irang rivers form a moat on three sides, but are, during the cold weather, easily fordable once or twice in every mile of their course.

The Laimaták, indeed, is fordable almost at any point.

The high road, as before stated, enters at the north-west corner.

After crossing the Irang (350 feet above the sea), it ascends a spur, at first easy, but becoming steeper higher up.

For the last 1,000 feet it zig-zags up the steep face of the hill through thick bamboo jungle and enters at a comparatively low saddle (2,600 feet above the séa).

The ground is precipitous on either side of the entrance, and a line of stockade work has been erected across it. Behind the line of stockade is a Manipuri post of observation, which consists of one house surrounded by a weak stockade and garrisoned by four or five sepoys under a non-commissioned officer.

East and west of the entrance are the Kaupui Naga villages of Lilonong (from which the post takes its name) and Tuyang; both are out of sight of the entrance. Between the entrance and each village the ridge is very narrow (at some points not more than 10 feet broad), with a precipitous drop on each side.

The high road, after crossing the rim of the basin, zig-zags down the inner side, passing below the Political Agent's rest-house, and follows the nothern edge of the plateau. Midway across, it passes through a stockade hornwork thrown out in front of the Kaupum thannah.

This post has a garrison of 1 officer, 2 non-commissioned officers, and 20 sepoys; is defended by a stockade in good order and a water ditch, 15 feet broad and 4 feet deep.

The road, on touching the hills on the east, ascends gradually along the inner side of the basin at an easy gradient, passes below the village of Loanglo, and crosses at an elevation of

This entrance is not (1885) defended artificially, but the ground is very favourable for resistance to an approach from either side.

On the plateau itself a force of 5,000 men could get ample camping-ground, water, and grazing for its transport, at any season of the year, and water from it is available at the southern end, where the stream falls down to the level of the Irang valley.

There is plenty of excellent timber, including oak and bamboo, and abundant grass for making huts. It possesses an excellent signal station in the Kaupum peak, situated on the western side and visible from any point along the eastern interior edge.

Besides the main road, four paths enter the Kaupum basin,—one on the south side close by the exit of the stream, another opposite Mukhti, a third opposite Nungba.

All three come straight up the face of the hill, and ladders have to be used in several places. Each could be defended by a dozen men against a regiment.

The fourth path leads from Nongnang village to Loanglo, and though difficult gives the assailant a more even chance with the defender.

The main approach along the high road is commanded for the last 600 yards. If the road were quitted and a direct ascent through the jungle attempted, it would be impossible to keep the men in hand, and the last 100 feet of the ascent is everywhere almost precipitous.

Should a party succeed in gaining the crest, it would find itself on a narrow ridge; in front a very steep hill-side, covered with jungle and planted with pangies (bamboo spikes stuck into the ground by way of obstacles), a descent over which must inevitably result in disorganization.

Turning to right or left along the ridge, it would encounter villages with stockaded entrances, commanding narrow open approaches with precipitous sides.

If all the approaches above detailed be found to be guarded, the best alternative that can be suggested by the present writer would be to continue up the valleys of the Irang and the Laimaták. The latter flows in a wide open valley, almost free from jungle, and the position could thus be turned without much difficulty. An opposing force too would have to fight on equal terms with respect to ground.

KAUPUM—

A stream draining the Kaupum plateau, between the Irang and the Laimaták. It affords the best water-power in Manipur, and from its situation close to the Cachar road it may prove useful in the future. It has never yet (1885) been utilised.

KEK-KA—

A village on the Ava-Kendat route, containing about 90 houses. Level road over plain.

Water.—Sufficient.

Supplies.—Cattle numerous; extensive cultivation.

KEMUM—

A village on the Ava-Kendat route, containing about 50 houses, at a distance of one day's cart travelling from Moung-yaum. Road good.

KENDAT (GENDAT)—

A town called by the Burmese Nat-Kyoungaung-Myo, on the left bank of the Ningthee river, immediately opposite to Sanayachil Ghát (about latitude 23° 45′ and longitude 95° 42′), from whence is the principal pass into the Kubbo and Manipur valleys. There are about 100 houses.

Defences: Garrison.—This was formerly a Burmese frontier post, with a stockade of solid teak, without ditch or outer earth-works, and was garrisoned by a considerable force; but the stockade was burnt early in February 1882 by a fire which also destroyed a great part of the town; and since the Burmese standing army has been disbanded, there has been no garrison.

Communications.—Specially constructed trading steamers belonging to the King of Burma have been brought up at all times of the year to Kendat. The Burma Trading Company are also building vessels with the same object. The town is on the route from Tamoo to Ava; the road, however is bad in places. The Khambat Woon, who governs the Khambat district, resides here.—(*Lieut. Dun, 1881-82.*)

KENGMAL—

A Manipuri village on the Thobal river, not far from its junction with the Imphal.

Elevation.—
Temperature.— } *Vide* page 77, Changangai.
Climate.—

Houses.—25, Manipuri pattern.
Inhabitants.—125, sepoy class.
Fighting-men.—25.
Water.—Plentiful.
Camping-ground.—
Products.— *Vide* page 77, Changangai.
Timber.—
Harvest.—
Live-stock.—50 cows, 27 buffaloes.
Carriage.—25 carts.
Approach.—By good mule-path along the Thobal river from north and south.

KENGOI—

A Hawkib village, built after the usual Kuki pattern, about 4,000 feet above the sea-level. There are 50 houses.

Inhabitants.—The inhabitants belong to the Hawkib subdivision of the Kongjai Kuki tribe. Population 250, of whom 75 may be fighting-men. The chief's name is Chunghin, and he has most influence.

Climate.—The climate is unhealthy from beginning of August to end of October.

Supplies.—Rice-straw procurable. Fair grazing. Principal grains are Indian-corn, job's-tears, rice, and múm. Firewood plentiful. Pumpkins, beans, yams, and sugarcane. Rice harvest in November; múm in December; other crops, November and early part of December.

Live-stock.—Pigs, poultry, and a few metna.

Transport.—For coolie purposes, 75 men and women.

Timber.—Chiefly small bushy oaks.—(*Lieut. Dun, 1881.*)

KHAMBAT—

One of the four districts to the east of the Ningthee. It is governed by the Khambat or Khan-pat Woon. Bounded on the north by Samjok; the village of Mentha is the boundary.—(*Phayre, 1882.*)

A town (called by the Burmese Khan-pat) situated in the Kubbo valley, on the road from Sanayachil Ghât to Tamoo and Manipur. The Khambat Woon derives his title from this ancient town; his jurisdiction extends to the Noajeree hills, three days' journey north of Kendat, and south to Moukadan-Myo. He resides at Kendat.

KHAMROIKONG—

One of the streams of the Somrah basin. It is simply a mountain stream, and fordable anywhere.

KHARAN—

A village in Manipur, 3 miles beyond Ingorok on the Manipur-Kongal road.

Camping-ground.—There is a small camping-ground.

Approach.—The road from the west ascends a steep spur up to the village.

Signal Station.—To the north of the village there is a peak where a signal station might be placed to communicate with Manipur city.

Water.—A small supply.—(*Lieut. Dun, 1881-82.*)

KHARMA—

A Manipuri village, 4 miles from Imphal on the Cachar road.

Elevation.—
Temperature.— *Vide* page 77, Changangai.
Climate.—

Houses.—60, Manipuri pattern.
Inhabitants.—300, sepoy class.
Fighting-men.—60.
Water.—
Camping-ground.—
Grazing.—
Products.—
Timber.—
Harvest.—
Vide page 77, Changangai.
Live-stock.—120 cows, 90 buffaloes.
Carriage.—60 carts.
Approaches—By Cachar road from north and south.

KHAYANG PHUNG—

A twin peak to Kachauphung. Elevation 9,295 feet. A path leads over the top connecting Manipur and the Somrah valley. There is a little water and camping-ground close to the top of the peak.

KHEBICHING—

A small Kaupui Naga village in North-West Manipur.

KHETRI LIKAIE—

A Manipuri village on the Thobal river, south of Yárapók and north of the Thobal villages.

Elevation.—
Climate.—
Temperature.—
Vide page 77, Changangai.
Houses.—25, Manipuri pattern.
Inhabitants.—125, sepoy class.
Fighting-men.—25.
Water.—
Camping-ground.—
Products.—
Timber.—
Harvest.—
Vide page 77, Changangai.
Live-stock.—Fifty cows, 37 buffaloes.
Carriage.—Twenty-five carts, 10 boats.
Approaches—By good mule-path along either bank of the Thobal from north and south.

KHOMBAON—

A small Manipuri village in the north-west portion of the valley, about 7 miles west of Imphal.

KHOMJOM—

A peak (elevation 5,985 feet) bounding the upper portion of the course of the Iril on the east.

KHONDANG—

A small Kaupni village in North-West Manipur.

KHONDANG-KONKAIBA—

A small Kaupui village in North-West Manipur

KHONGA KONG—

A small Chiru village in North-West Manipur.

KHONGNAPATH—

A small Kaupui Naga village at the northern end of the valley, 4 miles south of Sengmail.

KHONJIRON—

A small Kaupui Naga village in North-West Manipur.

KHONSAN KONG—

A small Koireng village in North-West Manipur, 6 miles from Sengmail, the first stage on the Kohima road.

KHOTEH—

A Marring village, built after the usual Marring pattern, about 3,000 feet above the sea-level. There are 40 houses.

Inhabitants.—The inhabitants belong to the Marring Naga tribe. Population 200, of whom 60 may be fighting-men. The chief's name is Kowpam.

Climate.—The climate is unhealthy from beginning of August to end of October.

Supplies.—Rice-straw procurable. Fair grazing. Principal grains, Indian-corn, rice, múm, and chayan. Firewood plentiful. Arum, beans, and pumpkins. Harvest in November and beginning of December.

Live-stock.—Pigs, poultry, and metna.

Transport.—For coolie purposes, 40 men and women.

Timber.—Chiefly oaks; no firs.—(*Lieut. Dun, 1881-82.*)

KHÚNGNÚNG—

A new Kuki village of the Simmté clan, situated in the valley of the Manipur source of the Tipai stream on the western side.

Elevation.—3,000 feet above the sea.

Temperature.—42° at sunrise in December.

Climate.—Unhealthy from 1st May to December.

Houses.—One hundred, Kuki pattern.

Inhabitants.—Four hundred.

Fighting-men.—One hundred, many of whom possess guns.

Water.—
Camping-ground.—
Products.—
Timber.—
Harvests.—
Grazing.—
} *Vide* page 77, Chanjang.

Live-stock.—Thirty metna, pigs, and poultry.

Carriage.—Two hundred coolies.

Headman.—Punkhón, friendly,—a chief of some consequence among the Simmté.

KHUNHO—

The south-eastern peak of the mass of mountain better known under the name of Japvo.

It has an elevation of 8,809 feet above the sea and is surrounded by steep, precipitous cliffs. It is called Tahazo by the Angamis.

KHUNKU—

A Chiru village at the northern end of the Manipur valley just above Sengmail on the west.

KHUNTAK—

A Tankul village, built after the usual Tankul pattern, 3,000 feet above the sea-level. There are 16 houses.

Camping-ground.—There are sufficient camping-ground for 200 men and their coolies.

Approaches.—Very steep approaches, both from above and below the village.

Inhabitants.—The inhabitants belong to the south-western section of the Tankul Naga tribe. Population 80, of whom 16 are fighting-men. The most influential man is Iroikungba.

It is situated close to the Kongal thannah road, just above the Máglang river.

Climate.—The climate is unhealthy from beginning of August to end of October.

Water.—Plentiful supply close to village.

Supplies.—Rice-straw procurable. Scanty grazing. Principal grains are rice and múm. Firewood plentiful. Pumpkins, yams, and arum. Rice harvest in November; múm in December.

Live-stock.—Pigs and poultry.

Transport.—For coolie purposes, 16 men and women.

Timber.—Bamboos, oaks, and other timber.—(*Lieut. Dun, 1881-82.*)

KHUNTAK-KULEL—

A Tankul village, built after the usual Tankul pattern, about 5,000 feet above the sea-level. There are 100 houses.

Camping-ground.—Terraced rice-fields available.

Inhabitants.—The inhabitants belong to the north-eastern section of the Tankul Naga tribe. Population 500, of whom 100 may be fighting-men. The most influential man is Heising, who is friendly.

Climate.—The climate is healthy at all seasons.

Supplies.—Rice-straw procurable. Scanty grazing. Principal grains are rice and múm. Firewood plentiful. Pumpkins, yams, and arum. Rice harvest in November; múm in December.

Live-stock.—Pigs, poultry, and a few metna.

Transport.—For coolie purposes, 100 men and women.

Timber.—Chiefly oaks and firs.—(*Lieut. Dun, 1881-82.*)

It is situated on the Kongál thannah road.

KHURKAL—

A Manipuri village at the northern end of the valley west of the Kohima road.

KHYANG—

A Tankul village, built after the usual Tankul pattern, about 3,500 feet above the sea-level. There are 8 houses.

Inhabitants.—The inhabitants belong to north-eastern section of the Tankul Naga tribe. Population 40, of whom 8 may be fighting-men. The most influential man is Lendo, who is friendly.

Climate.—The climate is unhealthy from beginning of August to end of October.

Supplies—Rice-straw procurable. Scanty grazing. Principal grains are rice and múm. Firewood plentiful. Arum, yams, and pumpkins. Harvest in November and early part of December.

Live-stock.—Pigs and poultry.

Transport.—For coolie purposes, 8 men and women.
Timber.—Oaks, firs, and other trees plentiful.—(*Lieut. Dun, 1881-82.*)

KHYEN-DWEN (pronounced "Chin-dwin").

The Burmese name for the Ningthee. (*Vide* Ningthee.)

KHYENS (pronounced "Chins").

The Burmese word for all hill tribes, but applied more particularly to the Sukti Kukis. (*Vide* Sukti.)

KIÁM—

A Manipuri village on the Marakhon stream, 6 miles due west of Imphál.

KIGWEMA—

An Angami village on the road from Phunamah to Kohima, containing 190 houses.

Camping-ground.—Plenty of camping-ground in terraced rice-fields.
Approaches—Along a ridge about 200 yards broad, on a level with the village, from the west. There is no natural or artificial obstacle.
Inhabitants.—The inhabitants belong to the Angami Naga tribe, and are divided into the four following subdivisons, *viz.*, Kamema, Makuma, Merama, and Kiphoma. Population 950, of whom 190 are fighting-men. There is no chief or headman, but the most influential man is Kasakre.
Climate.—The climate is healthy at all seasons.
Water.—Plentiful supply close under village on the north side.
Supplies.—Rice-straw procurable. Fair grazing. Principal grains are rice, múm, and chayan. Rather moderate supply of firewood. Pumpkins and arum. Harvest in November and December.
Live-stock.—Cows in large numbers, pigs, and poultry.
Transport.—For coolie purposes, 190 men, women, and children.
Timber.—Very little fir or oak; small pollarded alders; bamboos scarce.
(*Lieut. Dun, 1881-82.*)

KIGWEMA—

A ridge and peak near Japvo peak. The ridge is crossed by the Phunamah-Kohima road just above the village of the same name. The peak rises on the west of the road and shows a bare precipitous face; it is separated from the Viswema peak by a densely-wooded gorge.—(*Lieut. Dun, 1881-82.*)

KIPHIMI—

A Kolya Naga village in Northern Manipur, at the head of the B[illegible]zar valley.
Elevation.—5,500 feet.
Temperature.—33° at sunrise in January.
Climate.—Healthy at all seasons.
Houses.—One hundred, Naga pattern.
Inhabitants.—Four hundred, wild and unsettled.
Fighting-men.—One hundred.
Water.—Scanty.
Camping-ground.—Scanty, unless fields have been kept unflooded. Sufficient for 200 men and transport.
Grazing.—Fair.
Produce.— }
Timber.— } *Vide* page 78, Charo.
Harvests.— }
Live-stock.—Ten cows, pigs, and poultry.

Carriage.—One hundred and fifty coolies.

KIRIHONG—

A Tankul village, built after the usual Tankul pattern, about 3,500 feet above the sea-level. There are 20 houses.

Inhabitants.—The inhabitants belong to the south-western section of the Tankul Naga tribe. Population 100, of whom 20 may be fighting-men.

Climate.—The climate is unhealthy from beginning of August to end of October.

Supplies.—Rice-straw procurable. Scanty grazing. Principal grains are rice and múm. Firewood plentiful. Arum, yams, and pumpkins. Harvest in November and early part of December.

Live-stock.—Pigs and poultry.

Transport.—For coolie purposes, 20 men, women, and children.

Timber.—Oaks, firs, and other trees plentiful.—(*Lieut. Dun, 1881-82.*)

KLAYA—

A subdivision of the Marring Naga tribe.

KODAI—

A new Kuki village of the Simmté clan in the valley of the Manipur, sources of the Tipai river.

Elevation.—3,000 feet.

Temperature.—42° at sunrise in December.

Climate.—Unhealthy from 1st May to 1st December.

Houses.—20, Kuki pattern.

Inhabitants.—80.

Fighting-men.—20.

Water.—
Camping-ground.—
Grazing.—
Products.—
Timber.—
Harvests.—

Vide page 77, Changangai.

Live-stock.—Pigs and poultry, possibly two or three metna.

Carriage.—30 coolies.

Approaches.—*Vide* page 77, Changangai.

KODAN—

A village containing 40 or 50 houses on the road from Tamoo towards Mandalay.—(*Lieut. Dun, 1881-82.*)

KOHIMA—

An Angami village, built after the usual Angami pattern, 5,000 feet above the sea-level; containing 1,300 houses.

Camping-ground.—Plenty of camping-ground in terraced rice-fields.

Approaches.—The village is approached by a rough road up an easy slope from the west, the road in parts being commanded by the village. It is not artificially defended.

Inhabitants.—The inhabitants belong to the Angami Naga tribe and are divided into seven subdivisions, *viz.*, Hepoma, Hurisama, Siama, Puchatsama, Rusuma, Dakusuma, and Setenoma. Population 4,500, of whom 1,300 are fighting-men. There is no chief or headman, but the most influential men are Ung-loo, Hos-alé, and Nisamo.

Climate.—The climate is healthy at all seasons.

Water.—Several springs round the village, but the total amount is very small.

Supplies.—Rice-straw procurable. Fair grazing. Principal grains are rice, múm, and chayan. Rather moderate supply of firewood. Arum and pumpkins. Harvest in November and December.

Live-stock.—Cows in large numbers, pigs, and poultry.

Transport.—For coolie purposes, 1,300 men, women, and children.

Timber.—Very little fir or oak; only small pollarded alders; bamboos scarce.—(*Lieut. Dun, 1881-82.*)

KOHIMA—

The head-quarter station of the Naga hills district.

The civil officers consist of a Deputy and Assistant Commissioner and a Surgeon.

A battalion of Assam Light Infantry is stationed here and a battalion (600 men) of Frontier Police commanded by two British officers.

There is not as yet (1885) any stockade or fort.

Houses have been built for all officers, both civil and military.

Communications.—There are good roads to Manipur and the Assam valley suitable for mule carriage, and one is now being made to Khonoma.

Two miles of the road to Manipur is a cart-road and the remainder of the trace is quite suitable for wheeled traffic. A cart-road trace to the Assam plain is now being laid out.

There is a terminal telegraph station at Kohima connected with India through Assam, and a weekly post runs to Manipur.

The station is situated on an open saddle between the village of Kohima, than which it is some 500 feet lower in elevation, and the peak of Polivadzo, a projecting bluff of the main mass of mountain known as Japvo.

KOIRENG*—

A subdivision of the Kom Kuki tribe. Mr. Damant, late Political Agent of Manipur, and afterwards of the Naga hills, classes the Koirengs as Kukis by their language, they formerly having been classed as Nagas. He writes:—

"The Koirengs are a small and insignificant tribe dwelling in eight small villages situate on the hills north of the valley of Manipur. They inhabit 120 houses, and number about 600."

KOKSHAI—

A small Manipur village in the centre of the valley. The Raja's elephants graze in the vicinity.

Elevation.—
Climate.—
Temperature.— } *Vide* page 77, Changangai.

Houses.—20, Manipur pattern.

Inhabitants.—100, sepoy class.

Fighting-men.—20.

Camping-ground.—Unlimited (if grass jungle be cleared) between 1st December and 1st April.

Water.—Plentiful.

Grazing.—Good.

* This is a mistake, though a very natural one. There are two tribes of Koirengs bearing the same name, but entirely distinct; one tribe is of the old Kuki stock, and its members are scattered here and there in the hills bordering the valley.

Products.—
Timber.—
Harvests.— } *Vide* page 77, Changangai.
Live-stock.—40 cows, 30 buffaloes.
Carriage.—20 carts, 10 boats.
Approaches—By good mule-path from the north from central valley road branching off at Maiyang, Imphal bazaar.

By banks of Nambol river from Bishanpur (Lamlángtong) between 1st January and 1st April.

KOKSHINGH-KULEL—

A Manipuri village in the south-east portion of the valley, 2 miles from the Aimol-Moray route just before it reaches Pallél.

Elevation.—
Temperature.—
Climate.— } *Vide* page 77, Changangai.
Houses.—45, Manipur pattern.
Inhabitants.—225 Loi.*
Fighting-men.—45.
Water.—
Grazing.—
Products.— *Vide* page 77, Changangai.
Timber.—
Harvests.—
Camping-ground.—Good and unlimited all the year round along foot of low hills on the south and west.
Live-stock.—90 cows, 67 buffaloes.
Carriage.—45 carts, 45 coolies.
Approaches—By small paths from the Aimol road, practicable only in the cold weather. By a good path always open from the Shugunu road, crossing low ridge half a mile from the village.

KOKSHINGH-KUNAO—

A Manipuri (Loï) village in the south corner of the valley, about 12 miles north of Shugume.

Elevation.—
Temperature.—
Climate.— } *Vide* page 77, Changangai.
Houses.—40, Manipuri pattern.
Inhabitants.—200 (iron-workers).
Fighting-men.—40.
Water.—
Grazing.—
Camping-ground.— } *Vide* page 77, Changangai.

* They were Lois, but now call themselves Hindoos, having some time since 1867 been adopted into the Hindoo community by the Raja, and they give themselves all the airs of Hindoos.—(*J. Johnstone, 1885.*)

The others are the remnants of a once powerful and numerous tribe allied to the Northern Nagas, more closely to the Murams. They now inhabit eight small villages near Kaithemabi, but their former quarter is shown by the many bechive-shaped cairns erected by their ancestors and scattered over the grassy slopes in the neighbourhood of the road between Sengmal and Mayang Khang, chiefly near Kaithemabi. M'Culloch says that they were great road-makers, and that many hill-roads cut by them are still to be seen.—(*J. Johnstone, 1885.*)

Products.—
Timber.— } *Vide* page 77, Changangai.
Harvests.—

Live-stock.—80 cows, 60 buffaloes.

Carriage.—40 carts, 40 coolies.

Approaches.—By a narrow path through grass jungle and rice-fields from the Shugume road.

KOLAO—

A very small Marring village, built after the usual Marring pattern, about 3,500 feet above the sea-level, containing 4 houses.

Inhabitants.—The inhabitants belong to the Marring Naga tribe. Population 20, of whom 6 may be fighting-men. Headman, Moddon.

Climate.—The climate is unhealthy from beginning of August to end of October.

Supplies.—Rice-straw procurable. Fair grazing. Principal grains, Indian-corn, rice, múm, and chayan. Firewood plentiful. Arum, beans, and pumpkins. Harvest in November and early part of December.

Live-stock.—Pigs and poultry; 10 metna.

Transport.—For coolie purposes, 7 men and women.

Timber.—Chiefly oaks; no firs.—(*Lieut. Dun, 1881-82.*)

KOLONGTEN—

A very small Marring village, built after the usual Marring pattern, about 3,500 feet above the sea-level, containing 5 houses.

Inhabitants.—The inhabitants belong to the Marring Naga tribe. Population 25, of whom 7 may be fighting-men. Headman, Miran.

Climate.—The climate is unhealthy from beginning of August to end of October.

Supplies.—Rice-straw procurable. Fair grazing. Principal grains are Indian-corn, rice, múm, and chayan. Firewood plentiful. Arum, beans, and pumpkins. Harvest in November and early part of December.

Live-stock.—Pigs and poultry.

Transport.—For coolie purposes, 5 men and women.

Timber.—Oaks and other kinds; no firs.—(*Lieut. Dun, 1881-82.*)

KOLYA—

One of the Naga tribes (*vide* Naga).

KÓMGÁNG—

KOM-KUKIS—

A division of the Kuki tribe. They are scattered about the hills near the Manipur valley.

KOMENAILENGPA—

A small Chiru village on the western slope of Kaupru peak in North-Western Manipur.

KÓMYÁNG—

A new Kuki village of the Singsón clan, situated on the Kailam range, south-east of the Kaupúm plateau.

Elevation.—3,500 to 4,500 feet.

Houses.—About 80, Kuki pattern.

Water.—Probably scanty.

Camping-ground.—No.

Products, &c.—*Vide* page 77, Chanjang.

Headman.—Yamchung, believed to be unfriendly.

This village has come from the Lushai country, and has not yet been brought under the influence of civilization.

KONGAL (THANA)—

A Manipur frontier post, forming one of the third or outer line along the eastern edge of the Yumadoung range. The thana is situated on the broad flat end of a spur about 30 feet above the level of the valley. This portion of the Yumadoung hills is called by the Burmans the Malian range. The new thana, like the old one which was burnt by the Samjok people in December 1877, is close to the Nammea stream, and faces the east, being only a few hundred yards from the northern boundary of the Kubbo valley. Kongal Thana has always been well within the Manipur boundary, whether by the line of Pemberton's map or the strict letter of the treaty of 1834. It was established some 15 years ago to keep the Lahupa Tankuls in check.

Camping-ground.—There is any amount of camping-ground.

Defence and attack.—The stockade is between 60 and 70 yards square, with flanking defences. It is composed of two or three rows of timbers 6 inches to 1 foot in diameter, most of which are rotten. They are not bound together. On the north, south, and west sides, stakes projecting 1 foot 6 inches above the ground have been driven in a few inches apart, forming a good obstacle.

Surrounding Country.—The thana could most easily be attacked from the south and the west. The ground slopes away towards the south, east, and north at a few yards from the stockade. The forest comes up to within 20 yards on every side but the east, where it is clear to the Nammea, which is distant about 250 yards.

Garrison.—Its ordinary garrison consists of 1 subadar, 1 jemadar, 1 havildar, and 60 sepoys.

Water.—Water has been brought from the hills on the west, along a small channel, into the stockade; but this supply could easily be cut off. Plentiful supply from the stream.

Supplies.—Firewood plentiful. Scanty grazing.

(*Col. Johnstone, 1882; Lieut. Dun, 1882.*)

KONGANG—

An Anal village, built after the usual Kuki pattern, about 3,000* feet above the sea-level. It is situated on the Aimol-Moray route, 11 miles south of Aimol, and is where the Manipuris made a great stand against the Burmans in 1819. There are 7 houses.

* Over 4,250, tested three times carefully with an aneroid.

Camping-ground.—Camping-ground for one regiment.

Approaches.—The road is partly commanded by the village.

Inhabitants.—The inhabitants belong to the Anal Kuki tribe. Population 35, of whom 10 may be fighting-men.

Climate.—The climate is unhealthy from beginning of August to end of October.

Water.—Water-supply distant and scanty.

Supplies.—Rice-straw procurable. Fair grazing. Principal grains are rice, múm, chayan, and oil-seed. Firewood plentiful. Plantains, yams, and pumpkins. Harvest in November and early part of December.

Live-stock.—Pigs and poultry.

Transport.—For coolie purposes, 7 men and women.

Timber.—No heavy timber; small oaks, &c.; no firs.

(*Political Agent, Manipur, 1877-78; Lieut. Dun, 1881-82.*)

KONGBA—

A small stream draining the southern side of the mass of hills between the Jiki and the Iril.

It dries up completely in the cold weather, a little water being retained in its bed, on the eastern side of the city, by throwing dams across.

KONGJAI-OR NEW KUKI—

A division of the Kuki tribe, of which they form the greater part. They are scattered over nearly the whole of the hill territory of Manipur. Numbers are found in the western ranges of hills, in the Yumadoung hills, and in the ranges south of the Manipur valley.

They are subdivided as under:—

(1) Thado.
(2) Vungson.
(3) Changsen.
(4) Shingsol.
(5) Mangvung.
(6) Khlangam.
(7) Chungloe.
(8) Changput.
(9) Haukib.
(10) Simmté.
(11) Kambau.

Physical Characteristics.—The Kukis, generally speaking, are shorter than the Nagas, the usual run of all the Kuki tribes being of medium and frequently of low stature. Amongst those of low height are found the long-armed individuals, which length of limb is said by some observers to be a characteristic of the Kuki race.

The oblique eye is perhaps the most persistent feature amongst them, showing their probable Mongolian origin; but even this is by no means well marked, and is as common to the Manipuri as to the Kuki.

Lieutenant Dun writes in 1882:—

"In appearance they exactly resemble the Lushai Kukis, who have settled this year in Cachar, but they are slightly superior in physique.

"Nearly all could converse readily with a Thadoe Kuki, whose family has been settled for a long time in Cachar.

"They have the most independent air of any of the hill tribes, and the Manipuris treat them with a certain amount of respect. They are the best carriers in the State, and for military transport possess the great advantage of being able to protect themselves to a great extent.

"They are apt to give way to fits of childish rage and passion if hurried or annoyed on the march.

"They drink a good deal of liquor; but I never saw one intoxicated."

They are keen hunters, pay their chiefs a religious devotion, and are delighted at any opportunity of a fight.

Costume.—The dress of both sexes is very scanty. The men wear a loin cloth and a sheet, and the women a short blue kilt and a kind of small shawl, usually dyed dark blue.

Like the Lushais, every Kongjai carries a netted bag containing flint and steel, pipe and tobacco, and various odds and ends.

The hair of the men is worn long, combed back, and tied in a knot on the nape of the neck.

The women part theirs in the middle, plait it on each side of the head, cross these plaits at the back of the head, and bring them up to the top of the head in a crown, making a very pretty coiffure.

The men also wear a puggree with a fringe, frequently made of small scarlet feathers.

The men do not distend their ears as the old Kuki tribes do; this is reserved for the women, who distend the lobes with huge silver cylinders or discs of wood or ivory, but usually have a string supporting a couple of cornelian beads passed through a small hole in the lobe of the ear.

The men also wear a few beads and a pig's or tiger's tusk on a string round the throat.

Village Government.—The local or village chiefship is hereditary. In return for ruling, the chief is supported by his subjects. They till his fields, give him a certain portion of their produce, game and labour, and he receives presents at the time of all domestic occurrences.

They do not appear to swear an eternal fealty to the head of their clan, for a popular chief who has selected a good site for his village and a good piece of ground for cultivation attracts a large following.

A younger son usually succeeds in outstripping his elder brother in importance as a chief, as the eldest son stays at home with his father, while the younger are assigned a certain following, and he is sent off to make his own way in the world.

This is very observable in Lushai country, where a similar custom prevails.

Marriages, &c.—They usually choose their own partners; but a girl of ancient lineage is sought for by parents. A man, if he cannot pay the price asked for the object of his affections by her parents, performs from two to five years' service.

Religion.—They have indistinct notions on this subject, but worship two principal deities—Teval and Sangron. They believe in a future state and in a heaven and hell, and have regular catalogues of good acts and sins.

In behaviour they are solemn and dignified; they speak in deep measured tones and without gesticulation.

Their songs are mournful but harmonious chants, sung in parts, sometimes by as many as a hundred men together. Only the lowest bass notes are employed, and these are prolonged and long drawn out. The effect is most weired and impressive.

They are inveterate smokers, and even little children may be seen with pipes in their mouths. The women smoke pipes with a receptacle below to catch the nicotine oil. This is preserved and is sipped by the men.

Villages.—They move their villages every three or four years. These are not stockaded, but sometimes a palisade about 4 feet high is made round each

NOTE.—The question of the origin of the Kukis is a most interestingIone. They have, as a rule, far finer features than the typical Mongolian, and they have generally the very marked wave in the hair observable in the Kolarian and Papuan races, whom in some ways they resemble so much as to suggest affinity. They are, however, fairer by many degrees than either of these races, but, as a rule, distinctly darker than any of the northern Nagas. A really good monograph on the Kuki race, language, and original habitat would be extremely interesting

If they came originally from the Malay Peninsula, as from their constant march northwards might be inferred, it is very probable that they are allied to the Kolarian and Papuan races. The question, however, arises—"Did they originally come from the south, or are they originally from the north and now returning from a wandering of many generations to the south?" I am inclined to consider them a composite race.—(*J. Johnstone.*)

house. The houses are built after the usual Kuki pattern, entirely of bamboo, raised about 4 feet from the ground. There is a great similarity in sites chosen, water and jooming ground being the influences which decide them in their choice.

Arms.—About 10 per cent.* are armed with guns, chiefly flint-locks. These are much prized, and are purchased on the Burmese side for Rs. 30 or 40 each. They have dhaos, but no spears. They manufacture their own powder.

* Now (1885) at least 50 per cent., if not more, have firearms.—(*J. Johnstone*).

Crops.—They grow rice, múm, and chayan, occasionally dhall and a little cotton; also Indian-corn, arums, yams, and pumpkins. Produce per house, 5 maunds of rice, 5 maunds of mum, and 2 or 3 maunds of chayan, which even with root crops seems insufficient for their consumption.

Liquor.—They brew a refreshing kind of beer from rice and an intoxicating drink from a white bean.

(*Political Agent's Report, 1877-78; Lieut. Dun, 1881-82.*)

KONG-JAL—

A Tankul village, built after the usual Tankul pattern, about 4,500 feet above the sea-level, containing 12 houses.

Inhabitants.—The inhabitants belong to the south-western section of the Tankul Naga tribe. Population 60, of whom 12 may be fighting-men.

Climate.—The climate is unhealthy from beginning of August to end of October.

Water.—Scanty supply.

Supplies.—Rice-straw procurable. Scanty grazing. Principal grains are rice and múm. Firewood plentiful. Arum, yams, and pumpkins. Harvest in November and early part of December.

Live-stock.—A small number of pigs and poultry.

Transport.—For coolie purposes, 10 men, women, and children.

Timber.—All kinds of timber in profusion, except firs.—(*Lieut. Dun, 1881.*)

KOPAMEDZA—

A peak on the northern frontier of Manipur.

Elevation.—8,375 feet.

KOPRU—

The highest peak on the range bounding the Manipur and Tiki valleys on the west.

Elevation.—8,409 feet.

KORTAK—

The stream which carries the drainage of the Logták lake into the Imphal river.

In the cold weather it is still deep and unfordable, and flows in a nala with perpendicular banks but little raised above the water's edge.

KUBBO VALLEY—

A flat valley lying between Manipur and the Ningthee, and separated from the former by the Yumadoung range and from the latter by the Angoching range; it is called by the Burmans Tamoo Khan-pat Myo Atwen Chyoung. The Kubbo valley has not changed its general aspect since Pemberton's time. It is still a narrow strip of forest land, with spaces cleared here and there for paddy cultivation. It is almost flat. The trees are tall and far apart;

there is very little brushwood, and the ground is covered with grass, which at the northern end grows to about 4 feet in height. The valley appears to be traversable in every direction. There are a few patches of swamp, but of no great extent. To the north are several large open grass patches.

Timber.—The commonest tree is a kind of sâl, said to be fast-growing. It is not the ordinary sâl of commerce. Much teak has been cut down, and only young trees remain. There is a good deal of kio (lacquer tree), yango (oil-tree), and bastard teak. The cultivation of the valley seems to have decreased of late years, the sâl growing in abandoned places.

Streams.—The Nammea river drains the northern portion of the valley and flows into the Maglung, the main river of the valley.

Climate.—The climate from the beginning of May to the end of November is excessively unhealthy, the northern portion being least so.

Elevation.—At Kongal thannah the valley is about 1,000 feet above the sea-level.

Temperature.—In December 75° to 80° in the middle of the day. In a grass-hut the cold is not felt at night. There is little or no fog in the Yumadoung hills and Kubbo valley to interfere with signalling.

Inhabitants.—The inhabitants are almost exclusively Shans. There are a few Manipuri settlers at Tummoo and Moray, and two Marring villages, one a Kwon-doung and one called Songatel.—(*Lieut. Dun, 1881-82; Phayre, 1882.*)

KUCHAI OR MEVURHI—

A small western confluent of the Lanier river.

KUDUMPOPI—

A Manipuri village, 6 miles from Imphal, on the Cachar road.

Elevation.—
Temperature.—
Climate.— } *Vide* page 77, Changangai.

Houses.—40, Manipuri pattern.

Inhabitants.—200, sepoy class.

Fighting-men.—40.

Water.—
Camping-ground.—
Products, &c.— } *Vide* page 77, Changangai.

Live-stock.—80 cows, 60 buffaloes.

Carriage.—40 carts.

Approaches—Along Cachar road; (2) along village path from Khanna and Maibam.

KUIHOW—

A Manipur village east by south of the Imphal.

KUJAIROK—

A river of Manipur which flows into the Maglung. It is crossed by the Pallel-Moray route, and also by the Tanga-pokpi-Moray road. At the point where the latter crosses it, the river is 30 yards broad, with 5 feet perpendicular banks, and bad crossing. Good open camping-ground, and plenty of water near Moray Thana.

KUJMAN—

A Manipuri village, 2 miles south-east of Bishenpur (Lamlángtong).

Elevation.— }
Temperature.— } *Vide* page 77, Changangai.
Climate.— }
Houses.—30, Manipuri pattern.
Inhabitants.—150, sepoy class.
Fighting-men.—30.
Water.— }
Camping-ground.— } *Vide* page 77, Changangai.
Grazing.— }
Products, &c.— }
Live-stock.—60 cows, 45 buffaloes.
Carriage.—30 carts, 7 boats.
Approaches—By bad village paths from Kujumal and Moirang road.

KUJUMAL—

A Manipuri village, 1½ miles south-east of Bishenpur (Lamlángtong).
Elevation.— }
Temperature.— } *Vide* page 77, Changangai.
Climate.— }
Houses.—30, Manipuri pattern.
Inhabitants.—150, sepoy class.
Fighting-men.—30.
Water.— }
Camping-ground.— } *Vide* page 77, Changangai.
Products, &c.— }
Live-stock.—60 cows, 45 buffaloes.
Carriage.—30 carts.
Approaches—By indifferent field-paths from Bishenpur and neighbouring villages.

KUKILONG OR DAKKA—

A Tankul Naga village on the north-eastern frontier of Manipur not far from the junction of the Lanier with the Ningthee river.
Elevation.—About 3,500 feet.

There are said to be 300 houses in the village.

The people are very savage, and no Manipuris ever visit the village.

They can be communicated with through the people of Somrah Maialúng.

The best route to the Sarameti peak would lie through this village.

The valley in which it is situated is filled with magnificent forest and quite different to that in the Somrah basin, which touches it on the west.

KUMKAILAK—

A small muddy stream which issues from a jheel in the Manipur valley due west of Imphal.

KUNNI-MYO—

One of the principal towns on the right bank of the Chindwen (Ningthee) river, about 60 miles from its junction with the Irrawaddy. Here the country is thickly studded with villages, monasteries, and temples, surrounded by groves of cocoa and palmyra trees, and possessing large herds of very superior cattle.—(*Pemberton.*)

KUNOKONG—

A river of Manipur, which unites with the Meiay stream and forms the Napanga.—(*Lieut. Dun, 1881-82.*)

KUNPI—

A Marring village, built after the usual Marring pattern, about 3,500 feet above the sea-level, containing 40 houses.

Inhabitants.—The inhabitants belong to the Marring Naga tribe. Population 200, of whom 60 may be fighting-men. The chief's name is Akah.

Climate.—The climate is unhealthy from beginning of August to end of October.

Supplies.—Rice-straw procurable. Fair grazing. Principal grains are Indian-corn, rice, múm, and chayan. Firewood plentiful. Arum, beans, and pumpkins. Harvest in November and early part of December.

Live-stock.—Pigs, poultry, and metna.

Transport.—For coolie purposes, 40 men and women.

Timber.—Oaks and other kinds; no firs.—(*Lieut. Dun, 1881-82.*)

KUNSOWA—

A subdivision of the Marring Naga tribe (*vide* Naga).

KÚRBÓK—

A small Tankul village of the Kharán subdivision, situated on the western slope of the Yumadoung above Chandwakong and Ningyel.

Elevation.—4,500 feet above the sea.

Temperature.—40° at sunrise in February.

Climate.—Healthy at all seasons.

KUSSOM-KULEL—

A Tankul village, built after the usual Tankul pattern, about 4,000 feet above the sea-level, containing 60 houses.

Inhabitants.—The inhabitants belong to the south-western section of the Tankul Naga tribe. Population 300, of whom 60 may be fighting-men.

Climate.—The climate is unhealthy from beginning of August to end of October.

Water.—Scanty supply.

Supplies.—Rice-straw procurable. Scanty grazing. Principal grains, rice and múm. Firewood plentiful. Arum, yams, and pumpkins. Harvest in November and early part of December.

Live-stock.—Pigs and poultry.

Transport.—For coolie purposes, 60 men, women, and children.

Timber.—Chiefly oaks; no firs.—(*Lieut. Dun, 1881-82.*)

KUSSOM-KUNAO—

A Tankul village, built after the usual Tankul pattern, about 2,000 feet above the sea-level, containing 10 houses.

Inhabitants.—The inhabitants belong to the north-eastern section of the Tankul Naga tribe. Population 50, of whom 10 may be fighting-men. Most influential man, Hasi, who is friendly.

Climate.—The climate is unhealthy from beginning of August to end of October.

Water.—Scanty supply.

Supplies.—Rice-straw procurable. Scanty grazing. Principal grains are rice and múm. Firewood plentiful. Arum, yams, and pumpkins. Harvest in November and early part of December.

Live-stock.—Pigs and poultry.

Transport.—For coolie purposes, 10 men, women, and children.

Timber.—Chiefly oaks; no firs.—(*Lieut. Dun, 1881-82.*)

KWENDOUNG—

A Marring village, in the Kubbo valley, about 700 feet above the sea-level, containing 25 houses. The village is on the road from Yanga-pokpi to Moray Thana, being 14 miles from the former.

Camping-ground.—The village being on the broad flat end of a spur, there is plenty of camping-ground.

Approaches.—By easy road from the west, not stockaded. Cultivation lies below the village on the east.

Inhabitants.—The inhabitants belong to the Marring Naga tribe, though settled amongst Shans. Population 125, of whom 25 may be fighting-men.

Climate.—The climate is unhealthy from beginning of June to end of October.

Water.—Plentiful supply from Namchialo stream close to the village.

Supplies.—Rice-straw procurable. Fair grazing. Principal grain, rice. Firewood plentiful. Plantains, yams, and pumpkins. Harvest in November and early part of December.

Live-stock.—Pigs, poultry, and buffaloes.

Transport.—For coolie purposes, 25 men and women.

Timber.—Teak, sal, and bamboo.—(*Lieut. Dun, 1881-82.*)

Houses.—10, Naga pattern.

Inhabitants.—40.

Fighting-men.—10.

Water.—Scanty.

Camping-ground.—Sufficient for 100 men.

Grazing.—
Timber.—
Products.—
Harvests.— } *Vide* page 78, Charo.

Live-stock.—Pigs and poultry; a few metna and cows.

Carriage.—15 coolies.

Approaches.—Up steep open slope from the valley.

KYAYMOO or KYA-YOWA—

A village in Burma, about 200 houses, on the Ava-Kendat road. Cattle and water abundant; good road.

KYEN-DOUNG—

(*Vide* Kwendoung.)

L

LAIBI—

A Marring village, built after the usual Marring pattern, about 3,500 feet above the sea-level, containing 6 houses.

Inhabitants.—The inhabitants belong to the Marring Naga tribe. Population 30, of whom 9 may be fighting-men. The chief's name is Tongjuba.

Climate.—The climate is unhealthy from beginning of August to end of October

Supplies.—Rice-straw procurable. Fair grazing. Principal grains are Indian-corn, rice, múm, and chayan. Firewood plentiful. Arum, beans, and pumpkins. Harvest in November and early part of December.

Live-stock.—Pigs and poultry.

Transport.—For coolie purposes, 6 men and women.

Timber.—Chiefly oaks; no firs.—(*Lieut. Dun, 1881-82.*)

LAII (GAZIPHIMI)—

A Tankul village, built after the usual Tankul pattern, about 5,000 feet above the sea-level, containing 200 houses.

Camping-ground.—Terraced rice-fields.

Inhabitants.—The inhabitants belong to the Kolya-Mau Naga tribe. Population 1,000, of whom 200 may be fighting-men. The most influential man is Topa. Headman, Tongum.

Climate.—The climate is healthy at all seasons.

Supplies.—Scanty grazing. Principal grains are múm and chayan. Firewood plentiful. Arum, yams, and pumpkins. Harvest in November and early parts of December.

Live-stock.—Pigs and poultry.

Transport.—For coolie purposes, 300 coolies.

Timber.—Chiefly oaks and firs.—(*Lieut. Dun, 1881-82.*).

LAIMATAK—

A river crossed by the Cachar road.

It is of no great breadth—from 20 to 35 yards,—but with a strong current; it is crossed either by fording or by a suspension bridge, according to the state of the river.

It is liable to sudden floods, which have frequently carried away the suspension bridge, and sometimes the Manipuri Thana on the bank.

LAIMATOL—

The portion of the range which bounds the Manipur valley on the west, crossed by the Cachar road, is called Laimatol.

There is a fine stream of water near the summit of the pass.

LAIMENA—

A small Kanpui village in South-West Manipur. There are only 10 houses.

Products, &c.—*Vide* page 78, Charo.

LAIRENG-KABI—

LAIRENG-KABI—

LAIRENG-SENYI—

A Manipuri village in the north-east portion of the valley.

LAIRIT—

A Kom village in the Túrbúng valley, South-West Manipur.

Elevation.—2,800 feet.
Temperature.—43° at sunrise in December.
Climate.—Unhealthy from 1st May to 1st December.
Houses.—20, Manipuri pattern.
Inhabitants.—80.
Fighting-men.—40.
Water.—Good and plentiful.
Camping-ground.—Unlimited.
Grazing.—Good.
Timber.—
Products, &c.— } *Vide* page 77, Chanjang.
Live-stock.—A few metna, pigs, and poultry.
Carriage.—40 coolies.
Approaches.—Up easy slope through light jungle from Moirang on the east.

LAISANG-KONG—

A Manipuri village, 11 miles from Imphal, on the Longtival road.
Elevation.—
Temperature.— } *Vide* page 77, Changangai.
Climate.—
Houses.—40, Manipuri pattern.
Inhabitants.—200, sepoys.
Fighting-men.—40.
Water.—
Camping-ground.— } *Vide* page 77, Changangai.
Products, &c.—
Live-stock.—80 cows, 60 buffaloes.
Carriage.—40 carts, 10 boats.
Approaches—From north and south along central valley road; along the Thobal river by a good mule-path.

LAISEN—

An almost isolated mass of hills on the east bank of the Iril; elevation of highest point 5,173 feet.

LAISHANGTEN—

A Manipuri village on the Thobal river below the Thobal villages.
Elevation.—
Temperature.— } *Vide* page 77, Changangai.
Climate.—
Houses.—25, Manipuri pattern.
Inhabitants.—125, sepoy class.
Fighting-men.—25.
Water.—
Grazing.—
Camping-ground.— } *Vide* page 77, Changangai.
Products, &c.—
Live-stock.—50 cows, 37 buffaloes.
Carriage.—25 carts, 12 boats.
Approaches—By good mule-path along the Thobal.

LAISOM—

A peak on the range which forms the eastern boundary of the Maiyan khang Marthaipham valley and on a level in latitude with Karong.

It is thickly wooded with oak.

Elevation.—7,094 feet.

LAMDEM—

A small Manipuri village in North-West Manipur, 6 miles from Imphal.

LAMGANG—

A Hiroi village in the south-west corner of Manipur.

Elevation.—About 4,500 feet

Houses.—100, Manipuri pattern.

Inhabitants.—400.

Fighting-men.—100.

Water.—
Camping-ground.— } Both probably plentiful.

Products, &c.—*Vide* page 78, Charo.

Live-stock.—20 metna, pigs, and poultry.

Carriage.—150 coolies.

Name of headman.—Pómaching.

LAMGANG KUNTAK—

Similar in all respects to Lamgáng Kulel, of which it is an offshoot.

There are only 10 houses.

LAMJANG—

A new Kuki village of the Simmté clan, situated on the Manipur source of the Tipai river.

Elevation.—3,500 feet.

Temperature.—42° at sunrise in December.

Climate.—Unhealthy from 1st May to 1st December.

Houses.—200, Kuki pattern.

Inhabitants.—800.

Fighting-men.—200.

Water.—
Grazing.—
Camping-ground.—
Products, &c.— } *Vide* page 77, Chanjang.

Live-stock.—40 metna, pigs, and poultry.

Carriage.—300 coolies.

Approaches.—Not personally visited.

The chief of this village, Sumkám by name, is recognised as the head of the Simmté clan. He is a rather sulky-looking youth, of about 25 years of age.

LAMKÁNG—

An Anál (Hól) village in South-East Manipur.

Elevation.—4,000 feet.

Houses.—30.

Live-stock.—A few metna, pigs, and poultry.

Water and Camping-ground.—Probably plentiful.

Products, &c.—*Vide* page 78, Charo.

Carriage.—45 coolies.

LAMLAI—

A Tankul village east by north of the Imphal, built after the usual Tankul pattern, 3,500 feet above the sea-level, containing 15 houses.

Camping-ground.—Small camping-ground on the west of village.

Approaches.—Steep ascent and descent to village from west and east. Naturally difficult, not artificially defended. The eastern approach commands the village.

Inhabitants.—The inhabitants belong to the Tankul Naga tribe, but tie their hair like the Marrings. Population 75, of whom 15 are fighting-men. The chief and most influential man is Milan, who is friendly.

Climate.—The climate is unhealthy from beginning of August to end of October.

Water.—Scanty supply.

Supplies.—Rice-straw procurable. Very scanty grazing. Principal grains are rice and múm. Firewood plentiful. Pumpkins and yams. Rice harvest in November; múm in December.

Live-stock.—None.

Transport.—For coolie purposes, 10 men, women, and children.

Timber.—Oaks and other forest trees plentiful.—(*Lieut. Dun, 1881-82.*)

LAMLAI-KUNAO—

A Tankul village, built after the usual Tankul pattern, about 3,500 feet above the sea-level, containing 6 houses.

Camping-ground.—From the position of the village, there should be plenty of ground for camping.

Inhabitants.—The inhabitants belong to the Tankul Naga tribe, but tie their hair like Marrings. Population 30, of whom 6 may be fighting-men. The head and most influential man is Mikraug.

Climate.—The climate is unhealthy from beginning of August to end of October.

Supplies.—Rice-straw procurable. Very scanty grazing. Principal grains are rice and múm. Firewood plentiful. Yams and pumpkins. Rice harvest in November; múm in December.

Live-stock.—Pigs and poultry.

Transport.—For coolie purposes, 6 men, women, and children.

Timber.—Oaks and plenty of other forest trees.—(*Lieut. Dun, 1881-82.*)

LAMLÁNG—

A Tankul village on the Hytuk-pokpi-Yanga-pokpi route, built after the usual Tankul pattern, 5,000 feet above the sea-level, containing 120 houses.

Camping-ground.—Terraced rice-fields available.

Approaches.—The village is above, but does not command the Yanga-pokpi road.

Inhabitants.—The inhabitants belong to the north-eastern section of the Tankul Naga tribe. Population 600, of whom 120 may be fighting-men. The chief's name is Luong. Gnobah, who is friendly, has much influence.

Climate.—The climate is healthy at all seasons.

Water.—Water from river below the village on the south side.

Supplies.—Rice-straw procurable. Very scanty grazing. Principal grains are rice and múm. Firewood plentiful. Yams and pumpkins. Rice harvest in November; múm in December.

Live-stock.—Pigs, poultry, and a few buffaloes or metna.

Transport.—For coolie purposes, 120 men, women, and children.

Timber.—Chiefly oaks and firs; bamboos scarce.—(*Lieut. Dun, 1881-82.*)

LAMLANGTONG—

A Manipur (Loï) village on the Cachar road, close to the Bishenpur thannah.

Houses.—150, Manipuri pattern.

Inhabitants.—750, employed in collecting pan-leaf.
Fighting-men.—150.
Water.—Good and plentiful.
Camping-ground.—Sufficient for a large force all the year round, and requires little clearing, especially in the neighbourhood of the thannah.
Elevation.—
Temperature.— } *Vide* page 77, Changangai.
Climate.—
Supplies, &c.—*Vide* page 77, Changangai.
Live-stock.—300 cows, 225 buffaloes, 30 ponies.
Carriage.—150 carts.
Approaches—By the Imphal-Silchar road and the Moirang road. Both are good and lie through flat open country.

LAMLONG-KAI—

A small Koireng village in the north-west corner of the Manipur valley.

LAMLONG-KULEL—

A Marring village, built after the usual Marring pattern, about 3,500 feet above the sea-level, containing 10 houses.
Inhabitants.—The inhabitants belong to the Marring Naga tribe. Population 50, of whom 15 may be fighting-men.
Climate.—The climate is unhealthy from beginning of August to end of October.
Supplies.—Rice-straw procurable. Fair grazing. Principal grains are Indian-corn, rice, múm, and chayan. Firewood plentiful. Arum, beans, and pumpkins. Harvest in November and early part of December.
Live-stock.—Pigs and poultry.
Transport.—For coolie purposes, 30 men and women.
Timber.—Oaks and other kinds; no firs.—(*Lieut. Dun, 1881-82.*)

LAMLONG-KUNAO—

A Marring village, built after the usual Marring pattern, about 3,500 feet above the sea-level, containing 7 houses.
Inhabitants.—The inhabitants belong to the Marring Naga tribe. Population 35, of whom 11 may be fighting-men. The chief's name is Mowba.
Climate.—The climate is unhealthy from beginning of August to end of October.
Supplies.—Rice-straw procurable. Fair grazing. Principal grains are Indian-corn, rice, múm, and chayan. Firewood plentiful. Arum, beans, and pumpkins. Harvest in November and early part of December.
Live-stock.—Pigs and poultry.
Transport.—For coolie purposes, 5 men and women.
Timber.—Oaks and other kinds; no firs.—(*Lieut. Dun, 1881-82.*)

LAMPAL—

A Manipuri village in the north-west of the valley.

LAMPHÉL—

A large sheet of water at the north-west corner of Imphal.

LAMPUI—

A Tankul village on the road from the Imphal to Poshing, built after the usual Tankul pattern, about 5,000 feet above the sea-level, containing 30 houses.

Inhabitants.—The inhabitants belong to the south-western section of the Tankul Naga tribe. Population 150, of whom 30 may be fighting-men. The chief's name is Malepu.

Climate.—The climate is healthy at all seasons.

Water.—Scanty supply.

Supplies.—Rice-straw procurable. Fair grazing. Principal grains are rice and múm. Firewood plentiful. Yams and pumpkins. Rice harvest in November; múm in December.

Live-stock.—Pigs and poultry.

Transport.—20 coolies.

Timber.—Oaks, firs, and other kinds plentiful; bamboos scarce.

(*Lieut. Dun, 1881-82.*)

LAMTÂNG—

A small Manipuri village in the north-west portion of the valley.

LAMTÁNG—

A Kaupui village on the Laimatol range in South-Western Manipur, south of the Cachar road.

Elevation.—About 4,500 feet.

Temperature.—37° at sunrise in January.

Climate.—Healthy at all seasons.

Houses.—70, Naga pattern.

Inhabitants.—280.

Fighting-men.—70.

Water.—
Camping-ground.— } Probably plenty.

Grazing.—
Products, &c.— } *Vide* page 78, Charo.

Live-stock.—Pigs and poultry.

Carriage.—100 coolies.

Approaches.—Up easy open spur from the Manipur valley.

LAMTING—

A Manipuri village close to the eastern valley road, 20 miles from Imphal.

Elevation.—
Climate.—
Temperature.— } *Vide* page 77, Changangai.

Houses.—40, Manipuri pattern.

Inhabitants.—200, sepoy class.

Fighting-men.—40.

Water.—
Camping-ground.—
Products.— } *Vide* page 77, Changangai.

Live-stock, &c.—80 cows, 60 buffaloes.

Carriage.—10 carts.

Approaches—By good mule-path along the Ingorok (or Wangching) stream from the high road or from Ingorok.

LANG—

A Tankul village, built after the usual Tankul pattern, about 4,500 feet above the sea-level, containing 10 houses.

Inhabitants.—The inhabitants belong to the south-western section of the Tankul Naga tribe. Population 50, of whom 10 may be fighting-men. The chief's name is Mashowhang.

Climate.—The climate is unhealthy from beginning of August to end of October.

Water.—Scanty supply.

Supplies.—Rice-straw procurable. Scanty grazing. Principal grains are rice and múm. Firewood plentiful. Yams and pumpkins. Rice harvest in November; múm in December.

Live-stock.—Pigs and poultry.

Transport.—For coolie purposes, 10 men, women, and children.

Timber.—All kinds, including oak; fir plentiful.—(*Lieut. Dun, 1881-82.*)

LÁNGATEL—

A Manipuri village situated at the inner or western foot of the Yumadoung range between Hytukpokpi and Pallel.

Elevation.—
Climate.—
Temperature.— } *Vide* page 77, Changangai.

Houses.—75, Manipuri pattern.

Inhabitants.—375, sepoy class.

Fighting men.—75.

Water.—Plentiful.

Camping-ground.—Plentiful.

Grazing.—Good.

Products, &c.—*Vide* page 77, Changangai.

Live-stock.—110 buffaloes, 150 cows.

Carriage.—75 carts.

Approaches.—By indifferent paths through rice cultivation.

LANGDANG—

A Tankul village, built after the usual Tankul pattern, about 6,000 feet above the sea-level, on the north-east frontier of Manipur, containing 50 houses.

Inhabitants.—The inhabitants belong to the north-eastern section of the Tankul Naga tribe. Population 250, of whom 50 may be fighting-men. The chief's name is Chángsón.

Climate.—The climate is healthy at all seasons.

Water.—Small supply close to village on north-east.

Supplies.—Rice-straw procurable. Scanty grazing. Principal grains are rice and múm. Firewood plentiful. Arum and pumpkins. Rice harvest in November; múm in December.

Live-stock.—Pigs, poultry, and a few buffaloes or metna.

Transport.—For coolie purposes, 50 men, women, and children.

Timber.—Chiefly oaks and firs, which are plentiful; bamboos scarce.

(*Lieut. Dun, 1881-82.*)

LANGKUN—

A small Kaupui village in north-west Manipur.

LANGÓL—

A hill rising out of the Manipur plains and the spurs from which cover Imphal on the north and west.

LANGOL—

A Marring village, built after the usual Marring pattern, about 3,000 feet above the sea-level, containing 30 houses.

Inhabitants.—The inhabitants belong to the Marring Naga tribe. Population 150, of whom 45 may be fighting-men.

Climate.—The climate is unhealthy from beginning of August to end of October.

Supplies.—Rice-straw procurable. Fair grazing. Principal grains are Indian-corn, rice, múm, and chayan. Firewood plentiful. Arum, beans, and pumpkins. Harvest in November and early part of December.

Live-stock.—Pigs and poultry.

Transport.—For coolie purposes, 30 men and women.

Timber.—Oaks and other kinds; no firs.—(*Lieut. Dun, 1881-82.*)

LANGOL*—

A long spur stretching from the northern end of the Imphal city, where its highest point, 1,100 feet above the level of the valley, is situated, almost to Sengmaie on the Kohima road.

It affords a means of protecting Imphal on the northern side against an attack from that direction; but *vide* page 94, Imphal city.

LANIER OR TUZU—

The principal river of North-Eastern Manipur. It flows through remarkably flat open valleys throughout the whole of its course, and its bed makes an admirable road, as there are few rocky places or masses of boulders, and camps can be formed at any point.

In January 1885 it was 2 feet deep between Jessami and Mellomi and was easily fordable, the stream being by no means swift.

Native information declares that, after receiving the eastern branch (called Tuzu only), it becomes quite unfordable; but this is open to doubt. (*Lieut. Dun, 1885.*)

LAPUPO—

An Anal village on the Pallel-Moray route, built after the usual Kuki pattern, on the Nupitel Ridge 3,000 feet above the sea-level, containing 5 houses.

Camping-ground.—Sufficient camping-ground for half a battalion at east end of village.

Approaches.—From east and west the village is approached along a tolerably broad and level ridge, which neither is commanded by, nor commands, the village. There are no defences. The village slightly commands the Moray road.

Inhabitants.—The inhabitants belong to the Anal Kuki tribe. Population 25, of whom 7 are fighting-men. The headman's name is Birow.

Climate.—The climate is unhealthy from beginning of August to end of October.

Water.—Fair supply east of village.

Supplies.—Rice-straw procurable. No grazing. Principal grains are rice and múm. Firewood plentiful. Plantains, yams, and pumpkins. Harvest in November and early part of December.

Live-stock.—Pigs and poultry.

Transport.—For coolie purposes, 5 men and women.

Timber.—No heavy timber; small oaks, &c.; no firs.—(*Lieut. Dun, 1881-82.*)

* The Langol hill supplies the famous hockey canes.—(*J. Johnstone.*)

LAPUTHUROK—

A Manipuri hamlet on the western edge of Imphal.

LATTAH—

A Shan village, built after the usual Shan pattern, about 700 feet above the sea-level, containing 4 houses.

Camping-ground.—Any amount of camping-ground available, the ground being quite flat and free from thick undergrowth.

Approaches—By broad path through forest land perfectly flat, and not artificially defended.

Inhabitants.—The inhabitants belong to the Shan tribe. Populatior 20, of whom 4 may be fighting-men.

Climate.—The climate is unhealthy from beginning of June to end of October.

Water.—Plentiful supply.

Supplies.—Rice-straw procurable. Fair grazing. Principal grains are Indian-corn, rice, múm, and chayan. Firewood plentiful. Arums, beans, and pumpkins. Harvest in November and early part of December.

Live-stock.—Pigs, poultry, and a few buffaloes.

Transport.—For coolie purposes, 4 men and women.

Timber.—Teak, sál, bamboos, and other kinds.—(*Lieut. Dun, 1881-82.*)

LEELONG—

A river of Manipur, formed by the junction of the Iril and Imphal streams. There is a temporary bridge across it, where the road to Pallel crosses at 6½ miles from the capital. At this point the river is 50 yards broad at the top, with banks 25 feet high, and in the cold weather 3 to 4 feet of water. (*Lieut. Dun, 1881-82.*)

LEESA—

A village of the Anal tribe in South-East Manipur.

LEICHING—

A hill in Manipur, suitable for a signal station, from which to communicate with South Nupitel peak.—(*Lieut. Dun, 1881-82.*)

LEICHING-KULEL—

A Marring village, built after the usual Marring pattern, about 3,000 feet above the sea-level, containing 10 houses.

Inhabitants.—The inhabitants belong to the Marring Naga tribe. Population 50, of whom 15 may be fighting-men. The headman's name is Kongshangba.

Climate.—The climate is unhealthy from beginning of August to end of October.

Supplies.—Rice-straw procurable. Fair grazing. Principal grains are Indian-corn, rice, múm, and chayan. Firewood plentiful. Arum, beans, and pumpkins. Harvest in November and early part of December.

Live-stock.—Pigs and poultry.

Transport.—For coolie purposes, 10 men and women.

Timber.—Oaks and other kinds; no firs.—(*Lieut. Dun, 1881-82.*)

LEICHING-KUNAO—

A Marring villiage, built after the usual Marring pattern, about 3,000 feet about the sea-level, containing 5 houses.

Inhabitants.—The inhabitants belong to the Marring Naga tribe. Population 25, of whom 7 may be fighting-men. The headman's name is Lairengba.

Climate.—The climate is unhealthy from beginning of August to end of October.

Supplies.—Rice-straw procurable. Fair grazing. Principal grains are Indian-corn, rice, múm, and chayan. Firewood plentiful. Arum, beans, and pumpkins. Harvest in November and early part of December.

Live-stock.—Pigs and poultry.

Transport.—For coolie purposes, 10 men and women.

Timber.—Oaks and other kinds; no firs.—(*Lieut. Dun, 1881-82.*)

LEIRAM-KULEL—

A Tankul village, built after the usual Tankul pattern, about 3,000 feet above the sea-level, containing 13 houses.

Inhabitants.—The inhabitants belong to the south-western section of the Tankul Naga tribe. Population 65, of whom 13 may be fighting-men. The head and most influential man's name is Lalomba.

Climate.—The climate is unhealthy from beginning of August to end of October.

Supplies.—Rice-straw procurable. Scanty grazing. Principal grains are rice and múm. Firewood plentiful. Arum and pumpkins. Rice harvest in November; múm in December.

Live-stock.—Pigs and poultry.

Transport.—For coolie purposes, 13 men, women, and children.

Timber.—Chiefly oak and fir, plentiful; bamboos scarce.

(*Lieut. Dun, 1881-82.*)

LEIRAM-KUNAO—

A Tankul village, built after the usual Tankul pattern, about 3,000 feet above the sea-level, containing 14 houses.

Inhabitants.—The inhabitants belong to the south-western section of the Tankul Naga tribe. Population 70, of whom 14 may be fighting-men. The head and most influential man's name is Walokpa.

Climate.—The climate is unhealthy from beginning of August to end of October.

Water.—Scanty supply.

Supplies.—Rice-straw procurable. Scanty grazing. Principal grains are rice and múm. Firewood plentiful. Arum and pumpkins. Rice harvest in November; múm in December.

Live-stock.—Pigs and poultry.

Transport.—For coolie purposes, 14 men, women, and children.

Timber.—Chiefly oak and fir, plentiful; bamboos scarce.

(*Lieut. Dun, 1881-82.*)

LEIRAM-PUNGA—

A Tankul village, built after the usual Tankul pattern, about 3,000 feet above the sea-level, containing 9 houses.

Inhabitants.—The inhabitants belong to the south-western section of the Tankul Naga tribe. Population 45, of whom 9 may be fighting-men. The head and most influential man's name is Ako.

Climate.—The climate is unhealthy from beginning of August to end of October.

Supplies.—Rice-straw procurable. Scanty grazing. Principal grains are rice and múm. Firewood plentiful. Arum and pumpkins. Rice harvest in November; múm in December.

Live-stock.—Pigs and poultry.

Transport.—For coolie purposes, 9 men, women, and children.

Timber.—Chiefly oak and fir, plentiful; bamboos scarce.

(*Lieut. Dun, 1881-82.*)

LEIRENG—

A Tankul village on the road between the Imphal and Poshing, built after the usual Tankul pattern, about 3,000 feet above the sea-level, containing 4 houses.

Camping-ground.—There is camping-ground for a large force near the village.

Inhabitants.—The inhabitants belong to the south-western section of the Tankul Naga tribe. Population 20, of whom 4 may be fighting-men.

Climate.—The climate is unhealthy from beginning of August to end of October.

Water.—Plentiful supply at a short distance on the east.

Supplies.—Rice-straw procurable. Very scanty grazing, but grass for making huts. Principal grains are rice and múm. Firewood plentiful. Arum and pumpkins. Rice harvest in November; múm in December.

Live-stock.—Pigs and poultry.

Transport.—For coolie purposes, 4 men, women, and children.

Timber.—Chiefly oak and fir, plentiful; bamboos scarce.

(*Lieut. Dun, 1881-82.*)

LEISHEE—

A Tankul village, built after the usual Tankul pattern, about 5,000 feet above the sea-level, containing 20 houses.

Inhabitants.—The inhabitants belong to the south-western section of the Tankul Naga tribe. Population 100, of whom 20 may be fighting men. The most influential man is Sási.

Climate.—Climate is healthy at all seasons.

Water.—Scanty supply.

Supplies.—Rice-straw procurable. Scanty grazing. Principal grains are rice and múm. Firewood plentiful. Arum and pumpkins. Rice harvest in November; múm in December.

Live-stock.—Pigs and poultry.

Transport.—For coolie purposes, 20 men, women, and children.

Timber.—Oaks, firs, and other kinds plentiful; bamboos scarce.

(*Lieut. Dun, 1881-82.*)

LEITAL—

A Hawkib village, built after the usual Kuki pattern, about 4,000 feet above the sea-level, containing 20 houses.

Inhabitants.—The inhabitants belong to the Hawkib subdivision of the Kongjai Kuki tribe. Population 100, of whom 30 may be fighting-men. The chief and most influential man is Hinglep.

Climate.—The climate is unhealthy from beginning of August to end of October.

Supplies.—Rice-straw procurable. Principal grains are rice and múm. Firewood plentiful. Arum, beans, and pumpkins. Rice harvest in November; múm in December.

Live-stock.—Pigs and poultry.
Transport.—For coolie purposes, 30 men and women.
Timber.—Chiefly small bushy oaks.—(*Lieut. Dun, 1881-82.*)

LEITING—

A Tankul village, built after the usual Tankul pattern, about 5,000 feet above the sea-level, containing 6 houses.
Inhabitants.—The inhabitants belong to the south-western section of the Tankul Naga tribe. Population 30, of whom 6 may be fighting-men. The most influential man is Rung-jing.
Climate.—The climate is healthy at all seasons.
Water.—Scanty supply.
Supplies.—Rice-straw procurable. Scanty grazing. Principal grains are rice and múm. Firewood plentiful. Arum and pumpkins. Rice harvest in November; múm in December.
Live-stock.—Pigs and poultry.
Transport.—For coolie purposes, 8 men, women, and children.
Timber.—Oaks, firs, and other trees plentiful; bamboo scarce.
(*Lieut. Dun, 1881-82.*)

LENGBA—

A small stream runs at the foot of the hill near Nungba, a village which lies midway between Cachar and Manipur, and nearly the same between the two principal rivers, the Barak and Irang. This stream is not navigable by boats, and easily fordable at all times.

LENGKUN—

A small Kaupui Naga village in North-West Manipur.

LENGLONG—

A new Kuki village of the Shingsól clan, on the west bank of the Irang, south of Kaupum.
Elevation.—About 3,000 feet.
Houses.—30, Kuki pattern.
Inhabitants.—120.
Fighting-men.—30.
Water.—
Camping-ground.— } *Vide* page 77, Chanjang.
Products.—
Live-stock.—A few metna, pigs, and poultry.
Carriage.—40 coolies.

LIYÁNG OR RAZAMEH—

A Katcha Naga village in the north-west corner of Manipur territory, above the Barak river, on the north side.
Elevation.—5,300 feet.
Temperature.—45° at sunrise in March.
Climate.—Healthy at all seasons.
Houses.—35, Naga pattern.
Inhabitants.—140.
Fighting-men.—35.
Water.—Very good and plentiful. Two large streams and a small tarn, a mile above the village to the east.

Camping-ground—Unlimited and very good. The village appears to be on an old moraine, judging from the shape of the plateau it is placed upon, and the (apparently) ice-worn boulders scattered about its surface.

The village is situated on the western edge of the plateau. The surface of the latter is gently undulating and covered in patches with light clumps of oak and alder.

Grazing.—Good.

Products, &c.—*Vide* page 78, Charo.

Live-stock.—50 cows, pigs, and poultry.

Carriage.—50 coolies.

Approaches.—The immediate approaches to the village from north and east are easy, lying over open rolling country for a mile before the village is reached.

A steep path leads up from the valley of the Barak on the south side.

The north and east paths, however (from Kenoma and Wuelong respectively), rise up to the plateau very steep, and, on the east, precipitous ascents.

LOANG-LOL—

A Manipur thannah, on the Cachar road on the western side of the Laimatak valley.

There is no stockade, and the garrison consists of 1 non-commissioned officer and 4 or 5 sepoys.

It is chiefly used as an octroi post.

LOANG-LOL-KULEL—

A Kaupui Naga village on the Cachar road, at the north-east corner of the Kaupum basin.

Elevation.—4,100 feet.

Temperature.—40° at sunrise.

Climate.—Healthy at all seasons.

Houses.—25, Naga pattern.

Inhabitants.—100.

Fighting-men.—25.

Water.—Fairly plentiful.

Camping-ground.—Below the village on the edge of the main road there is ground for 400 men, with water not far off to the east.

Products, &c.—*Vide* page 78, Charo.

Live-stock.—13 buffaloes, pigs, and poultry.

Carriage.—35 coolies.

Approaches—Up broad easy road through light jungle from Cachar road (?) by a narrow path from the north from the Irang.

LOANG-LOL-KUNAO—

A small Kaupui Naga village on the western side of the Laimatol valley, half a mile to the north of the Cachar road.

Elevation.—3,600 feet.

Temperature.—37° at sunrise in January.

Climate.—Unhealthy from 1st May to 1st December.

Houses.—17, Naga pattern.

Inhabitants.—68.

Fighting-men.—17.

Water and Camping-ground.—Scanty; sufficient for 200 men only.

Grazing.—
Products, &c.— } *Vide* page 78, Charo.
Live-stock.—
Carriage.—20 coolies.
Approaches—Up steep jungle-covered spur from Cachar road above Loang-lol thannah.

Ditto ditto from the Laimatol on the east and from the Irang on the north.

LOANGSŬNG BŬM—

A small Kaupui Naga village, 4 miles from Imphal on the Kohima road.

LOGTĀK—

The largest piece of water in Manipur. (*Vide* chapter I.)

LOKCHAO—

The name properly means "large stream," but it is applied more particularly to a mountain stream in the Yumadoung range, flowing eastwards and entering the Kubbo valley at Moré thanna. It is crossed by the Pallel-Moray route, near Sitpong village. At this point it is 50 yards broad, but has only 6 inches of water in the cold season.

LOMANG—

A small Tankul Naga village on the right bank of the Máglang river, close to its junction with the Tuyungba.
Elevation.—4,000 feet.
Temperature.—42° at sunrise in February.
Climate.—Unhealthy from 1st May to 1st December.
Houses.—7, Naga pattern.
Inhabitants.—28.
Fighting-men.—7.
Water and Camping-ground.—Sufficient for 200 men.
Grazing.—
Products, &c.— } *Vide* page 78, Charo.
Carriage.—10 coolies.

LONGHEL—

A new Kuki village of the Hawkib clan in the valley of the Manipur source of the Tipai river.
Elevation.—2,800 feet.
Temperature.—
Climate.— } *Vide* page 77, Chanjang.
Houses.—10.
Water.—
Camping-ground.— } *Vide* page 77, Chanjang.
Products, &c.—
Live-stock.—4 metna, pigs, and poultry.
Carriage.—20 coolies.

LONGJENGMAIE OR KABUIKHOLEL—

A small Kaupui village in North-Western Manipur.

LONGMAITEL—

A Manipuri village at the foot of the Yumadoung range, 3 miles north of Ingorok.

LONGTIVAL—

A Manipuri village, 4 miles from the Raja's palace, Imphal, on the Central Valley road.

Elevation.— }
Temperature.— } *Vide* page 77, Changangai.
Climate.— }

Houses.—60.

Water.—Plentiful.

Grazing.—Good.

Camping-ground.—East of the village and of the Atchamba river. There is a piece of ground formerly occupied by the Manipur Levy, which would accommodate a division.

It would be too damp for use, during the rains, with any safety to health.

Products, &c.—*Vide* page 77, Changangai.

Live-stock.—120 cows, 90 buffaloes.

Carriage.—60 carts, 15 boats.

Approaches—By the central valley road from north and south. The village almost adjoins Imphal.

LONGTIVAL—

A Kaupui Naga village on an eastern spur of Longtival hill.

Houses.—100.

Products, &c.—*Vide* page 78, Charo.

LONGTIVAL [generally spelt Langthabal]—

A hill rising out of the centre of the Manipur plain, 4 miles south of Imphal. Its highest peak is 420 feet above the plain. It is almost denuded of trees and the sides are steep.

One of the eastern spurs was in old times the Raja's residence, and a brick building is still standing there. There is a large canal made for boat-racing along the eastern side, and on the northern side between it and the city a large open space, formerly occupied by the Manipur Levy, and now the most suitable cold weather camping-ground for any large force stationed at Manipur.

LOREMBAM—

A Manipuri village at the foot of the Yumadoung range on the western side, 3 miles north of Ingorók.

Elevation.— }
Climate.— } *Vide* page 77, Changangai.
Temperature— }

Houses.—25.

Inhabitants.—125, sepoy class.

Water.— }
Camping-ground.— } *Vide* page 77, Changangai.
Products, &c.— }

Live-stock.—37 buffaloes, 50 cows.

Carriage.—25 carts.

Approaches—By good mule-path from Sárapók and Ingorók.

LOSAO—

A new Kuki village of the Simmté clan, situated on the western slopes of the Kailám peak in Southern Manipur.

Elevation.—About 4,000 feet.

Houses and fighting-men.—200.
Water.—
Camping-ground.—
Products, &c.
} *Vide* page 77, Chanjang.
Live-stock.—Believed to be about 70 metna, besides pigs and poultry.
Carriage.—300 coolies.
Approaches.—Not visited.
Headman.—Pumlal, friendly.

LOSEOMI—

A Kolya Naga village in Northern Manipur.

LOSHING—

A Tankul village, built after the usual Tankul pattern, about 4,500 feet above the sea-level, containing 14 houses.

Inhabitants.—The inhabitants belong to the south-western section of the Tankul Naga tribe. Population 60, of whom 14 may be fighting-men. The chief's name is Kaieelung.

Climate.—The climate is healthy at all seasons.

Water.—Scanty supply.

Supplies.—Rice-straw procurable. Scanty grazing. Principal grains are rice and múm. Firewood plentiful. Arum and pumpkins. Rice harvest in November; múm in December.

Live-stock.—Pigs and poultry.

Transport.—For coolie purposes, 15 men.

Timber.—All kinds peculiar to the country, including oak and fir.

(*Lieut. Dun, 1881-82.*)

LOWDUI—

A Manipur village, east by north of the Imphal.

LOWTAIE—

A Tankul village, built after the usual Tankul pattern, about 3,500 feet above the sea-level, containing 31 houses.

Inhabitants.—The inhabitants belong to the south-western section of the Tankul Naga tribe. Population 155, of whom 31 may be fighting-men. The most influential man is Marosung

Climate.—The climate is unhealthy from beginning of August to end of October.

Supplies.—Rice-straw procurable. Scanty grazing. Principal grains are rice and múm. Firewood plentiful. Arum and pumpkins. Rice harvest in November; múm in December.

Live-stock.—Pigs, poultry, and a few metna.

Transport.—For coolie purposes, 31 men, women, and children.

Timber.—All kinds peculiar to the country, including oaks and firs.

(*Lieut. Dun, 1881-82.*)

LOZAPHIHOMI—

A Kolya Naga village in Northern Manipur.

LUCHAIE-KULEL—

A Tankul village, built after the usual Tankul pattern, about 5,000 feet above the sea-level, containing 150 houses.

Inhabitants.—The inhabitants belong to the south-western section of the Tankul Naga tribe. Population 750, of whom 150 may be fighting-men. The most influential man is Phambah.

Climate.—The climate is healthy at all seasons.

Supplies.—Rice-straw available. Scanty grazing. Principal grain is múm. Firewood plentiful. Arum and pumpkins. Rice harvest in November; múm in December.

Live-stock.—Pigs and poultry.

Transport.—For coolie purposes, 150 men, women, and children.

Timber.—All kinds peculiar to the country, including oaks and firs; bamboos scarce.—(*Lieut. Dun, 1881-82.*)

LUCHAIE-KUNAO—

A Tankul village, built after the usual Tankul pattern, about 5,000 feet above the sea-level, containing 20 houses.

Inhabitants.—The inhabitants belong to the north-eastern section of the Tankul Naga tribe. Population 100, of whom 20 may be fighting-men. The most influential man is Yamáng.

Climate.—The climate is healthy at all seasons.

Supplies.—Rice-straw procurable. Scanty grazing. Principal grains, rice and múm. Firewood plentiful. Arum, yams, and pumpkins. Rice harvest in November; múm in December.

Live-stock.—Pigs and poultry.

Transport.—For coolie purposes, 20 men, women, and children.

Timber.—All kinds peculiar to the country, including oaks and firs.

(*Lieut. Dun, 1881-82.*)

LULAKPA—

A small Koireng village on the eastern slopes of Kopru peak.

LUMBUNG—

A Manipuri hamlet of two or three houses on the northern edge of the Lamphel Thíl.

There is very good grazing here. Water and good camping-ground for a regiment.

It is close to one of the Raja's firewood preserves.

LUNGOW—

A Tankul Naga village on the north-east frontier of Manipur.

LUSAD—

A Tankul village, built after the usual Tankul pattern, about 4,500 feet above the sea-level, containing 5 houses.

Inhabitants.—The inhabitants belong to the south-western section of the Tankul Naga tribe. Population 50, of whom 10 may be fighting-men. The headman is Mowba.

Climate.—The climate is healthy at all seasons.

Water.—Plentiful supply on east of village.

Supplies.—Rice-straw procurable. Scanty grazing. Principal grains are rice and múm. Firewood plentiful. Arum, yams, and pumpkins. Rice harvest in November; múm in December.

Live-stock.—Pigs and poultry.

Transport.—For coolie purposes, 5 men, women, and children.

Timber.—Chiefly oak and fir.—(*Lieut. Dun, 1881-82.*)

M

MACHI—

A Marring village, close to the Hytuk-pokpi-Yanga-pokpi route, on the south side, built after the usual Marring pattern, about 3,500 feet above the sea-level, containing 20 houses.

Camping-ground.—None.

Approaches.—Steep ascent from both east and west along a narrow ridge.

Inhabitants.—The inhabitants belong to the Marring Naga tribe. Population 100, of whom 30 may be fighting men. The chief is Chingsanglokpa.

Climate.—The climate is unhealthy from beginning of August to end of October.

Water.—Scanty supply.

Supplies.—Rice-straw procurable. Good grazing. Principal grains are Indian-corn, rice, múm, chayan, and dhall. Firewood plentiful. Arum, yams, and pumpkins. Harvest in November and early part of December.

Live-stock.—Pigs and poultry, 50 metna, 40 cows, and 10 goats.

Transport.—For coolie purposes, 20 men and women.

Timber.—All kinds except fir; oak not common.—(*Lieut. Dun, 1881-82.*)

MAGLANG—

A mountain stream in the Yumadoung, flowing in a very narrow steep-sided valley. Where crossed by the regular Kongál route (No. VI.), it is barely fordable, as the water, though shallow, flows with some violence out of one deep pool into another.

It is bridged at this point by strong bamboo matting laid on baskets of stones.

It is called by the Burmese Yoo Chyoung, drains the northern portion of the Kubbo valley, and eventually flows into the Ningthee. The road from Yanga-pokpi to Tummoo through the Kubbo valley crosses the Maglang at about a mile from Tummoo; the river is 60 yards broad at the crossing, but shallow and impassable for boats on account of rapids. About 5 or 6 miles below this point, however, it is navigable for small boats of 100 baskets burden.—(*Phayre, 1881-82; Lieut. Dun, 1881-82.*)

MAHA—

A thannah, about 1 mile from Pallel, on the Pallel-Nasinga route, situated on the western foot of the Yumadoung range, and forming one of the first or inner line of Manipur frontier posts.—(*Lieut. Dun, 1881-82.*)

MAHAKHON—

The name of two small Chiru villages on the inner or eastern slope of the Kopru-Laimatol range.

MAIBAM KUNJIL—

A Manipuri village on the Imphal river, below the point where it receives the Thobál.

Houses.—25, Manipuri pattern.

Inhabitants.—125, sepoy class.

Elevation.—
Temperature.—
Climate.—
Water.—
Camping-ground.—
Products.—

Vide page 77, Changangai.

Live-stock.—50 cows, 37 buffaloes.
Carriage.—25 carts, 12 boats.
Approaches—By central valley road from north and south.

MAIBI—

A Hawkib village, built after the usual Kuki pattern, about 4,000 feet above the sea-level, containing 30 houses.

Inhabitants—The inhabitants belong to the Hawkib subdivision of the Kongjai Kuki tribe. Population 150, of whom 45 may be fighting-men. The chief and most influential man is Mangshom.

Climate.—The climate is unhealthy from beginning of August to end of October.

Supplies.—Rice-straw procurable. Good grazing. Principal grains are Indian-corn, job's-tears, rice, and múm. Firewood plentiful. Pumpkins, beans, and arum. Rice harvest in November; múm in December.

Live-stock.—Pigs and poultry.
Transport.—For coolie purposes, 45 men and women.
Timber.—Chiefly small bushy oaks.—(*Lieut. Dun, 1881-82.*)

MAIRING—

A Tankul Naga village at the southern end of the Sakok-Lang range.

Elevation.—5,000 feet.
Houses.—20.
Water and Camping-ground.—Scanty (said to be sufficient for 300 men).
Grazing.—
Products, &c.— } *Vide* page 78, Charo.
Carriage.—30 coolies.
Approaches—Up very steep slope from the west; from above from the east.

MAITHAIPHAM—

A subdivision of the Koyla Naga tribe. (*Vide* Naga.)

MAITHAIPHAM THANNAH—

A thannah on the Manipur-Kohima route, situated on the west bank of the stream of the same name.

Defences.—The thannah is defended by an earthen bank 4 feet high.
Camping-ground.—Unlimited camping-ground.
Water.—Unlimited supply.
Supplies.—Grazing for 200 animals for one day in the valley.
(*Lieut. Dun, 1881-82.*)

MAITOMBOK—

A Manipuri village in the north-western part of the valley on the Operok stream.

MAITRAM—

A Manipuri village of about 40 houses on the Thobal river, south of the Thobál villages.

MAIYANG IMPHAL—

A Manipuri village on the central valley road, 14 miles from Imphal and on the bank of the Imphal (or Atchowba) river.

Elevation.—
Temperature.— } *Vide* page 77, Changangai.
Climate.—
Houses.—80, Manipuri pattern.
Inhabitants.—400 Mussulmans, sepoy class.

Fighting-men.—Eighty.

Water.—Plentiful.

Camping-ground.— } *Vide* page 77, Changangai.
Products, &c.— }

Live-stock.—160 cows, 120 buffaloes.

Carriage.—80 carts, 20 boats.

This place was the original settlement of the Mussulman immigrants from Cachar. It was deserted for long time, but was reoccupied in 1854. There is no trace of the large earthwork mentioned in Dr. Brown's Report on Manipur.

MAIYANG LANGCHING—

A small Chiru village at the foot of the western slope of the Langol hill.

MAKEL—

A village on the road from the Imphal to Phunama Mao.

(*Lieut. Dun, 1881-82.*)

MAKKU—

A Tankul village on the Pong-Kongal route, built after the usual Tankul pattern, 4,500 feet above the sea-level, containing 10 houses.

Camping-ground.—Sufficient for 200 men to south of village; remaining ground has a steep slope.

Approaches.—From the Konookong stream on the east, up a steep and in some places narrow spur. The village commands a very small portion of the road. There is also a very steep path coming down from behind the village and through thick jungle.

Inhabitants.—The inhabitants belong to the south-western section of the Tankul Naga tribe. Population 50, of whom 10 are fighting-men The chief is Missorong.

Climate.—The climate is unhealthy from beginning of August to end of October.

Water.—Plentiful supply, but at some distance.

Supplies.—Rice-straw procurable. Scanty grazing. Principal grains are rice and múm. Firewood plentiful. Arum, pumpkins. Rice harvest in November; múm in December.

Live-stock.—Pigs and poultry.

Transport.—For coolie purposes, 12 men, women, and children.

Timber.—Chiefly oak and firs.—(*Lieut. Dun, 1881-82.*)

MAKUNGA—

A subdivision of the Marring Naga tribe.

MALHONG—

A Chussad village, built after the usual Chussad pattern, about 2,000 feet above the sea-level, containing 10 houses.

Inhabitants.—The inhabitants belong to the Chussad subdivision of the Kongjai Kuki tribe. Population 50, of whom 15 may be fighting-men. Chief and most influential man is Komtu.

Climate.—The climate is unhealthy from beginning of August to end of October.

Supplies.—Rice-straw procurable. Principal grains are rice and mum. Firewood plentiful. Pumpkins, beans, and arum. Rice harvest in November; múm in December.

Live-stock.—Pigs and poultry.—(*Lieut. Dun, 1881-82.*)

MALLONG—

A Tankul village, built after the usual Tankul pattern, about 4,000 feet above the sea-level, containing 4 houses.

Inhabitants.—The inhabitants belong to the south-western section of the Tankul Naga tribe. Population 20, of whom 4 may be fighting-men.

Climate.—The climate is unhealthy from beginning of August to end of October.

Water.—Scanty supply.

Supplies.—Rice-straw procurable. Scanty grazing. Principal grains are rice and múm. Firewood plentiful. Arum and pumpkins. Rice harvest in November; múm in December.

Live-stock.—Pigs and poultry.

Transport.—For coolie purposes, 4 men, women, and children.

Timber.—Chiefly oak and fir.—(*Lieut. Dun, 1881-82.*)

MAMOKONG—

A mountain stream flowing almost to the point where it joins the Viratar in a narrow rocky gorge. It drains part of the outer slope of the hills which form the edge of the Somrah basin.

It is everywhere fordable during the cold weather.

MANCHNIBUNG—

A peak at the eastern end of the eastern spur from Sanaching Yumadoung range.

MÁNGNÉ—

A new Kuki village of the Simmté clan, in valley of the Manipur source of the Tipai river.

Elevation.—3,500 feet.

Temperature and climate.—*Vide* page 77, Chanjang.

Houses.—20, Kuki pattern.

Inhabitants.—80.

Fighting-men.—20.

Water.—Good and plentiful.

Camping-ground.—Good and plentiful.

Grazing.— }
Products, &c.— } *Vide* page 77, Chanjang.

Live-stock.—A few metna, pigs, and poultry.

Carriage.—30 coolies.

Approaches.—Easy and open from the stream.

Headman.—Mángné, friendly.

MANGSANG—

An Anal village in South-Eastern Manipur

MANGYÓL—

A new Kuki village in the valley of the Turbung. The inhabitants are of the Simmté clan.

There are only 5 houses.

MANOI—

A village containing 4 houses on the road from Moreh thannah to Samjok.

(*Major Badgeley, 1881-82.*)

MANTUIKUL—

An Anal village in South-Eastern Manipur.

MAO1

(*Vide* Phunamah.)

MAPAN—

A small Tangal Naga village on the hills immediately north of the Manipur valley.

MAPHITEL OR NUPITEL—

The range bounding the Thobal valley on the east. It connects the great mass of hills north and north-east of Manipur with the Yumadoung range.

Its highest peak is 6,716 feet above the sea. The western face is very steep and covered with dense forest on the eastern side. The spurs are longer and easier and the jungle lighter.

From the south peak, communication with flag or heliograph could be kept up with Makku-Leiching and several points on the Chandwakong and Ingovok routes.

MAPUM—

A Tankul village, built after the usual Tankul pattern, about 5,000 feet above the sea-level, containing 40 houses.

Inhabitants.—The inhabitants belong to the north-eastern section of the Tankul Naga tribe. Population 200, of whom 40 may be fighting-men. The chief is Lushaie.

Climate.—The climate is healthy at all seasons.

Water.—Small supply on west of village.

Supplies.—Rice-straw procurable. Scanty grazing. Principal grains are rice and múm. Firewood plentiful. Arum and pumpkins. Rice harvest in November; múm in December.

Live-stock.—Pigs and poultry.

Transport.—For coolie purposes, 40 men, women, and children.

Timber.—Chiefly oak and fir.—(*Lieut. Dun, 1881 82.*)

MARAM—

A peak on the southern (Khunho) spur of Japvo.

Elevation.—6,167 feet.

MARÁM-KULEL—

A Kolya village of the Marám section, west of the Manipur-Kohima road, on a level with Maithaipham thannah.

Elevation.—6,000 feet.

Climate.—Healthy at all seasons.

Houses.—500, Naga pattern.

Inhabitants.—2,000.

Fighting-men.—150.

Water.—Plentiful.

Camping-ground.—Sufficient for 400 men, south of the village.

Grazing, Products, &c.—*Vide* page 78, Charo.

Live-stock.—300 cows, pigs, and poultry.

Carriage.—200 coolies.

Approaches—Up gentle open spur from the south. From the Barak river and from where the Kohima road crosses the ridge on which it is situated.

These people are untrustworthy and somewhat savage.

The headman is now in hiding from the Manipuri authorities, his Kheyl having recently murdered an Angami Naga.

MARAM KUNAO—

A Kolya Naga village on the spur west of the Manipuri-Kohima road between Karong and Maithipham.

Elevation.—4,500 feet.

Climate.—Healthy at all seasons.

Houses.—17, Naga pattern.

Population.—10, Maram clan.

Water and Camping-ground.—Sufficient for 200 men.

Products, &c.—*Vide* page 78, Charo.

Live-stock.—20 cows, pigs, and poultry.

Carriage.—25 coolies.

MAREM-KULEL—

A Tankul village, built after the usual Tankul pattern, about 5,000 feet above the sea-level, containing 60 houses.

Inhabitants.—The inhabitants belong to the north-eastern section of the Tankul Naga tribe. Population 300, of whom 60 may be fighting-men. The most influential man is Kui-Kui (interpreter).

Climate.—The climate is healthy at all seasons.

Supplies.—Rice-straw procurable. Scanty grazing. Principal grains are chayan and múm. Firewood plentiful. Arum and pumpkins. Harvest in November and early part of December.

Live-stock.—Pigs, poultry, and a few metna.

Transport.—For coolie purposes, 60 men, women, and children.

Timber.—Chiefly oak and fir.—(*Lieut. Dun, 1881-82.*)

MAREM-KUNAO—

A Tankul village, built after the usual Tankul pattern, about 5,000 feet above the sea-level, containing 30 houses.

Inhabitants.—The inhabitants belong to the north-eastern section of the Tankul Naga tribe. Population 150, of whom 30 may be fighting-men. The most influential man is Asawa.

Climate.—The climate is healthy at all seasons.

Supplies.—Rice-straw procurable. Scanty grazing. Principal grains are chayan and múm. Firewood plentiful. Arum and pumpkins. Harvest in November and early part of December.

Live-stock.—Pigs, poultry, and a few metna.

Transport.—For coolie purposes, 30 men, women, and children.

Timber.—Chiefly oak and fir.—(*Lieut. Dun, 1881-82.*)

MARO—

A Tankul village, built after the usual Tankul pattern, about 4,000 feet above the sea-level, containing 10 houses.

Inhabitants.—The inhabitants belong to the south-western section of the Tankul Naga tribe. Population 50, of whom 10 may be fighting-men. The headman is Maletopa.

Climate.—The climate is unhealthy from beginning of August to end of October.

Supplies.—Rice-straw procurable. Scanty grazing. Principal grains are rice and múm. Firewood plentiful. Arum, yams, and pumpkins. Rice harvest in November; múm in December.

Live-stock.—Pigs and poultry.

Transport.—For coolie purposes, 10 men, women, and children.
Timber.—Oak and fir plentiful.—(*Lieut. Dun, 1881-82.*)

MARONGKONG—

One of the streams of the Somrah basin, North-East Manipur.

MATSEN—

A Burmese village on the Ava-Kendat road. It is a few miles east of the Ningthee river, situated in a valley about a mile in width, nearly all under cultivation, with a good many black cattle and buffaloes. It is bounded on the west by a low range of hills, and to the east by high hills running off in ridges to the north. The little villages in this valley, through which the Choung Magyee flows from the Thanaka hills, go by the general name of Matsen, and are said to amount in all to about 400 houses.

(*Dr. Richardson.*)

MAUKOT—

A Chussad village on the Ponk-Kongal road, built after the usual Chussad pattern, about 2,400 feet above the sea-level.

The village, together with that of Chowhoom, covers any advance on Tounghoo from the north, but is itself commanded by the road.

Camping-ground.—There is open ground, fairly level, for a small force on the east side of the village.

Approaches—Down easy slope from north; no jungle. From this side the village is commanded. Up easy slope from south, thick jungle, and no view of the village.

Defences.—The northern approach is defended by a palisade across a narrow part of the ridge.

Inhabitants.—The inhabitants belong to the Chussad subdivision of the Kongjai Kuki tribe. Population 115, of whom 35 are fighting-men. The head and most influential man is Daulet.

Climate.—The climate is unhealthy from beginning of August to end of October.

Water.—Plentiful supply close to village.

Supplies.—Rice-straw procurable. Fair grazing. Principal grains are Indian-corn, job's-tears, rice, and múm. Firewood plentiful. Arum, beans, and pumpkins. Rice harvest in November; múm in December.

Live-stock.—Pigs and poultry.

Transport.—For coolie purposes, 23 men and women.

Timber.—Many kinds; oaks and firs plentiful.—(*Lieut. Dun, 1881-82.*)

MAW-LONE—

A village in the Kubbo valley, about 23 miles from Samjok.

(*Phayre, 1881-82.*)

MAYANG-KHANG—

A subdivision of the Koyla Naga tribe. (*Vide* Naga.)

MAYANG-KHANG THANNAH—

The third march from Kohima on the Manipur-Kohima route.

Camping-ground.—Plenty of camping-ground.

Surrounding Country.—The thannah is situated on the flat bottom of a valley, which is here about 500 yards broad, and is commanded by the hills on the west.

Water.—Plentiful supply.

Supplies.—Grazing very scanty, even when the grass has been burnt at the proper time.—(*Lieut. Dun, 1881-82*).

MEIE—

A stream in Manipur which, uniting with the waters of the Kunokong, forms the Napanga river.—(*Lieut. Dun, 1881-82.*)

MEKITHODZOMI or MAITHAIPHAM—

A Kolya Naga village of the Maithaipham section, east of the Kohima road, and south-east of Maithaipham thannah.

Elevation.—5,300 feet.

Climate.—Healthy at all seasons.

Houses.—140, Naga pattern.

Water and Camping-ground.—Plentiful.

Products, &c.—*Vide* page 78, Charo.

Live-stock.—200 cows, pigs, and poultry.

Carriage.—160 coolies.

MELLOMI—

A Naga village as yet unclassified, and the people of which are merely called "Naked," Nagas.

Elevation.—About 3,000 feet.

Climate.—Unhealthy for the greater part of the year.

Houses and Fighting-men.—About 700.

Water.—Scanty.

Camping-ground.—Sufficient open ground for 200 men on the southern side of the village, and for 1,000 men with transport along the spur one mile to the south.

There is ample accommodation on the banks of the Lanier, below the spur, on which the village is built, and plenty of excellent water.

Products, &c.—*Vide* page 78, Charo.

There are some magnificent clumps of giant bamboo on the southern and western borders of the village.

Approaches—By a path at an easy slope through light jungle from Persami, on the south-west a similar path but steeper, from the Lanier on the south east, and by path along the face of the hills to the next village to the east. The entrances to the village are stockaded and have flanking defence. The inhabitants are armed with cross-bows, which give them great prestige with the neighbouring villages.

MELNUI—

A Shan village, built after the usual Shan pattern, about 700 feet above the sea-level, containing 8 houses.

Inhabitants.—The inhabitants belong to the Shan tribe. Population 40, of whom 8 may be fighting men.

Climate.—The climate is unhealthy from beginning of June to end of October.

Supplies.—Rice-straw procurable. Scanty grazing. Principal grains are Indian-corn, rice, múm, and chayan. Firewood plentiful. Arum, beans, and pumpkins. Harvest in November and early part of December.

Live-stock.—Pigs and poultry.

Transport.—For coolie purposes, 8 men and women.

Timber.—No oaks or firs; other kinds plentiful.—(*Lieut. Dun, 1881-82.*)

MENEE—
One of the principal towns on the Moo river.

MENTHA—
A Shan village on the road from Yanga-pokpi road to Tummoo, through the Kubbo valley, about 2 miles from the former place.—(*Phayre, 1881-82.*)

MIKHIR—
A little stream crossed by the Kohima road, just above Maithaipham.

MIMA—
An Angami village, built after the usual Angami pattern, about 4,500 feet above the sea-level, containing 100 houses.

Inhabitants.—The inhabitants belong to the Angami Naga tribe, and are divided into three subdivisions, *viz.*, Jama, Safema, and Risomai. Population 500, of whom 100 may be fighting-men. There is no chief, but Tazole has most influence.

Climate.—The climate is healthy at all seasons.

Supplies.—Rice-straw procurable. Fair grazing. Principal grains are rice, múm, and chayan. Rather moderate supply of firewood. Arum and pumpkins. Harvest in November and December.

Live-stock.—Cows in large numbers, pigs, and poultry.

Transport.—For coolie purposes, 100 men, women, and children.

Timber.—Very little fir or oak; small pollarded alders; bamboos scarce. (*Lieut. Dun, 1881-82.*)

MITHNA.—Manipuri name for hill cattle.

MOLNUI—
A Chussad village close to Chunyang and Changlé, on the Pong-Kongal route, built after the usual Chussad pattern, about 2,000 feet above the sea-level, containing 15 houses.

Camping-ground and Approaches.—*Vide* Chunyang, the villages being close together.

Inhabitants.—The inhabitants belong to the Chussad subdivision of the Kongjai Kuki tribe. Population 75, of whom 23 are fighting-men. The head and most influential man is Kamtong.

Climate.—The climate is unhealthy from beginning of August to end of October.

Water.—Plentiful supply close.

Supplies.—Rice-straw procurable. Fair grazing. Principal grains are Indian-corn, job's-tears, and rice. Firewood plentiful. Arum, beans, and pumpkins. Harvest in November and December.

Live-stock.—Pigs and poultry.

Transport.—For coolie purposes, 23 men and women.

Timber.—Many kinds; oaks and firs plentiful.—(*Lieut. Dun, 1881-82.*)

MONAING-MYO—
An important town on the Moo river.

MONBI—
A new Kuki village of the Mangvung clan, situated at the head-waters of the Chakpi in South-East Manipur.

Elevation.—3,500 feet.

Houses.—60, Kuki pattern.

Water and Camping-ground.—Said to be plentiful.
Products, &c.—*Vide* page 77, Chanjang.
Headman.—Mulshong, friendly and a man of some consequence.
Live-stock.—Fifteen metna, pigs, and poultry.
Carriage.—100 coolies.

MONDRO-KULEL—

A Kaupui Naga village, north of the Cachar road, close to Irang thannah.
Elevation.—3,500 feet.
Houses.—35, Naga pattern.
Water and Camping-ground.—Apparently very little of either at the village, but sufficient for 200 men on the Lengba stream just below.
Products, &c.—*Vide* page 78, Charo.
Live-stock.—Pigs and poultry.
Carriage.—50 coolies.
Approaches—Along steep jungle-covered spurs from the Lengba river and Irang thannah.

MONGHLAM—

A new Kuki village of the Hawkib clan in the Turbung valley.
Elevation.—2,800 feet.
Temperature and Climate.—*Vide* page 77, Chanjang.
Houses.—9.
Water and Camping-ground.—Plentiful.
Products, &c.—*Vide* 77, Chanjang.

MONGTEU—

A new Kuki village of the Simmté clan in the valley of the Manipur branch of the Tipai river.
Elevation.—3,000 feet.
Houses.—20.
Water.—
Camping-ground.— } *Vide* page 77, Chanjang.
Products, &c.—
Headman.—Ginshing, friendly.

MONTHOW—

A Manipur village, about 15 miles east of the Imphal.

MOOLONG—

A Shan village, 12 miles from Kongal thannah on the Kongal-Samjok road, built after the usual Shan pattern, about 700 feet above the sea-level, containing 10 houses.
Inhabitants.—The inhabitants belong to the Shan tribe. Population 50, of whom 10 may be fighting-men.
Climate.—The climate is unhealthy from beginning of June to end of October.
Water.—Plentiful supply.
Supplies.—Rice-straw procurable. Scanty grazing. Principal grains are Indian-corn, rice, múm, and chayan. Firewood plentiful. Arum, beans, pumpkins, and plantains. Harvest in November and early part of December.
Live-stock.—Pigs, poultry, and buffaloes.
Transport.—For coolie purposes, 18 men and women.
Timber.—Teak, sál, &c.—(*Lieut. Dun, 1881-82.*)

MORAY* THANNAH—

A Manipur frontier post, on the eastern edge of the Yumadoung range north-west of Tummoo, forming one of the third or outer line of posts.

It is situated on the broad flat end of a spur coming down from the hills, and is about 30 feet above the level of the valley. It lies between two considerable streams, the Kujierok and the Lierok, which unite at its north-eastern corner.

Defences.—It is about 80 yards square, and would accommodate a large garrison than there is at present.

The stockade is composed of one row of 6-inch timbers, 25 feet high. No flanking defences and no obstacles. The timbers are wide apart, and an attacking force could fire into the thannah just as easily as the defenders could fire out.

Surrounding Country.—It is not commanded on any side; the jungle around is light, but comes up to the stockade on the south and west; on the north is a village; on the east the ground is cleared for 300 yards.

Attack.—The Kujierok stream offers good cover to assailants, but on the whole the west and south would be the best points from which to attack.

Camping-ground.—There is plenty of good camping-ground.

Garrison.—The garrison consists of 1 subadar, 1 jemadar, 1 havildar, and 40 sepoys.

The place is used also as a penal settlement for women who have committed murder.—(*Lieut. Dun, 1881-82; Major Badgeley, 1881-82.*)

MORLUNG—

A Burmese town, about 16 miles nearly south of Kongal thannah.

(*Major Badgeley, 1881-82.*)

MOUKKADAN-MYO—

A Burmese village, containing about 100 houses, close to the left bank of the Ningthee. A good deal of trade in timber and carpentering work. Boats of considerable size are built here, and good-sized teak is cut in the neighbourhood.

This village is the most southern place subject to the Khampat Woon.

(*Lieut. Dun, 1881-82.*)

MOUNG YAUN—

A Burmese village of considerable size at a little distance from the Ningthee. Carts can be obtained here.—(*Lieut. Dun, 1881-82.*)

MOUNT ZOBO—

This is the walled Burmese city of 2 miles square, famous as the birth-place of Alompra; the walls, principally of bricks and partly of a kind of slate, are in pretty good repair, though the city was at one time entirely abandoned, and has only of late years been reoccupied. It is said to contain 1,000 houses, and there are extensive paddy-fields to the north and westward between the inner brick walls and outer wall or mound round which is the ditch.

To the southward there is no earthen wall, and the ditch is close to the brick walls. It is without flanking defences to any extent. The inner small fort, or palace enclosure, is entirely without inhabitants. There is a pagoda of considerable size.—(*Richardson.*)

* Usually spelt and marked on the map "Moreh."

MOWAIE—

A Tankul village, built after the usual Tankul pattern, about 4,000 feet above the sea-level, containing 40 houses.

Inhabitants.—The inhabitants belong to the south-western section of the Tankul Naga tribe. Population 200, of whom 40 may be fighting-men.

Climate.—The climate is unhealthy from beginning of August to end of October.

Supplies.—Rice-straw procurable. Scanty grazing. Principal grains are rice and múm. Firewood plentiful. Arum, yams, and pumpkins. Rice harvest in November; múm in December.

Live-stock.—Pigs and poultry.

Transport.—For coolies purposes, 40 men, women, and children.

Timber.—Oaks and firs plentiful.—(*Lieut. Dun, 1881-82.*)

MOWKEET—

A Chussad village containing 20 houses, belonging to Tonghu's group. (*Col. Johnstone, 1881-82.*)

MOYJING—

A Manipuri village on the Thobal river, south of the Thobal villages.

Elevation.—
Temperature.—
Climate.— } *Vide* page 77, Changangai.

Houses.—25, Manipuri pattern.

Inhabitants.—125, sepoy class.

Fighting-men.—25.

Products, &c.—*Vide* page 77, Changangai.

Water.—Plentiful.

Live-stock.—50 cows, 37 buffaloes.

Carriage.—25 carts, 12 boats.

Approaches—By good mule-path along the banks of the river.

MOYONG-KULEL—

An Anal village in South-Eastern Manipur.

Garrison.—The garrison consists of 1 subadar, 1 jemadar, 1 havildar, and 40 sepoys.

The place is used also as a penal settlement for women who have committed murder.—(*Lieut. Dun, 1881-82; Major Badgeley.*)

MUITHOW—

A Tankul village, built after the usual Tankul pattern, about 4,000 feet above the sea-level, containing 10 houses.

Inhabitants.—The inhabitants belong to the south-western section of the Tankul Naga tribe. Population 50, of whom 10 may be fighting-men.

Climate.—The climate is unhealthy from beginning of August to end of October.

Supplies.—Rice-straw procurable. Scanty grazing. Principal grains are rice and múm. Firewood plentiful. Arum, yams, and pumpkins. Rice harvest in November; múm in December.

Live-stock.—Pigs and poultry.

Transport.—For coolie purposes, 815 men, women, and children.

Timber.—Oak and fir plentiful.—(*Lieut. Dun, 1881-82.*)

MUKRU-RIVER—

Rising east of the Jiri from the hills to the north near the Burail range, which separates the watershed of Assam from that of Manipur, it flows south and falls into the Barak, about 18 miles below the point at which it is crossed by the road to Cachar. The Mukru is not navigable for any part of its course. This stream is beautifully clear, about 45 yards board, and well stocked with mahseer fish. It is easily fordable in the dry season; the bottom is of large pebbles and round water-worn stones; the water about knee-deep.

A cane suspension bridge, strengthened with wire and passable by laden coolies in single file, spans the river at a height of about 100 feet above the stream.

MUNGHLAM—

A Hawkib village, built after the usual Kuki pattern, about 3,500 feet above the sea-level, containing 50 houses.

Inhabitants.—The inhabitants belong to the Hawkib subdivision of the Konjai Kuki tribe. Population 250, of whom 75 may be fighting-men.

Climate.—The climate is unhealthy from beginning of August to end of October.

Supplies.—Rice-straw procurable. Scanty grazing. Principal grains are Indian-corn, job's-tears, rice, and múm. Firewood plentiful. Arum, beans, and pumpkins. Rice harvest in November; múm in December.

Live-stock.—Pigs and poultry.

Transport.—For coolie purposes, 40 men and women.

Timber.—All kinds plentiful, except oak and fir.—(*Lieut. Dun, 1881-82.*)

MUNGPAH—

A Tankul village, built after the usual Tankul pattern, about 3,500 feet above the sea-level, containing 10 houses.

Inhabitants.—The inhabitants belong to the south-western section of the Tankul Naga tribe. Population 50, of whom 10 may be fighting-men.

Climate.—The climate is unhealthy from beginning of August to end of October.

Supplies.—Rice-straw procurable. Scanty grazing. Principal grains are rice and múm. Firewood plentiful. Arum, yams, and pumpkins. Rice harvest in November; múm in December.

Live-stock.—Pigs and poultry.

Transport.—For coolie purposes, 10 men and women.

Timber.—Bamboos, a few oaks, and firs; other kinds plentiful.

(*Lieut. Dun, 1881-82.*)

MUNGSA—

A Shan village in the Kubbo valley, on the route from Khanpat to Taap thannah, built after the usual Shan pattern, about 700 feet above the sea-level, containing 15 or 20 houses.

Camping-ground.—There should be any quantity available.

Approaches—By broad path through forest land, perfectly flat and not artificially defended.

Signal Stations.—A suitable station might be found from which to communicate with Kambang thannah.

Inhabitants.—The inhabitants belong to the Shan tribe. Population 75, of whom 15 may be fighting-men.

Climate.—The climate is unhealthy from beginning of June to end of October.

Water.—Plentiful supply.

Supplies.—Rice-straw procurable. Fair grazing. Principal grain is rice. Firewood plentiful. Plantains, yams, and pumpkins. Harvest in November and early part of December.

Live-stock.—Pigs, poultry, and buffaloes.

Transport.—For coolie purposes, 15 men and women.

Timber.—Teak, sál, and bamboo.—(*Lieut. Dun, 1881-82.*)

MURI-YANG-KUNAO—

An Anal village in South-Eastern Manipur.

MYAGO—

A Burmese village on the Ava-Kendat route, close to a small nala, in a richly cultivated country.

MYE-DU—

An important Burmese town on the Moo river. It is celebrated as having been the scene of many contests between the Burmese and Manipuris.

N

NAIKONG—

A Manipuri village, 1½ miles east of Bishenpur.

Elevation— }
Temperature.— } *Vide* page 77, Changangai.
Climate.— }

Houses.—40, Manipuri pattern.

Inhabitants.—200, sepoy class.

Water.— }
Camping-ground.— } *Vide* page 77, Changangai.
Products.— }

Live-stock.—80 cows, 60 buffaloes.

Carriage.—40 carts, 10 boats.

Approaches—By narrow path through rice cultivation from Bishenpur.

NALTHANGIT—

A village, containing 30 houses, between Toungban and Samjok; from the latter place it is 1 mile distant, on the Kongal-Samjok road.

Camping-ground.—A fine plain, half a mile square.

(*Major Badgeley*, 1881-82.)

NALTHANGIT—

A river crossed by the road from Kongal to Samjok, at the village of Tschdaugon. In the cold weather there is 1 foot of water.

(*Major Badgeley*, 1881-82.)

NAMBOL (EASTERN)—

One of the streams which flows through Imphal. It enters at the northern end, but brings in little water. It is apparently an old bed of the stream, called in various parts of its course, Tiki, Achanba and Imphal, and it has cut deep into the alluvial soil. Shortly after entering Imphal and at the western end of the main bazaar it receives the surplus water of the Lamphal jheel; just below this point it passes under the only brick bridge now standing in the Manipur. The nala in which the Nambol runs is here some 60 yards round at the top, 20 deep, and has steep earth sides. There are only a few feet of water in the cold weather, and it is then fordable at any point; but in the rains the water rises regularly to within 3 or 4 feet of the top of the channel.

The bridge is of solid construction, has three spans, and a 15 feet roadway (inside measurement).

NAMBOL (WESTERN)—

A stream, 9 miles from Imphal on the Cachar road.

The road crosses it at this point. It is here 20 yards wide. The banks are steep and earthy, 20 feet high and 40 yards apart at the top.

There is a bridge of bamboo matting laid upon a frame, and uprights of wood, and practicable for mules, though not for wheeled-carriages.

NAMBOL OR FOYJING OR BORI BAZAAR—

A Manipuri village on the Cachar road, 9 miles from Imphal.

Elevation.— }
Temperature.— } *Vide* page 77, Changangai.
Climate.— }

Houses.—150, Manipuri pattern.
Inhabitants.—750, sepoy class.
Fighting-men.—150.
Water.—Plentiful.
Camping-ground and Products.—*Vide* page 77, Changangai.
Live-stock.—300, cows, 225 buffaloes, poultry.
Carriage.—150 carts, 50 ponies, 30 boats.
Approaches.—(1) along Cachar road; (2) by path through rice-fields from Ulao. There is a large bazaar held here daily.

NAMCHIELO—

A stream crossed by the road from Yanga-pokpi to Moray thannah, at which point it is 40 yards broad, has 6 inches of water, and a 6-foot perpendicular bank.—(*Lieut. Dun, 1881-82.*)

NAMLI—

A Tankul village, built after the usual Tankul pattern, about 5,000 feet above the sea-level, containing 30 houses.

Inhabitants.—The inhabitants belong to the north-eastern section of the Tankul Naga tribe. Population 150, of whom 80 may be fighting-men. The most influential man is Changson (interpreter).
Climate.—The climate is healthy at all seasons.
Supplies.—Rice-straw procurable. Scanty grazing. Principal grains are rice and múm. Firewood plentiful. Arum, yams, and pumpkins. Rice harvest in November; múm in December.
Live-stock.—Pigs, poultry, and a few metna.
Transport.—For coolie purposes, 30 men and women.
Timber.—Bamboos, a few oaks and firs, and great many other trees.
(*Lieut. Dun, 1881-82.*)

NAMMEA—

A river of the Kubbo valley, and forming the boundary between Manipur and Burma for some distance as far as its source. It passes near Kongal thannah, at which point it is 40 feet wide, low banks, and 6 inches of water, with pebbly bottom.

The Nammea is characteristic of the rivers of the Kubbo valley, being a bright little stream running swiftly over a pebbly bed. Its banks are about 4 feet high, cut perpendicularly out of the sandy loam which forms the soil of the valley.—(*Lieut. Dun, 1881-82.*)

NAMNAIVÚNG—

A new Kuki village of the Changsen clan, south-west of Kanpum plateau.
Elevation.—About 4,000 feet.
Temperature and Climate.—*Vide* page 78, Charo.
Houses.—60, Kuki pattern.
Water.—, *Camping-ground.*—, *Products.*— } *Vide* page 77, Chanjang.
Live-stock.—A few metna, pigs, and poultry.
Carriage.—70 coolies.
Approaches.—Not visited; the path from Manipur territory to this village passes through Lenglong.
Headman.—Namnaivung, said to be friendly.

NAMPESAH—

A Tankul village, about 6 miles from the Burmese frontier, built after the usual Tankul pattern, 3,000 feet above sea-level, containing 150 houses.

A strong post of observation was established here by the Manipuris in 1878 to repel attacks of Burmese Nagas.

Camping-ground.—There appears to be small amount.

Approaches—Along a narrow ridge from both east and west. Steep ascent from the east. Easy descent from west.

Inhabitants—The inhabitants belong to the south-western section of the Tankul Naga tribe. Population 150, of whom 30 may be fighting men. The most influential man is Kassirong (interpreter).

Climate.—The climate is unhealthy from beginning of August to end of October.

Supplies.—Rice-straw procurable. Scanty grazing. Principal grains are rice and múm. Firewood plentiful. Arum, yams, and pumpkins. Rice harvest in November; múm in December.

Live-stock.—Pigs and poultry.

Transport.—For coolie purposes, 36 men and women.

Timber.—Bamboos, a few oaks and firs, and a great number of other trees.

(*Lieut. Dun, 1881-82.*)

NAMTREE—

A Kubbo village on the Tamoo-Taap road.

NAMUSI—

A Tankul village, a little way off the Ingorok-Kongal road, built after the usual Tankul pattern, about 3,000 feet about the sea-level, containing 12 houses.

Approaches.—The village is out of sight of the road.

Inhabitants.—The inhabitants belong to the south-western section of the Tankul Naga tribe. Population 60, of whom 12 may be fighting-men. The most influential man is Kumputamba.

Climate.—The climate is unhealthy from beginning of August to end of October.

Supplies.—Rice-straw procurable. Scanty grazing. Principal grains are rice and múm. Firewood plentiful. Arum, pumpkins, and yams. Rice harvest in November; múm in December.

Live-stock.—Pigs and poultry.

Transport.—For coolie purposes, 12 men and women.

Timber.—Bamboos, a few oaks and firs, and a great number of other trees.

(*Lieut. Dun, 1881-82.*)

NANG—

A Chussad village, built after the usual Chussad pattern, about 2,000 feet above the sea-level, containing 10 houses.

Inhabitants.—The inhabitants belong to the Chussad subdivision of the Kongjai Kuki tribe. Population 50, of whom 15 may be fighting-men. The chief and most influential man is Kanpu.

Climate.—The climate is unhealthy from beginning of August to end of October.

Supplies.—Rice-straw procurable. Principal grains are Indian-corn, job's-tears, rice, and múm. Firewood plentiful. Arum, beans, and pumpkins. Rice harvest in November; múm in December.—(*Lieut. Dun, 1881-82.*)

NANTHE—

A Burmese village of 40 or 50 houses with extensive paddy-fields, many black cattle, and a few horses. It is on the Ava-Kendat route, about 16 miles from the latter place.

NANUNG—

A subdivision of the Angami Naga tribe. (*Vide* Naga.)

NAPANGA—

A river draining a portion of the Yomadoung range, formed by the junction of the Kinokong and Meié waters. For some distance it is the boundary between Manipur and Burma.

NARAINDHUR—

(*Vide* Looshai.)

NARUM—

A Marring village, built after the usual Marring pattern, about 3,000 feet above the sea-level, containing 6 houses.

Inhabitants.—The inhabitants belong to the Marring Naga tribe. Population 30, of whom 9 may be fighting-men. The headman is Tolah.

Climate.—The climate is unhealthy from beginning of August to end of October.

Water.—Scanty supply.

Supplies.—Rice-straw procurable. Fair grazing. Principal grains are Indian-corn, rice, múm, and chayan. Firewood plentiful. Arum, beans, pumpkins, and plantains. Harvest in November and early part of December.

Live stock.—Pigs, poultry, and 10 metna.

Transport.—For coolie purposes, 6 men and women.

Timber.—All kinds except fir; oak not common.—(*Lieut. Dun, 1881-82.*)

NASINGA THANNAH—

A Manipur frontier post, forming one of the third or outer line, on the eastern edge of the Yomadoung range. It is half a day's journey from Punsa, 10 hours from Tamoo.—(*Lieut. Dun, 1882.*)

NATA-KOIRENG—

A small Koireng village on the eastern face of the Laimatol-Kopra range, due west of Imphal.

NATA-KUN—

A small Koireng village, a mile to the south of Nata-Koireng.

NATCHI—

A Manipuri village in South-West Manipur, 3 miles south of Bishenpur Thanna.

Elevation.—
Temperature.—
Climate.— } *Vide* page 77, Changangai.

Houses.—40, Manipuri pattern.

Inhabitants.—200, grass-cutters to the Raja.

Water.—
Camping-ground.—
Products, &c.— } *Vide* page 77, Changangai.

Live-stock.—80 cows, 60 buffaloes.

Carriage.—40 carts, 10 boats.

Approaches—Over rice cultivation by narrow paths from Bishenpur, Kujmán, and the Moitrang road.

NAT-THANYIT—

A village close to Samjok on the Kongal-Samjok route.

(*Phayre, 1881-82; Lieut. Dun, 1881-82.*)

NAT-THANYIT—

A small stream on which the village of the same name is situated.

NAUYANGTE—

A new Kuki village of the Hawkib clan on the western face of the Laimatol range, close to and north of the Cachar road.

Elevation.—4,900 feet.

Temperature.—38° at sunrise in January.

Climate.—Healthy at all seasons.

Houses.—19, Kuki pattern.

Water.—Scanty. Below village both on the north and south sides.

Camping-ground.—No level ground and no uncleared ground. 100 men could find accommodation on the edge of the Cachar road.

Live-stock.—A few metna, pigs, and poultry.

Products, &c.—*Vide* page 77, Changangai.

Carriage.—25 coolies.

Approaches—Up a steep jungle-covered spur from the Cachar road on the south.

NELIKONG—

The eastern branch of the Chattik-Kassom valley stream.

NENGTA-NEGOL—

A small Kaupui hamlet, close to the western edge of Imphal.

NEUPHONG—

A peak on the range, sometimes known as Sakoak-Ling, from the name of two villages situated at its northern and southern ends respectively, and between the Tuyungba and the Maglang.

Elevation.—5,818 feet.

NGAIRONGBAM—

A Manipuri village, 8 miles to the east of Imphal.

NGAKARHONG—

A Kaupui village in North-West Manipur.

NGA-PA-YA—

A Burmese village between Dubayen and the Ningthee.

NGAREAMBAM—

A Manipuri village, 4 miles north-west of Imphal.

NINGTHAUKONG—

A Manipuri village on the road between Bishenpur and Moirang, 5 miles from Bishenpur.

Elevation.—
Temperature.— } *Vide* page 77, Changangai.
Climate.—

Houses.—60, Manipuri pattern.

Inhabitants.—300, employed as servants to the Maiyang Ningthan or Western Raja, an hereditary chief who lives at this village.

Fighting-men.—60.

Camping-ground.—Unlimited on slightly raised grassy land, west of the road.
Water.—Good and plentiful. Stream from the hills.
Products, &c.—*Vide* page 77, Changangai.
Live-stock.—120 cows, 20 buffaloes.
Carriage.—60 carts, 15 boats.
Approaches.—Bishenpur-Moirang or western valley road.

NINGTHI—

Tankul village, built after the usual Tankul pattern, about 3,000 feet above the sea-level, containing 7 houses.
Inhabitants.—The inhabitants belong to the south-western section of the Tankul Naga tribe. Population 35, of whom 7 may be fighting-men.
Climate.—The climate is unhealthy from beginning of August to end of October.
Water.—Scanty supply distant.
Supplies.—Rice-straw procurable. Scanty grazing. Principal grains are rice and múm. Firewood plentiful. Arum, yams, and pumpkins. Rice harvest in November; múm in December.
Live-stock.—Pigs and poultry.
Transports.—For coolie purposes, 7 men and women.
Timber.—Bamboos, a few oaks and firs, and a great number of other trees.
(*Lieut. Dun, 1881-82.*)

NINGTHI OR CHIN-DWEN—

A large river of Burma. At Samjok, in December, it is 700 yards broad and 50 feet deep (in the stream). It flows at the rate of one mile an hour. Probably the Ningthi is little affected by the melting of snow in the hot weather.
Navigability.—Specially built trading steamers, belonging to the King of Burma, have at all times of the year been brought up as far as Kendat. The Burma Trading Company are now building vessels with the same object. A steam launch drawing 4 feet of water has been up as far as Kaksa, but was there stopped by the rapids. Small boats, however, ascend two months' journey higher up.
Means of crossing.—At Samjok there are six large boats of 500 maunds burden. At Kendat there are large numbers of boats of all sizes.
Fords.—There are no fords at either Kaksa, Samjok, or Kendat.
The banks being covered with forest, means of crossing troops could easily be devised.—(*Lieut. Dun, 1881-82.*)

NINGYEL—

A Manipuri (Loï) village at the western foot of the Yumadoung range, a little south of the exit of the Thobal river from the hills.
Elevation.—
Temperature.— } *Vide* page 77, Changangai.
Climate.—
Houses.—25, Manipuri pattern.
Inhabitants.—25, salt-makers.
Water.—Good and plentiful.
Camping-ground, Products, &c.—*Vide* page 77, Changangai.
Live-stock.—50 cows, 37 buffaloes.
Carriage.—45 coolies, 25 carts.
Approaches—By mule-path; good in dry weather, through rice cultivation.

NONAI—

A small Kaupui village in North-Western Manipur.

NONEH—

A small Kaupui village in North-Western Manipur.

NONGMAICHING—

A peak within the Manipur valley and separating the Thobal valley from that of the Iril and Imphal.

It is the chief firewood preserve for the Raja and royal household.

The top of the peak is 5,133 feet above the sea.

NONGNANG—

A Kaupui village in Western Manipur, a day's march north of the Cachar road and within the drainage of the Irang.

Elevation.—About 3,000 feet.

House.—70, Naga pattern.

Fighting-men.—70.

Water and Camping-ground.—Believed to be plenty of both.

Products.—*Vide* page 78, Charo.

Carriage.—Probably 100 coolies.

Approaches.—From the point where the Cachar road crosses the Irang by a narrow path through dense forest.

NONGTEK—

A small Kaupui Naga village in North-West Manipur.

NUNDEH—

A Tipperah village, about 3,000 feet above the sea-level, containing 7 houses.

Inhabitants.—Population 35, of whom 7 may be fighting-men. The headman is Meitak.

Climate.—The climate is unhealthy from beginning of August to end of October.

Supplies.—Rice-straw procurable. Fair grazing. Principal grains are rice and múm. Firewood plentiful. Plantains, yams, and pumpkins. Harvest in November and early part of December.

Live-stock.—Pigs and poultry.

Transport.—For coolie purposes, 7 men and women.

Timber.—No heavy timber; small oaks, &c.; no firs.—(*Lieut. Dun, 1881-82.*)

NUNGBI—

A Tankul village, built after the usual Tankul pattern, about 5,000 feet above the sea-level, containing 100 houses.

Camping-ground.—Terraced rice-fields available.

Inhabitants.—The inhabitants belong to the north-eastern section of the Tankul Naga tribe. Population 500, of whom 100 may be fighting-men. The most influential man is Pheiomatol.

Climate.—The climate is healthy at all seasons.

Water.—A small supply on the east.

Supplies.—Rice-straw procurable. Scanty grazing. Principal grains are rice and múm. Firewood plentiful. Pumpkins, yams, and arum. Rice harvest in November; múm in December.

Live-stock.—Pigs, poultry, and a few buffaloes or metna.

Transport.—For coolie purposes, 100 men and women.

Timber.—Bamboos scarce; oaks, firs, &c., plentiful.—(*Lieut. Dun, 1881-82.*)

NUNG-DUM—

A Manipuri village, about 15 miles east of the Imphal.

NUNGHAR—

A Tankul village, built after the usual Tankul pattern, about 5,000 feet above the sea-level, containing 70 houses.

Camping-ground.—Terraced rice-fields available.

Inhabitants.—The inhabitants belong to the north-eastern section of the Tankul Naga tribe. Population 350, of whom 70 may be fighting-men. The chief is Múbah.

Climate.—The climate is healthy at all seasons.

Water.—A small supply, both on the north and south.

Supplies.—Rice-straw procurable. Scanty grazing. Principal grains are rice and múm. Firewood plentiful. Arum, yams, and pumpkins. Rice harvest in November; múm in December.

Live-stock.—Pigs, poultry, and a few buffaloes or metna.

Transport.—For coolie purposes, 70 men and women.

Timber.—Bamboos scarce; oaks, firs, &c., plentiful.—(*Lieut. Dun, 1881-82.*)

NUNGPUNG—

A Tankul village, built after the usual Tankul pattern, about 4,000 feet above the sea-level, containing 30 houses.

Inhabitants.—The inhabitants belong to the north-eastern section of the Tankul Naga tribe. Population 150, of whom 30 may be fighting-men. The most influential man is As-awah (interpreter).

Climate.—The climate is healthy at all seasons.

Supplies.—Rice-straw procurable. Scanty grazing. Principal grains are rice and múm. Firewood plentiful. Arum, yams, and pumpkins. Rice harvest in November; múm in December.

Live-stock.—Pigs and poultry.

Transport.—For coolie purposes, 30 men and women.

Timber.—Bamboos scarce; oaks, firs, &c., plentiful.—(*Lieut. Dun, 1881-82.*)

NUNG-SHANG—

A Tankul village, built after the usual Tankul pattern, about 5,000 feet above the sea-level, containing 70 houses.

Inhabitants.—The inhabitants belong to the south-western section of the Tankul Naga tribe. Population 350, of whom 70 may be fighting-men. The most influential man is Nowba.

Climate.—The climate is healthy at all seasons.

Water.—Scanty supply.

Supplies.—Rice-straw procurable. Scanty grazing. Principal grains are rice and múm. Firewood plentiful. Arum, yams, and pumpkins. Rice harvest in November; múm early in December.

Live-stock.—Pigs and poultry.

Transport.—For coolie purposes, 10 men and women.

Timber.—Bamboos scarce; oaks, firs, &c., plentiful.—(*Lieut. Dun, 1881-82.*)

NUNGSHANGKONG—

An eastern tributary of the Thobal river. It is easily fordable throughout the year. Where crossed by the Imphal-Ukrul road, it flows in an open valley affording excellent camping-ground.

NUNGSHIGUM—

An elevated spur of the range between the Tiki and the Iril on the northern edge of the valley.

NUNGSHUNG—

A Tankul village, built after the usual Tankul pattern, about 5,000 feet above the sea-level, containing 100 houses.

Camping-ground.—Terraced rice-fields available.

Inhabitants.—The inhabitants belong to the north-eastern section of the Tankul Naga tribe. Population 500, of whom 100 may be fighting-men. The most influential man is Kamjaie.

Climate.—The climate is healthy at all seasons.

Water.—Small supply both on north and south of village.

Supplies.—Rice-straw procurable. Scanty grazing. Principal grains are ric and múm. Firewood plentiful. Arum, yams, and pumpkins. Rice harvest in November; múm early in December.

Live-stock.—Pigs, poultry, and a few metna.

Transport.—For coolie purposes, 100 men and women.

Timber.—Bamboos scarce; oaks, firs, &c., plentiful.—(*Lieut. Dun, 1881-82.*)

NUNGTAK—

A Mangvung village, about half a mile from the Hytuk-pokpi-Yanga-pokpi road, built after the usual Kuki pattern, about 3,800 feet above the sea-level, containing 10 houses.

Approaches—By a steep ascent from west, commanded by the village, which also commands the route.

Inhabitants.—The inhabitants belong to the Mangvung subdivision of the Kongjai Kuki tribe. Population 50, of whom 5 may be fighting-men. The headman is Ultong, the most influential man being Oondo.

Climate.—The climate is unhealthy from beginning of August to end of October.

Water.—Plentiful supply, but distant.

Supplies.—Rice-straw procurable. Plenty of grazing. Principal grains are Indian-corn, rice, múm, chayan, and oil-seed. Firewood plentiful. Arum, beans, and pumpkins. Harvest in November and beginning of December.

Live-stock.—Pigs, poultry, 20 or 30 metna, and 20 goats.

Transport.—For coolie purposes, 15 men and women.

Timber.—Chiefly oaks; a few bamboos.—(*Lieut. Dun, 1881-82.*)

NUNJAIBONG—

A small Manipuri post on the Cachar road, between the Piri and the Mukru rivers. It is situated at the top of the range which separates the two rivers. There is a rest-house here for officers.

NUNKOINO—

A Mangoung village, built after the usual Kuki pattern, about 3,500 feet above the sea-level, containing 6 houses.

Inhabitants.—The inhabitants belong to the Mangoang subdivision of the Kongjai Kuki tribe. Population 30, of whom 9 may be fighting-men. The head and most influential man is Halten.

Climate.—The climate is unhealthy from beginning of August to end of October.

Supplies.—Rice-straw procurable. Good grazing. Principal grains are Indian-corn, rice, múm, and chayan. Firewood plentiful. Arum, beans, and pumpkins. Harvest in November and beginning of December.
Live-stock.—Pigs, poultry, and a few metna.
Transport.—For coolie purposes, 9 men and women.
Timber.—Chiefly oaks; a few bamboos.—(*Lieut. Dun, 1881-82.*)

NUNSHIGUM—
An almost isolated block of hill on the northern edge of the valley between the Kongba and Iril rivers.

O

OGAL—

A Manipuri village at the western foot of the Yumadoung range, 2 miles west of Injorok.

Elevation.— } *Vide* page 77, Changangai.
Temperature.—
Climate.—

Houses.—25, Manipuri pattern.
Inhabitants.—125, sepoy class.
Fighting-men.—25.
Water.—Good and plentiful.
Camping-ground.— } *Vide* page 77, Changangai.
Products, &c.—
Live-stock.—50 cows, 37 buffaloes.
Carriage.—25 carts.

OINAM—

A Manipuri village, 12 miles from Imphal, on the Cachár road.

Elevation.— } *Vide* page 77, Changangai.
Temperature.—
Climate.—
Houses.—40, Manipur pattern.
Inhabitants.—200 carriers.
Water.— } *Vide* page 77, Changangai.
Camping-ground.—
Products, &c.—
Live-stock.—80 cows, 60 buffaloes.
Carriage.—40 carts, 40 men, 8 boats.

OINAM SAIREMBUNG—

A Manipuri village, 9 miles south of Imphal, and on the central valley road.

Elevation.— } *Vide* page 77, Changangai.
Temperature.—
Climate.—
Houses.—20, Manipuri pattern.
Inhabitants.—100, grass-cutters.
Water.— } *Vide* page 77, Changangai.
Camping-ground.—
Products, &c.—
Live-stock.—40 cows, 30 buffaloes.
Carriage.—20 carts, 5 boats.
Approaches.—Central valley road (Longtival-Kokshing) from north and south.

OIRONGBA—

A small Kaupui Naga village in North-West Manipur.

OKCHINGKEI—

A Manipuri village, 11 miles from Imphal, on the Cachar road.

Elevation.— } *Vide* page 77, Changangai.
Temperature.—
Climate.—

Houses.—25, Manipuri pattern.
Inhabitants.—125, Loï.

OKTANG—
A small Kaupui Naga village in North-Western Manipur.

ONJAME—
A small Kaupui village in North-Western Manipur.

OPEROK—
A small muddy stream which issues from a jheel in the north-western corner of the Manipur valley.

OSEI POKPI—
A stream crossed by the Pallel-Moray route.

P

PACHAMA—

An Angami village, built after the usual Angami pattern, about 4,500 feet above the sea-level, containing 27 houses.

Inhabitants.—The inhabitants belong to the Angami Naga tribe, and are subdivided as follows, *viz.*, Kanowri and Nisemi. Population 135, of whom 27 may be fighting-men. The most influential man is Merisé.

Climate.—The climate is healthy at all seasons.

Supplies.—Rice-straw procurable. Fair grazing. Principal grains are rice, múm, and chayan. Rather moderate supply of firewood. Arum and pumpkins. Harvest in November and December.

Live-stock.—Cows in large numbers; pigs and poultry.

Transport.—For coolie purposes, 27 men, women, and children.

Timber.—Very little fir or oak; small pollarded alders; bamboos scarce. (*Lieut. Dun, 1881-82.*)

PADANG—

A Tankul village, built after the usual Tankul pattern, about 5,000 feet above the sea-level, containing 150 houses.

Inhabitants.—The inhabitants belong to the north-eastern section of the Takul Naga tribe. Population 750, of whom 150 may be fighting-men. The most influential man is Turukám.

Climate.—The climate is healthy at all seasons.

Supplies.—Rice-straw procurable. Scanty grazing. Principal grains are rice and múm. Firewood plentiful. Arum, yams, and pumpkins. Rice harvest in November; múm early in December.

Live-stock.—Pigs and poultry.

Transport.—For coolie purposes, 150 men and women.

Timber.—Bamboos scarce; oaks, firs, &c., plentiful.—(*Lieut. Dun, 1881-82.*)

PALLEL—

A Manipuri village on the foot of the Yumadoung range where the Moray and Nasinga routes enter the hills.

Elevation.—
Climate.— } *Vide* page 77, Changangai.
Temperature.—

Houses.—15, Manipuri pattern.

Inhabitants.—75, sepoy class.

Fighting men.—15.

Water and Camping-ground.—Both good and very plentiful.

Products, &c.—*Vide* page 77, Changangai.

Live-stock.—30 cows, 12 buffaloes.

Carriage.—15 carts.

Approaches.—Eastern valley road. Cross Sengmail streams, north of village, 1 foot deep 18 feet broad in cold weather. There is a thannah here unstockaded, and supplied with a garrison from the village.

PANGAN KAIBUNG—

A Manipuri village on the Thobal river, south of the Thobal villages and before it joins the Imphal.

Elevation.—
Temperature.— } *Vide* page 77, Changangai.
Climate.—

Houses.—25, Manipuri pattern.
Inhabitants.—125, sepoy class.
Fighting-men.—25.

Water.—
Camping-ground.— } *Vide* page 77, Changangai.
Products, &c.—

Live-stock.—50 cows, 37 buffaloes.
Carriage.—25 carts, 12 boats.
Approaches.—By good mule-path from north and south, along the banks of the Thobal river.

PANYĀAM—

A small new Kuki hamlet in the valley of the Manipuri branch of the Tipai river.

It contains 10 houses.

The inhabitants belong to the Simmté clan.

PASUL—

A small Manipuri village in the north-west part of the valley, 6 miles south-west of Imphal.

PAUTANG—

A small Kuki village, said to be Lushai, about a day's journey, south of Kanpum.

It is said to contain 20 houses.

PEISAD—

A Hawkib village, built after the usual Kuki pattern, about 4,000 feet above the sea-level, containing 30 houses.

Inhabitants.—The inhabitants belong to the Hawkib subdivision of the Kongjai Kuki tribe. Population 150, of whom 45 may be fighting-men. The chief is Ongoto. The most influential man is Tangsho.

Climate.—The climate is unhealthy from beginning of August to end of October.

Water.—Plentiful supply.

Supplies.—Rice-straw procurable. Plenty of grazing. Principal grains are Indian-corn, rice, múm, and chayan. Firewood plentiful. Arum, beans, and pumpkins. Harvest in November and beginning of December.

Live-stock.—Pigs, poultry, and 10 metna.

Transport.—For coolie purposes, 45 men and women.

Timber.—Chiefly oak bushes.—(*Lieut. Dun, 1881-82.*)

PHAIIKONG—

A fair-sized mountain stream in the valley below Chattik on the east. In the cold weather it is not more than 2 feet deep, where the Chairkong joins it and flows with a steady current. It is, however, 40 or 50 yards broad.

PHALANGOON—

A large scattered Burmese village of over 150 houses on the Ava-Kenda road. It is about 6 miles north of Dubayen and 12 miles west of the Moo river.

Grain is plentiful and tolerably cheap; paddy sells at from 15 to 20 tikals (*2s. 6d.* Yule) per 100 baskets (basket = 56lb). A large quantity of palm sugar is also made here. Cattle are very plentiful, and common draught cattle sell from 10 to 15 tikals.—(*Richardson.*)

PHALLANG—

A Tankul village, built after the usual Tankul pattern, about 4,000 feet above the sea-level, containing 7 houses.

Inhabitants.—The inhabitants belong to the south-western section of the Tankul Naga tribe. Population 35, of whom 7 may be fighting-men.

Climate.—The climate is unhealthy from beginning of August to end of October.

Supplies.—Rice-straw procurable. Scanty grazing. Principal grains are rice and múm. Firewood plentiful. Arum, yams, and pumpkins. Rice harvest in November; múm early in December.

Live-stock.—Pigs and poultry.

Transport.—For coolie purposes, 7 men and women.

Timber.—Bamboos scarce; oaks, firs, &c., plentiful.—(*Lieut. Dun, 1881-82.*)

PHALOK—

A small Kaupui village in North-Western Manipur.

PHANGÉ-LANGCHUNG—

A Tankul village, built after the usual Chussad pattern, about 2,000 feet above the sea-level, containing 30 houses.

Inhabitants.—The inhabitants belong to the Tankul Naga tribe, but are subject to the Chussad Kukis. Population 150, of whom 30 may be fighting-men. The chief is Mangsál.

Climate.—The climate is unhealthy from beginning of August to end of October.

Water.—Plentiful supply close to village.

Supplies.—Rice-straw procurable. No grazing. Principal grains are Indian-corn, rice, múm, and chayan. Firewood plentiful. Arum, beans, and pumpkins. Harvest in November and early part of December.

Live-stock.—Pigs and poultry.

Transport.—For coolie purposes, 30 men and women.

Timber.—No oaks or firs; other kinds plentiful.—(*Lieut. Dun, 1881-82.*)

PHAU—

A small Tankul village just north of and outside of the Somrah basin. There are said to be 25 houses and the people are friendly.

Vide Jessami for Products, Timber, &c.

PHAUTEL—

A Manipuri village on the Thobal river between Yarapok and the Thobal villages.

Elevation.—
Temperature.—
Climate.— } *Vide* page 77, Changangai.

Houses.—25, Manipuri pattern.

Inhabitants.—125, sepoy class.

Fighting-men.—25.

Water.—
Camping-ground.—
Products, &c.— } *Vide* page 77, Changangai.

Live-stock.—50 cows, 37 buffaloes.
Carriage.—25 carts, 12 boats.
Approaches.—By good mule-path along the banks of the Thobal river, from north and south.

PHEKROKEZAMAI—

A Kolya Naga village on the northern frontier of Manipur.

PHESAMA—

An Angami village, built after the usual Angami pattern, about 4,500 feet above the sea-level, containing 64 houses.

Inhabitants.—The inhabitants belong to the Angami Naga tribe, and are divided as follows :—*viz.*, Sikamai and Meramai. Population 320, of whom 64 are fighting-men. The most influential man is Tezúr.
Climate.—The climate is healthy at all seasons.
Water.—Scanty supply in the village, but plenty in ravines on either side.
Supplies.—Rice-straw procurable. Fair grazing. Principal grains are rice, mûm, and chayan. Rather moderate supply of firewood. Arum and pumpkins. Harvest in November and December.
Live-stock.—Cows in large numbers, pigs, and poultry.
Transport.—For coolie purposes, 64 men, women, and children.
Timber.—Very little fir or oak; small pollarded alders; bamboos scarce.

(*Lieut. Dun, 1881-82.*)

PHIBU—

A Manipuri village, south of the Thobal villages and Waito.

Elevation.—
Temperature.— } *Vide* page 77, Changangai.
Climate.—

Houses.—25, Manipuri pattern.
Inhabitants.—125, sepoy class.
Fighting-men.—25.

Products, &c.—
Water.— } *Vide* page 77, Changangai.
Camping-ground.—

Live-stock.—50 cows, 37 buffaloes.
Carriage.—25 carts, 12 boats.
Approaches—By good mule-path along the banks of the Thobal.

PHOZAMEH—

A "naked" Naga village, a few miles south of the junction of the main streams of the Lanier river, in North-Eastern Manipur.

Elevation.—About 4,000 feet.
Houses.—About 200.

This village is similar in all respects to Mellomi, except that it is on the Manipuri side of the Lanier. The men of the neighbouring villages were afraid to go near this village.

There is probably both water and camping-ground in plenty.

PHUNAMAH-MAU-SOPVOMAH—

A Kolya Naga village on the Kohima road, and on the northern frontier of Manipur.

Elevation.—5,000 feet.
Temperature.—40° degrees at sunrise in December.
Climate.—Healthy at all seasons.

Houses.—120, Naga pattern.
Inhabitants.—480.
Fighting-men.—120.
Water.—Good and plentiful.
Camping-ground.—Sufficient for one company of 100 men, with transport on the ridge on which the village is built, and enough for two regiments (1,500 men) and transport in the terraced rice-fields south of the village, if not irrigated during the cold weather.
Products, &c.—*Vide* page 78, Charo.
Live-stock.—150 cows, pigs, and poultry.
Carriage.—200 coolies.

PHUNAN—

A Marring village on the hills east of Shugunu, South-East Manipur.
Elevation.—About 3,500 feet.
There are only five houses.
Products, &c.—*Vide* page 156, Machi.

PHUNAN—

A comparatively low peak, 3,717 feet above the sea, on a southern spur of Nongmaiching. It overlooks Andro and the Thobal valley on one side and the main valley on the other. It would be a useful signalling station to connect the capital with the Yumadoung range.

PHUNDRE—

A Manipuri (Mussulman) village at the foot of the Yumadoung range, due east of Sorah.
Elevation.—
Temperature.— } *Vide* page, 77 Changangai.
Climate.—
Houses.—50, Manipuri pattern.
Inhabitants.—250, sepoy class.
Fighting-men.—50.
Water.—
Camping-ground.— } *Vide* page 77, Changangai.
Products, &c.—
Live-stock.—100 cows, 75 buffaloes.
Carriage.—50 carts.
Approaches—By narrow and indifferent field-paths, through rice-fields, from the eastern valley road.

PHUNGAM—

A Tankul village, built after the usual Tankul pattern, about 5,000 feet above the sea-level, containing 200 houses.
Inhabitants.—The inhabitants belong to the north-eastern section of the Tankul Naga tribe. Population 1,000, of whom 200 may be fighting-men. The most influential man is Mangai (interpreter).
Climate.—The climate is healthy at all seasons.
Supplies.—Rice-straw procurable. Scanty grazing. Principal grains are rice and múm. Firewood plentiful. Arum, yams, and pumpkins. Rice harvest in November; múm early in December.
Live-stock.—Pigs, poultry, and a few metna.
Transport.—For coolie purposes, 200 men.
Timber.—Bamboos scarce; oaks, firs, &c., plentiful.—(*Lieut. Dun, 1881-82.*)

PHUSAMAH—

A Kolya Naga village of the Mau section on the northern frontier of Manipur, between the Sijjo and Zullo streams.

Elevation.—5,000 feet.

Houses and Fighting-men.—100.

Water.—
Camping-ground.—
Products, &c.— } *Vide* page 185, Phunamah.

Live-stock.—120 cows, pigs, and poultry.

Carriage.—130 coolies.

POERON KUNJIL—

A Manipuri village on the Thobal river, between Yarapok and the Thobal villages.

Elevation.—
Temperature.—
Climate.— } *Vide* page 77, Changangai.

Houses.—25, Manipuri pattern.

Inhabitants.—125, sepoy class.

Water.—
Camping-ground.—
Products, &c.— } *Vide* page 77, Changangai.

Live-stock.—50 cows, 37 buffaloes.

Carriage.—25 carts, 12 boats.

Approaches—By good mule-path along the banks of the Thobal river.

POI—

A Tankul village, built after the usual Tankul pattern, about 5,000 feet above the sea-level, containing 100 houses.

Inhabitants.—The inhabitants belong to the north-eastern section of the Tankul Naga tribe. Population 500, of whom 100 may be fighting-men. The most influential man is Asáwah (interpreter).

Climate.—The climate is healthy at all seasons.

Supplies.—Rice-straw procurable. Scanty grazing. Principal grains are rice and múm. Firewood plentiful. Arum, yams, and pumpkins. Harvest in November and early part of December.

Live-stock.—Pigs and poultry.

Transport.—For coolie purposes, 100 men and women.

Timber.—Bamboos scarce; oaks, firs, &c., plentiful.—(*Lieut. Dun, 1881-82.*)

POI OR SHINDU—

A Kuki tribe situated south of the Lushais and Sukties.

POILEN—

A Hawkib village, built after the usual Kuki pattern, about 4,000 feet above the sea-level, containing 10 houses.

Inhabitants.—The inhabitants belong to the Hawkib subdivision of the Kongjai Kuki tribe. Population 50, of whom 15 may be fighting-men. The head and most influential man is Komlo.

Climate.—The climate is unhealthy from beginning of August to end of October.

Supplies.—Rice-straw procurable. Plenty of grazing. Principal grains are Indian-corn, rice, múm, and chayan. Firewood plentiful. Arum, beans, and pumpkins. Harvest in November and early part of December.

Live-stock.—Pigs, poultry, and a few metna.
Transport. For coolie purposes, 15 men and women.
Timber.—Chiefly oak bushes.—(*Lieut. Dun, 1881-82.*)

PONG—

A Tankul village on the Manipur-Kongal route (*viâ* Chattik), situated on the east bank of the Maglang river; built after the usual Tankul pattern; containing 11 houses.

Camping-ground.—A few small terraced rice-fields below the village on the south-west.

Approaches—By a good level path, 6 feet broad, from the north. Up gradual spur from west, on which side is the valley of the Maglang. Down a steep narrow spur from above on the east. This last is defended by a ditch choked with jungle. The rest are easy and undefended.

Inhabitants.—The inhabitants belong to the south-western section of the Tankul Naga tribe. Population 55, of whom 11 are fighting-men.

Climate.—The climate is unhealthy from beginning of August to end of November.

Water.—Small supply at village; plenty half a mile distant, both east and west.

Supplies.—Rice-straw procurable. Fair grazing. Principal grains are rice and múm. Firewood plentiful. Arum, yams, and pumpkins. Harvest in November and early part of December.

Live-stock.—Pigs and poultry.

Transport.—For coolie purposes, 10 men and women.

Timber.—Bamboos scarce; oaks, firs, &c., plentiful.—(*Lieut. Dun, 1881-82.*)

PONG—

The Shan kingdom of Pong was formerly bounded on the north by the range of hills dividing Burma from Assam; south it extended to Khanpat; west to the Yoma range; east to the Yunan. The capital was Mogoung. After varying fortunes, it was annexed to Burma in 1752. The Pong kings used to give districts to their sons: hence the origin of the various Tsawbwaships, some of which still remain, such as Thoang, Thwoot, Wintho, and Kanto. (*Vide* Shans.)—(*Phayre, 1881-82.*)

POSHING—

A Tankul village on the Manipur-Chattik route (*viâ* Kangir), situated on the southern slope of the Sirdhifarar ridge, built after the usual Tankul pattern, about 5,000 feet above the sea-level, containing 50 houses.

Camping-ground.—Terraced rice-fields available.

Approaches.—The path, which is said to be fit for laden mules, ascends to the village both on the east and west side. There are no artificial defences.

Inhabitants.—The inhabitants belong to the north-eastern section of the Tankul Naga tribe. Population 250, of whom 50 may be fighting-men. The chief is Makati.

Climate.—The climate is healthy at all seasons.

Water.—Small supply close on the north side; plenty on south side.

Supplies.—Rice-straw procurable. Scanty grazing. Principal grains are rice and múm. Firewood plentiful. Arum, yams, and pumpkins. Harvest in November and early part of December.

Live-stock.—Pigs, poultry, and a few buffaloes.

Transport.—For coolie purposes, 50 men and women.

Timber.—Bamboos scarce; oaks, firs, &c., plentiful.—(*Lieut. Dun, 1881-82.*)

PRATUKONG—

A stream similar in character to the Nammea, crossed by the Kongal-Samjok route.—(*Lieut. Dun, 1881-82.*)

PROWI—

* Situated on a splendid plateau—a charming situation, with magnificent views all round.

A Tankul village,* built after the usual Tankul pattern, about 5,000 feet above the sea-level, containing 200 houses.

Inhabitants.—The inhabitants belong to the north-eastern section of the Tankul Naga tribe. Population 1,000, of whom 200 may be fighting-men. The most influential man is Mailu (interpreter).

Climate.—The climate is healthy at all seasons.

Water.—Fair supply.

Supplies.—Rice-straw procurable. Scanty grazing. Principal grains are múm and chayan. Firewood plentiful. Arum, beans, and pumpkins. Rice harvest in November; múm early in December.

Live-stock.—Pigs and poultry.

Transport.—For coolie purposes, 200 men and women.

Timber.—Bamboos scarce; oaks, firs, &c., plentiful.—(*Lieut. Dun, 1881-82.*)

PROWI THANNA—

A Manipur frontier post in the Tankul Naga country to the north-east.

Garrison.—One subadar, 1 havildar, 50 sepoys.—(*Lieut. Dun, 1881-82.*)

PUCHUNG—

A Tankul village, built after the usual Tankul pattern, about 3,500 feet above the sea-level, containing 7 houses.

Inhabitants.—The inhabitants belong to the south-western section of the Tankul Naga tribe. Population 35, of whom 7 may be fighting-men.

Climate.—The climate is unhealthy from beginning of August to end of October.

Supplies.—Rice-straw procurable. Scanty grazing. Principal grains are rice and múm. Firewood plentiful. Arum, yams, and pumpkins. Rice harvest in November; múm early in December.

Live-stock.—Pigs and poultry.

Transport.—For coolie purposes, 7 men and women.

Timber.—Bamboo scarce; oaks, firs, &c., plentiful.—(*Lieut. Dun, 1881-82.*)

PUEPI—

A small Chiru village on the western slopes of Kopru, North-West Manipur.

PUKRI—

A Kolya Naga village of the Marám subdivision.

Elevation.—4,500 feet.

Climate.—Healthy at all seasons.

Houses and Fighting-men.—13.

Products, &c.—*Vide* page 78, Charo.

Live-stock.—20 cows, pigs, and poultry.

Carriage.—18 coolies.

Water.—Good and plentiful, both stream and pond.

Camping-ground.—Good and of practically unlimited extent.

PUMBAH—

A Kuki village, built after the usual Kuki pattern, about 4,000 feet above the sea-level, containing 20 houses.

Inhabitants.—The inhabitants are Kukis; subdivision not known. Population 100, of whom 30 may be fighting-men. The head and most influential man is Hálvang.

Climate.—The climate is unhealthy from beginning of August to end of October.

Supplies.—Rice-straw procurable. Plenty of grazing. Principal grains are Indian-corn, rice, múm, and chayan. Firewood plentiful. Arum beans, and pumpkins. Harvest in November and early in December.

Live-stock.—Pigs, poultry, and a few metna.

Transport.—For coolie purposes, 30 men and women.

Timber.—Chiefly oak bushes.—(*Lieut. Dun, 1881-82.*)

PUNJUNG—

A Chussad village, built after the usual Kuki pattern, about 3,000 feet above the sea-level, containing 10 houses. This village, together with that of Kabyang, covers any advance on Tonghu from the west.

Inhabitants.—The inhabitants belong to the Chussad subdivision of the Kongjai Kuki tribe. Population 50, of whom 15 may be fighting-men. The chief and most influential man is Yangapow, a cousin of the Chief Tonghoo.

Climate.—The climate is unhealthy from beginning of August to end of October.

Water.—Plentiful supply.

Supplies.—Rice-straw procurable. No grazing. Principal grains are Indian-corn, rice, múm, and chayan. Firewood plentiful. Arum, beans, and pumpkins. Harvest in November and early in December.

Live-stock.—Pigs and poultry.

Transport.—For coolie purposes, 10 men and women.

Timber.—Oak and fir not common; all other kinds.—(*Lieut. Dun, 1881-82.*)

PUNSA—

A village in the Kubbo valley, south of Tummoo, on the road to Khambat.

PÚRÚM—

An old Kuki tribe, scattered about the hills close to the Manipur valley.

PUTSIMI or PUNGTAR KUNAO—

A Kolya Naga village in Northern Manipur. It is an offshoot from Jessami, and is situated between that village and the Thetzirr river.

Elevation.—5,000 feet.

Temperature.— 38° at sunrise in February.

Climate.—Healthy at all seasons.

Houses.—35, Naga pattern, small.

Inhabitants.—140.

Fighting-men.—35.

Water.—Scanty.

Camping-ground.—Sufficient only for 200 men.

Products, &c.—*Vide* page 78, Charo.

Live-stock.—Pigs and poultry only.

Carriage.—50 coolies.

Approaches—Up steep faces of spurs from east, west, and north, through high oak jungle.

Headman.—Yamang, friendly.

R

RADOUNG or **KADOUNG**—

A small Burmese village of 50 or 60 houses on the Ava-Kendat road. Surrounding country cultivated; cattle and water abundant; road good.
(*Richardson, 1833.*)

RAIMEH—

A Tankul Naga village in Northern Manipur, on the ridge between the Lanier on the east and the Tsolore on the west.

Elevation.—About 5,300 feet.

Houses and Fighting-men.—80.

Water and Camping-ground.—Sufficient only for 100 men.

Products, &c.—*Vide* page 78, Charo.

Live-stock.—A few cows, pigs, and poultry.

Approaches—Up steep slope through jungle from east and west.

RAKORRHI—

A small confluent of the Barak. It joins that river a few miles above Karong.

RASIBUNG—

An eastern spur from the range which comes down from Sirohifavar, between the Maglang and the Kunokong rivers. Elevation 5,656 feet.

RAZAMEH—

A large village (said to contain 700 houses) on the northern boundary of Manipur.

It is doubtful whether the inhabitants are more closely allied to Kolyas or to Angamis, or whether the village belongs to Manipur or the British Government.

RAZAMEH—

A small offshoot from Liyang, situated in the great northern bend of the Barak river under the Chakka cliffs.

RAZAMEH or **LIYANG**.—

Vide Liyang.

RAZARR—

A fair-sized mountain stream, a northern confluent of the Lanier, fordable at any point in the cold weather.

RIAR—

A Tankul village, built after the usual Tankul pattern, about 3,500 feet above the sea-level, containing 4 houses.

Inhabitants.—The inhabitants belong to the south-western section of the Tankul Naga tribe. Population 20, of whom 4 may be fighting-men.

Climate.—The climate is unhealthy from beginning of August to end of October.

Supplies.—Rice-straw procurable. Scanty grazing. Principal grains are rice and múm. Firewood plentiful. Arum, yams, and pumpkins. Rice harvest in November; múm in December.

Live-stock.—Pigs and poultry.

Transport.—For coolie purposes, 4 men and women.

Timber.—Oaks and firs scarce; bamboos and forest trees in large quantities.
(*Lieut. Dun, 1881-82.*)

RIOKONG—

A mountain stream flowing through a deep narrow gorge to its confluence with the Viratai, North-East Manipur.

RONG-JAO—

A Tankul village, built after the usual Tankul pattern, about 3,000 feet above the sea-level; containing 8 houses.

Inhabitants.—The inhabitants belong to the south-western section of the Tankul Naga tribe. Population 40, of whom 8 may be fighting-men.

Climate.—The climate is unhealthy from beginning of August to end of October.

Supplies.—Rice-straw procurable. Scanty grazing. Principal grains are rice and múm. Firewood plentiful. Arum, yams, and pumpkins. Rice harvest in November; múm in December.

Live-stock.—Pigs and poultry.

Transport.—Eight men and women.

Timber.—Oaks and firs scarce; bamboos and forest trees in large quantities.

(*Lieut. Dun, 1881-82.*)

RUCHIKONG—

A stream draining the northern slopes of Sirohi Farar and a tributary of the Viratai.

S

SADDA—

A small Tankul Naga hamlet on the Yumadoung range, close above Chandwakong. It has 5 houses.

SADDO—

A small Kaupui Naga village of 10 houses on the eastern face of the Laimatol range, a few miles south of the Cachar Road.

Products, &c.—*Vide* page 78, Charo.

SADIM—

A Kolya Naga village of the Maram section, situated on the ridge west of the Barak river, half way between Karong and Maithaipham.

Elevation.—About 5,000 feet.

Houses and Fighting-men.—35.

Water.—Plentiful.

Camping-Ground.—Unlimited.

Products, &c.—*Vide* page 78, Charo.

Approaches—Up easy open slopes from the east and along an almost level ridge from Pukri on the north.

SAIKOT—

A small new Kuki village of the Mangoung clan, situated on the Turbung stream, in Southern Manipur.

Elevation.—2,700 feet.

Temperature.—44° at sunrise in December.

Climate.—Unhealthy from 1st May to 1st December.

Houses.—10.

Products, &c.—*Vide* page 77, Chanjang.

Water.—Plentiful and good.

Camping-ground.—Unlimited.

Approaches.—Open and easy.

SAITUL—

A new Kuki village of the Vungson clan, on the Turbung stream, but within the main Manipur valley.

Elevation.—
Temperature.—
Climate.— } *Vide* page 77, Changangai.

Houses.—50, Manipuri pattern.

Inhabitants.—200.

Water.—Plentiful.

Camping-ground.—Unlimited, if the grass be cut or burnt, and in the cold weather only.

Products, &c.—*Vide* page 77, Changangai.

Live-stock.—Pigs and poultry; a few buffaloes.

Carriage.—75 coolies.

Approaches—Over open plain from the north-west, west, and south-east.

SAIYANG—

A small Chiru village on the Kopru-Laimatol range, due west of Imphal.

SAJIKONG—

A small stream crossed by the Hytuk-pokpi-Yanga-Pokpi road.

(*Lieut. Dun, 1881-82.*)

SAKAUPONG—

A Tankul village, built after the usual Tankul pattern, about 4,500 feet above the sea-level, containing 15 houses.

Inhabitants.—The inhabitants belong to the south-western section of Tankul Naga tribe. Population 75, of whom 16 may be fighting-men.

Climate.—The climate is unhealthy from beginning of August to end of October.

Supplies.—Rice-straw procurable. Scanty grazing. Principal grains are rice and múm. Firewood plentiful. Arum, yams, and pumpkins. Rice harvest in November; múm in December.

Live-stock.—Pigs, poultry, and a few buffaloes or metna.

Transport.—For coolie purposes, 15 men and women.

Timber.—Oaks and firs scarce; bamboos and forest trees in large quantities.

(*Lieut. Dun, 1881-82.*)

SAKOK—

A Tankul village, built after the usual Tankul pattern, about 4,000 feet above the sea-level, containing 10 houses.

Camping-ground.—A very little on the south side of the village.

Approaches.—From the south by a narrow path running along the face of a steep ridge. From the north up a steep spur. Both could easily be defended from the village.

Inhabitants.—The inhabitants belong to the south-western section of the Tankul Naga tribe. Population 50, of whom 10 may be fighting-men. The headman is Mapan. Raileng (interpreter) has much influence.

Climate.—The climate is unhealthy from beginning of August to end of October.

Water.—Scanty.

Supplies.—Rice-straw procurable. Scanty grazing. Principal grains are rice and múm. Firewood plentiful. Arum, yams, and pumpkins. Rice harvest in November; múm in December.

Live-stock.—Pigs and poultry.

Transport.—For coolie purposes, 10 men and women.

Timber.—Oaks and firs scarce; bamboos and forest trees in large quantities.

(*Lieut. Dun, 1881-82.*)

SAKOK LANG—

A ridge in the Yumadoung range, crossed by the Pong Chattik road.

(*Lieut. Dun, 1881-82.*)

SAKOMANG—

A small Kaupui Naga village in North-Western Manipur.

SALENGPHAM—

A Manipuri village on the Ingorok stream between its exit from the hills and the high road (eastern valley road).

Elevation.— }
Temperature.— } *Vide* page 77, Changangai.
Climate, &c.— }

Houses.—25, Manipuri pattern.

Inhabitants.—125, sepoy class.

Water.—
Camping-ground.— } *Vide* page 77, Changángai.
Products, &c.—
Line-stock.—50 cows, 37 buffaloes.
Carriage.—25 carts.
Approaches—By narrow and bad field-paths from all the neighbouring villages.

SAMJOK—

A Shan village, called by the Burmese Toung-thwoot, containing 60 houses, on the right bank of the Ningthee river.

The houses are built of wood and bamboo. About the middle of the town is the Tsawbwa's house, with a wooden spire and many gables; to the south and south-west is the spur of a little hill with numerous pagodas and a monastery. There are no fortifications.

Roads.—The town is a single street on the river bank.

Camping-ground.—There is a stretch of sand on the east bank of the river in cold weather, which might serve as camping-ground.

Surrounding Country.—The town is in a very defensible position, provided the hill to the south were fortified, as it has the broad deep river to the east, a stream with rotten banks and soft silty bottom to the north, and a great marsh to the west. Whoever holds the hill has the town; but there is no way of getting to the hill from the north, except through the town.

Inhabitants.—The inhabitants are Shans, and are mainly engaged in boat-building. Population from 1,500 to 2,000. On the opposite bank of the Ningthee are several small villages, chiefly occupied by boat-builders.

The Raja of the district resides here and has a body-guard of 30 or 40 men armed with flint-locks.

Manufacture.—The speciality of the town is a very good red pottery, unglazed, much used throughout the district.

Supplies.—The staple grain is rice, which sells in December at 6 maunds for one rupee. Harvest in December and a second in May or June.

Live-stock.—Plenty of buffaloes; no cows.

Timber.—Teak plentiful; mangoes, cocoanuts, palms, and other trees (*Major Badgeley, 1881-82; Lieut. Dun, 1881-82.*)

SAMJOK—

One of the districts east of the Ningthee river, governed by a Shan Tsawbwa, subject to Burma. This man has received regal honours, *viz.*, the privilege of using a white umbrella, and is said to be hostile to Manipur and the British Government.

To the south the district extends to within three days' journey of Kendat. It is estimated that the district contains about 500 houses, or 2,500 inhabitants.—(*Lieut. Dun, 1881-82.*)

SAMKOM OR TOG-WEMA—

A Kolya Naga village of the Marám section, situated on a southern spur of the Khunho peak and just north of the great northern bend of the Barak river.

Elevation.—5,500 feet.
Houses.—25, Naga pattern.
Inhabitants.—100.
Fighting-men.—20.

Water.—Scanty, and 500 feet below the village on the southern side.
Camping-ground.—None.
Products, &c.—*Vide* page 78, Charo.
Live-stock.—75 cows, pigs, and poultry.
Carriage.—75 coolies.
Approaches—Up very steep faces of spur from north and south. The village is placed in a very strong but confined position.

SAMOKOM—

A dâk station, 10½ miles from Hytuk-pokpi, on the road to Yanga-pokpi. Small supply of water; ground level.—(*Lieut. Dun, 1881-82.*)

SAMRAM—

A Manipuri village in Eastern Manipur, south of the village of Lamting.
Elevation.—
Temperature.— } *Vide* page 77, Changangai.
Climate.—
Houses.—30.
Inhabitants.—150, sepoy class.
Fighting-men.—30.
Water.—
Camping-ground.— } *Vide* page 77, Changangai.
Products, &c.—
Live-stock.—60 cows, 45 buffaloes.
Carriage.—30 carts.
Approaches—By narrow and indifferent paths, through rice-fields, from all the neighbouring villages.

SAMUKH—

A small Kuki village on the western slopes of the Kopru range.

SANACHING—

A peak on the watershed between the Manipur and Kubbo valleys and crossed by Route No. VI.
Elevation.—5,860 feet.

SANAM—

A Shan village, built after the usual Shan pattern, about 700 feet above the sea-level, containing 7 houses.
Inhabitants.—The inhabitants belong to the Shan tribe. Population 35, of whom 7 may be fighting-men.
Climate.—The climate is unhealthy from beginning of June to end of October.
Water.—Plentiful supply.
Supplies.—Rice-straw procurable. Fair grazing. Principal grain is rice. Firewood plentiful. Yams, plantains, pumpkins. Harvest in November and early in December.
Live-stock.—Pigs, poultry, and buffaloes.
Transport.—For coolie purposes, 7 men and women.
Timber.—Teak, sal, and bamboo.—(*Lieut. Dun, 1881-82.*)

SANAYACHIL—

A town in the Kubbo valley on the right bank of the Ningthee, opposite to Kendat. The Sanayachil-Khambat road is the best across the Ungoching hills.

SANGI—

A small Kaupui Naga village of 15 houses on the eastern face of the Laimatol range, a little way north of Bishenpur.

SANHEMI—

A naked Naga village on the northern frontier of Manipur.

SANGLEM—

A Mangoung village, built after the usual Kuki pattern, about 3,500 feet above the sea-level, containing 7 houses.

Inhabitants.—The inhabitants belong to the Mangoung subdivision of the Kongjai Kuki tribe. Population 35, of whom 11 may be fighting-men.

Climate.—The climate is unhealthy from beginning of August to end of October.

Supplies.—Rice-straw procurable. Fair grazing. Principal grains are Indian-corn, rice, múm, and chayan. Firewood plentiful. Arum, beans, pumpkins. Harvest in November and early in December.

Live-stock.—Pigs and poultry.

Transport.—For coolie purposes, 7 men and women.

Timber.—Oak and fir not common; all other kinds.—(*Lieut. Dun, 1881-82.*)

SANJAK—

A Tankul village, built after the usual Tankul pattern, about 5,000 feet above the sea-level, containing 40 houses.

Inhabitants.—The inhabitants belong to the south-western section of the Tankul Naga tribe. Population 200, of whom 40 may be fighting-men. The chief is Atomba.

Climate.—The climate is healthy at all seasons.

Supplies.—Rice-straw procurable. Scanty grazing. Principal grains are rice and múm. Firewood plentiful. Arum, yams, and pumpkins. Rice harvest in November; múm in December.

Live-stock.—Pigs and poultry.

Transport.—For coolie purposes, 40 men and women.

Timber.—Bamboos scarce; oaks, firs, &c., plentiful.—(*Lieut. Dun, 1881-82.*)

SANJEMBAM—

A small Kaupui Naga village in the north-eastern portion of the Manipur plain, 8 miles west of Imphal.

SANJING—

A Tankul village, built after the usual Tankul pattern, about 5,000 feet above the sea-level, containing 10 houses.

Inhabitants.—The inhabitants belong to the south-western section of the Tankul Naga tribe. Population 50, of whom 10 may be fighting-men. The chief is Rung-jing.

Climate.—The climate is healthy at all seasons.

Supplies.—Rice-straw procurable. Scanty grazing. Principal grains are rice and múm. Firewood plentiful. Arum, yams, and pumpkins. Rice harvest in November; múm in December.

Live-stock.—Pigs and poultry.

Transport.—For coolie purposes, 10 men and women.

Timber.—Bamboos scarce; oaks, firs, &c., plentiful.—(*Lieut. Dun, 1881-82.*)

SANNAU—

A small Kaupui Naga village in North-West Manipur.

SAPAM—

A Manipuri village south of the village of Lamting and one mile to the west of the eastern valley road.

Elevation.—
Temperature.— } *Vide* page 77, Changangai.
Climate.—

Houses.—Thirty-five, Manipuri pattern.

Inhabitants.—One hundred and seventy-five, sepoy class.

Fighting-men.—Thirty-five.

Water.—
Camping-ground.— } *Vide* page 77, Changangai.
Products, &c.—

Live-stock.—Seventy cows, 42 buffaloes.

Carraige.—Thirty-five carts.

Approaches—By narrow and indifferent paths through rice-fields from the high road and from the neighbouring villages.

SARAMETI OR CHING-ANGO-BA—

An elevated range, of which the highest known peak situated at the south-western end is 12,557 feet above the sea.

It is really an outlying spur of the main watershed between Assam and Burma, and apparently forms the western boundary of the portion of the Ningthee valley just south of Hukhong.

It has never been visited by Europeans.

In the month of January it has about 1,000 feet of snow on the northern side.

The Manipuris are afraid to visit it for superstitious reasons.

The boundary here is quite undefined, and it is an open question whether it belongs to Assam, Burma, or Manipur.

Its lower slopes would probably provide excellent sanitaria. It can be easily reached from the Ningthee river.

From Manipur it is most favourably approached through the Somrah country.—(*Lieut. Dun, 1885.*)

SARTE OR CHARTE—

A small Tankul village of 5 houses on the southern end of the Sakok-Lang ridge, Eastern Manipur.

SARTUNG—

A small Tankul village of 6 houses, situated at the junction of the Maglang and Tugungba streams in Eastern Manipur.

SARUI-KUNAO—

A Tankul village in Manipur.

SARUI-KULEL—

A Tankul village in Manipur.

SAWAMBA—

A Mangvung village on the Pallel-Moray route, built after the usual Kuki pattern, about 4,500 feet above the sea-level, containing 30 houses. This would be a favourable point for an enemy in possession of the hills to dispute the passage of troops.

Camping-ground.—Sufficient for 400 men, on south side of village only.

Approaches—From the east up a narrow spur, which could easily be defended half a mile from the village. The village does not command it. From the west along a broad level path, on the face of the hill, screened from the village, the path crosses the ridge just before the village is reached, and might be defended at that point with advantage. Also approached from the north; no details.

Inhabitants.—The inhabitants belong to the Mangvung subdivision of the Kongjai Kuki tribe. Population 150, of whom 45 are fighting-men. Their chief and most influential man is Sawam.

Climate.—The climate is unhealthy from beginning of August to end of October.

Water.—Scanty supply.

Supplies.—Rice-straw procurable. Fair grazing. Principal grains are Indian-corn, rice, múm, chayan. Firewood plentiful. Arum, beans, and pumpkins. Harvest in November and early in December.

Live-stock.—Pigs and poultry.

Transport.—For coolie purposes, 30 men and women.

Timber.—Oak and fir not common; all other kinds.—(*Lieut. Dun, 1881-82.*)

SEKPAO—

A Tankul village, on the Manipur-Kangjoi road, built after the usual Tankul pattern, about 5,000 feet above the sea-level, on the Nupitel ridge, containing 20 houses.

Inhabitants.—The inhabitants belong to the south-western section of the Tankul Naga tribe. Population 100, of whom 20 may be fighting-men.

Climate.—The climate is healthy at all seasons.

Water.—Scanty supply.

Supplies.—Rice-straw procurable. Scanty grazing. Principal grains are rice and múm. Firewood plentiful. Arum, yams, and pumpkins. Rice harvest in November; múm in December.

Live-stock.—Small number of pigs and poultry.

Transport.—For coolie purposes, 20 men and women.

Timber.—Bamboos scarce; oak, fir, and other kinds plentiful.

(*Lieut. Dun, 1881-82.*)

SEKTA—

A Manipur post on the western foot of the Yumadoung range, forming one of the first or inner line of frontier posts.—(*Lieut. Dun, 1881-82.*)

SENAM—

A Kuki village about 18 miles east by south of the Imphal.

SENGANG—

A Kuki village on the eastern face of the Kopru, Laimatol range, due west of Imphal.

SENGMAIE—

A Manipuri (Loï) village at the western foot of the Yumadoung range, a little south of the exit of the Thobal river from the hills.

Elevation.—
Temperature.—
Climate.— } *Vide* page 77, Changangai.

Houses.—25.

Inhabitants.—125, salt-makers.

Water.—Plentiful and good.
Camping-ground.— } *Vide* page 77, Changangai.
Products, &c.— }
Live-stock.—50 cows, 37 buffaloes.
Carriage.—25 carts, 12 boats.
Approaches—By field-paths through rice-field from all the neighbouring village.

SENGMAIE—

A Manipuri (Loï) village near the Tiki river, the first stage from Imphal, on the Kohima road.

There are 35 houses and the people are employed in liquor-making.

There is good and unlimited camping-ground near the Tiki, which is crossed by a weak bamboo bridge.

Products, &c.—*Vide* page 77, Changangai.
Live-stock.—Pigs and poultry only.

SENGMAIE—

A small stream, called higher up the Tusierok, and draining the valleys about Aimol. At Pallél it has in the cold weather 1 foot of water, but its bed is 50 yards broad.

SENGOPUNG—

A Kuki village. Now removed from the spot marked in the map.

SEPJANG—

A small new Kuki village of the Simmté tribe, consisting of 10 houses and one of the group in the Manipur source of the Tipai river.

Headman.—Sepjang, friendly.

SHANS*—

A tribe inhabiting the country east of the Ningthee river, and almost exclusively the Kubbo valley. They are governed by their own Tsawbwas (Rajas), but are subject to Burma.

Religion and Attitude.—The Shans are Buddhists, and would therefore undoubtedly prefer the rule of Burma always to that of Manipur; but they are very friendly towards Manipuris, and seem well inclined towards British officers. They would be glad of peaceful relations to revive trade.

The Tsawbwa of Samjok, however, does not appear friendly, and he might count on about 500 men, of whom 10 per cent. are armed with flint-locks, and probably also on the Chussad Kukis, whom he has indirectly abetted in their late courses, to assist him.

The Pagan Woon, a Burmese official, who resides at Tamoo and is supposed to control the foreign relations of Samjok and Kwendung, is personally friendly, but has little or no control over the Samjok Tsawbwa. The Khampat Woon rules the country south of Kwendung.

Language.—The Tat-hinoo (commander of stockade) of Mentha village and his followers, who were Shans, when interviewed by Mr. Phayre, spoke Burmese fluently. He said that the Shans of the Kubbo valley spoke different languages too, and could not understand the western Shans; but Mr. Phayre is of opinion that they belong to the same race, the difference of language being caused by long separation.

The Burmese language is taught in the monasteries, the inference being, though the Shans would not acknowledge it through fear or for some other

* For full account of Shans, see Report and Gazetteer of Burma, Part I, 1883.—*D. M.*

reason, that the Shan language is prohibited. There are still Shan manuscripts, however, in the monasteries.

Manners and Customs.—The Shans adopted the Burmese style of tying the hair and dressing in 1596—"two circumstances," says Pemberton, "which clearly prove their subjugation at that period to have been complete."

SHINGDA—

A small Manipuri hamlet, 6 miles to the north-west of Imphal.

SHIPROMI—

A Kolya Naga village, presumably of the Mau section, in Northern Manipur and on the western side of the Lanier valley.

Elevation.—About 4,500 feet.

Houses and Fighting-men.—One-hundred.

Water and Camping-ground.—Scanty.

Products, &c.—*Vide* page 78, Charo.

Live-stock.—A few cows, pigs, and poultry.

Carriage.—One-hundred and fifty coolies.

Approaches—Up gently sloping easy spur from the Lanier river.

SHONKITANG—

A new Kuki village of the Simmté clan in the valley of the Manipur source of the Tipai river.

Elevation.—About 3,000 feet.

Houses and Fighting-men.—Forty.

Products, &c.—
Water.—
Camping-ground.— } *Vide* page 77, Changangai.

Live-stock.—Ten metna, pigs, and poultry.

Carriage.—Eighty coolies.

Headman.—Mongbi, friendly.

SHUGUNU*—

A Manipuri (Loï) village at the extreme south-east corner of the main valley. The Imphal river here enters the hills.

Elevation.—
Temperature.—
Climate.— } *Vide* page 77, Changangai.

Houses.—Ten, Manipuri pattern.

Inhabitants.—Fifty.

Water.—Good and plentiful.

Camping-ground.—Unlimited.

Products, &c.—*Vide* page 77, Changangai.

Live-stock.—Twenty cows, 15 buffaloes.

Carriage.—Ten carts, 10 boats.

Approaches—Over open plain good broad road (unmetalled) from north and west; from the west cross the Imphal, 40 yards broad and 40 feet deep, in dug-out canoes. There is no bridge. The stream is scarcely perceptible.

SIEHAI—

A Tankul village, built after the usual Tankul pattern, about 5,000 feet above the sea-level, containing 15 houses.

* This used to be a penal settlement and place of execution for State criminals. During the present reign it has seldom been thus used.—(*J. Johnstone, 1885.*)

Camping-ground.—Terraced rice-fields available.

Inhabitants.—The inhabitants belong to the north-eastern section of the Tankul Naga tribe. Population 75, of whom 15 may be fighting-men. The chief is Changsol.

Climate.—The climate is healthy at all seasons.

Water.—Small supply west and north-east of village.

Supplies.—Rice-straw procurable. Scanty grazing. Principal grains are rice and múm. Firewood plentiful. Arúms, yams, and pumpkins. Rice harvest in November; múm in December.

Live-stock.—Small number of pigs and poultry.

Transport.—For coolie purposes, 15 men and women.

Timber.—Bamboos scarce; oak, fir, and other kinds plentiful.

(*Lieut. Dun, 1881-82.*)

SILCHAR—

The head-quarters of the Cachar district.

SILUK—

A Tankul village, built after the usual Tankul pattern, about 5,000 feet above the sea-level, containing 15 houses.

Inhabitants.—The inhabitants belong to the south-western section of the Tankul Naga tribe. Population 75, of whom 15 may be fighting-men. The chief is Kui-Kui.

Climate.—The climate is healthy at all seasons.

Water.—Small streams both on east and west of village.

Supplies.—Rice-straw procurable. Scanty grazing. Principal grains are rice and múm. Firewood plentiful. Arums, yams, and pumpkins. Rice harvest in November; múm in December.

Live-stock.—Pigs and poultry.

Transport.—For coolie purposes, 20 men and women.

Timber.—Bamboos scarce; oak, fir, and other kinds plentiful.

(*Lieut. Dun, 1881-82.*)

SINDHA—

A Tankul village, built after the usual Tankul pattern, about 4,000 feet above the sea-level, containing 10 houses.

Inhabitants.—The inhabitants belong to the south-western section of the Tankul Naga tribe. Population 50, of whom 10 may be fighting-men.

Climate.—The climate is unhealthy from beginning of August to end of October.

Supplies.—Rice-straw procurable. Scanty grazing. Principal grains are rice and múm. Firewood plentiful. Arums, yams, and pumpkins. Rice harvest in November; múm in December.

Live-stock.—Pigs and poultry.

Transport.—For coolie purposes, 10 men and women.

Timber.—Bamboos scarce; oak, fir, and other kinds plentiful.

(*Lieut. Dun, 1881-82.*)

SINGAL—

A Tankul village, built after the usual Tankul pattern, about 3,500 feet above the sea-level, containing 25 houses.

Camping-ground.—A little above the village on the west.

Approaches—By a gently sloping good path from the west, commanding the village. Up steep spur from the east, commanded by the village.

Inhabitants.—The inhabitants belong to the south-western section of the Tankul Naga tribe. Population 125, of whom 25 may be fighting-men. The chief is Mosáwa.

Climate.—The climate is unhealthy from beginning of August to end of October.

Water.—Plentiful supply north-west of village.

Supplies.—Rice-straw procurable. Very scanty grazing. Principal grain is rice. Firewood plentiful. Arums, yams, and pumpkins. Harvest in November.

Live-stock.—Pigs, poultry, and 5 metna.

Transport.—For coolie purposes, 25 men and women.

Timber.—Oak, fir, and many other forest trees.—(*Lieut. Dun, 1881-82.*)

SIPHONG—

A Tankul Naga village, of which little is known, in the next valley to the east of the Somrah basin. There are said to be about 300 houses. The country is covered with forest, but there is a good path to it from Somrah. It lies on the most direct route from Manipur to Sarameti.

SIROHI—

A Tankul village, built after the usual Tankul pattern, about 7,000 feet above the sea-level, containing 50 houses.

Camping-ground.—Terraced rice-fields available.

Inhabitants.—The inhabitants belong to the south-western section of the Tankul Naga tribe. Population 250, of whom 50 may be fighting-men. The chief is Maipah.

Climate.—The climate is healthy at all seasons.

Water.—Small supply on the south, close to village.

Supplies.—Rice-straw procurable. Scanty grazing. Principal grains are rice and múm. Firewood plentiful. Arums, yams, and pumpkins. Rice harvest in November; múm in December.

Live-stock.—Pigs, poultry, and a few metna.

Transport.—For coolie purposes, 50 men and women.

Timber.—Oak, fir, and many other forest trees.—(*Lieut. Dun, 1881-82.*)

SIROHIFARAR—

A peak in the centre of the mass of hills between the Kohima road and the Ningthee river. It sends down spurs on the north to the Lanier, on the south to the Kubbo valley.

There is plenty of water near the top of the peak. A road crosses over it, and there is plenty of camping-ground. The hill is chiefly covered with grass, alternating with patches of forest. The elevation of the summit is 8,420 feet above the sea.

SISEPHAMI—

A Kolya village on the Manipur road to Kohima, between Meitheipham thannah and Phunamah.

SITPONG—

An Aimol village on the Pallel-Moray route, built after the usual Kuki pattern, about 3,000 feet above the sea-level, containing 10 houses.

Camping-ground.—Sufficient in all for one regiment, at each end of the village.

Approaches.—From east and west along a tolerably broad and level ridge; very easy. Neither commands nor is commanded by the village. Palisades at each entrance.

Inhabitants.—The inhabitants belong to the Aimol subdivision of the Kom Kuki tribe. Population 150, of whom 30 are fighting-men.

Climate.—The climate is unhealthy from beginning of August to end of October.

Water.—Small stream south of village.

Supplies.—Rice-straw procurable. Fair grazing. Principal grains, rice and múm. Firewood plentiful. Yams, pumpkins, and plantains. Harvest in November and early in December.

Live-stock.—Pigs and poultry.

Transport.—For coolie purposes, 10 men and women.

Timber.—No heavy timber; small oaks; no firs.—(*Lieut. Dun, 1881-82.*)

SOMDAN—

A Tankul village, built after the usual Tankul pattern, above 5,000 feet above the sea-level, containing 150 houses.

Inhabitants.—The inhabitants belong to the north-eastern section of the Tankul Naga tribe. Population 750, of whom 150 may be fighting-men. The most influential man is Haying (interpreter).

Climate.—The climate is healthy at all seasons.

Supplies.—Probably rice-straw. Grazing believed to be fair. Principal grains are múm and chayan; rice doubtful. Firewood plentiful. Arums, yams, and pumpkins. Harvest in November and early in December.

Live-stock.—Pigs, poultry, and possibly a few metna.

Transport.—For coolie purposes, 30 men and women.

Timber.—Oaks, firs, and alders; bamboos not plentiful.—(*Lieut. Dun, 1881-82.*)

SOMRAH (NORTH PEAK)—

A sharp rocky peak at the northern end of the Somrah basin. It receives a good deal of snow in the winter. Some portions are covered with forest. Elevation 10,079 feet above the sea.

SOMRAH-GNÁCHÁN*—

A Tankul village, built after the usual Tankul pattern, about 5,000 feet above the sea-level, containing 30 houses.

* The people are the dirtiest I ever saw. The scenery is lovely.—(*J. Johnstone.*)

Inhabitants.—The inhabitants belong to the north-eastern section of the Tankul Naga tribe. Population 150, of whom 30 may be fighting-men.

Climate.—The climate is healthy at all seasons.

Supplies.—Probably rice-straw. Grazing believed to be fair. Principal grains are mum and chayan; rice doubtful. Firewood plentiful. Arums, yams, and pumpkins. Harvest in November and early in December.

Live-stock.—Pigs, poultry, and possibly a few metna.

Transport.—For coolie purposes, 30 men and women.

Timber.—Oaks,† firs, and alders; bamboos not plentiful.—(*Lieut. Dun, 1881-82.*)

† Chiefly firs.—(*J. Johnstone.*)

SOMRAH-KONGAI—

A Tankul village, built after the usual Tankul pattern, about 5,000 feet above the sea-level, containing 40 houses.

Inhabitants.—The inhabitants belong to the north-eastern section of the Tankul Naga tribe. Population 200, of whom 40 may be fighting-men.

Climate.—The climate is healthy at all seasons.

Supplies.—Probably rice-straw. Grazing believed to be fair. Principal grains are múm and chayan; rice doubtful. Firewood plentiful. Arums, yams, and pumpkins. Harvest in November and early in December.

Live-stock.—Pigs, poultry, and possibly a few metna.

Transport.—For coolie purposes, 40 men and women.

Timber.—Oaks, firs, and alders; bamboos not plentiful.—(*Lieut. Dun, 1881-82.*)

SOMRAH-KULEL—

A Tankul village, built after the usual Tankul pattern, about 5,000 feet* above the sea-level, containing 250 houses.

* 6,200 feet.—(*J. Johnstone.*)

Inhabitants.—The inhabitants belong to the north-eastern section of the Tankul Naga tribe. Population 1,250, of whom 250 may be fighting-men. The most influential man is Koito (interpreter).

Climate.—The climate is healthy at all seasons.

Supplies.—Probably rice-straw. Grazing believed to be fair. Principal grains are múm and chayan; rice doubtful. Firewood plentiful. Arums, yams, and pumpkins. Harvest in November and early in December.

Live-stock.—Pigs, poultry, and possibly a few metna.

Transporte.—For coolie purposes, 250 men and women.

Timber.—Oaks, firs, and alders; bamboos not plentiful.—(*Lieut. Dun, 1881-82.*)

SOMRAH-KÚNAO—

A Tankul village, built after the usual Tankul pattern, about 5,000 feet above the sea-level, containing 150 houses.

Inhabitants.—The inhabitants belong to the north-eastern section of the Tankul Naga tribe. Population 750, of wham 150 may be fighting-men.

Climate.—The climate is healthy at all seasons.

Supplies.—Probably rice-straw. Grazing believed to be fair. Principal grains are múm and chayan; rice doubtful. Firewood plentiful. Arums, yams, and pumpkins. Harvest in November and early in December.

Live-stock.—Pigs, poultry, and possibly a few metna.

Transport.—For coolie purposes, 150 men and women.

Timber.—Oaks, firs, and alders; bamboos not plentiful.—(*Lieut. Dun, 1881-82.*)

SOMRAH LIAM—

A Tankul village, built after the usual Tankul pattern, about 5,000 feet above the sea-level, containing 25 houses.

Inhabitants.—The inhabitants belong to the north-eastern section of the Tankul Naga tribe. Population 125, of whom 25 may be fighting-men.

Climate.—The climate is healthy at all seasons.

Supplies. Probably rice-straw. Grazing believed to be fair. Principal grains are múm and chayan; rice doubtful. Firewood plentiful. Arums, yams, and pumpkins. Harvest in November and early in December.

Live-stock.—Pigs, poultry, and possibly a few metna.

Transport.—For coolie purposes, 25 men and women should be available.

Timber.—Oaks, firs, and alders; bamboos not plentiful.—(*Lieut. Dun, 1881-82.*)

SOMRAH MAIALONG—

A Tankul village, built after the usual Tankul pattern, about 5,000 feet above the sea-level, containing 30 houses.

Inhabitants.—The inhabitants belong to the north-eastern section of the Tankul Naga tribe. Population 150, of whom 30 may be fighting-men.

Climate.—The climate is healthy at all seasons.

Supplies.—Probably rice-straw. Grazing believed to be fair. Principal grains are múm and chayan; rice doubtful. Firewood plentiful. Arums, yams, and pumpkins. Harvest in November and early in December.
Live-stock.—Pigs, poultry, and possibly a few metna.
Transport.—For coolie purposes, 30 men and women.
Timber.—Oaks, firs, and alders; bamboos not plentiful.—(*Lieut. Dun, 1881-82.*)

SOMRAH-PUNGTAR—

A Tankul village, built after the usual Tankul pattern, about 5,000 feet above the sea-level, containing 50 houses.
Inhabitants.—The inhabitants belong to the north-eastern section of the Tankul Naga tribe. Population 750, of whom 150 may be fighting-men.
Climate.—The climate is healthy at all seasons.
Supplies.—Probably rice-straw. Grazing believed to be fair. Principal grains are múm and chayan; rice doubtful. Firewood plentiful. Arums, yams, and pumpkins. Harvest in November and early in December.
Live-stock.—Pigs, poultry, and possibly a few metna.
Transport.—For coolie purposes, 150 men and women.
Timber.—Oaks, firs, and alders; bamboos not plentiful.—(*Lieut. Dun, 1881-82.*)

SOMRAH-TSEM.

A Tankul village, built after the usual Tankul pattern, about 5,000 feet above the sea-level, containing 30 houses.
Inhabitants.—The inhabitants belong to the north-eastern section of the Tankul Naga tribe. Population 150, of whom 30 may be fighting-men.
Climate.—The climate is healthy at all seasons.
Supplies.—Probably rice-straw. Grazing believed to be fair. Principal grains are múm and chayan; rice doubtful. Firewood plentiful. Arums, yams, and pumpkins. Harvest in November and early in December.
Live-stock.—Pigs, poultry, and possibly a few metna.
Transport.—For coolie purposes, 30 men and women.
Timber.—Oaks, firs, and alders; bamboos not plentiful.—(*Lieut. Dun, 1881-82.*)

SONGATEL—

A Marring village on the east side of the Kubbo valley.
Inhabitants.—The inhabitants belong to the Marring Naga tribe, and being amongst Shans might be useful in affording information.
(*Lieut. Dun, 1881-82.*)

SONGBU—

A subdivision of the Kaupui Naga tribe.

SONGHOL—

A village on the Pallel-Chakpi road to Nasinga thannah.
(*Lieut. Dun, 1881-82.*)

SORAH—

A Manipuri village, 1 mile west of the high road (eastern valley) and south of Lamting.
Elevation.—
Temperature.— } *Vide* page 77, Changangai.
Climate.—
Houses.—Thirty-five, Manipuri pattern.
Inhabitants.—One hundred and sixty-five, sepoy class.
Fighting-men.—Thirty-five.

Water.—
Camping-ground.— } *Vide* page 77, Changangai.
Products, &c.—
Live-stock.—Seventy cows, 42 buffaloes.
Carriage.—Thirty-five carts.
Approaches—By narrow and hard field-paths through rice-fields from neighbouring villages and from the high road.

SUKTI—

A tribe of Kukis living beyond Manipur jurisdiction, south of the valley. They are also called Kamhan and Wité.

SUMKHEL—

A new Kuki village of the Mangoung clan, in Northern Manipur and close to Karong thannah on the south-east.
Elevation.—About 4,500 feet.
Houses and fighting-men.—Thirty.
Water and Camping-ground.—Very little.
Products, &c.—*Vide* page 78, Charo.
Live-stock.—A few metna, pigs, and poultry.
Carriage.—Sixty coolies.
Headman.—Lankapau.
This man occupies a high place in Kuki estimation.

SUMMUMAI—

A subdivision of the Angami Naga tribe.

SUMPHEL—

A small Kuki village in North-West Manipur.

SUMRO TANGI—

A Manipuri village, 7 miles from Imphal on the Kokshingh-Longtival (central valley) road.
Elevation.—
Temperature.— } *Vide* page 77, Changangai.
Climate.—
Houses.—Fifty.
Inhabitants.—Two hundred and fifty, sepoy class.
Fighting-men.—Fifty.
Water.—
Camping-ground.— } *Vide* page 77, Changangai.
Products, &c.—
Live-stock.—One hundred cows, 75 buffaloes.
Carriage.—Fifty carts, 5 boats.
Approaches—By main road from north and south, two by a good mule-path from Sajing and Haurebi.

SUNKHALAL—

A small new Kuki village of 10 houses. The people are of the Simmté clan, and form part of the Simmté settlement in the valley of the Manipur source of the Tipai river.

SUSUKAMENG—

A Manipur post on the western foot of the Yumadoung hills, forming one of the first or inner line of frontier posts.—(*Lieut. Dun, 1881-82.*)

SWEMI OR CHINGJROI—

A Tankul Naga village in Northern Manipur, on the western side of the Lanier valley.

Elevation.—About 5,200 feet.

Houses and fighting-men.—Seventy.

Water and Camping-ground.—Scanty.

Products, &c.—*Vide* page 78, Charo.

Live-stock.—A few cows, pigs, and poultry.

Carriage.—One hundred coolies.

Approaches—Up a steep but open spur from the west.

The people are friendly.

T

TĀP THANNAH—

A Shan village, called by the Burmans Tat-ma-dar (main army), built after the usual Shan pattern, about 700 feet above the sea-level, on the site of Old Samjok. Formerly there was a stockade here and a considerable garrison; but since the Burmese standing army has been done away with, it has settled down into a peaceful village, and even the stockade no longer remains. There are 15 houses.

Camping-ground.—Any amount of ground.

Approaches.—From the village roads lead to Samjok, west to Manipur *viâ* Kanghom thannah and south to Tumoo.

Inhabitants.—The inhabitants belong to the Shan tribe. Population 75, of whom 15 may be fighting-men.

Climate.—The climate is unhealthy from beginning of June to end of October.

Water.—Plentiful supply.

Supplies.—Rice-straw procurable. Fair grazing. Principal grain is rice. Firewood plentiful. Yams, plantains, and pumpkins. Harvest in November and early in December.

Live-stock.—Pigs, poultry, and buffaloes.

Transport.—For coolie purposes, 15 men and women.

Timber.—Teak, sâl, and bamboo.—(*Phayre, 1881-82; Lieut. Dun, 1881-82.*)

TABO SNEEK—

A Burmese village on left bank of the Ningthee.

TAHOWPA—

A Chussad village, built after the usual Kuki pattern, about 2,000 feet above the sea-level, containing 6 houses.

This village, together with that of Channo, covers any advance on the Chussad Chief's village Tonghu.

Inhabitants.—The inhabitants belong to the Chussad subdivision of the Kongjai Kuki tribe. Population 30, of whom 9 may be fighting-men.

Climate.—The climate is unhealthy from beginning of August to end of October.

Supplies.—Rice-straw procurable. Indian-corn, rice, mum, and chayan. Firewood plentiful. Arums, beans, and pumpkins. Harvest in November and early in December.

Live-stock.—Pigs and poultry.

Transport.—For coolie purposes, 8 men and women.

Timber.—No oaks or firs; other kinds common.—(*Lieut. Dun, 1881-82.*)

TALOI—

A Tankul village, built after the usual Tankul pattern, about 4,500 feet above the sea-level, containing 200 houses.

Camping-ground.—Terraced rice-fields available.

Inhabitants.—The inhabitants belong to the north-eastern section of the Tankul Naga tribe. Population 1,000, of whom 200 may be fighting-men. The most influential man is Ang-owba (interpreter).

Climate.—The climate is healthy at all seasons.

Supplies.—Rice-straw procurable. Fair grazing. Principal grains are rice and múm. Firewood plentiful. Yams and pumpkins. Rice harvest in November; mum in December.

Live-stock.—Pigs, poultry, and a few metna.
Transport.—For coolie purposes, 200 men and women.
Timber.—Chiefly oak and fir.—(*Lieut. Dun, 1881-82.*)

TAMLAIE—

A Marring village, north of the Hytuk-pokpi-Yanga-pokpi route, built after the usual Marring pattern, about 3,000 feet above the sea-level, containing 10 houses. The village is out of sight of, and does not at all command, the road.

Inhabitants.—The inhabitants belong to the Marring Naga tribe. Population 50, of whom 15 may be fighting-men. The headman is Mépul.

Climate.—The climate is unhealthy from beginning of August to end of October.

Water.—Plentiful supply.

Supplies.—Rice-straw procurable. Good grazing. Principal grains are Indian-corn, rice, mum, and chayan. Firewood plentiful. Arums, beans, and pumpkins. Harvest in November and early in December.

Live-stock.—Pigs and poultry.

Transport.—For coolie purposes, 10 men and women.

Timber.—No forest trees; bushy oaks, &c.—(*Lieut. Dun, 1881-82.*)

TAMOO OR TUMMOO—

A Shan village, called by the Burmese Tat-oo-daw (advance guard), built after the usual Shan pattern, about 700 feet above sea-level, containing from 30 to 40 houses.

There was formerly a stockade here and a Burmese garrison, but the stockade no longer exists, and it is now a peaceful village.

The village is one mile distant from the Maglung (Yoo Choung) river.

Camping-ground.—Unlimited camping-ground, free from thick undergrowth.

Approaches—By a broad path through forest land.

Inhabitants.—The inhabitants belong to the Shan tribe. Population about 175, of whom 35 may be fighting-men. The most influential man is the Pagan Woon, Moung Pagan by name. The Bishop of Tamoo has spiritual jurisdiction over 37 villages in the district. His name is Oo-Endawara, and though a Yahan, he interferes a good deal in civil matters, though generally for the public good. He is much revered, and even feared somewhat, for he communicates direct with the Hlwoot.

Climate.—The climate is unhealthy from beginning of June to end of October.

Water.—Plentiful supply.

Supplies.—Rice-straw procurable. Fair grazing. Principal grain is rice. Firewood plentiful. Yams, plantains, and pumpkins. Harvest in November and early part of December.

Live-stock.—Pigs, poultry, and buffaloes.

Transport.—For coolie purposes, 35 men and women.

Timber.—Teak, sâl, and bamboo.—(*Lieut. Dun, 1881-82; Phayre, 1881-82.*)

TAMPUNG—

A Katcha Naga in the north-west corner of Manipur territory.

It is said to contain 50 houses, which would enable it to furnish 75 coolies and 50 fighting-men.

It is situated at an elevation of about 5,500 feet, and would therefore be healthy. There is probably plenty of water and camping-ground, judging from the villages in the vicinity.

It is connected by paths, more or less practicable, with all the neighbouring villages, including those in British territory.

TAMSAL—

A small Marring village of 10 houses, situated on the hills east of Shugum and south of Pallel.

The water-supply and camping-ground are scanty.

Products, &c.—*Vide* page 78, Charo.

Live-stock.—A few metna and cows, besides pigs and poultry.

TANAN—

A Shan village, 12 miles from Kongal thannah on the road to Samjok, containing 6 houses.—(*Major Badgeley, 1881-82.*)

TAN-BEN-GOONG—

A Burmese village on the left bank of the Ningthee river.

TANGBOONG—

(*Vide* Lushai.)

TANG-KULET—

A new Kuki village of the Simmté clan, situated in the valley of the Manipur branch of the Tipai.

Elevation.—About 3,000 feet; it is therefore unhealthy for Europeans between the 1st May and the 1st December.

Houses.—Forty, Kuki pattern.

Inhabitants.—One-hundred and sixty.

Fighting-men.—Forty.

Water.—
Camping-ground.—
Products, &c.— } *Vide* page 77, Chanjang.

Live-stock.—A few metna, pigs, and poultry.

Carriage.—Eighty coolies.

TANGO—

A Tankul village, built after the usual Tankul pattern, about 5,000 feet above the sea-level, containing 70 houses.

Camping-ground.—Terraced rice-fields available.

Inhabitants.—The inhabitants belong to the north-eastern section of the Tankul Naga tribe. Population 350, of whom 70 may be fighting-men. The most influential man is Koisumbah (interpreter).

Climate.—The climate is healthy at all seasons.

Supplies.—Rice-straw procurable. Principal grains are rice and múm. Firewood plentiful. Yams and pumpkins. Rice harvest in November; múm in December.

Live-stock.—Pigs, poultry, and a few metna.

Transport.—For coolie purposes, 60 men and women.

Timber.—Chiefly oak and fir.—(*Lieut. Dun, 1881-82.*)

TANGSOWA—

A subdivision of the Marring Naga tribe. (*Vide* Naga.)

TANGTOM—

A new Kuki village of the Simmté clan, situated in the valley of the Manipur source of the Tipai river.

It contains 20 houses, and is in every other respect similar to the village of Tang-kulet described above.
It could supply 20 fighting-men or 40 coolies.

TANKULS—
A division of the Naga tribe, sometimes also called Luhupas.

TARAPOKPI—
A small Kaupui village at the foot of the northern slope of Langol.

TAT-MA-DAW—
The Burmese name (meaning "the main army") for Tāp.

TÁT-OO-DAW—
The Burmese name (meaning "the advance guard") for Tummoo.

TAUBAL—
A Manipuri village, one mile north of Bishenpur and east of the Cachar road.
Elevation.—
Temperature.— } *Vide* page 77, Changangai.
Climate.—
Houses.—Forty, Manipuri pattern.
Inhabitants.—Two hundred, Keiroi.
Fighting-men.—Forty.
Water.—
Camping-ground.— } *Vide* page 77, Changangai.
Products.—
Live-stock.—Eighty cows, 60 buffaloes.
Carriage.—Forty carts.
Approaches—By narrow and indifferent tracks from Bishenpur and Naikong.

TAUBONGKO—
A small Manipuri village, 3 miles south-west of Imphal.

TAZEE-MYO—
A Burmese town in the Moo valley, about 5 miles north of Kyaymoo.

TEMIMI—
A Kolya Naga village on the northern frontier of Manipur. It has about 100 houses.

TENDOLYAL—
A small Kaupui Naga village, 1 mile to the west of the Kohima road and 8 miles from Imphal.

TENTA—
A Manipuri village on the Arung stream, on the eastern edge of the main valley.
Elevation.—
Temperature.— } *Vide* page 77, Changangai.
Climate.—
Houses.—25, Manipuri pattern.
Inhabitants.—125.
Fighting-men.—25.
Water.—Plentiful.
Camping-ground.— } *Vide* page 77, Changangai.
Products, &c.—

Live-stock.—50 cows, 37 buffaloes.
Carriage.—25 carts.

The people of this village have charge of about 100 buffaloes belonging to the Raja.

THANBOUK—

A Burmese village of 20 or 30 houses on the left bank of the Ningthee in about latitude 22° 55′; road fair.

From here to Kendat Dr. Richardson (1833) found the road impassable for any sort of carriage, but boats may be had on the river. From Thanbouk to Ava the road is good; and water, cattle, grain, and every necessary in greatest abundance.

THANDAM—

A Manipuri village, situated at the junction of the Imphal and Thobal rivers.

There are 25 houses, and it is similar in all respects to the village of Tenta. The inhabitants belong to the sepoy class.

THANG-KONG—

A stream in the Somrah basin.

THAUREJAM—

A Manipuri village on the western outskirts of Imphal.

THAURIPHI—

A small Manipuri village, 6 miles from Imphal, on the Kohima road.

THA-YA-GON—

A Burmese village on the Ningthee, opposite to Kunni-myo.

THEBOMAI OR KOHIMA*—

A subdivision of the Angami Naga tribe.

THEBONUMAH—

A Kolya Naga village in Northern Manipur on the western side of the Sijjo valley.

Elevation.—About 5,000 feet. It is therefore healthy at all seasons.
Houses.—100.
Fighting-men.—100.
Water.—
Camping-ground.— } *Vide* page 89, Hebubvomah.
Products, &c.—
Live-stock.—120 cows, pigs, and poultry.
Carriage.—140 coolies.

The people belong to the Mau section, and are friendly.

THETCHOLUMI OR TILOMI—

A Kolya Naga village in Northern Manipur and on the range forming the western side of the Razarr stream.

Elevation.—4,700 feet.
Temperature.—36° at sunrise in January.
Climate.—Healthy at all seasons.
Houses and Fighting-men.—75.
Water.—Fair supply below the village on the west.
Camping-ground.—Sufficient for 200 men.
Products, &c.—*Vide* page 78, Charo.

* Any Angami Naga village; Thepomai is the Manipuri name.

Live-stock.—Pigs, poultry, and a few cows.
Carriage.—100 coolies.
Approaches.—Up a steep slope through light jungle from the Lanier on the east.

THETZIRI—

One of the principal tributaries of the Lanier. It is everywhere favourable during the cold weather. It flows in a remarkably flat and open valley.

THEY-GOIN—

A small Burmese village on the Ava-Kendat road. Some remarkable pagodas.

THINGRA—

A small Kaupui Naga village in North-West Manipur.

THINGSA—

A Tangál Naga village near the mouth of the Tiki valley on the hills bounding it on the east.

THOBAL—

The second largest stream in the valley. In the hills it is a clear mountain stream, but in the plains flows in a muddy high-banked channel. At the Thobal bazaar, there are not more than 3 feet of water in it in the cold weather. It is bridged by a bamboo bridge passable by mules.

THOBÁL—

A Manipuri village on the river of the same name, situated at the southern end of the Nongmaiching spurs.

It is the most important of the Manipur villages, as the ground about it allows of indefinite expansion, and it is situated in a commanding position with regard to the routes to Burma.

Elevation.—
Temperature.— } *Vide* page 77, Changangai.
Climate.—

Houses.—One hundred and fifty, Manipuri pattern.
Inhabitants.—Seven hundred and fifty, sepoy class.
Fighting-men.—One hundred and fifty.
Water.—Plentiful.
Camping ground—Sufficient for 2,000 men and transport on the low hills and spurs north of the village.
Products.—*Vide* page 77, Changangai.
Grazing.—Very good in the cold weather.
Live-stock.—Three hundred cows, 225 buffaloes.
Carriage.—One hundred and fifty carts, 100 boats.
Approaches—By eastern valley road from the north-west, crossing a spur by a narrow pass 2 miles from the village. Open road from the south-east.

The village is owned by the Raja.

THOWNI—

A Manipuri village, about 18 miles north-east of the city.

THRENGBA—

A subdivision of the Kolya Naga tribe. (*Vide* Naga.)

THUMION—

A peak on the range east of Tiki stream and close above the head of that and the Mayang-Khang streams.

Elevation.—5,800 feet above the sea.

THUMION KULEL—

A Kolya Naga village of the Maram section, situated on the range west of the Tiki.

Elevation.—About 4,600 feet.

Houses and fighting-men.—Twenty.

Water.—Plentiful.

Products, &c.—*Vide* page 78, Charo.

Live-stock.—Twenty-five cows, a few buffaloes, and pigs and poultry.

Carriage.—Thirty-five coolies.

Headman.—Tappau.

THUMION KUNAO—

An off-shoot of Thumion Kulel and containing 8 houses, situated about the same position, but lower down in elevation.

THUNG-THWUT—

(*Vide* Samjok.)

THUNGUN—

A Burmese village of 80 houses, about 4 miles from the left bank of the Ningthee.

TIKI OR TURÉL ACHAUBA OR IMPHÁL TURÉL—

It is undoubtedly the stream which has laid down the greater part of the alluvium of the Manipur valley, the surface of which is raised 2,000 feet above the level of the valleys on either side.

The disparity between the quantity of soil deposited and the size of the stream which has brought it down is at once evident.

Of course the existence of a bar to the free egress of the stream, such as is known to exist at the Chindanhut, is sufficient to account for the damming of the water and the consequent deposition of silt above the bar, but hardly to the extent found in the Manipur valley.

The valley of the Tiki, moreover, is larger than that of the Barak river.

Proceeding up the Tiki along the Kohima road, we find gravel, and sandy spurs stretching almost across the valley from the range on the west, and the watershed between the Burmese and Indian drainage is simply one of these spurs, composed of gravel and sand which has successfully blocked up the valley.

The theory of the existence of glaciers at one time round the peak of Japvo, from which most of the drainage of Manipur starts, was raised by Colonel Godwin-Austen in 1873 from an inspection of the eastern and southern sides. This has been doubted by subsequent visitors; but an inspection of the ground at Pukri, at Togwema, and between that village and Kenoma, more especially the Liyang plateau, where huge water-worn boulders are scattered about, and the ground is evidently moraine formation, would satisfy any one of its correctness.

The botanical evidence too of the plants found on the ranges in this part point to the conclusion that the peaks were not long ago considerably more elevated than they are now.

Here, then, we have a possibly much larger stream of water caused by the melting of snow and ice.

At present the Barak valley carries off the major part of the water from Japvo, but it is impossible to see the country between Chakka on the south and Liyang on the north without coming to the conclusion that a vast split in the range has occurred here, and that the waters from the Maithaipham and other valleys, which used at one time to flow through the Mayangkhang-Tiki valley, now pour though this cleft in the range. Very similar splits are observable in the Barrail range a few miles west of Paona peak, through which the waters of the Kenoma stream must at once have narrowly escaped flowing, between the Sarameti peak and the northern peak of the Somrah basin and through which the Lanier empties itself into the Ningthee.

TINGIARU—

A tributary of the Thetzirr, Northern Manipur.

TINGLOPAL—

A halting place on the Pallel-Moray route.

Camping-ground.—Enough camping-ground for two regiments.

Water —Very scanty supply.—(*Lieut. Dun, 1881-82.*)

TINGRI—

A small Tangál Naga village, 8 miles from Imphal on the Kohima road.

TINLENG—

A small stream, forming the eastern source of the Nammia.

It drains part of the Chussad country on the northern end of the Kubbo valley.

TIPAI OR TURVAI—

This stream, though inconsiderable in the cold weather, is of large size during the rains, as its receives all the drainage of South Manipur. It joins the Barak at Tipai Mukh.

TIPAI MUKH—

The point where the Tipai or, as it is called by Kukis, the Tuivai, empties itself into the Barak.

At the extreme southern point of the Nunjaibong range, round which the Barak sweeps, there is a stone* with a Manipuri inscription showing the limit of Manipur dominions in this direction. There is ample camping-ground for a large force, and a bazaar kept up by Bengalis and Manipuris from the Cachar district.

* Set up by a Raja of Manipur on his return from an expedition against Tipperah in the middle of the last century.—(*J. Johnstone.*)

Four or five paths converge here—

From the Cachar district along the right bank of the Barak.

From the west across the Buban range.

From the North Cachar hills along the Nunjaibong range.

A made path into the Lushai country to the south, and a few paths to villages near.

TOKPO—

A subdivision of the Kolya Naga tribe.

TOLPI—

A new Kuki village of the Simmté clan, one of the groups in the valley of the Manipur source of the Tipai river. It has 20 houses. Its headman, Tolpi, is of no great importance.

TONGHLANG—

A Mangoung village, built after the usual Kuki pattern, about 3,500 feet above the sea-level, containing 50 houses.

Inhabitants.—The inhabitants belong to the Mangoung subdivision of the Kongjai Kuki tribe. Population 250, of whom 75 may be fighting-men. Their chief and most influential man is Sunet.

Climate.—The climate is unhealthy from beginning of August to end of October.

Supplies.—Rice-straw procurable. Fair grazing. Principal grains are Indian-corn, rice, múm, and chayan. Firewood plentiful. Arums, yams, and pumpkins. Harvest in November and early in December.

Live-stock.—Pigs and poultry.

Transport.—For coolie purposes, 50 men and women.

Timber.—No forest trees; bushes of oak, &c.—(*Lieut. Dun, 1881-82.*)

TONGHU OR CHUSSAD—

The chief village of the Chussad Kuki tribe, built after the usual Kuki pattern, about 2,000 feet above the sea-level, containing 100 houses.

Camping-ground.—There is sufficient scattered ground for one regiment to encamp, chiefly at the north-east end of the village.

Approaches.—From the north the path follows a gradually ascending ridge, open and narrow in several places. It is defended at 1¼ miles from the village by a palisade.

From the south the path, after passing between the villages of Chunnyang, Moluni, and Changlle, passes under a stockaded hill. The last part descends to Tonghu and commands the village. The road is very bad in parts.

The village is in the centre of the Chussad villages, Mankot and Chowhoom, cover any advance on it from the north; Rabyang and Punjoong from the west; Chunyang from the south; and Channo and Tahowpa from the east.

Inhabitants.—The inhabitants belong to the Chussad subdivision of the Kongjai Kuki tribe. Population 500, of whom 150 are fighting-men. Their chief is Tonghu, a boy. His mantri or minister, Rabyang, is a fine and intelligent man.

Climate.—The climate is unhealthy from beginning of August to end of October.

Water.—Scanty supply on east and west of villages.

Supplies.—Rice-straw procurable. Scanty grazing. Principal grains are Indian-corn, rice, múm, and chayan. Firewood plentiful. Arums, beans, and pumpkins. Harvest in November and early in December.

Transport.—For coolie purposes, 100 men and women.

Timber.—No firs; bamboos plentiful, and a fair supply of oaks.

(*Lieut. Dun, 1881-82.*)

TONG-KANG—

A Marring village, built after the usual Marring pattern, about 3,500 feet above the sea-level, containing 5 houses.

Inhabitants.—The inhabitants belong to the Marring Naga tribe. Population 25, of whom 7 may be fighting-men. The headman is Weirokpa.
Climate.—The climate is unhealthy from beginning of August to end of October.
Supplies.—Rice-straw procurable. Fair grazing. Principal grains are Indian-corn, rice, múm, and chayan. Firewood plentiful. Arums, beans, pumpkins. Harvest in November and early in December.
Live-stock.—Pigs and poultry.
Transport.—For coolie purposes, 5 men and women.
Timber.—No forest trees; bushes of oaks, &c.—(*Lieut. Dun, 1881-82.*)

TONGKULET—

A new Kuki village of the Simmté clan, situated in the valley of the Manipur source of the Tipai river.

It has 40 houses, and is in every respect similar to Chanjang. The headman, Tongkulet, is friendly. He is of no special importance.

TOOSHEL—

A Tankul village in the north-east of Manipur.

TOUNG-BAW—

A Shan village, 18 miles from Kongal thannah, on the eastern base of the Ungochin range, containing 18 houses.
(*Phayre, 1881-82; Major Badgeley, 1881-82.*)

TOUNG-DWEN-GYOUNG—

A Burmese town, south-west of Mengyen.

TOWAJE—

A Tankul village, built after the usual Tankul pattern, about 3,000 feet above the sea-level, containing 8 houses.
Inhabitants.—The inhabitants belong to the south-western section of the Tankul Naga tribe. Population 40, of whom 8 may be fighting-men. The most influential man is Marosung (interpreter.)
Climate.—The climate is unhealthy from beginning of August to end of October.
Water.—Plentiful supply.
Supplies.—Rice-straw procurable. Scanty grazing. Principal grains are rice and múm. Firewood plentiful. Pumpkin, yam, and ginger. Rice harvest in November; múm in December.
Live-stock.—Pigs and poultry.
Transport.—For coolie purposes, 5 men and women.
Timber.—Well wooded.—(*Lieut. Dun, 1881-82.*)

TOYUNGBA—

A small river of Manipur, crossed by the Kongal route *viá* Pong, 18 miles from the Thobal.

At this point it is 40 yards broad, a foot deep, and full of boulders.
(*Lieut. Dun, 1881-82.*)

TSAGAIN*—

A Burmese town on the right bank of the Irrawaddy, opposite to Ava. The Burmese have recently fortified this place (1882).

* For full account, see Burma Gazetteer, 1883, Part I.

TSAYE—

A large Burmese village on the Ava-Kendat road, about 8 miles north by west of Tsagain. Road level and good; much cultivation; cattle plenty.

The country from this place to Mount Zobo is said to be under water from July till September.

TSCHADANGON—

A village between Toung-baw and Samjok on the Nalthangit river, containing 6 houses.—(*Major Badgeley, 1881-82.*)

TSENDAT—

A Burmese village on the right bank of the Irrawaddy, about 10 miles west of Tsagain.

TSHAK-TA—

A Burmese village on the left bank of the Ningthee, containing 20 houses. (*Capt. Grant, 1882.*)

TSOLORE—

The upper course of the Iril river.

TUICHUM—

A new Kuki village of the Simmté clan, situated in the valley of the Manipur source of the Tipai river.

It has 20 houses and is in all respects similar to Chanjang.

TUIMUN—

A small western tributary of the Lanier.

TUIYANG—

A Kuki village on the western slope of Kopru.

TULÊM—

A Changput village, built after the usual Kuki pattern, about 3,500 feet above the sea-level, containing 30 houses.

Inhabitants.—The inhabitants belong to the Changput subdivision of the Kongjai Kuki tribe. Population 150, of whom 45 may be fighting-men. The chief and most influential man is Chungam (hun).

Climate.—The climate is unhealthy from beginning of August to end of October.

Water.—Scanty supply.

Supplies.—Rice-straw procurable. Fair grazing. Principal grains are Indian corn, rice, múm, and chayan. Firewood plentiful. Arums, beans, and pumpkins. Harvest in November and early in December.

Live-stock.—Pigs and poultry.

Transport.—For coolie purposes, 45 men and women.

Timber.—No firs; plenty of bamboos; a fair supply of oaks. (*Lieut. Dun, 1881-82.*)

TULMU—

A new Kuki village of the Simmté clan, situated in the valley of the Manipur source of the Tipai River.

It has 15 houses, and is similar in all respects to Chanjang.

TUMNOPOKPI—

A Tangal Naga village on the Thumion range, east of the Tiki stream.

Elevation.—About 3,300 feet.

Houses.—Twenty-five.
Water.—Plentiful.
Camping-ground.—Scanty.
Products, &c.—*Vide* page 78, Charo.
Live-stock.—A few cows, pigs, and poultry.
Carriage.—Forty-five coolies.

TUNGBYA—

A small Shan village in the Kubbo valley, at the foot of the Ungochin range, on the road from Tamoo towards Ava.—(*Lieut. Dun, 1881-82.*)

TUNGTANGNA—

A subdivision of the Marring Naga tribe. (*Vide* Naga.)

TUNGUM—

A stream crossed by the Hytuk-pokpi-Yanga-pokpi route.
(*Lieut. Dun, 1881-82.*)

TUNNAM—

A small Koireng village on the Turbúng, but within the main Manipur valley.

It has only 10 houses, and is similar in all respects to Chanjáng.

TUPHAN—

A Burmese village opposite to Samjok.

TURBUNG—

A fair sized stream which enters the Manipur valley at the south-west corner. It flows through a remarkably wide, flat-bottomed valley, which affords a most admirable place for camping-grounds at all seasons of the year. The bottom of the valley and the lower slopes of the hills are covered with grass. Higher up there is light oak forest and the top of the bounding ranges on either side are clothed with thick forest. The stream is fordable at every point except in the very height of the rains.

TURET—

A mountain stream of inconsiderable size, which drains the central section of the hills between the Manipur and the Kubbo valleys. It finds its exit close to Yanga-pokpi thannah in the Kubbo valley, and shortly afterwards empties into the Maglang.

TURI—

A northern confluent of the Iril river. A small stream of Cepri in the height of the rains.

TURNOONG—

A large Burmese village, about 3 miles inland, on the left bank of the Ningthee.

TURNOONG-SNEEK—

A Burmese village of 40 houses on the left bank of the Ningthee. Below this is shown on Captain Grant's map (1832) a Burmese stockade.

TUSEM—

A Tankul village, built after the usual Tankul pattern, about 6,000 feet above the sea-level, containing 100 houses.
Camping-ground.—Terraced rice-fields available.

Inhabitants.—The inhabitants belong to the north-eastern section of the Tankul Naga tribe. Population 500, of whom 100 may be fighting-men. The chief is Yensenba. Penakongha, the interpreter, has much influence.

Climate.—The climate is healthy at all seasons.

Supplies.—Rice-straw procurable. Scanty grazing. Principal grains are rice and múm. Firewood plentiful. Arums, yams, and pumpkins. Rice harvest in November; múm in December.

Live-stock.—Pigs, poultry, and a few metna.

Transport.—For coolie purposes, 100 men and women.

Timber.—Bamboos scarce; chiefly oaks and firs.—(*Lieut. Dun, 1881-82.*)

TUSIEROK—

A stream in the Yumadoung hills, the narrow valley of which is followed for some distance by the Pallel-Moray road after leaving Pallel.

(*Lieut. Dun, 1881-82.*)

TUSOM—

A peak on the western side of the Somrah basin and east of the village of the same name.

It is an isolated cone, covered with forest. Its sides are steep, but the road into the Somrah basin from the west crosses it a short way below the summit.

Elevation.—8,252 feet above the sea.

TUSOM-KULEL—

A Tankul village, built after the usual Tankul pattern, about 5,000 feet above the sea-level, containing 110 houses.

Camping-ground.—Terraced rice-fields available.

Inhabitants.—The inhabitants belong to the north-eastern section of the Tankul Naga tribe. Population 550, of whom 110 may be fighting-men. The most influential man is Yamang (interpreter).

Climate.—The climate is healthy at all seasons.

Supplies.—Rice-straw procurable. Scanty grazing. Principal grains are rice and múm. Firewood plentiful. Yams and pumpkins. Rice harvest in November; múm in December.

Live-stock.—Pigs and poultry.

Transport.—For coolie purposes, 110 men and women.

Timber.—All sorts plentiful, except bamboos.—(*Lieut. Dun, 1881-82.*)

TUSOM-KUNAO—

A Tankul village, built after the usual Tankul pattern, about 3,000* feet above the sea-level, containing 9 houses.

* Over 6,000 feet.—(*J. Johnstone.*)

Inhabitants.—The inhabitants belong to the south-western section of the Tankul Naga tribe. Population 45, of whom 9 may be fighting-men.

Climate.—The climate is unhealthy from beginning of August to end of October.

Water.—Scanty supply.

Supplies.—Rice-straw procurable. Scanty grazing. Principal grains are rice and múm. Firewood plentiful. Yams and pumpkins.

Rice harvest in November; múm in December.

Live-stock.—Pigs and poultry.

Transport.—For coolie purposes, 10 men and women.

Timber.—All sorts plentiful, except bamboos.—(*Lieut. Dun, 1881-82.*)

TUYANG—

A Kaupu Naga village at the north-west corner of the Kaupum plateau, just above Lilonong thannah on the west.

Elevation.—4,100 feet.

Houses and fighting-men.—Fifteen.

Water.—Scanty, distant, and difficult to reach, on western side below the village.

Camping-ground.—If the ground were cleared beforehand, 400 men could be accommodated. There is room without clearing for 100 men only.

Products.—*Vide* page 78, Charo.

Live-stock.—Twelve buffaloes, pigs, and poultry.

Carriage.—Twenty coolies.

Approaches—Up steep narrow jungle-covered ridge from Lilonong thannah.

Along a similarly steep and in places very narrow ridge from the Kaupum peak.

There is a precipitous path direct from the rice-fields below on the south-east.

TUYUNGBA—

The western branch of the Máglang Yumadoung range. It is fordable at any point except during the rains.

U

UAPHANG—

A small Chiru village on the western slopes of Kopru.

UCHIWA—

A Manipuri village on the Imphál river, south of its junction with the Thobál. It has 25 houses, and is similar in all respects to Changangai, page

Live-stock.—50 cows, 37 buffaloes.

Carriage.—25 carts, 12 boats.

Approaches—By good mule-paths along the Imphál and Thobál rivers.

UKHA—

A Changput village, built after the usual Kuki pattern, about 3,500 feet above the sea-level, containing 30 houses.

Inhabitants.—The inhabitants belong to the Changput subdivision of the Kongjai Kuki tribe. Population 150, of whom 45 may be fighting-men. The chief and most influential man is Chungam.

Climate.—The climate is unhealthy from beginning of August to end of October.

Water.—Scanty supply.

Supplies.—Rice-straw procurable. Good grazing. Principal grains are Indian-corn, rice, múm, and chayan. Firewood plentiful. Arum, beans, and pumpkins. Harvest in November and early part of December.

Live-stock.—Pigs, poultry, and a few metna.

Transport.—For coolie purposes, 45 men and women.

Timber.—Chiefly oaks; a few bamboos.—(*Lieut. Dun, 1881-82.*)

UKLONG OR WONLO—

A Kolya Naga village of the Marám section, situated on the range within the great northern bend of the Barák river.

Elevation.—5,500 feet.

Climate.—Healthy at all seasons.

Houses and fighting-men.—30.

Water.—Good and plentiful on the eastern side of the village.

Camping-ground.—Sufficient at the village for 200 men without clearing jungle.

Products, &c.—*Vide* page 78, Charo.

Live-stock.—100 cows, pigs, and poultry.

Carriage.—45 coolies.

Approaches—Up easy slopes through light jungle from north and south. The northern path traverses a spur with some narrow places not far below the village, and could be defended with ease at those points.

UKONG-SHANG—

A Manipuri village at the western foot of the Yumadoung range, 2 miles west of Ingorók.

There are 40 houses, the people belong to the sepoy class, and it is in every respect similar to Changangai—*Vide* page 77.

Live-stock.—80 cows, 60 buffaloes.

Carriage.—40 carts.

UKRUL—

A Tankul village, built after the usual Tankul pattern, about 5,000 feet above the sea-level, containing 250 houses.

Camping-ground.—Terraced rice-fields available.

Inhabitants.—The inhabitants belong to the north-eastern section of the Tankul Naga tribe. Population 1,250, of whom 250 may be fighting-men. The chief is Paraiching. Kong-yamba, the interpreter, has much influence.

Climate.—The climate is healthy at all seasons.

Supplies.—Rice-straw procurable. Scanty grazing. Principal grains are rice and múm. Firewood plentiful. Yams and pumpkins. Rice harvest in November; múm in December.

Live-stock.—Pigs, poultry, and 50 metna.

Transport.—For coolie purposes, 250 men and women.

Timber.—All sorts plentiful, except bamboos.—(*Lieut. Dun, 1881-82.*)

ULANG—

A new Kuki village of the Simmté clan. It is one of the clusters in the valley of the Manipur source of the Tipai river.

It has 20 houses, and is similar in all respects to Chanjang—page 77.

ULAU—

A Manipuri village on the Cachar road, 8 miles from Imphal.

There are 50 houses, the inhabitants are sepoys (artillery), but in all other respects it is similar to Changangai—page 77.

The live-stock is estimated at—

Cows, 100; buffaloes, 75; ponies 10.

Carriage.—50 carts, 10 boats.

UNCHUNG—

A new Kuki village of the Simmté clan.

Situated on the valley of the Manipur source of the Tipai river.

It has 10 houses, and is similar in every respect to Chanjang—page 77.

VAKOLPA—

A Kuki village in North-West Mánipur.

VIRATAI—

The eastern confluent of the Thetzirr, North Manipur.

It is fordable throughout the cold weather.

It flows in a wide open flat-bottomed valley without a violent current.

The whole of its valley is excellently suited for camping-grounds.

VISWEMA—

An Angami village, built after the usual Angami pattern, about 4,500 feet above the sea-level, containing 800 houses, situated between Phunamah and Kohima, on the ridge of the same name.

Camping-ground.—Plenty in terraced rice-fields.

Approaches.—Along a ridge, about 200 yards broad and on a level with village from the west.

No natural or artificial defences.

Inhabitants.—The inhabitants belong to the Angami Naga tribe, and are subdivided as follows, *viz.*, Ratzoma, Levama, Khiz-hazama, and Pabema. Population 4,000, of whom 800 may be fighting-men. The most influential men are Tebu and Nú-hé.

Climate.—The climate is healthy at all seasons.

Water.—Small supply at the village itself; plenty half mile to the north.

Supplies.—Rice-straw procurable. Fair grazing. Principal grains are rice, múm, and chayan. Rather moderate supply of firewood. Arums and pumpkins. Harvest in November and December.

Live-stock.—Cows in large numbers, pigs, and poultry.

Transport.—For coolie purposes, 800 men, women, and children.

Timber.—Very little oak or fir; small pollarded alders; bamboos scarce.

(*Lieut. Dun, 1881-82.*)

VUMLÁM—

A new Kuki village of the Simmté clan in the valley of the Manipur source of the Tipai river.

There are only 10 houses, and the village is similar in all respects to Chanjang.

W

WABACHING—

A Marring village near the Hytuk-pokpi-Yanga-pokpi road, built after the usual Marring pattern, about 3,500 feet above the sea-level, containing 6 houses.

The village is out of sight of the road, and does not command it at all.

Inhabitants.—The inhabitants belong to the Marring Naga tribe. Population 30, of whom 9 may be fighting-men.

Climate.—The climate is unhealthy from beginning of August to end of October.

Water.—Plentiful supply, but distant.

Supplies.—Rice-straw procurable. Good grazing. Principal grains are Indian-corn, rice, múm, and chayan. Firewood plentiful. Arums, beans, and pumpkins. Harvest in November and early in December.

Live-stock.—Pigs and poultry.

Transport.—For coolie purposes, 6 men and women.

Timber.—No forest trees, oak, and other bushes.—(*Lieut. Dun, 1881-82.*

WAIPÉ—

A new Kuki village of the Mangvúng clan, situated on the western slope of the Yumadoung range, above the villages of Chandwakong and Ninggel. There are 30 houses.

There is sufficient camping-ground and water for 200 men. In all other respects it is similar to Chanjang—*vide* page 77.

WAITO—

Three miles north-west of Thobal, the high road from Imphal reaches a long spur coming down from the Phunán and Nongmaiching peaks.

The spur is here cleft by a stream which runs from a jheel on the western side into another on the eastern side.

A fishing weir has been made in the cleft and passengers along the road cross the stream in the cleft on a weak bamboo bridge, practicable, however, for mules and ponies.

The stream itself is easily fordable in the cold weather.

On either side of the bridge the road leads along the face of the spur by somewhat narrow paths, just large enough however, for an elephant to pass along.

During the cold weather there is excellent grazing in the jheels on either side of the spur, and the Raja keeps a couple of hundred buffaloes here There is no village.

The spur is free from jungle and is easily surmountable anywhere, but the position could be made exceedingly strong, especially towards the east.

WAKHONG—

A Tankul village, on some steep and precipitous cliffs between the Mamokong and Riokong streams in North-East Manipur.

There are said to be about 50 houses, and the people are not very friendly. There is but little water up at the village. But below at the point where the Mamokong issues from a gorge, and where the village fields are placed, there is ample camping-ground and water for a force of 2,000 men with transport.

Approaches.—From the west up a precipitous cliff; from the east over the hills from Somrah.

WAKSHU—

A stream in the Kubbo valley, crossed by the Yanga-pokpi road to Moray thannah at 9 miles from the former place, where the stream is 20 feet broad, with low banks, pebbly bottom, and 4 inches of water in the cold weather. (*Lieut. Dun, 1881-82.*)

WANGCHING—

A Manipuri village on the Ingorok stream, between its exit from the Yumadoung hills and the high road.

It has 25 houses, and is in every respect similar to Changangai.

The people are of the sepoy class.

Live-stock.—50 cows, 37 buffaloes.

Carriage.—25 carts.

Approaches—By fair mule-path along the Ingorok stream from east and west.

WANGKHAIKUL—

A deserted Tankul village in the Viratai valley, a few miles north of Wakhong. The inhabitants have for the present gone to live at Wakhong. The village was looted and partially burnt by the Mellomi men in 1883.

There is ample and good camping-ground and water here for a large force.

WANGNU—

A Manipuri (Loï) village on the Imphal river, 10 miles north of Shugunu.

Elevation.—
Temperature.—
Climate.— } *Vide* page 77, Changangai.

Houses.—30.

Water.—Plentiful.

Camping-ground and Products, &c.—*Vide* page 77, Changangai.

Live-stock.—60 cows, 45 buffaloes.

Carriage.—30 carts, 30 men, 12 boats.

WANGOI—

A Manipuri village, 9 miles south of Imphal, on the central valley road.

Elevation.—
Temperature.—
Climate.— } *Vide* page 77, Changangai.

Houses.—50, Manipuri pattern.

This village is in all respects similar to Changangai—page 77.

Live-stock.—100 cows, 75 buffaloes.

Carriage.—50 carts, 10 boats.

Approaches—Along central valley road from north and south.

WANTIK—

A stream in Manipur which joins the Tungum stream close to the Hytuk-pokpi-Yanga-pokpi route.—(*Lieut. Dun, 1881-82.*)

WAYANG—

A Changput village, built after the usual Kuki pattern, about 3,500 feet above the sea-level, containing 20 houses.

Inhabitants.—The inhabitants belong to the Changput subdivision of the Kongjai Kuki tribe. Population 100, of whom 30 may be fighting-men. The chief and most influential man is Mangoun.

Climate.—The climate is unhealthy from beginning of August to end of October.

Water.—Plentiful supply.

Supplies.—Rice-straw procurable. Good gazing. Principal grains, Indian-corn, rice, múm, and chayan. Firewood plentiful. Arums, yams, and pumpkins. Harvest in November and early in December.

Live-stock.—Pigs, poultry, and a few metna.

Transport.—For coolie purposes, 30 men and women.

Timber.—Chiefly oaks; no firs.—(*Lieut. Dun, 1881-82.*)

WEIPE—

A Chussad village, built after the usual Kuki pattern, about 2,000 feet above the sea-level, containing 10 houses. It is by the new frontier line in Burmese territory.

Inhabitants.—The inhabitants belong to the Chussad subdivision of the Kongjai Kuki tribe. Population 50, of whom 15 may be fighting-men.

Climate.—The climate is unhealthy from beginning of August to end of October.

Supplies.—Rice-straw procurable. Fair gazing. Principal grains are Indian-corn, rice, mum, and chayan. Firewood plentiful. Amptums, beans, and pumpkins. Harvest in November and early in December.

Live-stock.—Pigs, poultry, and a few metna.

Transport.—For coolie purposes, 15 men and women.

Timber.—Chiefly oaks; no firs.—(*Lieut. Dun, 1881-82.*)

WIKONG—

A Manipuri (Loi) village in the south-east corner of the Manipur valley, about 15 miles north of Sungunu.

Elevation.— }
Temperature.— } *Vide* page 77, Changangai.
Climate.— }

Houses.—50, Manipuri pattern.

Inhabitants.—250, salt-makers.

Water.—Good and plentiful.

Camping-ground.—Very good and sufficient for 2,000 men and transport.

Products, &c.—As at Changangai—page 77.

Timber.—Fir in addition to the ordinary kind.

Firewood.—Plentiful and close to village.

Approaches.—By eastern valley road from the south the road crosses a low kotal close to the village.

The road could be very advantageously blocked at the point against a force advancing along it from the south.

WILONG OR GUELONG—

A Kolya Naga village of the Maram section, situated on a south-western spur of the Khunho peak, and just above the great northern bend of the Barak.

Elevation.—5,800 feet.

Houses.—85, Naga pattern.

Inhabitants.—340.

Fighting-men.—85.

Water.—Very scanty supply on the eastern side of the village

Camping-ground.—Sufficient for 200 men at east end of village. A thousand feet below the village on the south the reare large open plateaux which would accommodate 10,000 men and transport, and there is plenty of water.

Products, &c.—*Vide* page 78 Charo.

Approaches.—The village is situated on a high, narrow, steep-sided spur, and steep narrow paths approach in from south, west, and north.

WINTHO—

A portion of the old Pong kingdom. (*Vide* Pong.)

WITOOP—

A village in the Kubbo valley between Khambat and Tamoo.

WOKTONG—

A village in the Kubbo valley south of Witoop.

YAJGO—

A Burmese town in the Kubbo valley, 27 miles south of Khambat.

YALLANG—

A small Simmté Kuki village of 7 houses in the valley of the Manipur source of the Tipai river.

YANGA-POKPI THANNAH—

A Manipur post, 20 miles from Kambang, on the eastern edge of the Yumadoung hills, forming one of the third or outer line of frontier posts.

Position.—The thannah is situated in an angle of the Tuyang stream on its north bank, about 300 yards from it.

It is on the rather flat end of a spur running down from the hills on the west.

Camping-ground.—There is plenty of good camping-ground.

Surrounding Country.—Forest jungle comes up to the stockade on every side, except on the east, where it is cleared as far as the Tuyang. The view of the Kubbo valley is hidden by a hill 800 yards distant to the east. The stockade is not commanded on any side, but it could most easily be attacked from the south or the west.

Defences.—The stockade is 70 yards square, and consists of thin poles, 20 feet high, placed close together in three or four rows.

It has no flanking defences.

About 4 feet from the outside of the stockade, there is a light, strong fence, with sharpened bamboos on it, which makes a good obstacle.

Garrison.—The garrison consists of 1 jemadar, 1 havildar, and 50 sepoys.

Water.—A small stream which supplies the garrison, just under the south side of the stockade, which might easily be cut off; but there is plenty from the river.

Supplies.—Scanty grazing. Firewood plentiful.—(*Lieut. Dun, 1881-82.*)

YARAPOK—

A Manipur village on the Thobal river and at the eastern foot of Nongmaichin. The first stage on the Chandwakong route to the Kubbo valley.

Elevation.— }
Temperature.— } *Vide* page 77, Changangai.
Climate.— }

Houses.—Seventy-five, Manipuri pattern.

Inhabitants.—Three hundred and seventy-five, sepoy class.

Fighting-men.—Seventy-five.

Water.—Plentiful.

Camping-ground.— }
Products, &c.— } *Vide* page 77, Changangai.

Live-stock.—One hundred and ten buffaloes, 150 cows.

Carriage.—Seventy-five carts, 25 boats.

Approaches—By good mule road across easy kotal, where the road is scarped and about 8 feet broad, from Imphal. By fair mule-path along the Thobal. By good mule-path to Ukongshang and Chandwakong, &c.

YENDING—

A Tankul village, built after the usual Tankul pattern, about 2,500 feet above the sea-level, containing 6 houses.

Inhabitants.—The inhabitants belong to the south-western section of the Tankul Naga tribe. Population 30, of whom 6 may be fighting-men. The most influential man is Rung-jing.

Climate.—The climate is unhealthy from beginning of June to end of October.

Supplies.—Rice-straw procurable. Scanty grazing. Principal grains are rice and múm. Firewood plentiful. Yams and pumpkins. Rice harvest in November; múm in December.

Live-stock.—Pigs and poultry.

Transport.—For coolie purposes, 6 men and women.

Timber.—All sorts plentiful, except bamboos.—(*Lieut. Dun, 1881-82.*)

YOKPA—

A small Koireng village of 5 houses on the range west of the Tiki, a few miles north of the latitude of Sengmail.

YONG-BALANG-KONG—

An elevated point on the range which bounds the Tiki valley on the east. Elevation 5,527 feet above the sea.

YOO-CHYOUNG—

The Burmese name for the Maglung river. (*Vide* Maglung.)

YUMADOUNG—

The range of hills on the east and south of the Manipur valley. These hills may be divided into two portions :—

Northern portion.—North of the latitude of Nupitel peak on the west and the Chussad Kuki villages on the east; the hills consist of long parallel ridges running north and south, having as a central starting point the peak of Shirdhifarar.

Ridges.—These ridges are the Nupitel, the Sakok-Lang, the Mokku or Noongow, the Chattik, and the Kassom, with others smaller and subsidiary to them.

Streams.—The valleys are drained by the Toyoongba, the Maglang, the Kunokong, and the Meié streams. The Kunokong and Meié unite and are then known as the Napanga.

The ridges are narrow, rather rocky, and steep.

The streams are shallow, but swift, and their beds full of boulders.

There are no good routes for troops.

Southern portion—The southern portion of these hills—that is between the Manipur and Kubbo valleys—has a different character.

The Nupitel ridge is prolonged and forms the watershed as far south as the village of Sawamba; it runs close to the Manipur valley, sending down short steep spurs on the western side, and long gently-sloping spurs, with a general south-easterly direction, on the eastern side.

From Sawamba the watershed turns east as far as Lapupo, where it turns south-east.

Streams.—The streams are all small, the Turet and Lokchao being the largest.

Forests.—From the Sirdhifarar peak southward to the Chandwakong route, the hills are thickly covered with forest, a great deal being of oak and fir.

The southern faces of the Sirdhifarar and Makku peaks are, however, bare. From the Chandwakong route to the Chapki route, the hills are more clear of jungle, many of the southern slopes indeed being covered only with grass. Fir trees are rare, and oaks comparatively scarce. There are, however, more bamboos.

Geological Formation.—Speaking generally, these hills are all composed of grey slates with quartzite. Near Kongal thannah trap formation occurs.

Tribes.—In the north there are mostly Tankul Nagas; in the south Kongjai, Anal, Namfow, and other Kukis; and in the west Marrings.

Attitude of Tribes.—There is very little fear that any of the tribes, either individually or collectively (with the exception of the Chussad Kukis), would interfere with the passage of a force across the hills.

(*Lieut. Dun, 1881-82.*)

YUNG-KUN—

A Marring village, built after the usual Marring pattern, about 2,500 feet above the sea-level, containing 10 houses.

Inhabitants.—The inhabitants belong to the Marring Naga tribe. Population 50, of whom 15 may be fighting-men. The headman is Anhol.

Climate.—The climate is unhealthly from beginning of August to end of October.

Water.—Scanty supply.

Supplies.—Rice-straw procurable. Fair grazing. Principal grains are Indian-corn, rice, múm, and chayan. Firewood plentiful. Arums, beans, pumpkins, and plantains. Harvest in November and early in December.

Live-stock.—Pigs, poultry, and 10 metna.

Transport.—For coolie purposes, 10 men and women.

Timber.—Oaks, &c.; no firs.—(*Lieut. Dun, 1881-82.*)

YUNG-PO—

A Tankul village, built after the usual Tankul pattern, about 4,500 feet above the sea-level, containing 30 houses.

Inhabitants.—The inhabitants belong to the south-western section of the Tankul Naga tribe. Population 150, of whom 30 may be fighting-men. The chief is Naşaleng.

Climate.—The climate is unhealthy from beginning of August to end of October.

Water.—Scanty supply.

Supplies.—Rice-straw procurable. Scanty grazing. Principal grains are rice and múm. Firewood plentiful. Arums, beans, and pumpkins. Rice harvest in November; múm in December.

Live-stock.—Pigs and poultry.

Transport.—For coolie purposes, 30 men and women.

Timber.—All kinds plentiful, including oak and fir; bamboos scarce.

(*Lieut. Dun, 1881-82*).

Z

ZEEAWADDY—

A Burmese village north-west of Myedu.

ROUTES.

1. Imphál to Kohima.
2. Silchar to Manipur.
3. Manipur to the Ningthi *viá* Poshing.
4. „ to Cháttik *viá* Susukameng and Kangoi.
5. „ to Kongál Thanna *viá* Susukameng, Pong, and Cháttik.
6. „ to Kongál Thanna *viá* Chandrakong.
7. „ to Kongál Thanna *viá* Ingorok
8. „ to Yanga-pokpi *viá* Haituk-pokpi.
9. Haituk-pokpi to Kwendaung.
10. „ to Moré Thanna *viá* Kámbáng.
11. Manipur to Moré *viá* Pallél.
12. „ to Nasinga Thanna *viá* Pallél.
13. Kongál Thanna to Samjok.
14. Tummu to Myinmu towards Mandalay.
15. Yanga-pokpi to Moré Thanna.
16. Manipur to Monfu *viá* Helau.
17. Monfu to Sanayachil *viá* Ningthi River.
18. Sanayachil to Tummu *viá* Ningthi and Máglang Rivers.
19. Ava to Kendát.
20. Tummu to Sanayachil Ghât.
21. Tummu to Monphu.
22. Imphal to Lapvomé.
23. Lapvomé to Somrah Guáchán.
24. Kongál Thanna to Somrah Guáchán.
25. Imphal to Thobál *viá* Longtival.
26. Imphal to Shugunu.
27. „ „ *viá* Thobál.
28. „ „ *viá* Moirang.
29. „ to Silchar *viá* Aqui.
30. Bishenpur to Thobál.
31. Kongál Thanna to Samjok.
32. Yanga-pokpi Thanna to Samjok.

ROUTE No. 1.

FROM IMPHÁL TO KOHIMA.

Territory—MANIPUR. Authority—LIEUT. DUN.

Date—*May 1882.*

Names of Stages, &c.	Distance. Intermediate. Miles.	Distance. Total. Miles.	Rivers.	Remarks.
SENGMAIE	11½*	11½	....	† The road is perfectly level the whole of this stage. The breadth of roadway is 40 feet altogether, but there is a raised portion in the middle 12 feet broad. Between C and D it is much overgrown with grass, and there is a single foot-path along the centre of the roadway. The surface along the whole distance is rough, and, though practicable, cannot be said to be in its present state suitable for carts. It is not metalled, and is raised about 1 foot above the fields. The ground it passes through is nowhere swampy. For part of the way it is enclosed by mud walls 4 feet high and 30 yards apart. It is commanded either on one side or the other by steep, bare, and not very high hills along the whole distance. A.—Irrigation channel full of water, 4 feet broad, 2 feet deep; small bamboo bridge. B.—Naga village of about 25 houses; not stockaded. Bazaar held here daily. C.—The Tiki stream, 50 yards broad at the top, steep sandy banks 40 feet high, 2 feet of water, flowing swiftly in pebbly bed, crossed by a bamboo bridge 20 feet long and 6 feet broad. The right bank commands the left at the crossing. D.—The Tiki stream, 30 yards broad, 1 foot of water at crossing, bed pebbly, banks about 4 feet high; bamboo bridge 6 feet broad. At Sengmaie there is unlimited camping-ground close to the river; water and a little grazing north-east of the village.
KAITEMABI	12	23½	....	Leaving Sengmaie, the road, a track about 15 feet broad, crosses an open grass-covered plain with a very slight slope from west to east. It crosses several nalas, some of which contain a little water, all with steep ascents and descents. At the Atonglo stream at 5 miles the spurs become more marked and have steeper sides. The Atonglo flows through a broad bed of shingle. The road then skirts the base of the low spurs which stretch across from the hills bounding the valley on the west, rising occasionally about 20 feet above the base. It is 6 feet broad from this point, with occasional rather narrow places;

* This has always been estimated at 13 miles.—*J. J.*

† See sketch.

Names of Stages, &c.	Distance. Intermediate. Miles.	Total. Miles.	Rivers.	Remarks.
KAITEMABI—*contd.*	...	...	......	crosses many small streams, and is passable only for laden mules or coolies; finally at 12 miles it rises to the top of a plateau, and Kaitemabi Thanna is reached. The thanna is in a good position, is not commanded, but commands the road, and has a good view up the valley to the north. It is not stockaded or defended in any way. There is unlimited and excellent camping-ground, plenty of water, and if the grass has been burnt at a favourable time, there is at this season of the year (March) a fair amount of grazing, sufficient probably for 2,000 mules for a day. The Atonglo is the largest stream crossed; it has only a few inches of water in each channel in the cold weather, but apparently becomes of considerable breadth after heavy rain. The Tiki stream, which is not crossed, flows in an almost flat-bottomed valley filled with very tall grass, the hills on the east rising up from it very steeply indeed.
MAYANG-KHANG.	10*	33½	......	From Kaitemabi the road crosses an open plain, with a hardly perceptible slope from west to east, reaching some low hills which stretch across the valley at 3½ miles. Several streams cross the road in this portion; all of them are in nalas 7 or 8 feet deep and have steep ascents and descents. None of them contain more than a few inches of water. The road is 12 feet broad and is simply a track across the plain. On reaching the low hills it contracts to 6 feet and even less in some places. At 5½ miles it crosses the Tiki stream, which is here about 10 feet broad and a few inches deep, flowing in a shingly bed, and ascends the watershed between Burmese and Indian territory by an easy gradient. From the top of this ridge there is a very gradual descent to Mayang-Khang Thanna. The road throughout is passable for laden mules and coolies only. The gradient throughout, as in the previous stage, is excessively easy. The jungle is very slight, oak forest alternating with open grass-land, as in previous stage. There is plenty of camping-ground at Mayang-Khang Thanna and water, but grazing can only be obtained in the cold weather, if the long grass has been burnt at the right time. There is very little under the most favourable circumstances. Mayang-Khang Thanna is not stockaded. It is commanded by the hills on the west, and is situated on the flat bottom of the valley which is here about 500 yards broad.

* I make it 12 miles.—*J. J.*

Names of Stages, &c.	Distance. Intermediate. Miles.	Distance. Total. Miles.	Rivers.	Remarks.
KARONG THANNA.	8*	41½	......	From Mayang-Khang to Karong the road, as in previous marches, runs along the eastern faces of the spurs which come down from the hills on the west. On the left, and at from 10 to 20 feet below, is the stream flowing in a narrow flat valley bounded on the east by steep hills covered with tree-jungle. The spurs above the road on the west slope gently and have few trees on them; the road is escarped to a breadth of from 3 to 6 feet, and is therefore not passable for laden mules, but in its present state can only be traversed by coolies. The old road, which is on the same side of the stream, about 100 feet higher up, offers no impediments to mule carriage. At 7½ it crosses a stream 15 feet broad and a foot in depth, and gradually ascends to Karong Thanna, situated on the flat end of a spur which comes down from the hills on the east. The road throughout is almost level, and the streams crossed, with the exception of one, are very small indeed. At Karong Thanna there is unlimited good camping-ground and water, but no grazing at the thanna itself. If the old grass has been burnt, and if the ground has not been broken up for cultivation, there is in March a day's grazing for 200 animals at 2 miles to the south along the course of the old road. The thanna is not stockaded. It is commanded on east and west at about 600 yards, but otherwise its position is naturally very strong.
MEITHEIPHAM THANNA.	12†	53½	......	The road crosses the Meitheipham river below Karong Thanna on the north, and then ascends the hill which lies north of the thanna passing along its western face. At 8 miles, opposite the village of Satim, it crosses the saddle which connects this hill with the Maram Peak and descends along the eastern face of the long spur which comes down southwards from that peak. The valley of the Barak river as far as the saddle is narrow, and has flat ground at the bottom. The spurs from the hills on the west have a gradual slope and are almost free from jungle; the spurs on the east traversed by the road are steep and clothed with light oak forest. From the saddle onwards the road lies within the Meitheipham valley, which, though narrow just above Karong Thanna, opens out here to a breadth of half a mile, perfectly flat and laid out in rice-fields. The spurs on the west (traversed by the road) have an exceedingly gentle slope, and are quite free from jungle. Those on the east are covered with forest in patches.

* I make it miles.—*J. J.*

† I make it 10 miles.—*J. J.*

Names of Stages, &c.	Distance. Intermediate. Miles.	Total. Miles.	Rivers.	Remarks.
MEITHEIPHAM THANNA—*contd.*				The roadway is from 3 to 8 feet broad and traversable by laden mules and coolies. The gradient is excessively easy. The only stream crossed is the Meitheipham, just under the Karong Thanna. In the cold weather it is 15 feet broad, and has a few inches of water only at the crossing; but it evidently rises a great deal and becomes impassable in the rains. The Meitheipham Thanna is situated on the west bank of the stream. It is defended by an earthen bank 4 feet in height. It is commanded by the hills on the east at 400 yards. There is unlimited camping-ground and water, and 200 animals could get a day's grazing in the valley.
PHUNAMAH ..	14*	70¼	...... *Mikhir*	From Meitheipham Thanna the road crosses the next spur to the north, follows the valley below, and east of the villages of Kami and Sisephaun, and passes north of that village round the head of the valley. It there crosses the next ridge just above the central of the three villages of Makel and round the head of the valley to Phunamah, known also to the Angamis by the names of Sopvomah and Kuoo; to the Manipuris by the name of Mao. The first spur crossed is covered with grass jungle only. From thence to Phunamah the hill-sides are covered with light jungle, chiefly pollarded alder alternating with terraced rice-fields. The roadway has a uniform breadth of 6 feet with one bad and narrow place close to the first stream and on its right bank. It would require improvement to admit of the passage of laden mules. The trace on this march has been spoilt by allowing earth, which has slipped down from above, to accumulate on the roadway, forming infinite and troublesome little ascents and descents, wearisome to march over, and calculated to unsettle the loads of baggage animals. The general gradient is easy, 1 in 20. A large number of small streams are crossed. Two only are bridged, and they are situated close to one another on the northern slope of the Sisephami spur. They are both small, but are absolutely necessary to the passage of the ravines in the present state of the road. At Phunamah there is unlimited camping-ground; water led along the spur which comes down from the west, and firewood, but grazing is scanty.

* I make it 18 miles by the new road.—*J. J.*

Names of Stages, &c.	Distance.		Rivers.	Remarks.
	Inter-mediate.	Total.		
	Miles.	Miles.		
PHUNAMAH—*contd.*				There is a Manipuri stockade at the west end of the village, but it does not command the latter, and is itself commanded by the hill on the west. It commands the road both on the north and south sides of the ridge. The water channel is led into a reservoir 20 yards from the door of the stockade. The village has no defences. It also commands the road on both sides of the ridge.
			Tributary streams of the Zullo.	From Phunamah the path descends slightly, passes round the head of the valley, keeping a fairly equal elevation, and crosses the Viswema, Jakhama, and Kigwema ridges, just above those villages at 6, 9, and 12 miles. The road is very level and good; the gradient 1 in 20. It is 8 feet broad. The hill-sides, which above the road are very steep, are clothed with forest, which, however, grows lighter as Kohima is approached. Below the road, there is a great deal of terrace cultivation, and the slopes are more gentle than above. The villages of Viswema and Jakhama command the path to a small extent; they have no defensive works.
KIGWEMA .	12	82½	......	On the north side of Kigwema and at many points along this stage, there is ample camping ground in the fields and plenty of water and firewood, but grazing is very scanty.
KOHIMA .	10	92½	......	Beyond Kigwema the road is exactly the same in character as in the last stage. It winds round the head of the valleys at the foot of steep bluffs, and the last 2 miles are a gradual descent along the Kohima ridge. The last mile is a regular cart-road, and all along it there is good camping-ground, fair grazing, and plenty of water and firewood.

ROUTE No. 2.

FROM SILCHAR TO MANIPUR.

Territory—CACHAR DISTRICT, MANIPUR. Authorities—POLITICAL AGENT, MANIPUR; LIEUT. DUN.

Names of Stages, &c.	Distance. Intermediate. Miles	Distance. Total. Miles	Rivers.	Remarks.
LAKHIPUR .	14	...	Chiri Barák, one nala.	A small town situated on the right bank of the Barák; supplies procurable after due notice; water plentiful; country cultivated; road good; first nalla bridged, passable for laden cattle. The river Jhiri is bridged in the cold weather and crossed in the rains on a ferry made of bamboo matting laid upon two canoes and capable of holding two laden mules at one time. The current is very swift. The Barak, crossed at 3 miles from Silchar, has a wooden platform ferry.
JÍRÍGHÁT .	10	24	Several nalas, all bridged.	A stockade and good dry camping-ground for 500 men and transport on the right bank of the Jírí. No supplies; water plentiful; fair grazing. The road crosses the Jujong or Hanoong range through very dense jungle. Officers' rest-house and Manipuri stockade on left bank of river.
MUKKU RIVER	12*	36	Jírí, a bamboo bridge, and fordable in the dry season; a ferry in the rains.	Camping-ground on both banks of the river for possibly 500 men and transport if jungle be cleared.
			Several nalas bridged.	The road crosses the Jírí; at commencement of the stage runs along flat ground for some miles under dense forest and crosses the Nunjaibong range. At the top of this range there is camping-ground for possibly 500 men. Water is distant to the south. The Jírí is the British Manipur boundary. It is broad and rapid in the rains, at other seasons it is about 20 yards wide; bed sandy; stream gentle. No village or supplies.
BARAK RIVER .	10†	46	Mukku, fordable; also a floating bridge and a suspension bridge.	Camping-ground for possibly 500 men on transport if the men be distributed on both side of the river. No supplies but fuel and wat. Cross the Mukku at the commencement of th stage; a steep ascent to Kala Naga stockad (hardly any water), about 3,400 feet above t' sea and a steep descent to the Barak. Offic rest-house at Kala Naga.

* Very much under the mark. From Jírí to Kala Naga has always been reckoned 24 miles, which I as follows, viz.,—

Jírí to Mukku 19
Mukku to Kala Naga 5

J.

† This should be 11 miles.—J. J.

Names of Stages, &c.	Distance.		Rivers.	Remarks.
	Intermediate.	Total.		
	Miles.	Miles.		
NUNGBA	15*	61	*Barak*, a floating bridge and a suspension bridge, sometimes fordable.	Ascend steep hill by winding road to thanna. Cross one fair-sized stream and reach Nungba village at 15 miles. There is very little camping-ground and a poor supply of water. Descend a steep hill by a zig-zag road to the Lengba, a stream fordable at all times, 3 miles further on, where there is plenty of camping-ground and water. There is an officers' rest-house at Nangba village.
KAUPÚM	12†	73	*Lengba* (fordable). Irang (a floating bridge and a suspension bridge).	Good encamping-ground near a stockaded thanna, sufficient for a large force, on grass-covered flat (*vide* Gazetteer). From the Lengba river the road runs along the face of the hills on the right bank of the Irang, crosses that river at a bend in its course, and zig-zags up a steep spur to a pass which leads into the Kaupúm basin. The pass is commanded by the Lilonong Thanna and is closed by a line of stockade through which there is a door. Half a mile east of the thanna there is an officers' rest-house. Kaupúm Thanna is 2 miles beyond the pass. Kaupúm is the only place on the road where anything in the way of food can be obtained. Rice is the only food-supply, and 10 maunds could be got with difficulty at harvest time.
LAIMATÁK RIVER.	10‡	83	.. ...	Plenty of camping-ground on flat, grassy terraces above the river on either bank. Leaving the Kaupúm basin, the road ascends a steep range to an elevation of , and then descends to the Laimaták.
BISHENPUR or LAMLÁNGTONG.	9§	92	... ...	Ascend the Laimatol range to an elevation of 5,200 feet, the last part of the ascent containing a flight of stone steps which might be troublesome to mules when slippery with wet. Descend by a winding road to Bishenpur Thanna. Here and at Lamlángtong village, one mile further on, there is camping-ground for a large force; plenty of good water and a little grazing. There is an officers' rest-house at Lamlángtong.

* Nongba and the Lengba rivers are 5 miles apart. From the Barák river to Nungba is 15 miles.

† From Nungba to Kaupúm is 19 miles, according to my estimate.—*J. J.*

‡ My estimate is 14 miles.—*J. J.*

§ This is simply impossible; the average gradient is said to be here more than 1 in 12 and the total ascent and descent include 6,300 feet, which would give a distance of over 14 miles; besides this there is at least a mile of nearly level ground. The distance cannot be *less* than 15 miles, unless the estimate for the gradients is wrong.

Dr. Brown's estimate is worthless, as he always travelled in a dooly.

Colonel Stewart, formerly Deputy Commissioner of Cachar, a good authority, estimated the total distance from Cachar to Manipur as 133 miles; other authorities put it at 138 to 146; I say it is not under 132. I have tried very carefully to form a correct estimate.—*J. J.*

Names of Stages, &c.	Distance. Inter-medi-ate. Miles.	Total. Miles.	Rivers.	Remarks.
IMPHÁL	16*	108	*Western Nambol, Eastern Nambol.* Several small nalas.	The road follows the base of the hills for a few miles, and then strikes across the rice-fields straight towards Imphál. It is unmetalled and raised a few feet above the fields. There are neither enclosing walls nor hedges nor trees along it. Cross the Nambol and pass through Foyjing village at 7 miles. There is a large bazaar here held daily and usually called Bori Bazaar. The Nambol runs in a deep nala, and has a bamboo bridge passable by laden cattle. Enter the city at 14½ miles and cross the eastern Nambol close to the Residency by a large and massive brick bridge. Imphál is the capital town and the residence of the Raja and Political Agent. Everything the country produces is obtainable here.

* This is 17 miles as the crow flies measured on the map; the road is not straight and cannot be less than 18 miles.—*J. J.*

ROUTE No. 3.

FROM MANIPUR TO THE NINGTHI.

Viâ *Poshing.*

Territory—MANIPUR. Authority—LIEUT. DUN.

Date—*May 1882.*

Names of Stages, &c.	Distance. Inter-medi-ate. Miles.	Total. Miles.	Rivers.	Remarks.
1. SUSUKAMENG.	...	...	......	*Vide* Route No. 4.
2. NEAR LAIRÉL.	A short day's march		......	As in Route No. 5 to the Thobál. Ascend the valley of that stream, which is flat and broad, to a point near Laireng, and opposite the mouth of a small stream coming down from the Nupitel ridge. There is camping-ground for a large force, firewood, water, and grass for making huts, but there is hardly any grazing.
3. NEAR HUNDUNG.	A short day's march.		......	Ascend to the top of the Nupitel ridge by a gentle sloping spur. Follow the ridge some distance and descend to the valley of the Nungshangkong; camp below Hundung on the south-west. Camping-ground for a large force, firewood, water, and grass for making huts, but no grazing.

Names of Stages, &c.	Distance. Intermediate. Miles.	Total. Miles.	Rivers.	Remarks.
4. Near Kangoi.	...	...	......	Cross the Hundung spur, south of that village; ascend the valley of the Nungshangkong and camp below Kangoi. Camping-ground for a regiment; plenty of water and firewood, but no grazing.
5. Poshing	...	...	......	Ascend the Kangoi spur, cross the Sirohifarah ridge, and ascend to Poshing by a path in which there are a good many steep ascents and descents, but is nevertheless fit for laden mules. Camp in terraced rice-fields, in which, if the irrigation channels had been turned off for some time previously, there would be unlimited accommodation. There is plenty of water and firewood and a little grazing.
6. Chingsow	...	...	......	Cross several streams and steep-sided spurs; road fairly good, though steep in places, and camp either in Chingsow in rice-fields or below in the valley near the stream. The fields would afford the most accommodation, if the water had been kept turned off beforehand. Plenty of firewood, water, and camping-ground, and a little grazing. Note.—Up to this point (Chingsow) the path is traversable for laden mules, and the greater part of it is good and easy-going, but it now becomes both steep and rough and hardly passable for mule-carriage. There are, however, plenty of Tankul Nagas all round, and a good path could easily be made in a few days.
7. Chummu Kulel.	...	...	......	Steep ascent and descent to Chummu Kulel. Road bad; plenty of camping-ground in the rice-fields; firewood and water, and a little grazing.
8. Chummu Kunao.	...	...	......	Cross several spurs and camp on the Nélékong stream below Chummu Kunao. Road very bad and requires to be made. Plenty of camping-ground, water, firewood, and a fair amount of grazing.
9. Ningthi River.	...	...	......	Ascend slightly, cross low part of the Kassom ridge, and descend by an easy slope to the Ningthi. An old road crosses the Kassom ridge, but it has not been used for about three years. It was chiefly used by Nagas and not as a regular trading route by the Manipuris.

ROUTE No. 4.

From MANIPUR to CHÁTTIK.

Viâ *Susukameng and Kangoi.*

Territory—Manipur. Authority—Lieut. Dun (from native information).

Date—*1882.*

Names of Stages, &c.	Distance. Intermediate. Miles.	Total. Miles.	Rivers.	Remarks.
Susukameng .	15	15	*Imphál, Kong-ba, Iril.*	Road good as far as the Iril, over which there is a temporary bridge; cross the Imphál in Manipur and the Kong-ba Nala just outside the town. Both have small bamboo bridges. The Imphál is about 50 yards broad at the top, bank steep and 15 feet high, and it has about 2 feet of water in the cold weather. The Kong-ba is 20 yards broad at top, 15 feet steep banks, and 2 feet of water in the cold weather. The Iril is 30 yards broad at top, about 30 feet perpendicular banks, and about 2 or 3 feet deep in the cold weather. None of these streams are very swift. After leaving the Iril the road is bad, and about a mile beyond, at the Raja's cattle farm, it crosses a difficult deep nala with precipitous high earthy banks, which would cause much obstruction on a march. It has a very small temporary bridge. The road is then tolerable till close to Susukameng, where there are some swampy places which require bridging or filling in. The ground on each side of the road is perfectly flat and covered either with rice cultivation or thatching grass. Susukameng lies between some low hills situated north and south of it.
Lampui .	...	...	*Thobál* .	Ascend ridge gradually after crossing the Thobál to Kassom and along ridge (Nupitel) passing Setspao to Lampui; road good and fit for laden mules.
Kangoi .	...	...	*Nungshang-kong.*	From Kangoi there is a rise to Kundung Kusom, and then a descent to the Nungshang-kong stream; ascend again to near Nungshang, which is situated above the road, and along ridge to Kangoi.
Poshing .	...	...	......	Cross high range nearly 7,000 feet, and descend again to Poshing.
Cháttik .	...	...	......	From Poshing down to the Konookong river and along left bank by a narrow scarped path unfit for laden mules. Route 2 meets this path about half-way between Poshing and Cháttik.

ROUTE No. 5.

From MANIPUR to KONGÁL THANNA.

Viâ *Susukameng, Pong, and Cháttik.*

Territory—Manipur. Authority—Lieut. Dun.

Date—*1882.*

Names of Stages, &c.	Distance.		Rivers.	Remarks.
	Intermediate.	Total.		
	Miles.	Miles.		
1. Susukameng.	15	15	*Imphál, Kong-ba, Iril.*	For road to this point, *vide* previous Route.
2. Thobál River.	9	22	Unnamed nala. *Thobál.*	From Susukameng the road passes over a perfectly level wide valley, enters some low rounded hills covered with a light jungle of oaks, crosses one or two low ridges, and down an easily-sloping spur to the Thobál at 9 miles. The Thobál is 30 yards broad, has 6 feet perpendicular banks, and is 4 or 5 inches deep in the cold weather. Bottom hard and pebbly. Plenty of good camping-ground, grazing, water, and firewood. Road very good all the way.
3. Camp .	13	35	*Toyungba* .	From the Thobál river up a steep spur of the Nupilet range, passing through the villages of Lamlaic and Chunyam, follows the ridge for a little distance, and then down the eastern side of the hill to Singal village at 8 miles. At the village there is very little camping-ground and a scanty supply of water. A steep descent from this point all the way to the Toyungba at 13 miles. Good camping-ground on east bank for any force, and plenty of water; much jungle would have to be cleared. The Toyungba is a small mountain stream a foot deep and full of boulders, about 40 yards broad. This day's road is bad, but passable for laden mules.
4. Máglang River.	10	45	......	From the Toyungba up a steep spur to the top of the Sakok-lang ridge turn north and follow by gradually ascending path to Sakok at the northern and highest point. Cross over and descend slightly to the Hundung Kulel ridge, at the end of which lies that village. Down steep spur to the Máglang, and camp on the east bank in dry rice-fields sufficient for two regiments. The road in this march is good. The Máglang is exactly similar in character to the Toyungba, but twice as broad. The ridges traversed are very narrow. Fir forest.

Names of Stages, &c.	Distance. Inter-mediate. Miles.	Distance. Total. Miles.	Rivers.	Remarks.
5. Makku	15	60	......	The road then ascends the narrow valley of the Máglang along the east bank, crosses a considerable and very swift mountain stream and up a gently-sloping ridge to the top of the Makku range, passing through the village of Pong at $4\frac{1}{2}$ miles. There is hardly any jungle to this point; scattered fir trees and grass. A good road travels north from Pong along the Máglang valley. The road then follows the Makku ridge due north over very bad ground and through dense jungle,—the path is really a disused village path —and finally at a clump of rhododendron trees plunges down the steep side of a spur, reaching the village of Makku at 15 miles. There is camping-ground here for 200 men, but the water is distant; firewood plentiful; no grazing. The road along this stage is very steep in places, and much jungle requires to be cut to make it passable for laden mules. There is no water along the whole of this stage.
6. Cháttik	15	75	*Konookong.*	The road still descends a very steep spur to near the Konookong, where it becomes precipitous. The Konookong is 80 yards broad in channel, and has 6 or 8 inches of water. The regular Cháttik road is reached about 100 feet up the precipitous side of the hill of the eastern bank; the road is very narrow but level, and passes along the face of a very steep hill-side, crossing many streams, among which are two rather large ones. It is not broad enough for laden mules. Just below the village of Cháttik it suddenly ascends the ridge, on which the village is placed, by a very steep path for about 2 miles, reaching camping-ground between the village and thanna at 15 miles. There is camping-ground on the ridge for two regiments, and plenty of water. The road along this stage is bad, except along the course of the Konookong, and it is there too narrow for laden mules.
7. Konookong	12	87	......	The road now leads down the Cháttik spur south-south-east. It is good and has a fairly easy slope the whole way to the Chussad village of Maukot and the Tankul village of Chowhoom at 7 miles. There is a stockade across the road, the open forest which exists along the Cháttik ridge ends, and thick tropical vegetation begins. The road from this point still has a gradual downward slope, but is not good. The village of Maukot is commanded and Chowhoom is on a level with, and partly commands, the road at 7 miles; at $10\frac{1}{2}$ it reaches the junction of two streams and follows the bed of their downward course to the Konookong for

Names of Stages, &c.	Distance. Inter-mediate. Miles.	Total. Miles.	Rivers.	Remarks.
7. Konookong—contd.				1½ miles. This part of the route is impassable for mules. The bed of the stream, in which there is plenty of water, is full of large boulders and descends rather rapidly. The sides of the ravine are rocky and precipitous. There appears to be no other road opposite the exit of this stream on the south-west bank of the Konookong. There is an excellent camp for 100 men with a very secure position. The Konookong is here 150 yards broad and is 1 to 2 feet deep, with a strong current.
8. Kongál Thanna.	20	107	......	From this camp the road ascends a long, and in some places a narrow, spur, by a very easy gradient, to the village of Chussad (Tonghoo), which it passes through, meeting with a stockade and the inner line of defence a mile from the village. This portion of the road is quite fit for mules. From Chussad the road is very bad and narrow, for some distance passing along the face of a steep hill, and is unfit for mules. At 8 or 9 miles there are streams and fair camping-grounds for about 100 men each. From the latter to Chunyang, Molnui, and Changli villages, which are close together on the road, the path is good, and also as far as Kongál Thanna, descending a very gradual spur the whole way; at 14 miles there is a stream and fair camping-ground for 200 men. At 4 miles beyond this the Kubbo valley is reached, and Kongál Thanna at 20 miles. The jungle along the whole of this stage is particularly light and open. At 11 and at 12 miles there are stockades. The road at 8 miles is commanded by a stockaded hill on the north-west. This march was performed in 10 hours, exclusive of halts.

ROUTE No. 6.

FROM MANIPUR TO KONGÁL THANNA.

Viâ *Chandrakong* (*Ningyel*).

Territory—MANIPUR. Authority—LIEUT. DUN.

Date—*1882.*

Names of Stages, &c.	Distance. Inter-mediate. Miles.	Distance. Total. Miles.	Rivers.	Remarks.
1. YARAPOK .	7*	17	*Iril, Oseipokpi.*	The road leaves the Pát a few yards west of the south-east corner, and continues through the city almost to the Iril at 6 miles. Here there is a bamboo bridge practicable for mules and ponies. The channel in which the Iril flows is 40 yards broad at the top, 20 feet deep, and in January there is from 2 to 3 feet of water. The road then rounds the foot of a spur which comes down from Nongmaiching, and crosses a stretch of swampy ground on a well-raised embankment to a kotal 500 feet above the plain. The hill-side has been scarped and the gradient is sufficiently easy to admit the passage of carts. It now follows the base of the hills for a short distance, and then strikes across the plain to Yarapok.
2. CHANDRAKONG.	15	32	*Thobál* .	Cross Thobál river by the usual bamboo bridge. Pass through a single line of low hills at 3 miles and follow base of Yumadoung hills to Chandrakong.
3. TURET RIVER	17	49	*Turet* .	From Chandrakong ascend a steep spur to the watershed, and then follow a long easy spur to the Turet.
4. MÁGLANG RIVER.	17	66	*Máglang* .	Steep ascent along ridge, and steep descent to the Máglang.
5. KONGÁL .	15	81	......	Steep ascent and along ridge and easy spur to Kongál. The route was not traversed and must be very similar in character to Route No. 7.

* 12 miles.—*J. J.*

ROUTE No. 7.

FROM MANIPUR TO KONGÁL THANNA.

Viâ *Ingorok.*

Territory—MANIPUR. Authority—LIEUT. DUN.

Date—*1882.*

Names of Stages, &c.	Distance.		Rivers.	Remarks.
	Intermediate.	Total.		
	Miles.	Miles.		
1. YARAPOK .	17*	17	*Iril, Osei-pokpi.*	To Yarapok along Manipur Valley, *vide* Route No. 6.
2. INGOROK .	10	27	*Thobál* .	Good road over the Manipur plain to Ingorok, which lies in a little valley close under the hills; good camping-ground and water for two regiments.
3. TURET RIVER.	17	44	*Turet* .	Ascend steep spur to Kharan village at 3 miles, where there is a small camping-ground and water. From this point the road winds gradually upwards along the south face of the spur, reaching the top at 5 miles. It then follows the top of the ridge with many short but steep ascents and descents to 11 miles, whence it descends a narrow spur at an easy gradient to 15 miles, whence there is a steep descent for 2 miles to the Turet. There is only heavy jungle along the top of the ridge; the spurs are covered with grass only or very open forest. Kharan is the only village on the road and the only place where water is obtainable. An enemy in possession of the hills might defend the passage of this stage with the greatest advantage at Kharan. There are other but unfavourable positions from 5 to 11 miles. The Turet is 30 yards broad, 1 foot deep, and bridged. There is possible but confined camping-ground for 400 men. There is a road from this point to the Chandrakong route; the latter can be signalled at 12-14 miles.
4. MÁGLANG .	18	62	*Máglang* .	Ascend very steep side of spur to 2 miles, passing the village of Khoontak Khonae and water at one mile. From thence along level ridge and pass close to the village of Namusí out of sight of road at 4 miles. Descend gradually with occasional levels along faces of hills and along ridges to Kangbom Thanna at 12 miles. The ridge in front (east) of the thanna is very narrow, beyond it widens out, and on the reverse slope out of sight is the village of Kanggum. The road to Kongál passes north of Kanggum and descends gradually along a spur to the Máglang river; another road passes south of Kanggum to

* 15 miles.—*J. J.*

Names of Stages, &c.	Distance.		Rivers.	Remarks.
	Intermediate.	Total.		
	Miles.	Miles.		
4. MÁGLANG—*contd.*				the Kubbo valley opposite. Taap-Kangbom thanna commands both, and Kanggum village neither of these two roads. The Kubbo valley by the southern road is one day's march from Kangbom. Four hundred men could camp at Kanggum, but the water-supply is scanty. On the Máglang there are two camping-grounds, large enough for one regiment each. Both are on the east bank of the river, one on the river, the other 100 feet above it. The lower ground requiring no clearing is generally used, but it is damp at the beginning of the cold weather. The Máglang is 100 yards broad in channel, has one foot of water, and is bridged with bamboo matting laid on baskets of stones. The jungle along this stage is thick only at the level parts of the ridge; on the spurs it is light. Between 4 and 5 miles there is favourable ground for disputing the passage either from the east or the west.
5. KONGÁL .	14	76	Small stream	Rather steep ascent to 3½ miles; at 4 miles a little water; very good and easy road along top of village, ascending and descending to 6½ miles, whence descend a long, narrow, but easy, sloping spur to the Kabbo valley at 11 miles. There is a small camping-ground and a very little water at 7 miles. From 11 to 12½ miles the road crosses a number of small spurs and ravines with bridges across them; these bridges are small, and with much traffic would soon wear out. Road thence level and good to Kongál thanna at 14 miles. The jungle along the level ridges is heavy; everywhere else it is slight. This stage has an excellent road, and is nowhere very steep. There is no ground for camping mules on the Turet.

ROUTE No. 8.

FROM MANIPUR TO YANGA-POKPI.

Viâ *Haituk-pokpi.*

Territory—MANIPUR. Authority—LIEUT. DUN.

Date—*1882.*

Names of Stages, &c.	Distance.		Rivers.	Remarks.
	Intermediate.	Total.		
	Miles.	Miles.		
1. THOBÁL KYAM VILLAGE	12	12	*Leelong, Osei-pokpi, Thobál, Arong, Wangching, Haituk-pokpi stream, Sajikong.*	For this stage, *vide* Route No. 11.
2. HAITUK-POKPI.	14	26		For road as far as *Wangching, vide* Route No. 11. From thence turn east, pass through Hueerok village and up a valley to Haituk-pokpi at 14 miles. The end (east) of Hueerok village is reached at 7½ miles; the valley commences at 8 miles. In the valley the Haituk-pokpi stream is crossed twice and the Sajikong stream once; they are both small. The village of Tamlai on the north and the villages of Wabaching and Kolongten on the south are passed; they are all out of sight of the road, and do not to any degree command it. At Haituk-pokpi fair camping-ground for two regiments and plenty of water.
3. KAMBÁNG	17	43	...... *Wantik.*	The hills on each side are grassy, rounded, and easily ascended. From Haituk-pokpi a path ascends a steep spur to the village of Machi and meets the regular road further on at Samokom. The regular road continues up the valley of the Haituk-pokpi stream, which becomes very narrow, the hills steeper and more jungle-covered, to the junction Wantik and Tungum streams; at 3 miles crosses the former and ascends an easy-sloping spur to the watershed at 9½ miles, passing under the village of Noongtak, which commands it very slightly at a distance of 800 yards. The valley of Machi is on the opposite side of the ravine. From 9½, where there is a road north to Bolon village, the road continues along the ridge with continual short but steep ascents and descents, gradually rising, however, to Kambáng peak at 15 miles; at 10½ there is a dák station called Samokom with a little water and level ground and the road to Machi. At Kambáng peak there is a road to Sawamba, a little west of Lapopo on the Pallél-Moré route; descend spur on the east to Kambang thanna, at 17 miles passing the village of Chitta, which is about 1 mile from the road on a subsidiary spur. Up to 8½ miles the jungle is light; beyond that, except on the southern side of the Kambáng ridge, which is bare of trees, there is thick forest jungle. Kambang

Names of Stages, &c.	Distance. Intermediate. Miles.	Total. Miles.	Rivers.	Remarks.
3. Kámbáng —*contd.*				Thanna would make a good signalling station. There is camping-ground here for a regiment, but water is scanty and distant.
4. Yanga-pokpi	18	61	......	From Kambang to Yanga-pokpi the road descends one long, easy-sloping spur, the descent of which from Kambáng peak was commenced the previous march. The spur is occasionally very narrow and nowhere broad; the jungle along the upper portion is light, but there is a good deal of bamboo lower down. It is steep in a few places, but on the whole good and fit for laden mules. At 1 mile below Kambáng the road to Kwendaung and Moré Thanna is passed close to a Naga stone grave. At $1\frac{3}{4}$ there is a dák station with a little level ground and water, and close by the road to Bolon, which is about a mile from the road on the north. The next village met with is Lamlong, which is above, but does not command, the road. A little water is procurable at the foot of a rather steep slope below Lamlong on the east. The Kubbo valley and the Tuyang stream are reached at 16 miles; from thence it travels north, over undulating ground, through an open forest of large trees, crossing the Tuyang twice again to Yanga-pokpi at 18 miles. The whole of this route is good and fit for laden mules; but the road between $9\frac{1}{2}$ and 15 on the 3rd stage, and some of the steep descents in the last stage, could be easily improved, and their improvement would make this an excellent route.

ROUTE No. 9.

From HAITUK-POKPI to KWENDAUNG.

Territory—Manipur. Authority—Capt. Gordon.

Date—1882.

Names of Stages, &c.	Distance. Intermediate. Miles.	Total. Miles.	Rivers.	Remarks.
3. Kámbáng	...	43	......	Along Route No. 8 to this point.
4. Kwendaung	15	58	......	Down steep spur from Kambáng. Road good beyond. Not personally visited.

ROUTE No. 10.

FROM HAITUK-POKPI TO MORÉ THANNA.

Viâ *Kámbáng.*

Territory—MANIPUR. Authority—CAPT. GORDON.

Date—1882.

Names of Stages, &c.	Distance. Inter-medi-ate.	Total.	Rivers.	Remarks.
	Miles.	Miles.		
3. KÁMBÁNG .	...	43	......	To this point along Route No. 8.
4. SITPONG .	15	58	......	Down steep spurs from Kámbáng and over low spurs to Sitpong on Pallél-Moré Route, No. 11.
5. MORÉ .	7	65	......	*Vide* Route No. 11.

ROUTE No. 11.

FROM MANIPUR TO MORÉ.

Viâ *Pallél.*

Territory—MANIPUR. Authority—LIEUT. DUN.

Date—1882.

Names of Stages, &c.	Distance. Inter-medi-ate.	Total.	Rivers.	Remarks.
	Miles.	Miles.		
1. THOBÁL KYAM VILLAGE.	12*	12	*Leelong River* *Osei-pokpi stream.* *Weeton nala.*	At 3¾ miles from the Raja's enclosure, the city of Imphal ends. The road is very good and broad to the junction of the Iril and Imphál, which together form the Leelong at 6½ miles. There is a temporary bamboo bridge here. Special arrangements required for passing over even a small party of, say, 25 men. The channel is 50 yards broad at the top, with banks 25 feet high, and in the cold weather 3 to 4 feet of water. The village of Aravati lies close to the road on the south bank. The road is good, but not so broad to within one mile of the Osei-pokpi stream, at 9½ miles, where it passes through a swamp where it is very high, and gradually diminishes to a breadth of 5 feet at the Osei-pokpi. It then follows the base of some low hills and crosses the Weeton Nala, 40 feet broad, 20 feet perpendicular banks,

* 12 miles as the crow flies; by road 15.—J. J.

Names of Stages, &c.	Distance. Inter-mediate. Miles.	Distance. Total. Miles.	Rivers.	Remarks.
1. Thobál Kyam Village—*contd.*				and deep water, by a weak bamboo bridge; crosses low hills and continues along their eastern base almost to Thobál Kyam, the nearest point of the Thobál river. There is open ground here in the rice-fields, and is therefore more suitable as a camping place than Thobál bazaar.
2. Pallel	15*	27	*Thobál*	Good road, with villages on each side along north bank of the Thobál to crossing and Thobál bazaar at 2 miles. Temporary bamboo bridges, bank 25 feet high and steep, 50 yards broad at top, 2 feet 6 inches of water in the cold weather. From the Thobál to the Wangching stream the road lies through a good deal of swampy ground (swampy even in the cold weather) over several small muddy nalas and one large one.
			Arong	The Arong, 40 yards broad, 4 feet perpendicular banks, and 1 foot water in the cold weather, but with a soft muddy bottom; weak bamboo bridge. There are villages along the road to the east bank of the Arong without any break from the Thobál Kyam. The eastern portion is called Thobál Howka. East of the Arong there is a good deal of swamp, but becomes better as the Wangching is approached at 5½
			Wangching.	miles. The Wangching is 40 feet broad, has 15 feet perpendicular banks, and has 1 foot of water running swiftly over a pebbly bed. Lamting village is on the right, and Wangching at half mile from the road on the left; at 9 miles the road, which, from the Wangching has been fair, reaches the hills, having passed over a flat plain partly cultivated with rice, but chiefly short, coarse grass, and continues along the western base to Pallél. At 9 miles there is a road to Langatel, and also an old road over the hills to Pallél.
			Kokshing	It passes over two swampy places, reaches the Kokshing stream, 20 feet wide, 10 feet perpendicular banks, and 1 foot of water, running
			Sengmaiee	swiftly at 14½ miles; and the Sengmaiee, 40 yards wide, 5 feet perpendicular bank, and 1 foot of water at Pallél at 15 miles. Water and camping ground unlimited.
3. Lokchao River.	17½†	50½	......	From Pallél the road traverses the narrow valley of the Tusieuk stream between the valleys of

* I do not like to be too critical; but I think this distance is nearer 20 than 15.—*J. J.*

† This is obviously incorrect; the distance is 17½ miles as the crow flies, and I make it at least 20 by road: it is an impossible march for ordinary troops, though Manipuris can do it. I divide it as follows:—

Pallél to Aimol	3
Khongaung	9
Lokchao	8

but two of the marches might be doubled up into one.

Names of Stages, &c.	Distance. Intermediate. Miles.	Distance. Total. Miles.	Rivers.	Remarks.
3. Lokchao River—*contd.*				Sengmaice and the Meiha, and ascends a steep spur to the village of Aimol at 5½.* This portion of the road is not very good and would be trying to laden mules, but is quite passable for them. The village of Aimol commands the road from Aimol, where there is camping-ground for two regiments, but the most scanty supply of water; the road ascends gradually with one steep place near Aimol to the peak at 1¾ miles, and descends from thence along a narrow spur by an excellent road at an easy gradient to Tingloqal, a hollow in the spur, where there is camping-ground for possibly two regiments, but hardly any water.† (The reservoir referred to is a wooden trough, 4 × 1 foot.) Very gradual ascent to the top of a ridge, the real watershed and the village of Sawamba. This would be a favourable place for an enemy in possession of the hills to dispute a passage. There is camping-ground here for 400 men, but water is distant and scarce. Descend gently-sloping spur, passing village of Lapupo, which slightly commands the road; a little camping-ground and water just below at 11 miles, and the same as Koungang at 14½. A regiment might, perhaps, camp here, but water distant and scanty. Koungang partly commands the road. Descent easy to the Lokchao at 17½, last ¼ mile very steep; on the west bank there is narrow camping-ground for 400 men, and higher up on the same bank for 400 more. The ground above would require levelling bamboo jungle. The Lokchao is 50 yards broad, and has 6 inches of water in the cold weather, and many large boulders.
4. Moré .	12	62½	*Lokchao* .	Cross the Lokchao and ascend very steep side of spur with occasional levels to Siebong village at 4¾ miles. A regiment might encamp in and about the village, but water is scanty. Road from here to Kámbang and Kwendaung. The road passes through the village, which has stockaded entrance, down broad and very gradually descending spur (with one steep descent to, and ascent from, Kujierok stream at 9¼ miles) to Moré Thanna at 12 miles. There is good open camping-ground for any number of men, and plenty of water in the Kujierok stream. The latter part of this route is particularly free from jungle, and along the whole distance, except between Aimol village and Aimol peak, it is very light indeed. The road is very good the whole way. Tummu is 3 miles from Moré along a good flat road through open forest.

* From Pallél to Aimol is 6¾ miles as the crow flies; at least 8 by road.—*J. J.*

† This is in the dry season; in rainy weather there is plenty.—*J. J.*

ROUTE No. 12.

FROM MANIPUR TO NASINGA THANNA.

Viâ *Pallél.*

Territory—MANIPUR.

Authority—LIEUT. DUN (from native information).

Date—*1882.*

Names of Stages, &c.	Distance.		Rivers.	Remarks.
	Intermediate.	Total.		
	Miles.	Miles.		
1. THOBAL KYAM.	...	...	......	*Vide* Route No. 11.
2. MAHA THANNA.	...	...	......	*Vide* Route No. 11 to Pallél. Maha Thanna is about one mile from Pallél by a good road across level ground.
3. SONGHUL .	...	...	......	From Maha to Chakpi Thanna the road lies along the level valley of the Chakpi stream. From Chakpi ascend a hill by a good road to Songhul. The road, which is a good bridle-path fit for laden mules as far as Chakpi Thanna, follows the course of a stream the whole way. There is sufficient water the whole way along for a force of 500 men and transport, and there are many points where a force of this strength could encamp.
4. OONGBO .	...	...	......	Along the ridge to Oongbo. This is not a full stage, but is the most convenient halting-place for water.
5. BENUNG .	...	...	*Tuda* .	Descend to the Tuda, follow course of stream, and ascend slightly to Benung.
6. NASINGA .	...	...	......	Descend slightly to small stream and ascend high hill to Nasinga. This route was received from a resident of Chirapur (prolongation of Lamting). The marches given are probably long ones, occupying a whole day; Nasinga is half a day's journey from Punsa and 10 hours from Tummu. The thanna has been lately withdrawn to its present position from the Kubbo valley. The villages along the route are occupied by peaceful Anal Kukis. Camping-ground for 400 men, and high up on the same bank for 400 more. The ground above would require levelling; bamboo jungle.

ROUTE No. 12.

FROM KONGÁL THANNA TO SAMJOK.

Territory—MANIPUR. Authority—LIEUT. DUN (from native information).

Date—1882.

Names of Stages, &c.	Distance.		Rivers.	Remarks.
	Intermediate.	Total.		
	Miles.	Miles.		
1. TANAN	16	16	*Nammea* . *Pratukong* .	The road crosses the Nammea, 40 feet wide, low banks, and 6 inches of water, pebbly bottom, and goes south-east over flat ground, through open forest with little undergrowth. Cross the Nammea again at 6 miles and the Pratukong, which is just like the Nammea, at 9 miles, and reach the Shan village of Tanan at 16 miles. The road crosses some marshy places and several open patches covered with grass about 3 feet high. Two miles south of Tanan, on or near another road which connects Samjok and Tanan, there is an open patch of ground suitable for camping purposes. This route (Tanan-Samjok) is, according to native report, passable for laden cattle. The village of Moolong is passed at 12 miles.
2. TOUNGBAN .	18	34	......	The road over the Ungochings to Toungban, a Shan village at the foot of the eastern slope, is fit for laden cattle. The highest point crossed is 1,500 feet above the plain. There are several small streams along the route as far as the eastern slope, but no camping-ground. It has a few very steep places in the ascent, which occupies 4 miles; the remaining 14 miles are down a gently-sloping spur. The village of Toungban is half a mile south of the road. On the road level with it there are rice-fields, which would afford camping-ground to a regiment. Forest seen over the village and cultivation. The jungle along this stage consists of open forest.
3. SAMJOK .	5	39	......	The road from Toungban passes over a level plain covered with open forest like that of the Kubbo valley; at 3 miles the village of Natanyet. There is an open plain here half a mile square fit for encamping purposes; forest again to Samjok at 5 miles. There is no camping-ground here, except in the rice-fields. Samjok is situated on the west bank of the Ningthi. On the east bank there is a large stretch of sand in the cold weather, which might serve as a camping place.

ROUTE No. 14.

From TUMMU to MYINMU towards MANDALAY.

Territory—Manipur.

Authority—Lieut. Dun (from native information).

Date—*1882.*

Names of Stages, &c.	Distance.		Rivers.	Remarks.
	Intermediate.	Total.		
	Miles.	Miles.		
1. Ituk .	One day's journey.		*Mdglang* .	Small Shan village on the Kubbo valley. Road level and good.
2. Tungleya	Do. .		......	Small Shan village at the foot of the Ungochings.
3. Camp on the Ungochings.	Do. .		......	The road is said to be bad, but buffaloes and ponies used to be brought along it when trade was good, and it is the customary route between the two places.
4. Kendat .	Do. .		*Ningthi* .	Kendat is a town of about 100 houses, and is on the east bank of the Ningthi. It has a stockade capable of containing 200 or 300 men.
5. Kodan .	Do. .		......	By bad road through forest along the banks on the Ningthi, pass the hamlet of Malaki on the way. Kodan has about 40 or 50 houses.
6. Balet .	Do. .		...	Road bad, passes through forest as before and leaves the Ningthi at Maching, a village on the way. Balet has 24 houses. It is not far from the Ningthi.
7. Camp in Jungle.	Do. .		.....	From Balet it is usual on account of dacoits to travel to Moukhadan by boat. There is a shorter route by land. Road as before through forest.
8. Moukhadan.	Do. .		......	Road as before, about 100 houses, and a good dealing trade in timber and carpentry work. Most southern place subject to the Khampat Woon.
9. Moungyaun.	Two days' journey.		......	By boat to near Moungyaun, which is a little distance from the river. It is a large place from this point; carts can be obtained.
10. Kemun .	......		......	Road good, one day's cart travelling; about 50 houses.
11. Myinmu .	......		......	On the Irrawaddy, a short distance south of the mouth of the Moo river, described as about the size of Goalundo.

ROUTE No. 15.

FROM YANGA-POKPI TO MORÉ THANNA.

Territory—MANIPUR. Authority—LIEUT. DUN.

Date—*1882*.

Names of Stages, &c.	Distance. Inter-mediate. Miles.	Distance. Total. Miles.	Rivers.	Remarks.
			Tuyang .	To 1 mile along the Tuyang through open forest and cross the Tuyang as before (Route 8). Thick forest, swamp, and low hills to 2 miles. Old site of Machi village.
MORÉ THANNA	22	22	...... *Wakshu.* *Namchielo.* *Kujierok.*	From thence along the whole route there is an open forest of a kind of sál with other large trees in less numbers and an undergrowth of short grass and small plants. The road is perfectly flat and level, and, except for the nalas and streams noted, is perfectly traversable by carts. At 3 miles course south, the road to Mungsa, which is 1 mile distant, is passed; at 6 miles, another road to Mungsa, both from the east. At 7½ an old road on the west to deserted village, name unknown. At 9 miles the Wakshu stream, 20 feet broad, low banks, pebbly bottom, 4 inches of water; at 10½ a small stream, at 12 a low ridge, at 13 two old roads on the west; nothing about them was known, probably roads from Kámbang and Sitpong. At 14 miles the village of Kwendoung on the broad flat end of a spur from the west, not stockaded. The cultivation lies below the village on the east. Plenty of camping-ground, water, firewood, and grazing. On the south edge of the village, the Namchielo stream, 40 yards broad, 6 inches of water, and 6 feet perpendicular bank on far side. At 15 miles a stream and at 16 miles; at 16¾ a very deep rocky-sided nala, 15 feet broad; at 17½ nala with perpendicular banks, but good crossing place, 30 yards broad, very little water; at 18 a deep nala, 10 feet broad; at 18¾ a deep nala, 15 feet broad; at 19½ a deep nala, 30 feet wide, very little water; at 20½ a road to Tummu; turn west, cross the Kujierok; at 21 miles a deep nala, 30 yards broad, 5 feet perpendicular banks, bad crossing. Moré Thanna at 22 miles. This march was performed by coolies carrying 26 seers in 8¼ hours.

ROUTE No. 16.

FROM MANIPUR TO MONFU.

Viâ *Helau.*

Territory—MANIPUR. Authority—CAPT. GRANT.

Date—*January 1832.*

Names of Stages, &c.	Distance. Intermediate. Miles.	Distance. Total. Miles.	Rivers.	Remarks.
1. THOBAL .	11	11	......	A depôt for grain.
2. HUBBROK .	8	19	......	Inhabitants came from Tipperah a hundred years ago.
3. MUCHI .	9	28	......	A Naga village on the most western range of Murring hills.
4. KOMBANG	12	40	......	Hence three roads lead to the Kubbo valley; violent hoar frost on 15th January.
5. KWALOBI .	10	50	......	Good road.
6. KONDOUNG	5	55	......	A very good road.
7. MAGLANO NALA.	9	64	......	Road passes through a forest of keoo, teak, sál, cotton, and other trees; many wild animals.
8. NAMPHA-KAMHALA.	7	71	......	East of first range of Ungoching Hills.
9. NAM-SING-YIT.	8	79	......	A nala east of second range.
10. SOURCE OF HELAU NALA.	13	92	......	Road good; crossed the highest range of the Ungoching Hills.
11. HELAU .	12	104	......	On the banks of the Ningthi; just opposite a large nala called the Moo, Nimmoo, or Moowa, empties itself into the Ningthi. *Remarks by* CAPTAIN GRANT.—"The foregoing route across the Ungoching hills I consider equally good with those to Monfu and Sanayachil, and it might, with very little trouble, be made practicable for every description of cattle. Not having been travelled for many years and never before by Europeans, it is at present (1832) impeded by large trees, which have fallen across it, and also by bamboos which unite from both sides in many places at about 7 or 8 feet high above it. It possesses an advantage over the before-mentioned routes in a more abundant supply of water. The whole of the hills throughout this route to the

Names of Stages, &c.	Distance.		Rivers.	Remarks.
	Intermediate.	Total.		
	Miles.	Miles.		
11. Helau—*contd.*				Ningthi are covered with a dense bamboo jungle, which grows to an immense size. In that part of the last day's march, where the road runs along the bed of the Helau Nala, there is a second road, on the bank just above, which is at present so overgrown with forest and jungle as to be impracticable.
12.	9	113	......	The road from Tummu direct to Helau joins this one at about 2 miles distance from the latter village. It is much shorter, but so very bad as to have obtained the name of "stone-leaping road." Loaded coolies can, however, manage to travel it.
13.	9	122	......	
14.	9	131	......	
15. Monfu	9	140	......	The road from Helau to Monfu is 36 miles, of four marches, along the valley of the Ningthi, and might also be made available for all military purposes. Elephants have travelled the whole way from Manipur. As no boats larger than canoes were procurable, two of these were fastened, about 4 feet apart, by small timbers, and a bamboo platform laid over the whole. This formed a raft sufficiently large to hold 60 men. A raft of this description would answer well to cross troops were no boats procurable. The current of the Ningthi at the present season (end of January) is very slow. A short distance below Monfu a small range of hills crosses the river, composed of a reddish sand; much gold found here. Pass Marada on the right bank at 4 miles, Kuong-Goong right bank, and Ishak-ta left bank (20 houses) at 6 miles, Yaoong Karoo (20 houses) left bank at 8 miles, Cahndoo Sueek left bank at 9 miles, Turuoong Sueek (40 houses) left bank at 10½ miles. Reach Kneesung in 5 hours, right bank.

ROUTE No. 17.

From MONFU to SANAYACHIL.

Viâ *Ningthi River.*

Territory—Kubbo Valley. Authority—Capt. Grant.

Date—*1832.*

Names of Stages, &c.	Distances. Intermediate. Miles.	Distances. Total. Miles.	Rivers.	Remarks.
1. Kneesung	11	11	......	On the opposite bank of the river is a Burmese stockade. Leaving Kneesung pass a small nala, on the east bank of river, at 1½ miles called Khyookma-Kyoung. At 2 miles pass village of Lapan Goong (10 houses); at 4½ miles reach Mangya in 2½ hours.
2. Mangya	4½	15½	......	This is a village of 300 inhabitants. Leave Mangya and pass Ya-byen (8 houses) at 1½ miles, left bank; close to south of this is a small nala. At 5½ miles pass Nanyen Sueek on left bank (8 houses). Just below this on right bank pass Engda-Baoong. At 8 miles pass Taboo Sueck on left bank, opposite to which, on the right bank, is a small nala. At 10 miles pass Nam-Moorek on right bank and Magee Gnoong (20 houses) on left; immediately south of the latter place is a branch of the River Nummoo.
3. Helau	11	26½	......	At 11 miles reach Helau, a village of 300 inhabitants, time 5½ hours. On the opposite bank is a small village, Kyen-dwen. After leaving Helau pass Kyo-Goon at 1½ miles on right bank and Kwe-gnoo (4 houses) on opposite bank. The river, a mile from this, bends to the north-west and continues to flow in that direction for 5 miles. It then flows south for 2 miles, and south-east for 4 miles. At 13 miles from Helau pass the village of Gee-Goong (14 houses) on left bank. At 15 miles pass Khoon, a small village.
4. Malu	16	42½	......	At 16 miles reach Malu after 7 hours' journey. Leaving Malu pass at 4 miles Tanben-loon (80 houses from Tummu) on left bank. At 6 miles pass Swa-be-leng. At 13½ halt at a small nala called Chwook-Kan-Choung; no village; 6 hours.
5. Chwook-Kan-Choung (a small nala).	13½	56	......	The current generally slow, in some places almost still. At a short distance below the village of Tan-ben-loong is an extraordinary hill called Swe-ba-beng. It rises abruptly from bed of the river, forming a natural wall of about

Names of Stages, &c.	Distance. Intermediate. Miles.	Total. Miles.	Rivers.	Remarks.
5. Chwook-Kan-Choung (a small nala)—*contd.*				300 feet. The face of the hill turns the river suddenly from a southerly to a westerly direction. It appears to be the sudden commencement of a range, differing from the other hills in its vicinity, being free of trees with which the others are overgrown, and running in a succession of cones to the south-west as far as the eye could reach. The river here is very narrow, and just previous to its resuming its course to the south, a tremendous block of rock just nearly half across, which repels the stream backwards and causes in the rains a whirlpool which renders the navigation most dangerous to any one not acquainted with the locality. In January, however, it was a perfect mill-pond. Pass three nalas on east bank, and at 7 miles pass the village of Koon-dong on left bank (5 hours). At 8 miles pass the Mágiang river on right bank and on left Angoon. On south bank of the Mágiang is Yuwa, and a mile south on left bank a Burmese thanna of 10 men. At 11½ miles on left bank is Sepan-Gnee Goong. At 14 miles on left bank a small nala, and on its southern bank an old village called Ang-oong. At 15 miles on left bank a small nala, and on its north bank the village of Maru-oong-dza (10 houses). At 15½ miles left bank Pantha (25 houses) from Kubbo valley. At 21 miles pass Manoola village (10 houses). At 22½ a small nala on right bank, and Phe-ga-iza (30 houses) on left. At 23 or 24 miles reach Sanayachil. Time 11 hours.
6. Sanaya-chil.	23	79	......	The current of the Ningthi at this time of the year (January) is very slow, not much more than a mile an hour. On the eastern side sand-banks extend for 400 yards into the bed of the river, offering favourable points for the crossing of troops, which, at this season of the year, might be effected on rafts; row-boats not procurable.

ROUTE No. 18.

FROM SANAYACHIL TO TUMMU.

Viâ Ningthi and Máglang Rivers.

Territory—KUBBO VALLEY. Authority—CAPT. GRANT.

Date—*1832.*

Names of Stages, &c.	Distance.		Rivers.	Remarks.
	Intermediate.	Total.		
	Miles.	Miles.		
1. WEGA-DZA .	6	6	......	On 10th February started in a *dingy* for Yuwa, where the Máglang joined the Ningthi; reached Wega-dza in six hours; halted here; no village. Heavy dew falls here, fogs till 9 A. M.; reach Yuwa in three hours, being only two hours more than it took the boat to go the same distance down-stream. After proceeding up the Máglang for three hours halted for night. The Máglang discharges itself with some force into the Ningthi, and a boat or raft coming out of it would be carried without any exertion nearly to the opposite side.. After getting fairly into the Máglang, the water is not more than 2 feet in depth.
2. HALT ON SANDBANK.	12	18	......	Put to for night on sandbank; plenty of coal about. Tracks of innumerable wild beasts. Started at daylight; after three hours passed site of Yangnam village. There are salt-wells in this village. Two hours from this village reached the site of a second Nummoo, where also are salt-springs, and in another hour the junction of the Tadoi Choung Nala. From here to where the road to Sanayachil crosses the Tadoi Choung is five hours' journey. Halt at Tadoi Choung Nala.
3. HALT AT TADOI CHOUNG NALA. TADOI KHAO (?) ON PEMBERTON'S MAP.	...	...	......	The current during the day was generally very slow; passed three rapids, each of about 30 yards' continuance, but the fall so trifling as not to render it necessary to unload the boats. Total time travelled this day six hours. Three hours after leaving last halting-place reached a rapid called Khyuk-taeong, where the boats were obliged to be unloaded, and after about three hours more a second, where a like precaution was necessary. Neither of these rapids is of greater length than 40 yards; the last, which is named Chum-ka-le, is the worst, being a fall of about 10 feet; its difficulties are increased by large and loose rocks, over which it rushes. The obstacles offered to the navigation of the Máglang could be overcome by digging small canals, for which there is sufficient room; ever as it is the river is practicable for *dingies*, and

Names of Stages, &c.	Distance. Inter-mediate. Miles.	Total. Miles.	Rivers.	Remarks.
3. HALT AT TADOI—*contd.*	...	...	......	would be more so were the rocks in the bed removed. The only precaution necessary is to unload the loads for about 40 yards. Immediately above and below the falls is nearly as still as a pond. A short distance above the last rapid reached the site of a village called Chum-ka-le; halt for night. Here also are salt springs. Length of journey eight hours. Reach the junction of Khambat and Máglang rivers without any impediment from rapids. The point where the above rivers unite is about 8 miles east of Moo, and in the Kubbo valley. The village of Moo, whence is the ascent of the pass leading to Pa-tche-ne across the Ungoching, is distant from hence about 1½ miles. East of Pa-tche-ne village are most extensive salt-springs, which supply the whole southern division of Kubbo and Naga villages to the west of it with salt. Time 7½ hours.
4. CHUM-KA-TI	...	...		
5. JUNCTION OF KHAMBAT AND MÁGLANG STREAMS.	...	30?		
6. WETOOP	8	38	......	Leave boats and travel 8 miles west to Wetoop; road good and similar to that throughout all parts of the Kubbo valley. A village here of 40 inhabitants. The distance between Tummu and Manipur is given in Pemberton's map as 64 miles, divided into seven marches. In coming from Cachar one day at least would be saved in going direct across the valley, instead of diverging to the capital.
7. NAM-MALDA NALA.	...	...		NOTE.—The general width of the valley of the Máglang is about 2 miles; that of the river about 120 yards; its course upwards nearly east and west, except where it rounds the bases of the different ranges of hills, which it does by turning for a short distance to the north. In places throughout its course it is confined by a steep face of rock.
8. PASSA NALA	...	...		The hills on both sides terminate at, and slope gradually down to, its bed, leaving a gap for its egress to the Ningthi. A road might be made through the valley; it would, however, be very circuitous and the river crossed frequently—drawbacks which would more than counterbalance the advantages to be derived from it. The river might be made available for transporting grain and other stores by boats from Kubbo valley to the Ningthi. The banks on either side are covered to the water's edge with a forest of teak, sál, cotton, wood-oil, and other noble trees similar to those of the Kubbo valley, and swarm with wild beasts. There is no direct road across the valley. The ground can only be traversed towards the end of the cold weather. It is usually swampy.
9. TUMMU	...	...		

ROUTE No. 19.

FROM AVA TO KENDAT.

Territory—BURMA. Authority—DR. RICHARDSON.

Date—*1831.*

Names of Stages, &c.	Distance. Intermediate. Miles.	Distance. Total. Miles.	Rivers.	Remarks.
AVA	...	...	*Irrawaddy.* Boat.	Leave Ava at noon, cross river to Tsa-gain. Pass Pa-be-dan or "blacksmith's village" at 3-25; 70 to 100 houses, all inhabited by blacksmiths from Tsa-gain. At 3-35 pass Kyouk-tsheet, nearly same number of houses. At 4 pass Magee-tzen, village of same size. At 4-30 pass within a furlong of Koung-mhoo-dau-gyee pagoda, to the south-west of which, about half a mile, is a swamp of some extent, and to the east of it and of the road another called Yekha, the waters of which are extremely bitter. At 5-20 halt at Tsa-ye, a large village; the road throughout is good and level, the soil light and sandy; nearly the whole country on both sides of the road has been under cultivation.
1. SA-YE	8	8	......	Leave Sa-ye at 9 A.M., pass through Padoo, a large village, perhaps 160 houses. Appearance of country the same as in latter part of last march; cattle numerous, water sufficient, and cultivation extensive. Road level, light and sandy, runs along a plain between the Sa-gain hills to the eastward, 3 miles distant, and a ridge of elevated ground to the west, 8 miles distant; great part of this plain is, or might be, brought under cultivation. At 12-5 arrive at Kek-ka, about 90 houses. Time 3-5 hours, distance 7 miles, direction north 20° west.
2. KEK-KA	7	15	......	At 8 A.M. leave Kek-ka; at 8-50 pass Thughe, a small village, perhaps 20 houses. At 9-45 pass Ooung-ngay-bouk, about 70 houses; 10-20 Kamday, a small village in palmyra tope; 11-10 En-bay-toung-oong; 11-40 En-bay, a large village; 1-20 They-yoin, small village, some remarkable pagodas, the road light and sandy, as before, as far as They-yoin, from which commences a rich loamy clay. The range of hills on the right terminates at Kek-ka. After leaving En-bay, up to which place cultivation was almost uninterrupted, with large and numerous herds of cattle, and villages at short distances, the horizon to the west was bounded by apparently a thin strip of palmyra trees running some way north, then coming round to the east, and crossing the road; immediately within these to the westward is a grassy,

Names of Stages, &c.	Distance.		Rivers.	Remarks.
	Inter-medi-ate.	Total.		
	Miles.	Miles.		
2. Kee-ka—*contd.*				apparently marshy, plain of some miles in extent, and on the borders of this, about a quarter of a mile from the road, is a small cluster of huts called Sha-doun, the inhabitants of which are salt-makers. Between these and the road the paddy-fields continue to He-len. At 3-8 reach He-len, a large village, about 150 houses. Time 7 hours, distance 16 miles, direction north 20° west.
3. He-Len .	16	31	......	At 8 A.M. leave He-len, cross for a few minutes some high broken ground, at the foot of which cross some marshy grounds in the salt-fields; at 8-30 pass paddy-fields and cattle of village; at 9-30 grassy plain with open jungle; at 9-45 jungle closer; 10 pass small village called "Tha-men-Khyet-Shain" or "cooked-rice shop," 10 or 12 houses; here three people may dine for a quarter tikal; at 10-30 pass small village, paddy-fields and cattle; 11-50 arrive at Mout-zobo, a walled city of 2 miles square, the birth-place of Alompra. The walls, partly of brick and partly of a thin slate, still (1831) in pretty good repair. It is said to contain 1,000 houses. There are extensive paddy-fields between the inner brick walls and the outer one, or mound to the north and westward. To the south there is no earthen wall, and the ditch is close to the brick walls. The walls are without flanking defence. At 12-20 start, and at 1-25 pass out of the Kathay gate of the outer wall; the ditch, which on the south side is empty and might be crossed without notice, is here in tolerable repair; it is said that the ditch can at any time be filled from the Kan-dau-gyee or great Royal Lake which lies about 2 or 3 miles to the nor[illegible]east. At 2-25 pass a small village; at 3 pass K[illegible]aun, a village of 50 or 60 houses; at 4 halt at Kya-ywa, a village of 200 houses. The first part of this day's march has been less under cultivation than any former part of the route from Mout-zobo; cattle and water abundant; the road good throughout; hills visible to eastward; no highland visible to westward; many villages surrounded with cocoanut trees, the palmyra numerous throughout. Time 8 hours, distance 17 miles, direction north 40° west.
4. Kya-ywa .	17	48	*Moo*—Easily fordable in dry weather from bank to bank, 400 yards.	At 8 A.M. leave Kya-ywa; at 9-15 pass a second Kya-ywa; pass a small grassy lake and the third Kya-ywa; 10-30 pass Mendoung. To the north of this is jungle scantily inhabited. (At the time Dr. Richardson wrote there was a herd of 50 or 60 wild elephants, which did much damage to the crops.) 12-45 cross Moo River; in dry

Names of Stages, &c.	Distance. Intermediate. Miles.	Total. Miles.	Rivers.	Remarks.
4. Kya-ywa—*contd.*				weather there are two streams of nearly equal size, with 100 yards of land between them; from bank to bank, 400 yards. It is easily fordable in dry weather, but not so in the rains. On the western bank is a large village, Yee-oo. At 3-15 halt at Pha-lan-goun. Inhabitants, cattle, cultivation, and water plentiful, and the roads good for any description of carriage at this season. Pha-lan-goun is a large scattered village, about 150 houses. Dubay-en, the town from which the Myo-woon takes his title, is 6 miles south-west of this, but nearly depopulated and its walls entirely out of repair. This Government, which extends from the Tsagain territory to the Chin-dwen, furnishes 3,000 soldiers and 6 *bos*. Grain is plentiful and cheap; cattle are plentiful. Time 7-10; distance 16 miles; direction north 65° west.
5. Pha-lan-goun.	16	64	...... Small nala.	Leave Pha-lan-goun at 8-55, pass Sedi-mee, a small village of 30 houses; at 9-25 Weythey, same size; at 10-10 pass Ywatheet, 100 houses; this is called Yuama or "chief village"; 11-25 cross a small nala; and at 12-55 reach Mya-goo. The whole march is one uninterrupted sheet of cultivation; the soil rich, clayey loam, crops heavy and close, the whole country studded with palm trees. Time 4 hours; direction north 60° west.
6. Mya-goo .	$10\frac{1}{2}$	$74\frac{1}{2}$	......	At 7-35 leave Mya-goo; at 8 pass a small village, where sugar is made; at 9-30 another small village, 5 or 6 houses and small stream; at 12 pass the wide bed of a nameless mountain stream, in which water is not ankle-deep in dry weather; from this there is a gradual ascent; at 4 pass the village of Ywa-Ngay, 20 houses; 4-50 halt at Benthi in the jungle. No village and very little water; road as good as usual, but entirely in the jungle. Since 9-30, except the little village of Ywa-Ngay, no inhabitants, cultivation nor cattle seen; jungle open and principally composed of eng trees. Time 9-15; direction north 80° west.
7. Benthe .	20	$94\frac{1}{2}$	A small stream, in broad bed.	At 7-30 leave Benthe; at 8-15 pass the end of a deep ravine running north from road; since noon yesterday have been ascending, now descend into the broad bed of a river (without name), along which, in deep sand, the road runs all the way to Thoun-bouk, when it falls into the Chindwen, and along which a small stream of water finds its way, occasionally on the surface, occasionally lost in the sand; the banks are of soft sandstone, 20 to 100 feet high, often perpendicular, sometimes covered with jungle to their

Names of Stages, &c.	Distance. Intermediate. Miles.	Distance. Total. Miles.	Rivers.	Remarks.
7. Benthe—*contd.*				edges. In width the river varies from 40 to 120 yards or more, and in the sand are many large rolled masses of granite and syenite. At 11 pass Kimdonge, a small village with 10 or 12 houses; some cattle, buffaloes, and cultivation about it. There is a ravine running away to the north-west, and a small stream comes down from the west in much the same sort of bed as that in which the route has lain which joins here. The ground here is swampy, with long grass; the road is still very passable for any common carriage. At 1, low range of hills, 6 miles to south 70° west; road along bank of river. At 2 reach Thoun-bouk, a village of 20 or 30 houses on the banks of the Chin-dwen. Time 6-30, direction south 60° west.
8. Thoun-bouk.	17	111½	......	The road from hence to Kendat is impassable for all sorts of carriages, but boats may be had on the river by which the greater part of the communication to the north-west is carried on. At 8-30 leave Thoun-bouk for a few minutes; travel through thick jungle, then ascend a low but steep hill, down the descent of which it is necessary to dismount and lead the horses. At 9-10, in sight of the Chin-dwen, proceeding along the broad bed of a mountain torrent in deep white sand with high perpendicular banks running off in ridges from the stream; at 9-35 enter jungle and ascend another hill; pass along a narrow ridge and make a very steep descent; continue crossing steep ridges of low sandy hills covered with jungle and winding amongst them in the dry beds of torrents till 13-15, when pass small villages in cultivated plain; 12-30 cross a small stream about knee-deep with quicksands; 12-41 reach Mouk-ka-dan, 80 or 100 houses, close to banks of Chin-dwen. Large boats are made here, and teak timber of good size is proenrable in the neighbouring jungles. Time 4-15, direction north 75° west.
9. Mouk-ka-dan.	9	120½	......	
			Small stream.	At 7-30 leave Mouk-ka-dan and descend slightly into the valley of the stream with quicksands; pass along a bad swampy road through wet paddy-fields; cross and recross the stream till 9-45, when proceed up small branch more to the west with high sandstone banks on the westward and jungle on the eastward side till 11-25, when water is lost in sand. Reach Pa-doo-yee at 3-15 in the jungle. The road much the same as last march: the ravines close to the road appear dangerous; both sides of the first stream are well cultivated and inhabited; many buffaloes and some black cattle. The jungle composed principally of eng and teak; numerous marks of deer, wild hogs,
10. Pa-doo-yee	14½	135	......	

Names of Stages, &c.	Distance. Intermediate.	Total.	Rivers.	Remarks.
	Miles.	Miles.		
10. Pa-doo-yee —*contd.*			.	&c., during march. Time 6-20, direction north 30° west.
11. Balet .	15	150	......	At 7-45 leave Pa-doo-yee and proceed along a jungle path, same as last two marches, till 4 P.M., when pass some paddy-fields with buffaloes and reach small village of Balet, consisting of 4 or 5 houses. Village situated within a few miles of Chin-dwen, on the west of which are some high hills. Time 7-45, direction north 35° west. At 5-30 leave Balet by sandy road, beside a small stream, with paddy-fields along its banks, till 8-30, when reach Matsen; 10-25 leave Matsen by pretty good buggy road along the edge of the stream followed from Balet, and which here runs in a valley about a mile wide. This valley is nearly all under cultivation, with a good many black cattle and buffaloes; it is bounded on the west by a low range of hills and to the east by high hills running off in ridges to the northward. The little villages in this valley go by the general name of Matsen and amount in all to about 400 houses. At 12-30 leave valley and cross some steep but low hills by a rugged path in rather thick jungle. At 1-20 pass small village. From this to Nan-thi the course of the river is exceedingly circuitous amongst low rugged hills across which the path lies: after passing three small villages, each in its little valley by the stream, here about 2½ feet deep, reach Nan-thi, village of 40 or 50 houses, with extensive paddy-fields, many black cattle, and a few horses. Time 9 hours, direction north 20° west.
12. Nan-thi .	17	167	......	At 7-50 leave Nan-thi and proceed along the banks of a little valley 2 or 3 miles wide, in which the Nan-thi villages are scattered in the same way as those of Matsen; road partly good. At 9-30 enter jungle, and path becomes like the jungle path of previous marches; from 1-30 till 2-30 the road is level and the country open and cultivated to the north-west as far as the Chin-dwen, immediately on the western side of which the rugged hills of the Manipur territory rise to some height and run away in close and broken ranges to the north-east close to the edge of the river. Kendat is a long narrow jungle wood stockade close to the east bank of the river, situated in a long narrow swampy valley lying along the river about 15 or 20 miles in length, and averaging 1½ or 2 in width, with a strip of swampy ground to the eastward of it; population from 1,200 to 1,400. The number of cattle is smaller in proportion to the number of the inhabitants than in the villages nearer the capital.

Names of Stages, &c.	Distance.		Rivers.	Remarks.
	Intermediate.	Total.		
	Miles.	Miles.		
13. Kendat .	9	176	......	Note.—Kendat is now Burmese territory, and a new stockade is said to have been built there. The river here is about 600 yards wide from bank to bank, but towards the end of the dry weather the water is confined to a narrow channel on the western side. Dr. Richardson on his return came down the Chin-dwen by boat in three days to Thoun-bouk; the water was so shallow in places that the boat occasionally grounded; for the greater part of the way the banks were high sandstone hills covered with jungle to the edge. The course of the river is very circuitous. From Thoun-bouk to Ava he travelled by the same route as before. Kendat (100 houses) is the residence of a Woon, no military force, inhabitants armed. No sepoys are usually sent from Mandalay; a good many of the people have guns. When the Woon moves about he takes these people. They form the garrison of Tummu, when necessary; no one usually kept there. The harvest in Manipur and in Kendat occurs about the same time. A fresh crop is put in in February; the second crop an inferior crop. There are no officials under the Woon except the heads of villages. There is a stockade which would contain 200 or 300 on bank of river. Plenty of boats to cross river in. No milk or ghee obtainable from inhabitants till Moongyaune is reached. Steamers can come up at all seasons to Kendat.

ROUTE No. 20.

From TUMMU to SANAYACHIL GHÂT.

Territory—Kubbo Valley, Burmah. Authority—Capt. Pemberton.

Date—*1883.*

Names of Stages, &c.	Distance.		Rivers.	Remarks.
	Intermediate.	Total.		
	Miles.	Miles.		
1. Punsa Nala	7¾	7¾	Small nala *Namhaee Muring.* Nala. Nala. *Punsa nala.*	At 2 miles cross small nala; at 3½ cross the Namhaee Muring, a small stream with sandy bed; at 4¾ cross a small nala; at 5¼ pass the village of Punsa and small nala; at 7·6 cross Punsa Nala, bed pebbly, water abundant. The road lies on flat ground, tree-forest, with occasional clearings.

Names of Stages, &c.	Distance. Inter-medi-ate. Miles.	Total. Miles.	Rivers.	Remarks.
2. Namangka Nala.	11¼	18¾	Nala. Nala. Nala. Cross five small nalas. *Namangka Nala.*	After Punsa nala road passes through swamp for about a mile, and then crosses small nala; in the next mile two other small nalas are crossed. At 2¾ miles from Punsa nala road crosses Numooldah nala, 30 yards broad, bed pebbly, water knee-deep, and a second time in the next ¼ mile. Between this and Etoop, 8 miles further on, the road crosses four small nalas and two swamps. From Etoop to Namangka nala five small nalas are crossed and one swamp. The banks of this nala are steep, bed pebbly, water knee-deep.
3. Khambat River.	8¾	27½	*Khambat River (ford).*	At 2¼ miles reach Sarawontingkol; at 8¾ miles reach Khambat river; banks lofty, bed pebbly, 60 yards broad, stream thigh-deep.
4. Tadwe-Choung.	7¾	35¼	A river. *Vengoomakan nala; Tadwe-Choung.*	Half a mile from Khambat river the road crosses another and enters the hills; at two miles reach Vengoomakan, and at 7 Tadwe-Choung nala. The bed of this nala is filled with large sandstone boulders; in cold weather there is water in the pools; coal is found here.
5. Hueerang-pokpi.	10¼	45½	Small river .	At 6 miles cross the dry bed of a torrent; at 7 cross a very small rivulet, and at 10-2 reach Hueerang-pokpi.
6. Sanayachil Ghát.	4½	50	......	The road runs beside a nala for some distance, and is a gradual descent to Sonayachil Ghát on the Ningthee river.

ROUTE No. 21.

From TUMMU to MONPHU.

Territory—Kubbo Valley, Burmah. Authority—Capt. Pemberton.

Date—*1833.*

Names of Stages, &c.	Distance. Inter-medi-ate. Miles.	Total. Miles.	Rivers.	Remarks.
1. Kodong .	6¾	6¾	Four small nalas. River.	Direction north; at 1¾ miles pass road to Manipur on left side. At 3 miles cross a deep ravine on the trunk of a tree; between this and Kodong cross four small nalas and a branch of the Méglang just before reaching Kodong.

Names of Stages, &c.	Distance.		Rivers.	Remarks.
	Intermediate.	Total.		
	Miles.	Miles.		
2. Mungsa .	$10\frac{3}{8}$	$17\frac{1}{4}$	Three small nalas. Four small nalas. *W a k t o o nala.*	At $\frac{3}{4}$ mile cross small nala, at $1\frac{1}{2}$ cross small hill, at $2\frac{1}{4}$ cross small nala, and at $2\frac{1}{2}$ a deep ravine. In the next mile cross two small nalas; water abundant. At $4\frac{1}{2}$ miles road lead over swamp for a mile, and at $5\frac{1}{2}$ crosses a nala. At 8 miles crosses a nala with steep banks. At $9\frac{1}{2}$ pass the road from Kampang to the left, and crossing the Waktoo nala reach Mungsa.
3. Taap-Thanna (Old Samjok).	$10\frac{1}{4}$	$27\frac{1}{2}$	*Tureet nala* *Máglang.*	Leaving Mungsa the road lies through paddy-fields for some distance, and at $1\frac{1}{2}$ miles crosses the Tureet nala; water here abundant, 3 feet at ford, banks low, bed pebbly; at $2\frac{1}{2}$ cross Numtree Nala; at 5 cross a nala nearly dry; at $5\frac{1}{2}$ cross the Nummqlee, about 60 yards broad, bed pebbly, water knee-to-waist deep; high grass jungle on banks. Direction after passing Tureet nearly east; at $8\frac{1}{2}$ reach Choogne, near which is some cultivation. At 9 miles cross the Máglang, from 60 to 70 yards broad, banks steep, thigh-deep, bed stones and water-worn pebbles. At 10 miles reach Taap Thanna. This was formerly the old town of Samjok.
Noongpaktabee.	$10\frac{3}{4}$	$38\frac{1}{4}$		Direction almost due east. Shortly after leaving Taap the road enters Ungoching hills. (*Vide* Route No. 13, page 258.)

ROUTE No. 22.

From IMPHAL to LAPVOMÉ.

Territory— Authority—Lieut. E. W. Dun.

Date—*January 1885.*

Names of Stages, &c.	Distance.		Rivers.	Remarks.
	Intermediate.	Total.		
	Miles.	Miles.		
	$2\frac{1}{2}$	$2\frac{1}{2}$	*Kongba*, west of bund, 40 yards broad, 4 feet deep, 6 feet banks. East of bund, 40 yards broad, 2 feet deep, 6 feet banks.	Cross the Kongba at the edge of the town, $2\frac{1}{2}$ miles from the Pát. This portion of the road runs along the left bank of the Atchowba river, is good, and 20 yards broad, but unmetalled The Kongba is crossed on a 20 yards broad bund, over which water flows in the rains. The road then lies over a flat open plain, traversable in every direction. The plain is covered with low grass jungle on the west, cultivated on

Names of Stages, &c.	Distance. Inter-mediate. Miles.	Total. Miles.	Rivers.	Remarks.
				the east side of the road. A more circuitous road to Susukameng starts from the same point and lies further to the west and north.
	2	4½	*Iril* . .	The Iril is 30 yards broad at the top, 20 feet very steep banks, and has 2 feet of water. Stream 10 miles an hour. It is crossed on a weak wooden bridge.
	1½	6	......	At the Raja's cattle farm swamp on left of road, ascend steep spur 100 feet high by path practicable for mules, and descend along face of steep khud by a 6-feet path at 1 in 15. Cross this stream, 20 yards broad ,15 feet perpendicular banks, 1 foot of water, by weak wooden bridge and find good camping-ground for a large force. Plenty of water and grazing, but firewood distant.
			Okshu .	
	7	13		The road throughout this stage is 10 feet broad, and though rough, dry and in fair order. The ground on either side flat and covered with short coarse grass.
			Laimakhang	Ascend flat-bottomed valley at first along the left bank of the Laimakhang, then gradually approach eastern edge of valley, wind along easy spurs, and ascend a steep bit for 100 feet to top of ridge at 8 miles. Descend along face of easy spurs to Lairel thanna on the right banks of the Thobál river at 12 miles. In the Laimakhang valley the road is 15 feet broad and perfectly flat and in good order. The ground on either side is open and flat. Where it crosses the ridge it averages 8 feet in breadth, has a gradient of 1 in 20, except just below the crest on the eastern side where it is 1 in 10. The ridge is clothed with very light open oak forest. At Lairel there is good camping-ground for 800 men, and abundant water, grazing, and dry firewood.
	8	21	......	
LAIREL . .	4	25	*Thobál* .	
	2	27	Stream .	Follow the right bank of the Thobál over easy spurs covered with light jungle to a stream from the north at 2 miles. There is good camping-ground and all necessaries here for 200 men. Follow right bank of Thobál across face of steep hill-path 6 feet broad constantly ascending and descending, practicable for mules, but unsettling to loads. Cross the Thobál here 40 yards broad 4 inches deep at 4 miles. Camping-ground and all necessaries for 400 men.
	2	29	Thobál .	

Names of Stages, &c.	Distance. Inter-mediate. Miles.	Total. Miles.	Rivers.	Remarks.
	3	32	Stream	Ascend easy slope along face of hill to a small stream at 7 miles, 4,300 feet elevation.
Sokpao	1	33	......	Camping-ground, &c., for 100 men. Ascend very steep spur to Kassom Kulel at 5,300 feet. This village commands the road. Somewhat steep ascent to Sokpao at 5,800 feet. Road throughout 6 feet broad. Light jungle of fir, oak, &c. Good camping-ground at both villages for a large force, but the water kept in small tanks is bad.
Lampui	2	35	......	Level to Lampui at 10 miles. This piece of road is quite open. Camping-ground and water as at Sokpao and Kassom Kulel. Descend steep spur through light fir forest to the Nunshangkong at 12.
Camp	2	37	Nunshang-kong.	The valley here is triangular and affords camping-ground, water, and grazing for a force of 1,600 men. Elevation 4,000 feet. Ascend an open spur with 15° of slope to Tusom at 3 miles and pass the villages of Yanoubi and Pishnao. Ascend 200 feet of steep ascent to Hungdung at 4 miles. There is plenty of camping-ground and grazing at all these villages, but water (in tanks) scanty and bad. They all command the road. The road throughout is easy for mules. Hungdung is 5,600 feet above the sea. The road then traverses a broad-topped ridge covered with short coarse grass, and reaches Ukrul at 9 miles. There is no steep ascent to this village as shown in the map. It is 5,800 feet and level with the last part of the road.
Hungdung	4	41	......	
Ukrul	5	46	......	There is camping-ground and grazing for 1,200 men south of the village, but at a distance from the water-supply, which is below the village on the east. There is a fair-sized spring here, and close by it camping-ground for 400 men. Down broad easy spur (22° slope) through fir woods to junction of small stream with the Lanier, at 6 miles, 3,600 feet elevation. Camping ground for 1,600 men. Grazing only fair. Two hundred feet of steep ascent and a 2 feet ridge 50 yards in length. Could be avoided by a path up from some point higher up the small stream.
	6	52	Stream	Ascend an open grassy spur 23° slope to Phungam at 11 miles, 5,825 feet elevation. Road throughout easy for mules, except north of small stream. Unlimited camping-ground south of village. Water (to north of village) scanty; grazing indifferent.

Names of Stages, &c.	Distances. Inter-mediate. Miles	Distances. Total. Miles.	Rivers.	Remarks.
PHUNGAM	5	57	......	Traverse east face of Kapvo peak by narrow path, and through 200 yards of thick jungle. Descend easy and broad spur through open forest of large pollarded alders to 2 miles (5,100 feet). The spur then rises again and is quite open and broadens gradually to Prowi village at 5 miles (5,500 feet).
PROWI KULKL (old).	5	62	...... *Nishapui or Tuimun.*	The village is quite undefended and open. Camping ground unlimited, but water (tank) to west of village scanty and indifferent, and firewood and grazing very scanty. Easy descent to 8 miles, quite open, 3 feet grass jungle with rice-fields in the hollows. Descend rapidly through open oak forest to the junction of the Nishapui and the Lanier; camp at junction called Katong (fork) at 10 miles. The Lanier has a 50-yard broad shingly bed and 6 inches of water. Camping-ground for 3,000 men. Water and firewood. Grazing poor. Elevation 3,150 feet. Prowi Kunao, a small new village, situated above junction on the west.
CAMP KATONG	5	67	Lanier	The road throughout this stage is practicable for mules. Down the Lanier along the flat shingly bed, crossing the stream frequently, a few inches of water only; occasional pools. Camping-ground everywhere.
CAMP UNDER GAZIPHIMI.	13	80	......	Camp under Gaziphimi (Lyi) in rice-fields belonging to that village. Ground for 3,000 men, water and firewood. Grazing good. Path to Gaziphimi. Down the flat shingly bed of the Lanier as in previous march to 8 miles. Below this point river flows in a more rocky bed, and
	8	88	......	though rough the path along the sides is still practicable for mules. The hill-sides also become very steep and are clothed with thicket forest. Camp at the mouth of the Razarr stream at 17 miles. Camping-ground for 2,000 men, but requires clearing of thick reed jungle. Plenty of water and firewood. Excellent grass on the hill-sides, but difficult to get at. Elevation of camp 2,350 feet.
CAMP	19	97	Razarr	Follow the bed of the stream to 1½ miles, rice-fields. Ascend slope of 29° to 2,800 feet, pass round shoulder of spur to stream, and ascend slope of 28° to Jessami at 4 miles.
JESSAMI OR PUNGTAR.	4	101	......	Pass under village on the west. Camping-ground, firewood, grazing, and water for 3,000 men north of village. Streams (two) below camp on the east.

Name of Stages, &c.	Distance. Inter-mediate. Miles.	Tot. Miles.	Rivers.	Remarks.
JESSAMI OR PUNGTAR—*contd.*	...	...	......	Down steep and narrow path, north-east from camp through light jungle practicable for mules, except for the last 60 feet (which could, however, be easily zig-zagged) to the Lanier 20 yards broad, shingly bed, 1 foot of water.
	4	105	Lanier	Ascend steep side of spur and then along the top of the latter by a good easy path through light jungle to Mellomi. Camping-ground and a little water 1 mile south of village for 1,000 men, but clearing required. No grazing.
MELLOMI	9	110	......	
JESSAMI OR PUNGTAR.	...	101	......	Descend the Jessami ridge in a south-easterly direction by a good mule-path, cross a small stream, pass round a shoulder and down a short spur, getting gradually steeper to the Thetzirr, the last few yards being at present impracticable for mules. Elevation of Thetzirr 2,200 feet. Ascend a slope of 28° direct to Pungtar Kunao, 3,900 feet. Camping-ground for 200 men, but very little water and no grazing.
	4	105	*Thetzirr*	Descend a slope of 27° to a small stream, at 2,700 feet elevation, and up a very steep hill-side through thick jungle to Lapvomé at 4,900 feet.
LAPVOMÉ	7	112	......	Road practicable but very difficult for mules.

ROUTE No. 23.

From LAPVOMÉ to SOMRAH GNÁCHÁN.

Territory—

Authority—LIEUT. E. W. DUN.

Date—*February 1885.*

Names of Stages, &c.	Distance. Inter-mediate. Miles.	Total. Miles.	Rivers.	Remarks.
	2	...	*Stream.*	Down very steep face of ridge on the west at a slope of 29° to stream at 2,100 feet and ascend a similar slope to Pungtar Kunao at 4,000 feet.
PUNGTAR KUNAO.	4	...	......	Leave Pungtar Kunao on the west and descend a steep hill to the stream below Putsimi (this village is now deserted).
			Stream.	Cross a very steep spur along the face of a hill and along the bed of the Thetzirr to Wangkhaikul (deserted).
	4	...	*Thetzirr.*	Unlimited camping-ground, water, and fair grazing. Cross several steep-sided spurs and

Names of Stages, &c.	Distance. Intermediate.	Distance. Total.	Rivers.	Remarks.
	Miles.	Miles.		
	4	...	*Riokong.*	the Riokong, 10 yards broad and 1 foot of water just above its junction with the Thetzirr. On the left bank there is a difficult bit for mules, and as it is rocky, could only be made practicable with difficulty. Cross the spur below Wakhong. The latter is situated high up on steep cliffs. Camp at mouth of Mamokong gorge. Unlimited camping-ground, water, and good grazing. The path in many places in this stage is too steep for mules, but it could be easily taken along the bed of the Thetzirr the whole way.
	3	17	*Mamokong.*	
Tusom . .	10	27	.....	Ascend a spur, at first very steep, but passable for mules, and then easy through very open fir forest along this spur. Branch path to Karasom at 9 miles and Tusom on the top of the ridge at 10 miles at 5,700 feet. Pass along south-east face of main ridge and find camping-ground for 2,000 men and transport at 10½ miles.
Camp . .	½	27½	......	
Somrah Kulel.	16	43½	......	Straight up steep to very steep ridge to 8,000 feet close below Tusom peak, impracticable for mules without zig-zagging. Cross several steep-sided spurs, covered with fir forest, by irrigation channels too narrow (2 feet broad) for mules and down a broad spur to Somrah Kulel. There is excellent camping-ground, and plenty of water for 3,000 men above the village at an elevation of 6,200 feet. The water channels now used as paths could easily be widened sufficiently for mules, as the soil is light.
	6	..	*Marangkong.*	Descend through open rice-fields by narrow path. Cross rocky bed of stream (a difficult place for mules) at 2 miles, and pass below Pungtar out of sight of the village. Descend an easy open spur to the Marangkong at 6 miles, 3,700 feet. Three inches of water 20 yards broad. The last half mile lies along an irrigation channel and is too narrow for mules, but could easily be made passable. Ascend an easy hill-side covered with rice-fields, which irrigation during the cold weather converts into a swamp, and camp at the head of the fields at 5,600 feet north of and below the village of Kongailong. If the fields were kept dry, the camping-ground would be unlimited; if flooded, there remains sufficient for 1,000 men and transport close to water.
	4	53½	......	
	2 days' journey.	...	*Lanier.*	From Kongailong there is a good easy path over the next ridge on the east to the Ningthi valley through the villages of Kakilong and Sipong.
		...	*Ningthi.*	

Names of Stages, &c.	Distance. Inter-mediate. Miles.	Total. Miles.	Rivers.	Remarks.
	4	...	*Thangkong. Khanotirkong.* Stream.	By the Somrah Kulel road as far as the rocky bed of stream below Pungtar. Pass along east face of Somrah Kulel spur and down an easy slope to the junction of the Thangkong and Khanotirkong streams at 4 miles from Somrah Kulel. Cross stream (6 inches of water), and pass along face of hill by old irrigation channel (impracticable for mules at present) to the junction of the Gnáchán stream with the Khamroi stream. Cross stream and ascend an easy spur to Gnáchán. Scattered ground for 1,000 men and transport below the village on the east. Water and fair grazing.
	3	61½	......	

ROUTE No. 24.

From KONGÁL THANNA to SOMRAH GNÁCHÁN.

Territory— Authority—Lieut. E. W. Dun.

Date—*February 1855.*

Names of Stages, &c.	Distance. Inter-mediate. Miles.	Total. Miles.	Rivers.	Remarks.
Chattik .	...	32	......	*Vide* Route No. 4.
	6	...	*Phaiikong Chaiikong.*	The path (which throughout this route is never more than 4 feet wide) descends in a northerly direction along the eastern face of the Chattik ridge. It becomes very steep close to the foot of the hill, and though it could easily be rendered passable is here at present impassable for mules. Cross the Phaiikong and Chaiikong streams at their junction at 2,100 feet elevation. The former stream is here 40 yards broad, and has 2 feet of water with a very slight current. The latter is 20 yards broad and has 6 inches of water. There is camping-ground here for 1,000 men with transport, but much heavy jungle would have to be cleared.
	7	...	......	Ascend a gently-sloping spur on the left bank; cross several spurs from the Kassom range and that on which the village of Kassom is situated at 12 miles. Kassom Kulel is a small hamlet; it does not command the road. There is plenty of level camping-ground here if the jungle (which is light) be cleared, but the water is scanty. The path again crosses numerous spurs, some of them with steep sides, and reaches the

Names of Stages, &c.	Distance. Intermediate. Miles.	Distance. Total. Miles.	Rivers.	Remarks.
	6	...	*Nelekong*	Nelekong at 18 miles. This stream flows in a bed of gigantic boulders. It is bridged by a fallen tree, which has been carefully railed with bamboo and cane, and is practicable for mules.
Kachao	2	52	......	Ascend to the plateau east of Kachao by an easy spur. Unlimited camping-ground plenty of water and grazing anywhere east of the village, but little clearing required, 4,000 feet elevation. The path now ascends the southern face of the Kachaophung peak, crossing the
	1	...	*Nelekong*	Nelekong again at 1 mile. There is a capital piece of camping-ground here for 2,000 men with transport, but no grazing. The ascent is in many places precipitous, but it could be made practicable for mules by 200 men in a day. Camp on the south side of the peak, about 600 feet below. There are scattered bits of level ground here, which would in the aggregate afford room for 500 men and transport, but water is scanty and low down on the eastern slope. Elevation of camp about 7,000 feet.
Camp Kachaophung Peak.	8	60	......	There is a steep rise to the Kachaophung peak, 8,070 feet. A very extended view is obtainable from the top over the Ningthi valley, Upper Burma, Sarameti, and the Manipur hills. Descend by an easy spur through fine open forest,
	6	...	Small stream.	a small camping-ground and water at 6 miles. The fields of the deserted village of Lophao at 10 miles and by a precipitous bit (which could, however, be easily either avoided or zig-zagged) to the Chareli or Gnaraikong. There is only
	5	71	*Chareli or Gnaraikong.*	room for 200 men and transport on the stream. The deserted fields alone afford ample accommodation for 2,000 men and transport, and as the old irrigation channels are in existence, water could be brought to them. Elevation 2,700 feet. The ascent from the stream is again precipitous for 500 feet, but could easily be made practicable for mules. Thence there is at first a steep but good path up a spur and along the western face of the Arin or Somrah
	4	...	Small stream.	peak. There is a little water and a small camping-ground at 4 miles. Descend along a very gently-sloping spur, which in some places is very narrow, to Somrah Gnáchán. The highest point crossed is 7,400 feet. Somrah Gnáchán is 5,300 feet. There are scattered bits of camping-ground below the village on the
	8	83	......	east for 1,000 men and transport. Water and a little grazing.

ROUTE No. 25.

FROM IMPHAL TO THOBÁL.

Viâ *Longtival*.

Territory— Authority—LIEUT. DUN.

Date—*10th January 1885.*

Names of Stages, &c.	Distance. Intermediate. Miles.	Distance. Total. Miles.	Rivers.	Remarks.
	2	...	*Nambol*	A path leads south-east from Bishenpur Bazaar to the junction of two streams stated to be the eastern and western Nambols. It is quite open country and is practicable for mules in January, but not before. The stream below the junction is 40 yards broad and 2 feet deep, with a very slight current. It has a sound though muddy bottom and can be easily crossed by elephants; the banks are not more than 2 feet above the surface of the water. Either bank of the eastern stream can now be followed to a point where a small nalla joins from the east (believed to be an old bed of the Imphál). This portion is usually traversed in boats, and there is only a cold weather path; at other seasons the ground is covered with reed jungle. The right bank was traversed by an elephant which accompanied me. The left bank was in use by foot passengers. There is a good broad road through grass jungle and villages to Meiyang Imphál.
MEIYANG IMPHAL .	3	9		
	½	...	*Thobal* .	There is a good broad road through villages the whole way to Thobal Bazaar, crossing the Imphál by a bamboo bridge. The bridge is impassable for mules.
THOBÁL .	8½	...	*Imphál* .	This route may be said to be practicable for mules after the 15th January. Bridges or ferries would have to be constructed for the Nambol and Imphál streams, and the jungle along the banks of the Nambol cut some time previously to allow of the ground drying up.

ROUTE No. 26.

FROM IMPHAL TO SHUGUNU.

Territory— Authority—LIEUT. DUN.

Date—*January 1885.*

Names of Stages, &c.	Distance. Intermediate. Miles.	Distance. Total. Miles.	Rivers.	Remarks.
				Leave the Raja's enclosure by the western gate and proceed due west. Cross the Tiki or eastern Nambol by a strong brick bridge of three arches, with 20 feet roadway.* Turn due south and follow the right bank of that stream.

* *Vide* description of city.

Names of Stages, &c.	Distance. Inter-mediate. Miles.	Total. Miles.	Rivers.	Remarks.
			Eastern Nambol or Tiki.	The road is unmetalled and 30 feet wide. At 1½ miles there is a wooden bridge over the Nambol, and again at 2½ miles, both practicable for mules, the Thobal road here converges and again diverges. Leave the last house of the city at 3 miles and reach Longtival village at 4 miles straight on over open country to Hyenkhang at 5 miles. The road here crosses the Nambol between the Longtival and Kyenkhang Hills by a weak bamboo bridge (practicable for mules). The foot of the Longtival hill is here 600 yards from the foot of the Hyenkhang hill. The former rises 420 feet above the plain; the latter 100. The water at the above crossing is (in January) 5 feet deep. The banks are steep and 10 feet above the surface of the water. The current is very slight at both places. The road to this point is well raised and 30 feet broad, but it is unmetalled and the surface very rough. From 2½ to 5 miles it follows the right bank of the Nambol and has a swamp on the western side. On the eastern or left bank of the Nambol is a large open uncultivated piece of flat ground formerly occupied by the Manipur Levy and the station, and which is bounded on the south by the Longtival hill, the site of a former capital.
Hyenkhang .	6	...	Nambol .	From Hyenkhang the main road continues south-west, the Shugunu road branching off. It (the latter) is only 15 feet wide, not much raised, and is very rough. It crosses a perfectly flat country, chiefly cultivated with rice but with patches of grass interspersed. It leads over three small swamps spanned by bamboo bridges which are practicable for mules if in good repair and passes the villages of Samro Jangi and Wangor at 10 and 11 miles respectively.
Wangoi .	5	11	*Wangoi Nala.* .	At Wangoi there is a nala 30 feet wide, 4 feet deep in January, perpendicular sides 3 feet above the water, spanned by a bamboo bridge. A path leads to Wuetop on the Thobál Shugunu road from this place, but it is only practicable between 1st December and 1st May. From Wangoi the road proceeds as before crossing open rice-fields and small swamps and keeping the same character, passing Laisankhong at 2 miles and Meiyang Imphal at 5 miles (from each of these villages there are paths to Thobál) and reaching Kokshing Kulel at 12 miles. At Meiyang Imphal is touched the Imphal river, 8 feet deep, steep banks 20 feet above the water in the cold weather.
			Imphal .	
Kokshing Kulel .	12	21		
Shugunu .	18	39	...	*Vide* Thobál-Shugunu route.

ROUTE No. 27.

FROM IMPHAL TO SHUGUNU.

Viâ *Thobál.*

Territory—

Authority—LIEUT. E. W. DUN.

Date—*15th December 1884.*

Names of Stages, &c.	Distance. Intermediate. Miles.	Total. Miles.	Rivers.	Remarks.
THOBAL KYAM	12	12	......	*Vide* Route No. 10 of *Gazetteer*.
PALLÉL	12	24	......	Ditto ditto.
WUIKONG	12	36	......	By pathway to Kokshing Kulel at 2 miles across rice-fields from 3 miles short of Pallél. Cross the Sengmaie stream by bamboo bridge practicable for mules. Village on both sides of stream. In the winter there is 4 feet of water. The banks are steep, 20 feet high, and 40 yards broad at top, along well-raised though unmetalled and rough road, 18 feet wide, due west across a swamp to a low pass over a long spur coming down northward from the hills which form the eastern boundary of the Manipur valley, at 3 miles. Turn south, road as before crossing several swampy places on bundles of straw, the open valley of Manipur on the west, the hills just mentioned on the east. At 8 miles another long spur from the east juts out into the valley of Manipur running down north-west. The village of Wuikong is placed between it and the main range. There are salt springs here and a small mountain stream. There is excellent well-raised camping-ground and good grazing south of the village and on the spur for a large force. At 9 miles the road crosses a swampy stream coming down from the hills on the east by a narrow causeway and a 2-foot cutting in the latter.
SHUGUNU	8	44	......	Pass Kokshing Kunao at 10 miles, half a mile from the road. Cross a low spur and enter a valley about 1 mile wide, enclosed between the main range on the east and a spur coming out in a north-westerly direction from it as at Kokshing Kulel and Wuikong. Cross the spur by an easy rise, where it is not more than 100 feet above the plain, cross half a mile of open ground, and reach Shugunu at 20 miles.

ROUTE No. 28.

From IMPHAL to SHUGUNU.

Viâ *Moirang.*

Territory—

Authority—Lieut. E. W. Dun.

Date—*4th December 1884.*

Names of Stages, &c.	Distance. Intermediate. Miles.	Distance. Total. Miles.	Rivers.	Remarks.
			Eastern Nambol.	Unmetalled road, 20 feet broad. Crosses the Nambol at north-west corner of the Residency grounds by a brick bridge of three spans and very solid construction with 15 feet roadway. Follows right bank of the Nambol for ⅙ mile, and then branches off to the south-west. Leaves the city at 1⅓ miles. Crosses open rice-fields the whole way to Shugunu, interspersed with patches of grass. At 3 miles the village of Changangai abuts on the road. From 4 miles a line of villages lies parallel to the road at a distance of ½ a mile named in sections Kharma, Kudumpopi, Meitiam, Ulao, and approaching the road at Foyjing at 9 miles. At 8 miles on the western side, there are three forest-covered hills about 100 feet above the plain. The nearest is 400 and the most distant 800 yards from the road.
Foyjing	9	..	*Western Nambol.*	At Foyjing (where there is a large daily bazaar) cross the Nambol (western) by a frail wooden bridge (practicable for mules). The Nambol is here 20 yards wide. The banks are steep, 20 feet high, and 40 yards broad at the top. The road, preserving the same character, crosses foot of low hills on the east at 2 miles and the village of Okchingkei. At 3 and 4 miles respectively the villages of Oinam and Keino, 400 yards east of the road. At 6 miles it crosses the feet of low spurs of hills on the west. There are some very steep places which make this part impracticable for vehicles. The course of the road could be flat if taken a little lower down on the spurs. Reach Bishenpur at 7 miles.
Bishenpur or Lamlongtong.	7	16	.. ...	There is a rest-house here. A large bazaar is held here daily. There is excellent camping-ground, water, and fair grazing. The main road to Cachar branches off here. The Shugunu road passes through Bishenpur village and over a mound commanding a good view of the southern part of the valley. It would make a good signalling station, keeps the same character as hitherto, passes Ningthsokong at 6 miles, and reaches Moirang at 11 miles.

Names of Stages, &c.	Distance.		Rivers.	Remarks.
	Intermediate.	Total.		
	Miles.	Miles.		
MOIRANG	11	27	......	In the cold weather Moirang is separated from the Logtak Lake by a strip of marsh 1 mile wide; a direct cut capable of containing one canoe at a time has been made through it.
CHAIREL .	12	39	*Turbung* .	Road and country as before. A few marshes crossed on bundles of grass or straw. Ground chiefly covered with grass jungle 3 feet high. Kunbi at 5 miles. Cross the Turbung on edge of Kunbi village, 1 foot of water at ford, 8 feet banks, 30 yards broad. At 8 miles the village of close under the spur coming down from Saudong peak on the west. Pass Wangun, 1 mile from road to the east at 10 miles. At 16 miles cross the Imphal in boats. Chairel is situated on the left bank. The river is here 40 feet deep, 50 yards broad, perpendicular banks in the cold weather 6 feet above the water. There is a very slight current. The road now follows the left bank of the Imphal through high grass jungle, passing the village of at 4 miles. This place is famous for the quantity of fish procurable in the river just below it.
SHUGUNU	7	46	......	Shugunu (on the left bank) is reached at 9 miles. There is excellent camping-ground here for a large force and good grazing. The Chakpi stream falls into the Imphal about 3 miles below Shugunu; ½ a mile below the Chakpi there is a broad shallow ford. There is no road below Shugunu.

ROUTE No. 29.

FROM IMPHAL TO SILCHAR (*Cachar*).

Viâ *Aqui*.

Territory—MANIPUR.

Authority—LIEUT. E. W. DUN (from native information).

Date—*1st March 1885.*

Names of Stages, &c.	Distance.		Rivers.	Remarks.
	Intermediate.	Total.		
	Miles.	Miles.		
MAGLANG THANNA.	...	3 hours.	*Nambol* .	Flat road across the Manipur valley crossing the Nambol in the capital.

Names of Stages, &c.	Distance. Intermediate. Miles.	Distance. Total. Miles.	Rivers.	Remarks.
CAMP . .	1 day.	...	*Iaie, Leimatak.*	Pass through Kharam village ; camp at junction of the Iaie with the Leimatak.
CAMP . . (Barrack)	1 day.	...	(*Lesser*) *Irang,*	Follow the course of the Leimatak to the junction with the (Lesser) Irang. Camp at junction.
CAMP . .	1 day.	..	*Leimatak, Irang* (*real*).	Cross the next range to the east through Lamkhong village. Steep ascents; descent not fit for mule carriage. Camp on the Irang.
AGUI . (Barrack)	1 day.	...	*Barak* .	Very small camping-ground and scanty water-supply.
ATTINGBA (Alamba in map)	1 day.	...	......	Ditto ditto.
CAMP . .	1 day.	...	*Mukru.*	
AMANG HITTEN THANNA .	1 day.	...	*Tiri.*	
BALADHAN TEA GARDEN .	1 day.	...	......	Good road.
LAKHIPUR .	1 day.	...	......	Government road.
SILCHAR .	1 day. 24 miles. Total 10½ days.	...	......	Road throughout impracticable for mules.

ROUTE No. 30.

FROM BISHENPUR TO THOBAL.

Territory—MANIPUR. Authority—LIEUT. E. W. DUN.

Date—*10th January 1885.*

(Open 1st December to 1st May.)

Names of Stages, &c.	Distance. Intermediate. Miles.	Distance. Total. Miles.	Rivers.	Remarks.
			Eastern Nambol, Western Nambol.	The road is merely a track across fields and dried-up swamp to the junction of the eastern and western Nambol streams, at 3 miles, passing through the village of Thobál at 1 mile. At Thobál the track crosses a dangerously soft place which would require special attention if any traffic were required to run along this route.

Names of Stages, &c.	Distance. Intermediate. Miles.	Distance. Total. Miles.	Rivers.	Remarks.
			Eastern Nambol	Follow either bank of the eastern Nambol through high dense reed jungle to 8 miles. The Nambol streams after uniting are 6 feet deep and 40 yards broad. The banks a few feet above the water and the same above the swamp on each side through which the stream flows. There is a scarcely perceptible current. Natives seldom travel along the banks, but go along the Nambol in boats. They informed me at Bishenpur that Kokshai could not be reached across this piece of country; I took an elephant along the banks, and a good traversable path could easily be made, as there are no dangerous places. At 8 miles where a small stream enters the Nambol from the east, leave the latter, and proceed by a narrow path through high grass jungle to Kokshai at 8½ miles. The Maharaja keeps his elephants here, and there is excellent grazing for all cattle.
Meiyang Imphal .	9½	...	*Imphal* .	Pass through Kokshai and Shugunu Thanna villages by a broad through rough road to Meiyang Imphal bazaar on the right bank of the Imphal river. Cross the Longtival-Shugunu road (Route No.) (The Imphal is here 8 feet deep. Its banks are 20 feet above the water and are steep. There is a scarcely perceptible current), and follow the course of the Imphal and Thobál rivers by a path through villages to Thobál at 8 miles.
Thobal . .	8	17½	*Thobál* .	There is good and plentiful camping-ground at Meigang Imphal for a large force.

ROUTE No. 31.

From KONGÁL THANNA to SAMJOK.

Territory—

Authority—Major Badgeley.

Date—*December 1881*

Names of Stages, &c.	Distance. Intermediate. Miles.	Distance. Total. Miles.	Rivers.	Remarks.
Morlung .	16	...	......	A level path through open forest passing Thanán, a Shan village of 6 houses at 12 miles. Morlung is situate at the foot of the western slope of the Angoching range and consists of 14 houses.

Names of Stages, &c.	Distance.		Rivers.	Remarks.
	Intermediate.	Total.		
	Miles.	Miles.		
Taung-ban .	·18	34	......	Steep ascent to the crest of the range at an elevation of 1,500 feet above the sea and descend by a long gently-sloping spur.
Samjok .	5	39	*Nalthangit (one foot deep in December).*	Road level. Passes the Nalthangit river at one mile at Ischdangon (6 houses) and Nalthangit village (4 houses) at 4 miles. Between this and Samjok there are two small streams, the path following the river bank.
				There is water along this route at moderate distances apart, and in dry weather room for camping in the fields near the villages or when they are in bearing, in the jungle, which is thin tree forest with little undergrowth; at Nalthangit there is a plain half a mile square. The path is fit for all laden animals except elephants, but would be so for them with a little improvement.

ROUTE No. 32.

From YANGA-POKPI THANNA to SAMJOK.

Viâ *Morlung.*

Territory— Authority—Major Badgeley.

Date—*December 1881.*

Names of Stages, &c.	Distance.		Rivers.	Remarks.
	Intermediate.	Total		
	Miles.	Miles.		
Mungsa .	4	...	......	A Shan village of 20 houses.
			Tutel	Fordable throughout the year.
			Maglang.	Shingly bottom, fordable in the cold weather from November to May.
Taap (old Samjok). .	7	...	......	A Shan village of 10 houses.
Morlung .	4	15	......	A Shan village of 14 houses. For the rest of the route to Samjok, *vide* Route No. 31. Good flat roads up to this point.

APPENDIX A.

Advisability of entering the Shan country through Manipur.

It has been apparent of late years that the Shans of Upper Burma* could, if properly led and organized, make matters very unpleasant for their Burmese masters.

The control which the Burmese used to exercise over them has disappeared almost entirely, and though the capture of Mandalay would give out the keys of the nominal government of the country into the hand of the conqueror, the Shans would still have to be dealt with.

Strong as may be the dislike of the Shans to the present Burmese Government, we have no certain reason to suppose that they will receive a civilized Government with submission. In any case, it would probably be considered advisable to occupy the country they inhabit, *viz.*, the northern half of Upper Burma.

The distance from either Cachar or Assam to the Ningthee valley is as nearly as possible 200 miles.

From Mandalay to Samjok, the place of the greatest importance in the Ningthee valley, it is rather more than 200 miles.

Of the country between Mandalay and Samjok there is no modern information, whereas we have all details of the routes between Cachar or Assam, and that place up to 1881, and in some cases to 1885.

On the Manipur side the country is friendly up to within four marches of Samjok; between Mandalay and that place, every march may have to be made through a hostile or at least unfriendly population.

It would therefore appear not inadvisable to consider the possibility of sending a force through Manipur to Northern Burmah.

Manipur can be approached both from Cachar and Assam, and whichever route be adopted, all is plain sailing as far as Manipur territory, *i.e.*, two marches beyond Silchar on the one side and two marches beyond Kohima on the other.

Moreover, from these points onwards to the Kubbo valley, the roads are well known and have been recently reconnoitred and reported on, all details being given in the Manipur Gazeteer.

We will now consider—

(1) the best route into Manipur;

(2) the best route into the Kubbo valley;

(3) the force required;

(4) the supplies available—

  (*a*) rations,

  (*b*) carriages;

(5) the military assistance the State can afford.

Approaches to Manipur.

The valley of Manipur can be approached from British India along four routes—

Routes from Assam. Two from Assam on the north—first *viâ* Kohima, second *viâ* Rozepemah and Kenoma.

The first† could easily be made into a cart-road. A suitable trace now (1885) exists between Kohima and Manipur, and a trace is now being made from Dimapur to Kohima (state of Nichi Guard suspension bridge).

† Kohima route.

‡ Rozepmeah route.

The second‡ is simply a village path. It lies over an exceedingly broken country and crosses very steep ranges. It is difficult even for coolies.

Every village in the hills is, however, connected with every neighbouring village by some sort of a path, and it is probable that an easier line of approach than the last could be found *viâ* Henomah in the North Cachar hills.

Routes from Cachar. There are two lines of approach from the Cachar district on the west—

(1) By the Cachar road.

(2) By the Aqui route.

* By Upper Burmah was meant the country north of Shwebo. These remarks apply only to the Shans of Yazagyo, Thaungthut and Hontho, not in any way to the Shan east of the Irrawaddy.—*E. W. D.*

The first is a good mule path, the second impracticable for laden animals and difficult for coolies.

Comparison of the Cachar and Kohima roads.

The Kohima route is infinitely preferable to the Cachar route. On the former line troops can be brought all the year round in steamers to Nigriting.* On the latter, they would in the autmn have to do the last 50 miles of their journey in country boats—a tedious and dangerous process as the Lushai expedition showed.

* 163 miles from Imphal (Manipur).

At Golaghat, on the Kohima route, there is a transport depôt, and along the road to the Naga Hills there is plenty of camping-ground. In Cachar, until December, there is little dry ground to be obtained for camps.

The Kohima road could, if widened, be used by light carts; there is plenty of camping-ground, water, and grazing at every mile of the road within the hills, and as it follows the course of the valleys, the gradient is easy throughout. The Cachar road crosses seven ranges and five rivers. There is very little camping-ground at many stages, no grazing until Kanpum is reached, and it is very unhealthy until the cold weather is well advanced.

Every advantage, in short, is on the side of the Kohima road, at any rate for the movement of troops, but the Cachar road would be useful for bringing up stores, and would take off a great part of the pressure of traffic.

About 170 miles from Balagunge, the highest point to which steamers go in cold weather to Imphal (Manipur.)

The routes from Manipur to Upper Burmah.

All the routes beyond Manipur have the same character. They ascend a long spur up to a high peak on the watershed and descend along the crest of a corresponding spur on the other side.

They ascend on an average 3,500 feet above the level of the Manipur valley. There are many spots on them where water is scarce, the camping-ground small, and there are some steep gradients (in short distances).

They are all simple village paths, gradually improved by traffic.

No regular line of road has been laid out between the Manipur and Kubbo valleys.

There is, however, no reason why an easy route for laden animals or even for carts should not be made.

Between the peaks and at the heads of the streams, the watershed is not more than 1,000 to 1,500 feet above the level of the Manipur valley. The hill-sides are earthy and easily worked. There is but little jungle to be cut, and the streams on the Manipur side run in peculiarly flat-bottomed valleys, up which little or nothing in the way of road-making would be necessary.

It would, therefore, be no difficult matter, if labour were available, to run the road up a Manipur stream, zig-zag it over the Kotal and down an eastern stream to the Kubbo valley.

On such a line water would always be handy, camping-ground more plentiful, and the easier gradient would give lighter work to men and mules.

Labour available for improving communications.

The Taukul and Lahupa tribes are not forced by the Manipuris to carry loads out of their own hills, but they go all over Manipur to dig canals, tanks, &c., and at this kind of work they are exceedingly skilful. They number by the last census 32,952 souls.

This gives us 8,238 able-bodied men.

We may put the length of road to be constructed at 50 miles.

Taking a 6-feet roadway and an average slope of the hill-side of 45°, each man could be expected to cut 6 feet of road per diem.

The road could, therefore, be constructed by 3,000 men (a little more than one-third of the labour force available) in fifteen days—the period between the gathering of the harvest (1st December) and the 15th December when the troops should arrive in Manipur. *Vide* Gazetteer, page 11.

Implements.

Pick-axes and hoes would have to be imported to Manipur for the purpose, but as there are 800 men of the carriers, *vide* page 294, still available, there could be no difficulty about doing so.

Best line to adopt.

The most convenient line for such a road would be through Ingorok up the valley of the stream on which it stands, and then over the watershed into the valley of the Turet, entering the Kubbo valley as Yanga-pokpi thanna, a central point from which roads diverge to Samjok and Tummu *en route* to Kendat.

If it be decided to use the existing routes, the easiest are routes Nos. 8 and 11, which leave the valley at Haituk-pokpi and Pallel respectively.

The best existing routes.

They are also the most convenient; they lead direct upon that part of the Kubbo valley where there are most villages and to points on the direct routes to Samjok and Kendat, if it should be thought necessary for a force to visit that place.

The troops could not move across the hills in parties of more than 500 at a time, and special arrangements would have to be made for the supply of water at Kambáng (Route No. 8), and for level ground at the Lokchao (Route No. 11). *Vide* Colonel Johnstone's remarks upon the stages in the route.

Time occupied in passage.

If we divide the force, postulated on page 294, into six parties, the passage of the Yumadoung will take six days.

Routes from the Kubbo Valley to the Ningthee.

There are two routes from the Kubbo valley into the Ningthee valley—one direct to Samjok, the other towards the southern end of the valley towards Kendat. Both would appear to be passable by laden mules, though the description to hand of the southern route is somewhat vague. *Vide* Pemberton, page 57.

Other paths exist, *viz.*, near the Nampagua, over the Kassom range and two or three further north, but they have not been visited by Europeans, are little used, and are probably narrow paths, with occasional steep and difficult places.

We may look upon Routes Nos. 3 and 16 as those which would be selected by a force advancing upon the Ningthee valley.

Until they have been further explored and more carefully examined, it is impossible to make any suggestions for their improvement, or for the adoption of alternative routes.

The force required.

The two most important Shan towns in Northern Burma are Samjok and Bhamo.

If they were held by a battalion each, it would be easy, with the assistance of a mountain battery, to carry out successful punitive expeditions against any of the hill tribes who should evince hostility.

The possession of these two places, situated as they are upon the principal trade routes, and their connection by a chain of stockades, would make Northern Burma perfectly safe.

We will then, for the sake of calculating the supplies and transport available and required, assume that the force consists of two battalions of Native Infantry at full strength and a battery of mountain artillery.

Supplies.

Rations.—The Manipuri State can supply rice, dhall, ghee or oil, salt, bhoosa (under special arrangement), and goor.

Statement by Colonel Johnstone.

Of these articles it can give 2,000 men a two months' supply, or a total of 120,000 rations.

It can have these ready about the 15th December. A Native Infantry battalion, inclusive of transport followers and doolie bearers, would require 1,130 rations per diem.

A mountain battery would require 112 rations per diem.

The force would therefore want 2 × 1,130 + 212 = 2,472 rations per diem; or a total of 49,440 rations for the period it is passing through Manipur, which we estimate at 20 days.

Only rice-eating men could be employed, *viz.*, Assam regiments and 8 Frontier Police.

It will be observed that the ration is for rice-eating men, the supply of atta being practically *nil*.

Bison beef is procurable in fair quantity; poultry would be somewhat scarce.

Statement by Colonel Johnstone.

Transport.—The State of Manipur engages to supply coolie carriage to 2,000 men for a period of two months.

It is necessary to calculate what actual labour force this represents.

A Native Infantry battalion at full strength, and including mule-drivers, doolie-bearers, and carriage for tents and ammunition, but excluding rations, numbers about 1,130 souls.

It would require, on the last hot weather scale, carriage for 729 maunds per diem, inclusive of tents and spare and reserve ammunition, but exclusive of rations.

Two thousand men would therefore require carriage for 1,290 maunds per diem.

At 30 seers a load this would necessitate Manipur supplying a daily quota of 1,720

Total coolie force the State will supply while the force is passing through Manipur.

The State engages to supply this number for 60 days; but as they can be used for only 20 days, the period in which troops and stores would move across Manipur territory, 3×1720 = 5,160 would be required.

The chief carrying strength lies in the Kaukis and Kaupui Nagas, and amounts in these two tribes alone to 8,000 men.

The State might therefore be expected to supply 5,000 carriers for a period of 20 days without hardship.

Mule or coolie transport.

As the roads are quite suitable for mule carriage, and as grass and fodder are available throughout, it is presumed that it could be used in preference to coolie carriage, except indeed for the transport of rations.

The force will, if it employs mule carriage for personal baggage ammunition, &c., now have 120,000 rations and can have 5,160 loads of 30 seers each (3,870 maunds) of miscellaneous stores brought up to the last place in Manipur territory or even to the Ningthee valley.

Besides this the Manipuris could, with little difficulty, secure the crops, &c., in the Kubbo valley at harvest time. We may put this at 40,000 rations, one-third only of what Manipur supplies.

We have seen that while passing through Manipur the force consumes 49,440 rations. Arrived at the Ningthee valley. It has a balance in hand of 70,560 rations. One battalion and the battery (requiring 1,337 rations per diem) would go on, and this amount would be available for them. As it is equal to 53 days' rations, and the journey to Bhamo would not occupy more than 20 days, this would be an ample, not to say unnecessarily large, supply, considering the nature of the country passed through.

There is no doubt that the force remaining at Samjok could support itself from either the Kubbo valley or the Ningthee valley.

We see then that the 120,000 rations which the State will supply will meet all requirements without our drawing upon the labour supply (except to a small extent for special stores required for the troops), such as rum, tobacco, and the many little relishes and additions which, under the name of "masalla," are an indispensable part of the sepoys' food, and for transport of rations beyond Manipur.

The Ningthee valley, north of Samjok, is famous for the ponies bred there; but as they would at first and until trained be unfitted for carrying loads, it might be found necessary to indent upon the Manipur coolie supply for the transport of rations for the battalion proceeding to Bhamo.

Twenty days' rations for one battalion would amount to 680 maunds. It could be conveyed by 962 coolies, who would carry their own food for twenty days.

These men are available on the supposition that mule carriage has been employed by the troops.

As rations were consumed, a certain number of these men would be set free daily from the work of carrying loads.

They could be advantageously employed in scouting, clearing jungle, and erecting huts at camping-grounds, making stockades on communications, &c.

The 962 ration coolies would be away from their homes for 40 days, and would therefore represent a labour force of 1,924 20-day men.

Therefore, there would remain 3,238 20-day men at 30 seers each, leaving a total to be transported by the Manipur State from British to Burmese territory of 2,428 maunds.

Military assistance the State could give.

In 1879 the Political Agent estimated the Manipuri Army at—

500 Artillery.
400 Cavalry.
5,500 Infantry.
700 Kuki Irregulars.

hey were armed with two 7-lb. mountain guns, 8 old pattern brass 3-pounders, 2,700 old percussion cap muskets, and 1,250 Victoria muskets.

Of the Artillery, not more than 10 per cent. knew how to load and fire a gun.

The cavalry had little or no organization, no horses or ponies, and were not drilled.

The infantry alone received some sort of instruction, usually from the Raja himself.

Since 1879 there has been no increase to the armament, and no measures taken for instructing the troops.

The census of 1881 gives a grand total of 6,624 to the Army, of whom 250 are officers.

The fighting capability of the Manipuris is still an open question; and although the occupation of Upper Burma would be an easy task, and would probably be effected by a disciplined force almost without bloodshed, it would hardly be advisable to rely entirely upon the Manipur army.

A mixed force will probably recommend itself.

If then the occupation be effected by British troops, assisted by a force of deficient discipline and uncertain courage, many difficulties of transport, supply, and policy would be avoided by limiting the Manipuri detachment to a small picked body of men.

This might consist of 1,000 Manipuris and 500 Kuki irregulars. This force would be quite sufficient for the maintenance of posts upon the line of communications, and would also provide a useful body of scouts for service against hill tribes.

All Manipuris are good riders, and as Upper Burma produces large numbers of excellent ponies, communication could be kept up with great perfection right across the country by means of stockaded posts at intervals of, say, 20 miles and mounted orderlies.

At present, the telegraph line terminates at Silchar on the one side and Kohima on the other. The post reaches Manipur from Silchar in three days, and there is weekly postal communication with Kohima.

Communication with India.

Heliograph stations can be established from Assam and Cachar to the Ningthee, and would work well in the early part of the cold weather; but after the 1st February the atmosphere becomes hazy. Moreover, it will be seen (*vide* Appendix) that a very great number of stations are required, causing a great waste of money.

It will probably be found more convenient to lay down a field telegraph to Manipur at any rate, and probably to the Ningthee valley.

To sum up, the roads through Manipur are easy and well known. The population along them is more than friendly. It can and will give material assistance.

The vital points of the Northern Shan country can be as easily reached from Manipur as from Mandalay.

Rations can be supplied on the threshold of the enemy's country in sufficient quantity to enable the force to live until foraging parties have secured further supplies from a rich and well-cultivated country.

There is a reserve labour force, and a military force admirable for holding communications and for the particular style of warfare of the hill tribes.

The ease with which such an expedition could be carried out would appear to justify the experiment.

SIGNALLING POINTS.

Cachar Road.

1. Silchar.
2. 679 feet peak on the Tujong range.
3. Kala Naga village.
4. Kanpum.
5. Laimatol.
6. Imphal.

Kohima Road.

1. Kohima.
2. Phesama.
3. Mau.
4. Tehrenuma.
5. Mekithodzomi.
6. Peak east of Karong Thanna.
7. A point above Mayangkhang thanna on the west.
8. Thumion Peak.
9. Yongbalangkong.
10. Imphal (Langol hill).

Signal Stations on the two Southern Kubbo valley routes.

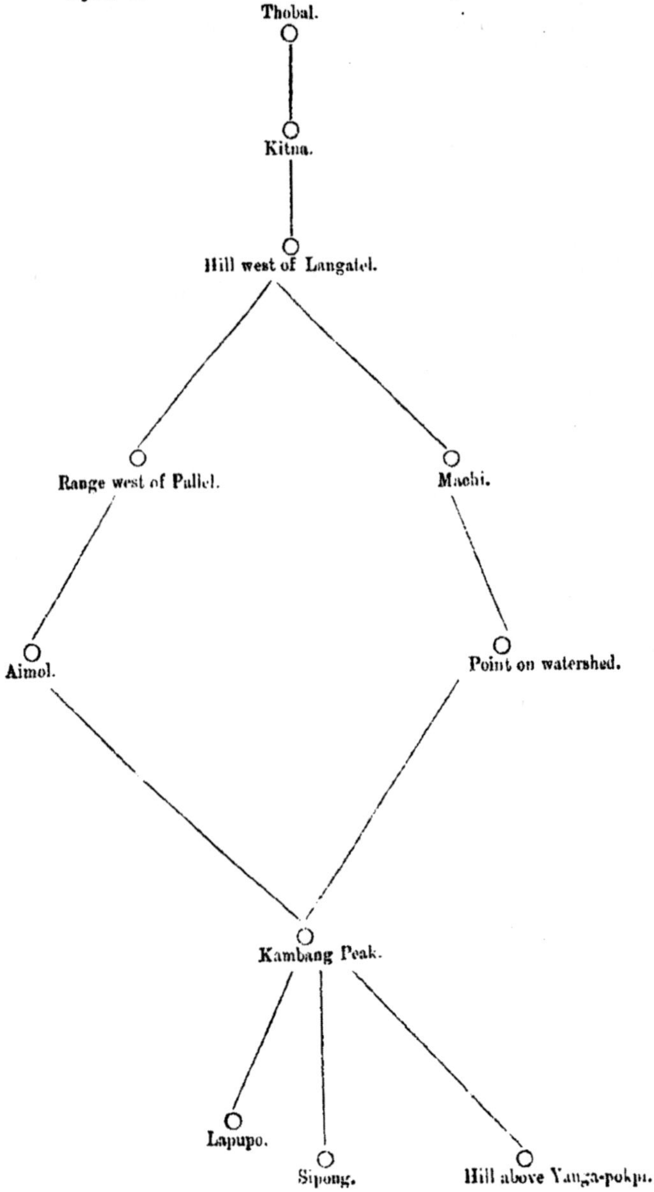

Valley stations.

Imphal. { Chingamukka.
Langol.
Polo ground. }
Nongmaiching.
Longtival.
Phunan.
Thobál.
Thánga (Logtak Lake).
Hill west of Pallel.

Signal Stations on the two Northern Kubbo valley routes.

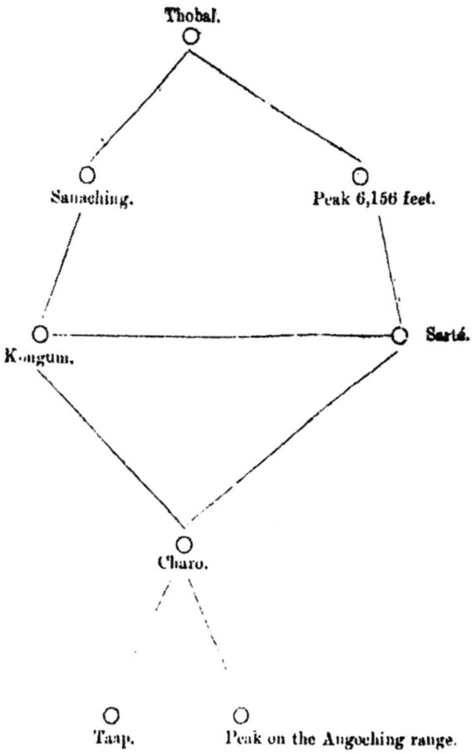

Coolies.

The report upon the Lushai expedition contains some suggestions which would be applicable in the present case, *viz.*, that for medical attendance and that for badges and vouchers.

The pay of the Manipur coolies would be the same as that for the coolies in the Lushai expedition with this exception, that the price of a 30-seer trip from Lakhipur to the Cachar district to Manipur is fixed at Rs. 5.

Four annas per diem may, however, be taken as the rate for calculation for any other part of the country.

The Manipuri coolie requires to be provided with nothing in the way of equipment excepting a dâo; *but this should be of a pattern to which he is accustomed.*

Equipment.

Some of the old Kuki tribes have been trained as doolie-bearers, and it is now their hereditary duty. I am unable to say with any exactitude what number of doolie-bearers would be forthcoming; but there would be sufficient to replace all casualties in the ranks of the regular Hindustani doolie-bearers.

Trained doolie-bearers.

Camp Equipage.

In calculating the number of coolies required for the transport of a battalion or battery full camp equipage has been assumed. It will, however, be found that expense and labour will be saved by taking lighter means of shelter than the sepoy pâl.

Tents were despensed with in the Lushai expedition. Men hutted themselves when they made any stay in a place, and the same can be done in Manipur and Upper Burmah.

Tarpaulins might be used as in the Lushai expedition.

The English circular single-fly, weighing 66lb and accommodating 20 men, was found an economical and useful tent in the Abyssinian campaign.

The most economical would be the Russian *tente d'abri*, which consists of two sheets 6·41 feet long and 2·88 feet broad, fastened together along one side by loops and eyes and with eyelet holes on the other side.

The tent without supporting sticks, but waterproofed, would weigh about 4lb and accommodate two men.

Inns and Billets.

It should be noted that there is nothing in Manipur in the shape of an inn such as is commonly found in China, and, I believe, in Burma. Every man cooks his own food and none can be bought ready cooked.

It would be impossible in a friendly occupation or passage through the country to billet troops upon the inhabitants.

They pretend that they cannot admit any but Hindus of the very highest castes into their houses; and as the houses contain but one room, it would, in any case, be a hardship to the owner.

Climate.*—Vide* Gazetteer.

Diseases.*—Vide* Gazetteer.

Cholera is said to appear frequently at Samjok in December.

Speaking generally, the climate of the region operated in would, during the cold weather, be very favourable, and there is no reason to suppose that any particular disease would make its appearance during that period.

APPENDIX B.

The most influential men in Manipur.

The present Raja is Sir Chunder Kirti Singh, K.C.S.I.
He has ten sons. The four eldest are known by their titles only.
The eldest is styled Joobraj or heir-apparent.
The second, Wankei Lakpa.
Wankei is one quarter of the capital; Lakpa signifies a chief.
The third, Samsherjuba or Lord of Elephants.
The fourth, Kotwal Quirreng or Chief of the Quirrengs.
The remainder are called by their names,—

Tambao.	Gandha Singh.
Pakka Senna.	Gopal Senna.
Angao.	Tillah Singh.

The Joobraj is 33 years of age, and his claim to the succession has been recognized by Government.

At his succession his brothers will be dependent upon his charity, and will probably sink into positions of poverty and obscurity.

The only two important and powerful subjects are the two ministers—Tangal Singh and Balram Singh. The former is 68 years of age, and the latter 58; they have been associated in the Raja's service for very many years, and are acutely jealous of one another.

Tangal Singh is the most forward and active and the readiest speaker of the two, and has most sympathy with Western notions. Balram Singh has the reputation of being the most astute. They may be fairly accurately described as representing in Manipur the Liberal and Conservative parties.

They command two regiments out of seven, which compose the Manipur army, and have the rank of General. They are usually addressed by this title.

The hill country is divided between them as follows:—

Tangal Singh.

The Cachar road and villages along it.
The Kohima road and as far east as the Thobal and the upper course of the Lanier.
A small wedge of country lying along the north of Route No. 5.
From route No. 7 southwards, including all dealings with the Kambows.

Balram Singh.

The Kukis at the southern end of the valley, and the whole of the hills west of the valley, with the exception of the Cachar road.
The north-eastern corner, including the Somrah basin.
Route No. 6 and the Kubbo valley.

Though at present possessed of great power, they depend entirely upon the favour of the Raja, and may lose everything at his death. Without the assistance of these officers, nothing can be obtained in their respective districts, whether coolies, supplies or interpreters, and it would be hopeless to attempt anything against their wishes.

There are no other individuals in the State who possess any power or wealth worth mentioning.

The throne is the source of rank, and the possession of rank is almost the only means of obtaining wealth. Social status is arranged on a system not unlike that which obtains in Russia.

E. W. DUN, *Lieut.*,
28th Bengal Infantry.

MANIPUR,
1st March 1885.

APPENDIX C.

Memorandum by Colonel J. Johnstone, C.S.I., late Political Agent of Manipur.

The best route for troops from Assam to Burmah is undoubtedly *vid* Manipur, as it is well known, has been traversed by me from one end to the other, and I can speak with certainty of it. Other routes may be good, but they are at the best hypothetical, and by adopting any of them without the possibility of making arrangements previously, there would certainly be a hitch. It must be remembered, too, that the route *vid* Manipur brings you out on Burmese territory, at a point where provisions can be obtained and where there is water carriage near at hand—no mean consideration in a country possessing no other means of carriage. Depend upon it that, unless for some special reason it be desirable to adopt another route, it would be exceedingly undesirable to do so. The Burmese entered Assam by a different route, it is true, for the very good reason that they knew of no other, and would in any case have been unable to force their way through the Angami country.

The following are the marches to Manipur, *vid* Cachar and *vid* the Naga Hills:—

(1) Cachar to—

1. Luckipore	14	miles.
2. Jeerighat	10	„
3. Mukkun river	18	„
4. Burak river	13	„
5. Lengba river	19	„
6. Rowpoom Thannah	13	„
7. Laimetuk river	15	„
8. Bissenpore	13	„
9. Mainpur (Langthabal)	19	„
Total	134	miles.

(2) Kohima to—

1. Kigwema	11	miles.
2. Mao	12	„
3. Mytiphum	14	„
4. Khurong	15	„
5. Mayankong	10	„
6. Kaithee mabee	11	„
7. Sengmaie	12	„
8. Manipur (Langthabal	17	„
Total	102	miles.

I give "Langthabal" as the halting place for the capital in both cases, as there is no good site near the Residency sufficiently large for a regiment to encamp. It would be necessary to arrange beforehand for the erection of huts for a standing camp. This could be done cheaply if the Durbar does not interfere with a view to making money by it. The proper course would be to fix a fair price and hand it over to the Durbar, and request that the work be done.

From Manipur to Kendat the marches are as follows:—

Manipur (Langthabal) to Thobal or better still to—

Wangshung	17 miles.
Pullel	14 „
Aimole	8 „
Lokehno river	17 „
Moreh Thanna	12 „
Mahmo	10 „
Weetoop	15 „
Owktong	10 „
Toungeeah	9 „
Yésone	15 „
Kendat	14 „
Total	141 miles.

Mules could be taken the whole distance with a little assistance from pioneering.

Time of year suitable.—In ordinary seasons, troops should rendezvous in the valley of Manipur about 1st December, and after halting a week or ten days to rest, and weed out men with fever, start on the 10th and reach the Kubbo valley by the 15th, by which date the large open tracts of rice land would be dry enough to encamp on, and the straw of the lately cut rice would serve the men for bedding. Any force coming to Manipur in early December is sure to suffer from fever. I had ten men sick out of sixty and had to leave them behind. I think this sickness must be faced, as it is essential to enter the Kubbo valley as early as possible as the cold season is so short. The Kubbo valley is very healthy in the dry season, and much the reverse in the rainy season, it is said. The rains ends about the middle of October, but the country is not thoroughly dry before December.

Most suitable kind of carriage.—If mules can be fed on paddy, they would undoubtedly be the most suitable carriage, but it would be necessary for an advance guard of pioneers to smooth the road occasionally. Elephants would do, if well looked after and equipped with guddies not liable to give sore-backs, but they are at the best unsatisfactory.

A coolie corps of 1,000 to 1,500 men might be raised in Manipur at about R7 per mensem per man in addition to rice, and it might be kept going till 31st March. The Durbar would probably raise it; but I am perfectly certain that were the Durbar to offer no obstacle, present or future, men would willingly come forward. The dishonesty and cupidity of the Durbar, which robs the coolies of their hard earnings, is the only possible obstacle. If it were a question of merely passing troops through Manipur, 3,000 coolies in all might be furnished between November 1st and March 1st.

Method of supply.—If a mule corps, or proper pack bullock train, were organized, it would be easy to establish a depôt of such provisions, as Manipur does not supply, in Manipur, without drawing on the cooly supply, or if time were given, coolies could be furnished. It would, however, probably be better to send such provisions of which very large quantities are required. *After leaving Manipur* to Kendat by steamers, one depôt might be formed in Manipur supplied from Cachar, and another at Tummoo, supplied from Kendat. Manipur can supply rice, but only in Manipur territory, and for consumption therein. Salt is very bad, and so exceedingly dear that it should be imported from Cachar or Rangoon. A pack bullock train properly managed, if possible, by professional bunjurries from the Central Provinces, would transport all requisite supplies from Cachar at a low rate. Coolies from Cachar to Manipur carry 30 seers each and generally get R5 for the journey, which can be done in seven days.

The Kubbo valley ought to be able to supply 10,000 to 15,000 maunds of rice to be stored at the different places *en route*, with a large depôt at Tummoo; but if it is desired to collect it, no time should be lost, as in December the old rice will be exhausted, and the new not prepared. Dhan will keep any time, and can be cleaned at short notice. If required, I would suggest offering a contract to Mr. Morgan, the Bombay-Burmah Corporation Agent at Tummoo. Mr. Morgan is a gentleman admirably qualified for the work by his thorough knowledge of the Burmese with whom he is a great favourite; but, I repeat, there is not a moment to be lost. Were there any demand for wheat or dhall, &c. in Manipur, it could and would be grown; and if supplies are required in 1887 (*i.e.*, after April 1887), it would be well to make arrangements for doing so.

I should add that coarse sugar ("goor") is tolerably plentiful, and potatoes can be purchased in small quantities; a larger demand would increase the supply. Oil can also be procured ("til"). Cows are not allowed to be slaughtered in Manipur, but fowls can be had at an average of 4 annas each; also ducks. Cows are not plentiful in the Kubbo valley, and are scarce at Kendat. Fowls are scarce in Kubbo, and very scarce at Kendat.

During the march of troops through Manipur, the Durbar would arrange for supplies of rice, and by giving *plenty of notice*, ghee and dhall might be provided by the Political Agent for consumption on the spot; but both these articles are so scarce, that they would have to be gradually brought up in small quantities.

I would add that after the 10th December the rivers in the Kubbo valley are no obstacle. If it is desired to strike the Chindwin at a higher point than Kendat at Thoungdoot (Sumjok), it would easily be reached in three days from Moreh Thanna. By previous arrangements, boats might be used from Maw (20 miles from Tummoo) to Kendat; but I hardly think they could be used with advantage for a greater distance.

J. JOHNSTONE, *Colonel.*

MANIPUR;
6th March 1886.

INDEX